TRACKS ON THE OCEAN

TRACKS ON THE OCEAN

A History of Trailblazing, Maps, and Maritime Travel

SARA CAPUTO

The University of Chicago Press

The University of Chicago Press, Chicago 60637
© 2024 by Sara Caputo
All rights reserved. No part of this book may be used or reproduced in any
manner whatsoever without written permission, except in the case of brief
quotations in critical articles and reviews. For more information, contact
the University of Chicago Press, 1427 East 60th Street, Chicago, IL 60637.
Published 2024
Printed in the United States of America

33 32 31 30 29 28 27 26 25 24   1 2 3 4 5

ISBN-13: 978-0-226-83792-5 (cloth)
ISBN-13: 978-0-226-83793-2 (e-book)
DOI: https://doi.org/10.7208/chicago/9780226837932.001.0001

First published in Great Britain in 2024 by Profile Books Ltd.

Library of Congress Cataloging-in-Publication Data

Names: Caputo, Sara, author.
Title: Tracks on the ocean : a history of trailblazing, maps, and
    maritime travel / Sara Caputo.
Description: Chicago : The University of Chicago Press, 2024.
    | Includes bibliographical references and index.
Identifiers: LCCN 2024006699 | ISBN 9780226837925 (cloth) |
    ISBN 9780226837932 (ebook)
Subjects: LCSH: Ocean travel—History. | Ocean travel—
    Maps—History. | Discoveries in geography—History.
Classification: LCC G540 .C26 2024 | DDC 387.509—dc23/
    eng/20240514
LC record available at https://lccn.loc.gov/2024006699

♾ This paper meets the requirements of ANSI/NISO Z39.48-1992
(Permanence of Paper).

For Cameron

CONTENTS

Color illustrations follow page 120.

INTRODUCTION

What hath pride profited us? or what good hath riches with
    our vaunting brought us?
All those things are passed away like a shadow, and as a post
    that hasted by;
And as a ship that passeth over the waves of the water,
    which when it is gone by, the trace thereof cannot be
    found, neither the pathway of the keel in the waves;
                  Wisdom of Solomon (KJV) 5, 8–10[1]

When you sit on a plane for a long-haul flight, the small screen
in front of you displays your ongoing journey as a sharp line,
cutting across khaki land masses and dark-blue oceans. The first
circumnavigation of the globe was painted by Renaissance artists
as a blazing silver trail. When Captain Cook, in the eighteenth
century, sailed deep into the Pacific, the tracks of his ships were
printed on nautical charts as cobweb-thin black threads. For centuries now, European maps have been strewn with the wakes of
ephemeral human passages, through land, air and water (Figure
0.1).[2]

    It was not always so, however. Journey route lines, a feature of
maps and charts that we now take for granted, have a complex and
relatively recent history.[3] This history only begins in the early sixteenth century: in the ancient and medieval West, as far as we can
tell, individual trips were never recorded as lines on a map. Maps
representing roads and land routes, to be clear, were not unknown.
But roads, paths and routes are static – they are not journeys.
They are collective possibilities, inviting future itineraries, not
particular stories, recounting a specific past deed.[4] The idea that

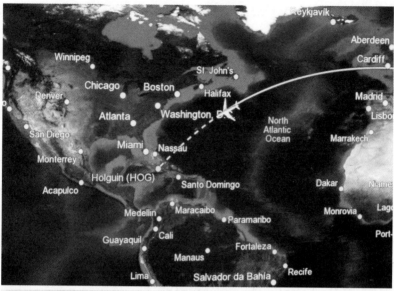

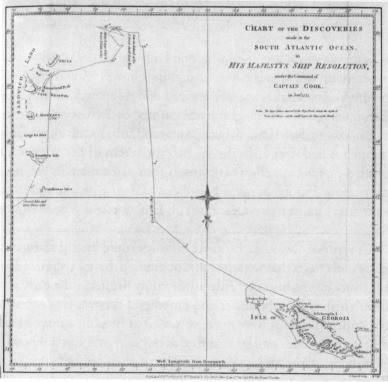

Figure 0.1: A transatlantic flight in the twenty-first century and
Captain James Cook's voyage across the South Atlantic in 1775.

each individual human journey can be made to leave a permanent, visible track not only on Earth but on the pathless sea is a
revolutionary one. It is also inextricable from the development of
European sea-bound empires.

As a practice, a convention and a conceptual and visual device,
the 'track' has embedded itself in Western understandings of
space and movement. Following its evolution over the last five
centuries, then, offers us a first-class view on some of the most significant developments in European and North American cultures.
Tracks speak of colonial occupation, of the rise of modernity and
globalisation, of the cults of accuracy, discovery, celebrity and individualism, of the birth of geo-surveillance, and of what happens
when humans enter a confrontation with the natural environment, set on transforming it and controlling it. *Tracks on the Ocean*
recounts the historical development of a particular mode of representing journeys. But, in doing so, it also asks questions about what
this mode expressed, and at times enabled: a momentous change in
the way in which many humans live and move on the planet.

The argument of this book is that journey lines were born, like
Venus, from the foam of the sea. Track lines mostly began at sea,
rather than on land, for a simple reason: it isn't fully possible – or
indeed necessary – to shape your own path when the path is already
there. And on land it usually is, if we discount places like deserts
and ice fields – which spatial theorists, in any case, like to compare
to seas.[5] Even in the absence of a trail, there are always hills, rocks,
trees, sheep: manifest features that, unless you are especially stub-
born, will determine the wending line of your footsteps. Out on
the open sea, on rivers and on lakes, the path does exist, as any sailor
can tell you. However, it is not always immediately visible, and
as such it can look like a choice: something that is built through
one's own movement, conjured out of thin water. Imagining this
personal course, in turn, helped European mariners to make sense
of the deceptively featureless ocean. Seafaring, with its practical,
problem-solving, 'crafty' heroes, sits at the core of modern Western
storytelling conventions; according to some scholars, it provided a
template for the genre of the adventure novel, and the notion of
a linear plot taking the reader along on the journey.[6] Similarly, the

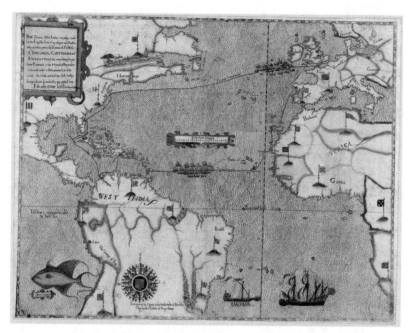

Figure 0.2: Francis Drake's fleet drawing a loop across the Atlantic in 1585–6.

practical realities of deep-sea navigation also prompted a new form of *graphical* storytelling: the track. Tracks mark particular occasions, events clearly defined in time, and with a named or nameable author. They are *Francis Drake*'s track, *James Cook*'s track, or the track of this or that vessel (Figure 0.2). So, whether they are drawn on a nautical chart during the journey, or on a narrative map made subsequently, they are excellent at documenting occurrences, adventure and skill.[7] The notion of the personal voyage line was, and is, usable on dry land, of course – and we'll touch upon that briefly. But its essence is fundamentally watery.

All this is not to say that the origin of the track is entirely 'Western'. Some Europeans imposed their mapping onto others, but its shape owed much to local ideas, terrains and contributions.[8] Tracks are no exception. At several points of this story, we encounter itinerary lines as deployed in other cultures – most notably in East Asia. Some of those lines, with very different meanings, already crossed the water. 'The West' did not invent the notion of a sea track. However, it did put it to use in unique ways, which suited some central traits of its imperial expansion: attempts at universal *schematisation*, the *occupation* of the unoccupiable, and *personal* claims of priority and impact.

The first of these characteristics is a drive to catalogue, collect and order. Reading the premise of this book, you may have wondered whether I am assigning too much importance to the tiny device of the track. Here I must agree with philosopher Bruno Latour, who argues that momentous change isn't to be explained through supposed momentous causes. In the history of modern science and technology, 'the most powerful explanations', he writes, 'are those that take writing and imaging craftsmanship into account': not huge cultural and material upheavals, but 'simple modifications in the way in which groups of people argue with one another using paper, signs, prints and diagrams'.[9] Most of all, one element is key here: 'objects which have the properties of being *mobile* but also' – supposedly, I would add – '*immutable, presentable, readable* and *combinable* with one another'.[10] Objects with the power to transport, display and collate: the power to 'draw things together'. The map, the tabular classification, the technical drawing using perspective, standardised units of measurement: these tiny devices don't represent the 'truth', but a deracinated model of it that is persuasive and easy to wield.[11] For this reason, they are also key instruments used by the modern state to make people 'legible'.[12] They are the building blocks of surveillance.

The cartographical track is a perfect example of one such object. It takes a voyage and makes it into a thing, relatively stable and portable. With a track, someone consulting a chart in Europe could hope to gain a grasp, at a glance, of the main outlines (literally) of something that had happened over days, months and years, on the other side of the globe.[13] Tracks were incredibly powerful ways of storing knowledge, pre-packaged and ready to use. But the track didn't simply help Europeans understand where their ships had been, neutrally: it made claims. This brings us to the Western track's second trait. The thing becomes a drawing, but the drawing also becomes a thing, back out there.

The track represented an evolving sense of humanity's position in the world: notions of destiny, permanence and possession, heroic craft and odds-defying relevance. It portrayed the individual standing in front of the wild environment, wrangling it and branding it, tattooing the image of the Earth with lines that say – 'I have been there'. *I am still there*, in fact: we shall see how the track is a form of occupation. A person wanting to mark water seems the epitome of folly, the perfect subject for a parable. In fact, the Bible says as much, in words apocryphally attributed to the wise King Solomon: 'a ship that passeth over the waves of the water, [...] when it is gone by, the trace thereof cannot be found, neither the pathway of the keel in the waves'.[14] But while these words never ceased to haunt navigators, they gradually came to ring more as a dare than an admonition.

Of course, as we have noted, tracks *do* have some pre-existing solidity. To the untrained eye, the oceans look like a uniform wavy expanse, but their surface and their depths flow and swirl with powerful structure.[15] While sailing across the Atlantic in 1960, during the first Single-handed Trans-Atlantic Race, navigator David Lewis could always tell the difference between the Labrador current and the Gulf Stream: 'one was pale bottle-green and the other deep indigo'.[16] Ships, and especially sailing ships, are buffeted, channelled, spun, misdirected and stopped by winds, currents, doldrums and tides. The sea may after all force you to go one way, forming some sort of 'road' – whether visible or not. Geography and the environment condition and constrain human activity. However, the tracks on modern European maps, as human artefacts, don't simply reproduce forces bigger and more ancient than people: they challenge them, trying to make those people's tiny voices heard. They try to bridge the distance between the 'long duration' of environmental timescales and maritime geomorphology and the fleeting events of human history – by placing the two on the same level.[17] How can a coastline that transforms over thousands of years and a ship flitting past in a day both be drawn as lines? In fact, often in track maps the seascape itself plays second fiddle, as plain, blank backstage. Portraying spaces like oceans as 'empty' and inert, 'passive or negative', is a fundamental habit of Western imperialism.[18] It's also the precondition necessary to clear the space for tracks. Tracks, then, are there explicitly to mark the sea, through the interface of the map. If the point was simply reproducing paths that *exist*, other devices would be available – devices that point to alternative models of living and moving in the world.

Tracks, instead, are in many ways typical harbingers of the 'Anthropocene' – a new event or proposed epoch in history, when the phenomena shaping the Earth are not only geological, but human-made. In the Anthropocene, humans have become a geological phenomenon.[19] They have exceeded the terms of their tenancy agreement, and transcended merely cosmetic adjustments to their abode: they have begun to put down their own sedimental horizons on the ground, altered the composition of the oceans, and hung new clouds in the sky. 'Ship track', today, is a technical term that transcends cartography altogether: it refers to line-shaped clouds made by ships' exhaust fumes. Ship engines, if unregulated, cough up vast amounts of sulphur dioxide; in the early 2000s, it was calculated that between 4 and 9 per cent of its global emissions came from the shipping industry. Sulphur dioxide, in turn, forms aerosol sulphate particles. Under specific atmospheric conditions, the glowing white plumes of ship tracks coalesce around them, modifying existing clouds. First detected in the 1960s, many of these striking formations are visible from space, stretching for hundreds of kilometres; and they can linger on for a day or more, long after the ship has passed (Plate 1).[20]

The beginnings of the Anthropocene are debated. The atomic era is an obvious candidate, but some historians and scientists backdate the kick-off to the seventeenth and eighteenth centuries. The fact that the proper boom in cartographical tracks took place then is no coincidence. Both the Anthropocene and tracks depended on a new faith in technology, and arguably a new mindset of confidence and control, brought about by the ambitious quest to tame global horizons.[21]

As such, however, tracks are subject to all the qualifications that one can apply to the concept of the Anthropocene. They are not the doing of all humanity, but of certain parts of it. The Anthropocene is not species destiny, but the result of specific historical choice and action.[22] Journey tracks may have depended on set environmental structures, and may have become nearly universal cognitive constructs, but they originated as the imperial stories and instruments of particular individuals and groups. 'Line-making', anthropologists have shown us, might be something that all creatures do, as they move in the world.[23] But *these* lines couldn't have existed anywhere and anytime: they were rooted in certain peculiar ways of understanding and exploiting oceanic spaces.[24]

Here we come to the third, most crucial trait of the track: we have seen that it works as a tool for gathering knowledge and as a tool for marking occupation, but it is also, more specifically, a *storytelling* tool. And stories are always *someone's* stories. Much of what we have just discussed – schematisation, appropriation, a close relationship with modernity and empire – applies quite well to maps in general.[25] But there is one thing that makes the track worth looking at in its own right. The concrete historical practices behind the production and consumption of each track are central here: the track is, itself, process. It's a temporal procedure lying flat on the map, somewhat incongruous among the spatial shrubbery.[26] Its power rests in its recounting the way in which it was made. Unlike most other features of the map, the track never pretends that it was always there. Quite the opposite: as we saw, it adver-tises action and impact. All maps are subjective, and all maps are statements of power: the more objective they claim to be, the less we should trust the notion that they represent 'reality'.[27] Europe, Asia and North America are bloated on our planispheres because of the quirks of cartographical projection; rivers are rarely blue; borders get drawn and toponyms assigned in the most arbitrary ways – and they are often in the eye of the beholder.[28] All maps 'lie' and fabricate, by approximation, addition, omission, distortion, or in a myriad other inventive or accidental ways.[29] And they usually do so behind a mask of respectable objectivity. The track, however, has a unique approach: there is no subtlety in its claims of author-ity. It is determinedly and programmatically individual, loud and unabashed. How do we square this fact with the common assump-tion that modernity has removed subjectivity from its arsenal of representations, in favour of geometrical 'truths'?[30] The answer is, we don't. So the track has a lot to tell us about the contradictions of modern mental frameworks. Storytelling may be often cast as a feature of 'primitive' societies, but it never went away. In fact, modernity's whole rational dominion is built on storytelling.[31]

In this sense, the presence of tracks even on the most technical charts shows us something important: the technological forces of modernity aren't necessarily as impersonal and universalising as they are often portrayed. The same subjectivity that characterises modern literary and artistic endeavours sits snugly at the very heart of modern scientific knowledge. To understand this point better, we can briefly put it in context within the history of mapping.

The seas on medieval and Renaissance maps were commonly filled with decorations: marine monsters, representing the terror of the unknown, and tall ships running before the wind, showing that humanity feared no monsters (Figure 0.3). By the end of the eighteenth century, these idiosyncratic images had nearly all vanished. Some historians have argued that the demise of drawings of ships and monsters signals a scientific and rational turn in Western cartography. New methods for reckoning latitude and longitude reassured navigators that they could pinpoint their exact position in the vast blue ocean. Allegedly, this emerging confidence helped to make such decorations redundant.[32] Then, so the story goes, there was a hiatus of a couple of hundred years, during which the delusion and obsession of Western mapmakers was total, objective, *true* representation of the world, without frills, without subjective angles and without decorative rubbish: depicting the world *as it truly was*. 'Objectivity', of course, is a modern construct. The idea that we can report reality *as is*, doing away with our subjective mediation, is historically contingent. It belongs, most undiluted and intoxicating, to the positivism of the late nineteenth century.[33] A hundred years later, with the rise of grid-based and digital mapping technologies, we supposedly witness another turn: 'embedded subjectivity' comes back. In maps, the here and present matter more, once again, than the universal, stable, 'God's-eye' representation.[34]

This account is plausible, but it omits one element. As ships and monsters faded, track lines arose, flanking them and then slowly replacing them. It is true that there was a shift towards objectivity,

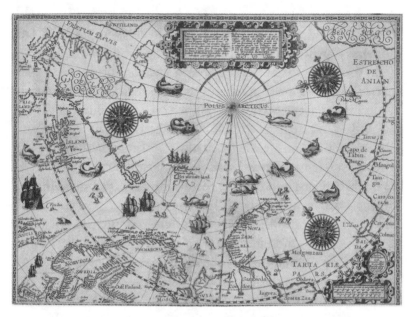

Figure 0.3: Arctic waters littered with ships, whales and
sea monsters (and Dutch ship tracks) (1598).

and then back to subjectivity. Yet, if we scratch just below the
surface, we can unearth a subterranean genealogy, linking the subjectivity of ancient itineraries to that of state-of-the-art GPS. The
common thread is the track, and we will follow it, in its twists and
turns, through this book.[35]

As we do so, however, we must keep in mind an important point.
The subjectivity of the track wasn't just a function of its nature, of
the impossibility of removing the middleman in mapping: it was
deliberate, and it made discovery claims – another very prominent
notion in the modern world. Much like 'objectivity', 'discovery'
doesn't exist, at least as we usually imagine it. The discrete heroic
moments and protagonists that we learn about in school are
somewhat arbitrarily plucked from the stream of lengthy, messy,
collaborative and incremental processes. Knowledge is never built
from scratch. The closer you look at any 'discovery' with the historian's hat on, the more the scope of that discovery breaks down.
What is interesting is *why* those specific moments and people

are picked: this usually has to do with the context in which they moved, and with the types of person, belief and behaviour that certain groups wished to legitimise.[36] Marking a specific event as 'discovery', rather than another, is a power move – and one that tracks do excellently.

This brings us to a key question: are all tracks the same, after all? Sociologists and anthropologists, in particular, are interested in building taxonomies. In his famous work on lines, the British anthropologist Tim Ingold distinguished between lines of 'wayfaring' – the meandering routes that all creatures draw as they live in the world – and lines of 'transport' – direct exercises in 'connecting dots', only giving importance to the departure and arrival points. Transport traces are cold, efficient and usually straight, spurning the cliché that locates fun in the journey rather than in the destination. They go 'across', not 'along'.[37] Wayfaring is the style of the hitchhiker on a gap year, not sure yet where she will land; transport belongs to the six-flights-a-week commuter, simply aiming to arrive. These categories of traveller seemingly have nothing in common, and neither, Ingold would possibly say, do their tracks. For him, the wayfaring track is the natural one, signifying 'habitation' of the world, whereas the straight transport track is the offspring of a modern and imperial 'occupation' mindset.[38] We will return to these connotations later. However, from a historical rather than an anthropological point of view, what we are interested in here is not a rigid taxonomy, but understanding how these types of tracks are *related*. How the ones stem from the others, and vice versa, changing and morphing over time. The route networks that have propped up colonialism and environmental destruction across 'pathless' seas and skies began as individual wayfaring journeys, those of imperial 'explorers' who really had limited knowledge of where they were going. Maritime and aerial highways are not as impersonal as they seem – for they, too, tell stories. In fact, if they didn't tell stories, they wouldn't be at all.

A second possible way of classifying tracks would consider the material history of cartography – the specificities in how and why maps are made. All too often, different 'modes' of mapping, such as nautical charting and geographical mapping, are flattened under a single, blurry notion of 'cartography', which ignores context and function.[39] It's important to avoid this trap. An ordinary captain plotting his course across the Atlantic and hoping to make landfall had little in common with a commercial mapmaker who glorified Drake's voyages in shining colours. Although I have written of tracks as if they were characters, we should never forget that specific people are behind them, with a range of personal and professional aims. Yet the track, as a tool and an idea, quickly spread across various 'modes' and practices of mapping, and in the process made the leap into more general conceptualisations of mobility and the world. Further, tracks moved from the environment to the map, and vice versa: foamy wakes crystallised into ink, and eventually vomited back onto the sea and sky as slashes of pollution. In their daily work, environmental historians have to wrangle this urgent paradox: ideas about nature and our impact on it are cultural constructs, but ecological collapse is not. How do we go from ideas to material reality, and vice versa?[40] The track inhabits precisely this twilight zone, where fantasy shades into solid hallucination. All its passages and transitions between imagination and reality are historically informed and, by and large, documentable, as we shall see in the coming chapters. Mapping, as 'both analogue and abstraction', has 'agency': it is capable not only of representing, but of constructing the world.[41] In doing so, it can well transcend its original main function. So, in many ways, this isn't a book about maps, but a book *through* maps.

Throughout what follows, then, we look at the track in two closely interconnected senses. First, and most fundamentally, we must see it as a navigational instrument, a technology for devising, completing and documenting oceanic journeys, and later carrying out maritime surveys. Here we are in the domain of the material history of mapping, of the concrete practices of calculation, tracking and drawing. However, we cannot observe the evolution of these practices without exploring their cultural meanings – which arguably had the largest impact on people's lives. Tracks weren't just a navigational tool: they were a symbolic tool. They schematised: they turned disorderly, lived, on-the-ground experience into a neat convention. They occupied – by marking

Figure 0.4: How does this become permanent?

the territory, and even the supposedly 'pathless' ocean. And they reeled out stories, by crystallising the flow of time into a permanent flow of ink – stretching a sequence of actions by mortal individuals into a spatial unbroken line. What unifies all these meanings is a single theme: in theory, tracks represent *control*. We shall see that the reality was far messier.

THE TRACKLESS WORLD

In 1932, the man who had been known as 'Lawrence of Arabia' published a translation of Homer's *Odyssey*.[1] T. E. Lawrence was an archaeologist, soldier and spy who became immensely famous during the First World War, and later retired into semi-anonymity; he read ancient Greek classics as a hobby. When he was a young Oxford student, as his ambitions of imperial glory brewed, he had carried the *Odyssey* in his pocket wherever he went. For men like Lawrence, empire was a blank map to be filled with personal stories: a 'screen on which European fantasies may be projected'. Two-and-a-half-millennia-old tales, blending epic adventure with wondrous legend, offered a perfect template.[2] Bruce Rogers, a renowned typographer, turned to Lawrence for this translation because he found all existing versions of the *Odyssey* 'lacking in speed'.[3] The result was a dynamic and forceful retelling of a familiar story: the tribulations of the Greek hero Odysseus as he attempts to return home after ten years of war on the windswept plains of Troy.

From at least 1934, in all American impressions, the inside cover of Lawrence's book featured a striking round map of the Homeric Mediterranean.[4] Odysseus himself loomed dramatically around the frame, alongside his divine protector Athena and his mortal enemy Poseidon, god of the sea. A track with small directional arrows marked, as promised by the map title, 'The Wanderings of Odysseus Son of Laertes, Lord of Ithaca, Kinsman of Zeus' (Figure 1.1). The hero's path bounces around the sea, buffeted by the winds and the anger of the gods, from the isle of the Lotus Eaters to that of the Cyclopes, almost in range of home, Ithaca, but then cruelly away again, deep into the Greek underworld, and back and forth

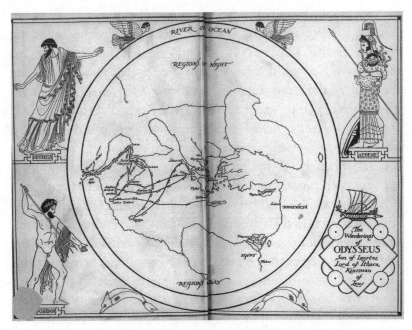

Figure 1.1: 'The Wanderings of Odysseus Son of Laertes, Lord of Ithaca, Kinsman of Zeus', in T. E. Shaw (Lawrence of Arabia), *The Odyssey of Homer: Newly Translated into English Prose* (New York: Oxford University Press, 1932, 9th popular impression, 1947).

on myriad other misadventures, for ten long years. Odysseus finally comes back to his family – a middle-aged wife harassed by suitors; a grown-up son; an elderly, widowed and distraught father; and the faithful dog Argos, who lived to extreme old age only to die of joy upon seeing his master come home. But this part of the story, although it occupies the whole second half of the *Odyssey*, finds no place on the map. What matters are the wanderings.

This graphical representation of the Homeric tale was built upon a long tradition. We can already recognise many of its features in a round map from the 1790s, which accompanied the first German translation of the *Odyssey*.[5] A flowing dotted line recounts the '*Irrfahrten des Odysseus*' ('wanderings of Odysseus'). The path of the vessel is much less rigid than on the Lawrence/Rogers map, but the geographical referents are in the same place: the islands of a mythical, imagined Mediterranean (Figure 1.2).[6] The convention of displaying this journey continued in the following decades: in the 1830s and 1840s, a reworked version of the round map was widely published across Europe, sometimes including the track of the Argonauts next to that of Odysseus (Figure 1.3).[7] The Lawrence imprints, it seems, directly recycled this template. While this specific format was popular throughout the century, other analogous visualisations of the story became quite common, too: school textbooks made Odysseus' tracks into philological and pseudo-scientific matters. William Gladstone, the future British Prime Minister, was another obsessive amateur classicist who would later become mired in the contradictions of Britain's Mediterranean empire. In the 1850s, he published a thematic diagram of the 'outer geography of the *Odyssey*', showing the hero's peregrinations in highly schematic fashion. Homeric quotes referring to the duration of each leg of the voyage, complete with citations of chapter and verse, accompanied the track lines. The plate was picked up by a Scottish cartographer and included in a new edition of his successful classical atlas for children. By this point, a travel story like that of the *Odyssey* was best told and taught with the visual aid of a map.[8] For European audiences, steeped in imperial propaganda, Odysseus' voyages resembled those of their own tragic explorers: 'discovering' new lands and peoples, battling against desperate odds, and, like Lawrence, we could add, frequently losing themselves amid delusions and bloodshed.

But if Odysseus, one night after dinner in his palace in Ithaca, had taken a look at any of these maps, reminiscing on his travels, all he would have seen is a series of squiggles. The modern 'cartographical' perspective – let alone tracks – likely had nothing to do with that of ancient Greek navigators. Their world knew and used maps, but in very different ways from ours. If we search for European ship tracks before the sixteenth century, we find none. In fact, we find hardly any proper journey lines, whether at sea or on land.

How did Odysseus (if he even existed) think of his movements across the seas? We have some clues to that because the *Odyssey* delves deep into maritime culture. For example, when the hero's

Figure 1.2: Homer's world and Odysseus' journeys as seen at the turn of the nineteenth century: 'Homerische Welttafel von J. H. Voss 1806'.

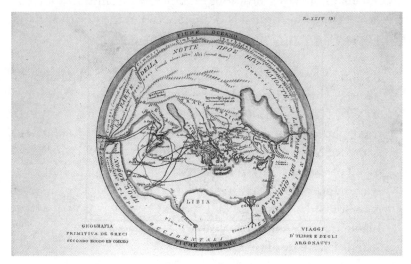

Figure 1.3: The journeys of Odysseus and the Argonauts, from an 1842 Italian atlas.

worried son Telemachus is looking for information about his lost father, he visits King Nestor in Pylos. The old man gives him a breakdown of the navigational options that had faced commanders after their departure from Troy: heading into the open sea, which Nestor himself did, was the most dangerous solution, but the quickest. As an alternative, the commanders 'mulled over the long sea route, unsure / whether to lay our course northward of Khios, / keeping the isle of Psyria off to port, / or inside Khios, / coasting by windy Mimas'.[9] The referents here are 'northward', leftward ('port'), 'inside' and 'by': the perspective, it seems, is at sea level, or just above. There is more: the modern translator I have just quoted (the American poet Robert Fitzgerald), seeing matters through his own worldview, writes of a 'long sea route'; however, if we check the original text, that actually says 'long sailing', 'long navigation' or 'long voyage' (*dolichòn plóon*, 'δολιχὸν πλόον') – with an emphasis on time and action rather than space.[10] This wasn't a long *line* on the sea, but a long *time* at sea, busy with the process of sailing. The difference is subtle, but crucial.

All this still tells us little about how journeys would have been represented and reported to others, if not through lines on maps. The closest hint we have is a typology of document that, unlike graphic maps, survives in various examples from antiquity. Here is an extract from one, probably drafted between the fourth and the sixth century AD, the long dusk of the Roman Empire:

IN THE SAME WAY BETWEEN SICILY AND AFRICA:
island of Cossura from Lilibeo of Sicily
are CLXXX stadia [*unit of distance*],
from Clipea out of Africa DXC stadia,
islands of Malta Ciefesta and Falacron,
island of Cercena, this from Tacapis
is a distance of DCXXII stadia,
island of Girba from Gitti of Tripoli XC stadia.
Island Traieia Syrota Cephallania
Asteris Itaca Paxos Propaxos Oxia.

[...]

The Strophades Islands, which were previously called Plote,
in the Ionian sea, by which Greece is bathed,
in these lived the Harpies;
islands Cephalanie Zacinthos and Dulcia,
here is mount Ithacus, where is Ulysses' homeland;[11]

According to archaeologists, the Bronze Age city of Troy fell –
if it did at all – in the twelfth century (*c.*1180) BC; the Homeric
poems were composed between 400 and 500 years later.[12] So,
looking at a fourth-century AD Roman imperial text to make sense
of worldviews during the Trojan War would be like reading a food
magazine today to make sense of how a Roman ate. And yet, some
continuities existed across 'antiquity': for example, in the verbally
and later textually oriented, memory-focused, storytelling culture
that in the eighth century BC begat the *Odyssey*, and 1,200 years
later begat seemingly dull lists like the passage I have just quoted.
Perhaps these lists look dull to us only because we have lost the
contextual skills to interpret them. How did a text like this work?

In order to answer this, we must first ask a radical question. Did
the ancient Graeco-Roman world at all know and use visual wayfinding maps? This doubt seems absurd, because to us maps are
entirely natural tools – they are the way the world *is*. How can
you imagine it, if not through a map? Yet, for some historians and
classicists, the answer is that Greeks and Romans didn't conceive
of 'scale' maps, especially when it came to ones representing large
swathes of territory, and to be used for practical wayfinding. The
ancients, these scholars claim, usually saw their surroundings in a
linear, 'path-shaped' way: from their own point of view rather than
a flat, on-scale, top-down or aerial perspective. The technical term
for this is 'hodological', from *hodós*, the Greek word for path.[13]
Here we may get excited – because what are we looking for in this
book if not journey paths? But there is a catch: this ancient form
of thinking by path is fundamentally different from our modern
journey-line paths.

The man who pioneered the theory of an ancient hodological vision, the Italian scholar Pietro Janni, explains this difference with a wonderful example. Imagine that you have organised a birthday party for your child, and at the end you must drive his friends back to their houses; unfortunately, one of them doesn't know his own address. As panic sets in, you realise you have kidnapped a toddler. What this clever toddler does know, however, is the route he takes every day to go home from school. So you drive him to the school, and patiently follow his instructions, turn by turn, until you get to his house – which is, it transpires, very close to yours. But the little boy had no idea, because his way of picturing places and movement was structured around a single dimension – a route line – rather than a bidimensional surface: direction rather than distance, concrete lived experience rather than abstract geometrical convention. Here, the parallel with a child's vision shouldn't lead us to infantilise ancient cultures, or speak of 'evolution'. Rather, it serves to demonstrate different, equally successful ways of navigating the world that we still regularly adopt – even in conjunction with scale maps.[14] When we stop a stranger to ask for directions, and try to focus as they rattle out half a dozen turns and landmarks; when we remember that we need to take the motorway exit just past the run-down McDonald's; when we are late for work and worry about those thirty seconds at the traffic light from hell – on all those occasions, we are mainly thinking about space hodologically. Modern journey lines unfold graphically *on a map*, but the ancient type of hodological journey line existed as a standalone item, whether mentally, verbally, textually or, more rarely, graphically. It didn't mark the territory – it came to life through it.

According to Janni's faction of the historical debate, then, all ancient wayfinding was done not through maps, but through words. That is, through mental, verbal or written descriptions of specific voyages, sometimes boiling down to simple lists of places, distances and landmarks: what we term itineraries. Such lists have a venerable tradition: some Babylonian ones have reached us from over four millennia ago.[15] The Bible, too, preserves a few itineraries. For example, in the last chapter of the Book of Numbers, Moses is ordered by God to write down the long list of encampments (forty years' worth!) that took his people from Egypt to Jericho: 'Here are the stages in the journey of the Israelites'. The word used for 'stages' in the Hebrew original, '*mas'ei*' (מסעי), also translated as 'journeys' in some English versions, literally means 'pullings-up of tent-pegs'.[16] This is a step-by-step way of visualising a journey, through concrete – and discrete – actions rather than an abstract unbroken line.

Ancient itineraries had a special name when they illustrated sea journeys: they were called *periploi*, which in Greek literally means 'sailings around'. Here we get a clue as to what kinds of journeys were usually completed by sea. Lacking the navigational tools to determine their exact position, and often the nautical infra-structure to sail against the wind in open waters, ancient ships rarely strayed out of sight of the shore. The exception were well-tested and short-distance seasonal routes, such as those crossing the southern Mediterranean, the 'Sicilian Sea', the Red Sea, or the Channel between today's England and France. Stellar navigation was known, but it mainly served to sail in a straight direction along what we would term a parallel.[17] The longer they spent away from known referents, the more ancient vessels risked ending up like Odysseus' fleet – hopelessly lost. Moreover, hugging the coast rather than shooting for a single destination meant that trade could be done in every port, instead of just a final one.[18]

In light of this information, let's recall that scattered list of islands we saw a minute ago. If you weren't straying into the empty blue oceans but just jumping between known bases, instructions like those made perfect sense. This model of moving in the world is tunnel-like, linear in the sense of being a channel through which the voyager proceeds, rather than a line that he or she paints behind themselves on a flat surface.[19] Places and landmarks are strung together like beads in a necklace, and nothing else exists beyond (or indeed between) them. The perspective is that of someone *in* the world, rather than *on* and *above* the world, and the voyager doesn't leave her trace on the land and sea, but simply looks at their features to guide her next step.

Some of the surviving itineraries and *periploi* are so bare that they might have been nigh-unusable for actual travel. The extract on islands that we encountered just now, a case in point, comes from a long collection known as *Itinerarium Antonini*. This source, surviving in various manuscript copies, covers vast areas of Europe, Britain, Africa and the Near East, as well as the intervening seas. It was once thought that 'Antoninus' might have referred to the Roman Emperor Marcus Aurelius Antoninus, usually known as Caracalla (AD 188–217) – famous for perpetrating vast slaughter and for granting citizenship to all free male imperial subjects. However, the itinerary likely has nothing to do with him, or indeed with any Emperor.[20] Looking at its form and at the specific toponyms used, it appears that the land half and the maritime one may have originated as independent texts, the latter much more recent than the former.[21]

Even setting aside the question of dates, trying to work your way through the endless lists of places and distances, particularly in the land part, is hardly straightforward. What emerges is a tangle of repetitions and inconsistencies, often spurning obvious routes and stops. Frustrated by the task of trying to make sense of this jumble, one historian has suggested that it was nothing more than a 'hobbyist's assemblage' of specific journeys – he reckons likely completed by imperial soldiers or officials, and reported in this dry format as part of 'a timesheet or expenses claim'.[22] The itinerary's maritime half is an equally chaotic list of disjointed crossings, and, later on, of islands with mythical facts. The most coherent stretch is a rundown of the ports one would touch when sailing along the coast of northern Italy, from Rome up to Arles in Gaul: 'from Pirgos at Panapione, anchorage, miles III; from Panapione at Castrum Novum, anchorage, miles VII; from Castrum Novum to Centum Cellis, anchorage, miles V', and so on.[23] The anonymous author(s) ran no risk of wasting words.

If we only looked at samples like this one, without the context to bring them alive, the itinerary-based worldview would seem dull and lifeless, shorn of colour and desiccated to the bones. Other itineraries, however, read a lot like guidebooks, of which they are the most direct ancestors. Here we can consider two examples, one maritime and one land-based – very different, but both vividly illustrating the spirit and perspective of the itinerary 'mode'.

*

The Greek *Periplus Maris Erythraei* ('circumnavigation of the Red Sea') was written in the first century AD, by an Egyptian Greek merchant. In Roman Egypt, the long arm of trade reached out to lands that were little more than legend. The *Periplus* skirts the shores of the whole north-western quarter of the Indian Ocean, before heading down the eastern coast of Africa, out as far as present-day Sri Lanka ('Palaisimundu', or 'Taprobanê'), and beyond. It is in this 2,000-year-old document that we find the first ever Western mention of China. 'Thina' is, according to the author, 'a very great inland city' lying 'right under Ursa Minor', 'from which silk floss, yarn, and cloth are shipped by land'; 'it is not easy to get to this Thina,' he adds, a place whence few have come to the outside world.[24] The route description ends shortly afterwards, on a powerful note that on a map would be a truncated line: 'What lies beyond this area, because of extremes of storm, bitter cold, and difficult terrain and also because of some divine power of the gods, has not been explored.'[25]

The *Periplus* overflows with political, commercial and navigational details useful for the traveller, as well as foreign terms from the trading world of the Indian Ocean, many of them not previously attested in Greek.[26] The form is that of a text in full sentences, and the images are often vivid and memorable. In each port we are given a handy list of the commodities that can be bought or sold. Coloured cloth, precious stones, silverware, gold, glass, brass, tin, lead, iron and copper, Roman coins, grain, cane sugar, axes, knives, pots and vessels, tortoise shells, ivory, rhino horn, nautilus shell, pearls, dates, myrrh, incense, indigo, dyes, spices, saffron, white marble, coral, pepper, wines, olive oil – all in various forms, qualities and quantities, depending on the place, and slowly transforming as the voyage proceeds eastwards: even if the aim is transmitting practical information, the reader is inevitably swept along on a journey of the senses, and paraded in the first person through the stalls of these local, ever-changing faraway markets. The various steps of the voyage echo with direct experience in other ways, too. For example, in the impervious gulf in front of Bharuch ('Barygaza', or 'Βαρύγαζα'), present-day Gujarat, the tides are so strong that they flood the river, making it flow upstream: ships are ripped off their anchorages and smashed on the shoals.

So much power is generated at the inrush of the sea even during the dark of the moon, particularly if the flood arrives at night, that when the tide is just beginning to come in and the sea is still at rest, there is carried from it to people at the mouth something like the rumble of an army heard from afar, and after a short while the sea itself races over the shoals with a hiss.[27]

Navigators are also warned off the treacherous shallows of the nearby Gulf of Barakê (Kutch), signalled by the swarming of 'snakes, huge and black'; 'around Barygaza', instead, 'snakes that are smaller and yellow and golden in color are met with'.[28]

Let's jump ahead two or three hundred years, and travel beside a weary but expectant pilgrim – quite possibly a woman – slowly progressing towards the most sacred core of her faith.[29] The text that allows us to do so is perhaps the most heartfelt example of land itinerary to have survived from the ancient world. It describes the route of (and may well be addressed to) some of the earliest European Christians embarking on the long pilgrimage to the Holy Land. The author outlines a specific journey taking place in AD 333: Christianity had been decriminalised by Emperor Constantine just two decades earlier. Known as the Bordeaux Itinerary (*Itinerarium Burdigalense*), this account starts on the estuary of the River Garonne in France, and continues until about halfway as a plain list of the kind that we saw above: from Bordeaux, 'change at Stomatas leagues VII; change at Sirione leagues VIIII; city of Vasatas leagues VIIII; change at Tres Arbores leagues V'. In this fashion it carries on along the Pyrenees and the north of Italy, across the Balkans, down to Constantinople and through present-day Turkey. But the closer we get to the destination, the more interesting facts seep into the droning catalogue. At 'Mount Syna', we learn, there is a spring that will make a woman pregnant if she bathes in it. At Isdradela, 28 miles further, one can see the place where Elijah made his prophecies, and the field in which David killed Goliath. Within a few days, our wide-eyed pilgrim passes the mountain where Abraham almost sacrificed his son, Joseph's tomb, the spot where his sister Dinah was raped by the

Amorites, the tree by which Jacob fought the Angel of God, and more. And thence to Jerusalem, which of course gets many paragraphs of its own – as do other biblical sites like Jericho and Bethlehem. Then the monotonous list of places and distances resumes, as the itinerary bends back on the home leg from Heraclea, crosses Macedonia and the length of Italy, and terminates in Milan.[30]

Some modern editions, of course, represent all this as a map with a journey line.[31] Perhaps you were mentally doing the same while reading through the paragraph above. However, that sanitised line doesn't capture the deep feeling and lived observation of place embedded in an itinerary like this: the point of view of a pilgrim from 1,700 years ago, counting their long dusty miles, overnight stays and horse changes, and discovering the land and its stories as they went along.[32] Arguably, that line is not one that he (or she) could have pictured at all.

The matter, of course, is a contested one. At least one source, a military manual from the fourth century AD, advises commanders to use 'itineraries not only written, but also pictured' ('itineraria non tantum adnotata sed etiam picta').[33] What was meant by this? Without diving too deep into the debate concerning the ancients' knowledge of scale maps, we can briefly consider what is left from antiquity that might resemble a journey route map. The material is scattered and flimsy, so it's best followed thematically rather than chronologically.

Topographical plans, showing a bird's eye view of small areas – fields, urban spaces and their surrounding roads – crop up across the millennia. Perhaps the oldest is a mural painting from the Neolithic site of Çatal Hüyük, in present-day Turkey. Created over 8,000 years ago, it looks like a collection of squares stacked into three or four rows. Archaeologists have read it as a map of the town and the volcano nearby. But how do we know whether it's our own cartographical mindset that leads us to think in such terms? What if this was a completely different form of decoration, a representation of an object, or a pattern? Are we seeing maps in objects that aren't maps, just as we see the man in the Moon?[34] This type of cognitive bias stalks and ambushes historians around every corner. As a human default, we look at the past as a mirror, but we cannot assume that people who turned to dust thousands of years ago would have seen and imagined the world through the same eyes as us.

If we move forward a few millennia, we do find clay tablets that more clearly represent street plans. For example, one from Nippur in Mesopotamia, datable from the second millennium BC, shows an aerial view of the city: its walls, stores, a park and a temple to the god of winds.[35] Another, roughly contemporary tablet from the same site displays the irrigation system in the surrounding fields as a twisting series of double lines (Figure 1.4).[36] And much later in time we encounter large mapping projects like the Severan Plan of Rome (*Forma Urbis Romae*), an architectural city plan of the whole sprawling imperial capital, carved onto marble around AD 210. One thousand, one hundred and eighty-six fragments have survived, plus eighty-seven of which we only have early modern drawings: this is thought to be about 10 or 15 per cent of the original total – an immense series of slabs that occupied 235 square metres on a wall of the Temple of Peace. Since the Renaissance, dozens of generations of researchers have toiled away to reconstruct this giant puzzle, using the grain and scuffs of the marble and a deep knowledge of Rome. Most recently, cutting-edge digital technologies and 3D modelling algorithms have hugely accelerated the process, and new methods based on similarities in cathodoluminescence and isotope ratios are being trialled, potentially allowing archaeologists to assign fragments to specific neighbouring pieces and slabs.[37] (In archaeology, no puzzle-solving techniques ever count as cheating.) The lines on the *Forma Urbis* mark, in considerable planimetric detail, the walls of houses, shops and monuments, but the streets are also clearly visible as the empty spaces between blocks (Figure 1.5).

These, however, are all static maps, made for the management of property and territory rather than wayfinding. Representing various blocks and the surrounding roads, or a system of ditches and canals, is not the same as depicting an itinerary, nor even as

Figure 1.4: Clay tablet from Nippur (*c.*1500 BC), showing a network of irrigation canals.

Figure 1.5: An eighteenth-century drawing of some fragments of the Marble Plan of Rome.

making movement routes the focus of a map. Instead, there are some other ancient maps in which routes receive substantial attention.

The prosperous reign of Ramesses III, a pharaoh of the Egyptian Twentieth Dynasty, ended in blood. His mummy shows that he was murdered, his throat deeply and brutally slit. His left big toe was also sliced off during the attack, the payoff of a harem conspiracy led by one of his queens. From this muddle of corruption and betrayal his successor, Ramesses IV, emerged triumphant, wiping out the murderers and ascending to the throne. However, we know little else about him. He may have been the son of Ramesses III, and he may or may not have continued his predecessor's military involvement in Canaan in the north, Libya in the west and Nubia in the south. This was the twelfth century BC, 300 years after the peak of the Egyptian empire under the Eighteenth Dynasty – a time when the Pharaohs' power had stretched from the edges of Anatolia to present-day Sudan. By the days of Ramesses IV, Egypt's might had started on its long way out.[38]

What we do know about Ramesses IV is that early on in his reign he ordered several quarrying expeditions to mines in the remote corners of his dominions, to extract stone, copper and turquoise for his grand building plans. Four of these expeditions went to the Wadi Hammamat. This is a rocky riverbed in the middle of the Eastern Desert, on the road that, from the vicinity of modern Luxor, snakes away towards the shores of the Red Sea. His men were tasked with fetching the local Bekhen-stone (greywacke), unique to this quarry, for various projects in the necropolis of Thebes. These quarrying expeditions were massive endeavours, counting an entourage of thousands, and supply lines intended to keep them fed and equipped. Thousands also died – reportedly 900, or 10 per cent of the complement, on the fourth expedition alone.[39]

It is one of these missions that has left us the oldest known specimen of a route map (and of a geological map, too): the so-called 'Turin Papyrus', dated about 1150 BC. The mercenary Italian excavator Bernardino Drovetti sold this exceptional find to the King of Sardinia in 1824. It came as part of the initial batch of antiquities that led to the foundation of one of the largest Egyptian museums in the world, in the unlikely site of Turin; there it has remained ever since. Likely oriented south-east (the Nile flows northwards, so south was up for the ancient Egyptians), and not drawn to scale, this fragment of pinkish-tinted papyrus contains a snapshot of two T-crossroads, running alongside and between the mountains and *wadis* of the region. As well as these roads, its captions point to a cluster of workmen's houses, a shrine for the god Amun, a stela dedicated to a previous pharaoh, and priceless deposits of gold and of the dark-greenish Bekhen sandstone (Plate 2).[40] We can see that this is a route map in the sense of a *road* map: it shows permanent features of the territory, rather than marking human passage with a line.

There is another ancient document that potentially portrays land roads, over a wider stretch of territory. Here we dip our toes into turbulent waters. The 'Artemidorus Papyrus' hit the classical academic world like a depth charge, in the late 1990s. Carbon-dated to within a few decades either side of the first century AD, its fragments suddenly came to light in a private collection. They had been rescued from a glut of 'recycled papyrus' that had been intended as stuffing, maybe of non-human mummies. The fabulous find was purchased by a large Italian banking foundation for an eye-watering 2.75 million euros.[41]

Why was this papyrus so valuable? It contains three things: written passages, partly matching some known texts by geographer Artemidorus of Ephesus (whence the name); very rare ancient sketches of animals, people and anatomical parts; and the oldest Graeco-Roman map ever discovered – possibly the earliest surviving representation of the Iberian peninsula (Figure 1.6). What matters for our purposes is that this map seems to show some wavy land routes, crossing its whole width. Some of them are single lines, but one at the bottom could well be a road, drawn as two parallel lines that fork around a settlement. Yet the map is utterly opaque to attempts at interpretation: are these marks actually 'routes', or in fact watercourses, mountain ranges and boundary lines? Without colour-coding, or even a clue as to the location represented, it's difficult to know.[42] Worst of all, there is a chance that this papyrus is, in fact, a nineteenth-century forgery.

Since its original publication, followed by a lavish international exhibition in Turin, Berlin and Munich, the document has racked up scepticism from various experts. The Italian classicist Luciano Canfora has poured rivers of ink into demonstrating that the papyrus was actually made by the Greek Constantine Simonides (*c.*1820–90), a larger-than-life forger and thief. For many decades, the ruthless, erudite and crafty Simonides fooled scholars and antiquarians across Europe and the Mediterranean. He produced a range of spectacular fakes – including, possibly, his own death of leprosy in Alexandria. Could the rediscovered 'Artemidorus' be, more than a century later, just another papyrus in his cap? With millions at stake, the matter landed in the hands of the authorities. In 2018, after a police investigation, an Italian magistrate ruled that the artefact had been fraudulently sold as genuine. But heated debates continued on matters ranging from the terms and characters used in the text to the chemical composition of the ink (which, unlike the papyrus support itself, wasn't immediately carbon-dated, to avoid irreparable damage). For over two decades now, conferences, books, articles and news pieces have relentlessly piled up, each of them dissecting specific aspects of the 'P.Artemid.': are its images plausible, or suspiciously similar to those in some eighteenth-century drawing manuals? How about the text, which bears an astonishing resemblance to the French translation of an early-nineteenth-century German geographical treatise? Is the ink genuinely ancient? Why do we know so little of the circumstances in which this papyrus suddenly came to light? We only have one photo of the stuffing glut in which it was allegedly retrieved – and some experts have accused this image of being digitally manipulated.[43]

As is often the case in these situations, the debates have spilled across the board to tarnish the reputation of the art dealer, and the credentials of the scholars on either side. Media outlets have bluntly taken one position or the other, turning a scholarly discussion into an international scandal.[44] Without specific expertise it's impossible to pass judgement here, and all we can do

Figure 1.6: Map portion of the 'Artemidorus Papyrus', currently in Turin. Are the horizontal lines routes, mountains, boundaries or rivers?

is move swiftly on. However, in our quest for journey lines, we do so still empty-handed.

We now come to the most famous ancient route map, a stunning masterpiece usually known as the 'Peutinger Map', or 'Peutinger Table'. A parchment strip about 7 metres long and 34 centimetres tall, it is preserved in pieces at the Austrian National Library. It shows the full extent of the Romans' known world, between Britain and Sri Lanka, although bits are now missing. The whole is heavily compressed into horizontal stripes, dotted with cities and fortifications. The thick blue-green veins of rivers pattern the pale surface of the land masses, together with a complex web of thin red lines – the route arteries that connected and sustained the empire.

How do we square an artefact like the Peutinger Table with the theory that the ancients had no 'map consciousness', or bidimensional geographical vision? For some historians, we don't.[45] However, we should note two things. First, we aren't absolutely sure that the Table is actually a Roman object. The version we have is a medieval copy. Most scholars place the original on which it's based sometime in the first few centuries of the Christian Era, but there is little certainty as to the exact period. The classicist Emily Albu has even suggested that the prototype map was not Roman at all, but itself medieval, from around the time of Charlemagne or his successors (ninth century AD).[46] Whatever the case may be, the Table is also most certainly not built to scale. Historians' go-to comparison here is the London Underground map: the mapmaker's aim was not reporting relative distances and directions faithfully, but turning the spotlight onto the structure of the connectivity system.[47] The Table's view from above is distorted and entirely schematic.

In the Peutinger Table we see the first instance of the temporality of an itinerary being squashed into a graphic representation. Here we need to take a quick dive into Latin grammar. Latin, like German or Russian, declines nouns into 'cases'. So if a Roman had wanted to say, 'I'm going to Rome', she could have changed the ending of the word, rather than using the preposition 'to'. *Roma* here would have become *Romam*, an economical way of deploying language. The same word could have many different endings, and thus come to mean an array of different things: to Rome, of Rome, in Rome, from Rome, and so on. The names of places on the Peutinger Table aren't always written in the standard 'static' form (the nominative case), but with endings that incorporate movement and mean '*from* place x' and '*to* place x'. That is the same way in which textual itineraries were formulated, and establishes a clear direction of travel along each line.[48] It's almost as if the place names were numbered. In short, these impressionistic red arteries do not strictly represent physical roads, but moving itineraries – that is, potential journeys.[49]

We see here the earliest roots of our tracks on the water, but with two caveats. First, these lines have little to say about specific, *individual* journeys. They may not be physical infrastructure, in the sense of actual roads, but they are collective and impersonal nonetheless. Second, the lines on the Peutinger Table dare not stretch onto the empty rust-green seas.

A few of them briefly cross the dark water of rivers and narrow gulphs, and their red ink is very nearly submerged in it: it's clearly not intended that they should be visible; the stroke, if at all continuous, is a matter of drawing convenience (Plate 3). Occasionally, some other route reaches the edge of the land – only to drown in the sea without a trace, before magically reappearing on a facing shore. Classicists also point to a few coastal line tracts that must have represented maritime itineraries, because the land passage in those parts is impracticable. Benet Salway suggests that these lines were drawn as land rather than sea routes because the artist was working from a written itinerary, and didn't realise that the instructions at that point were sending the voyager by sea.[50] But perhaps there is another, more momentous explanation: what if the person who drew the Table simply *couldn't* imagine a line on the water? This gives us an indication of how close to roads the Peutinger Map lines still were.

A similar issue crops up in the last ancient map we shall consider here. The mighty city of Dura-Europos, in present-day Syria, sat on the banks of the River Euphrates for over 2,300 years: originally at the crossroads of many civilisations, and then, for sixteen long centuries, buried and mostly forgotten. In 1920, during British military occupation, some Indian soldiers were digging up a trench on the site when they stumbled upon a marvellous find. Hidden wall paintings gleamed through the dust, bright and very well preserved. This accidental discovery triggered many decades of intermittent archaeological operations. The best sections of the ruins were dismantled and packed off to the National Museum in Damascus and the Art Gallery of Yale University, while the rest was eventually sacked and largely razed to the ground by ISIS in the early 2010s.[51] The city, however, had much more to offer. In 1922, the teams excavating there discovered the remains of some oval parade shields, with thick leathery parchment glued to the flat sides. The parchment bore the trace of decorations. The following year, a further fragment emerged: sketched on it was the earliest map ever found of the coast of the Black Sea – and of what today is Ukraine.[52]

On the left, in blue, is the water, with two ships and a rowing boat floating on it. Vertically across the middle runs the white line of the coast. And on the right, on the reddish land, is a Greek list of places and distances, with small brick buildings sketched beside most of them (Plate 4). Few specific geographical features are recognisable, apart from the occasional river: this is not a map in the modern cartographical sense as much as a textual itinerary written on a painted shore. Towards the end of its living history, in around AD 200, Dura-Europos had become a bustling garrison base on the eastern frontiers of the Roman Empire. This map was likely drawn by an archer deployed there, and is reckoned to depict the stages of his march. Is the journey represented on the shield a land or a sea one, and in what proportions?[53] We will never know, for one simple reason: there is no line.

What we have, then, from over two millennia of Mediterranean history, is a sketch of two crossroads, a line-less list of coastal stops painted by a soldier 1,400 years later, a possible forgery that *may* represent itineraries, and a giant diagram of land routes that was still deeply wedded to the concept of roads. Route maps don't seem to have been particularly fashionable in antiquity. The ancient world was also, as Janni puts it, 'totally unacquainted with nautical cartography'.[54] This view, like pretty much any academic position, has found its strong opponents, and it is certainly problematic to argue from absence.[55] But a proper maritime map from ancient Greece or Rome has yet to emerge. All the more so, then, a map showing the track of a ship. In all these mapped seas, the floor is lava: no path treads on the waves.

Why should we care about ship tracks in particular? Because ship tracks, unlike land routes, are artificial constructs. The foamy wake left behind by a vessel can only become a solid line if one adopts a specific cartographical mindset. The fact that pre-modern people privileged other ways of reporting navigation shows us that this mindset is not universal. Ship tracks don't simply exist: they were born, as a symptom of well-defined historical circumstances.

As we saw, there is a second feature of these ancient route maps that sets them apart from modern journey lines: they never depicted an individual voyage. They showed *structural* and static features of the territory, like roads and mountain passes, or at most common itineraries. They spoke of set possibilities rather than personal stories. We shall return to this type of route track later, for it is one that we use a great deal today. However, our modern route networks also took shape *through* the mediation of individual journey lines. Most importantly, they took shape as a result of a specific historical struggle against the pathlessness of the seas. In the ancient Mediterranean world, we may suspect, the lack of lines on the water and the lack of personal lines largely went hand in hand.

As we proceed into the Middle Ages, the hodological vision continues to prevail, although the number and variety of maps decidedly mushroom. Medieval Europeans had their own rich traditions of mapmaking, and people were far more mobile than we may think, at all social levels. For example, textual evidence allows us to reconstruct the months-long, meandering itineraries followed by kings and bishops across their land, with huge baggage trains, treasure, families and retinue. Medieval courts weren't perpetually entrenched in castles: monarchs were regularly on the move, bringing justice, war, taxes and awe to subjects in the furthest reaches of their domains. Those subjects, too, covered vast distances for trade, pilgrimage and military campaigns. A world in motion requires a good understanding of routes: a few land route and road maps survive, illustrating a thick web of possibilities for mobility. Some of these maps, like the fourteenth-century 'Gough Map' of Britain, look quite similar to the Peutinger Table – although the question of whether they were used for wayfinding remains unresolved (Plate 5).[56]

This isn't simply a story of continuity, however. In the late thirteenth century, two separate and decisive innovations prepared the ground for tracks. Within the same decade or so, in the 1290s, we encounter *both* the first proper storytelling route on a map and the first instance of maritime mapping.

Painted just before 1300, the so-called Hereford *Mappa Mundi* was displayed in that city's cathedral, in England, for the edification of visitors and pilgrims. This map is notable for many reasons, but one interests us here: the Exodus of the Israelites from Egypt – the forty years' march that is recounted as an itinerary in the Bible – was painted as a journey line.[57] To my knowledge, we have no earlier example. A colourful, round-shaped representation of the known world, the *Mappa Mundi* swirls with many episodes and characters, from the Old and New Testament, from tales of the saints or Alexander the Great's conquests, and even Greek and Roman myth. But only the path of the Children of Israel through the desert is shown as a route line.[58] This might potentially indicate how the innovation happened. The Exodus is no random trip. Its sacred and foundational weight, the quintessential truth of Scripture and the hefty symbolism of salvation, cement it onto the land *as if it was* a route. Additionally, a desert, in its ostensible featurelessness, may have invited a track-based depiction of movement for the same reason why the 'pathless' oceans would do so in later times. Not only are lay journeys excluded from this route-like representation, but other sacred ones are, too: we seemingly must wait until the 'Age of Discovery' before further biblical voyages join in the track fashion.[59] In the Hereford *Mappa Mundi*, we should also note, the hydrophobia of itinerary lines remains strong: the Red Sea is depicted in the snapshot moment when it was parted by Moses; the line doesn't get wet (Plate 6).[60] Linear representations of water-based journeys, biblical or not, were still over two centuries away.

The Hereford Map route, while apparently revolutionary in its conception, stemmed from a context in which not only were generic itineraries represented as lines (as in the Peutinger or Gough Maps), but a strong culture of pilgrimage had established a powerful link between routes and lived experience of travel. The path of the Exodus was easier to conceive of as a set route because Christian pilgrims could, spiritually, emotionally and symbolically, walk it. To clarify this point, let's look at a religious land itinerary map, made a few decades before, which embodied the 'on-the-ground' perspective of ancient travel.

The Abbey of St Albans, today a cathedral, sits in the green countryside some 20 miles north of London. By the time of Magna

Carta, it had been a site of Benedictine worship for over four centuries, and of Christian worship for even longer. In the first half of the thirteenth century, just after the death of King John, the community acquired a new novice, who was to become its greatest chronicler. Matthew Paris was a historian, an artist, a polymath and a meddler. His personal network encompassed kings and queens, knights and bishops, and powerful people across Britain and Europe; he was even sent to Norway by the Pope, in the late 1240s, to settle an episcopal squabble in the monastery at Nidarholm. The monks of St Albans segregated themselves from worldly concerns, but the world still came to St Albans. One of Matthew's contacts was Waleran, the Bishop of Beirut, who might have been one of his main sources of information on the route to Palestine.[61]

Matthew, indeed, didn't simply leave the fullest and most readable contemporary history of medieval Britain (and perhaps Europe). He also painted many maps – of the world, of England and Scotland, of Palestine, and of the route from London to southern Italy, on the way to the Holy Land (Plate 7). He may have gone to Norway, but the Holy Land was out of reach. Short of a real journey to the cradle of his faith, the next best option available to a medieval monk living 3,000 miles away was an 'imagined journey'. According to historians, that is exactly what the maps provided: you opened their flaps and pictured yourself on this long route, with colourful towns and landmarks flying by – drawn for the most part not from above, but as you'd see them from the ground. The territory beyond your sight was of no importance, and was thus left blank, blurry, 'marginal'.[62] The hodological view had been recruited into Christian spiritual practices; it now marked even more deeply subjective experiences of space, not simply traversed as a tunnel, but *imagined* as a tunnel. This tradition would have a long afterstory. Across Europe, well into the early modern period, devout Christians projected Calvary and biblical sacred sites onto their local 'Holy Mounts', and climbed the same route as Jesus in a different place and a different time.[63] In the fifteenth century, for example, in the cold cloisters of the Saxon convent of Wienhausen, the nuns walked round and round the Stations of the Cross, as their faith built Jerusalem around their footsteps.[64]

What about the sea? In each version, Matthew Paris's map, like all others we have seen so far, breaks up at the blue edge of the sea: it stops at the Channel and resumes in France, it stops in southern Italy and resumes in Palestine, on solid land. Once it's reached the end of Italy (growing messier in the last stretch), it offers written instructions on how to proceed on the water, exactly of the sort we have already encountered over and over again: keep Sicily to your left and Malta to the right, then you get to Crete ... (and so on and so forth).[65]

At sea, indeed, the verbal itinerary tradition continued un-abated. Scraps of 'back-of-the-envelope' itineraries crop up all over the place in medieval manuscript collections. For example, a four-teenth- and fifteenth-century Latin miscellany kept at the British Library, in London, contains a list of places and distances from Venice to Joppa – that is, the ancient port of Jaffa, in present-day Tel Aviv. In a handful of laconic lines, the brief extract drags us on a whistle-stop tour across the eastern Mediterranean, via southern Italy, Crete, Rhodes and Cyprus.[66] This list only served a generic descriptive function: for one, the distance between each stop is nearly always '300' miles, so we would be justified in procuring a better guide before setting off on the journey.

Where might one find such a guide? More elaborate descend-ants of *periploi*, the so-called '*portolani*' or 'rutters' ('*routiers*' in French), were also distributed and later printed to guide sailors. The earliest such printing appeared only thirty-five years after Gutenberg's Mainz Bible, in 1490, and was probably authored by a Venetian navigator called Alvise Ca' da Mosto; we shall meet him again.[67] Shortly thereafter, the French mariner Pierre Garcie 'Fer-rande' published the first known pilot book of the coasts of western Europe, with the title *Le Routier de la mer* – the 'route book of the sea'. Addressing the reader, he takes him by the hand along crossings and coastings, telling him how to behave with the various tides, where to anchor, what to do at each step. It's almost impossible to overstate the usefulness of this book. In 1520, it went through an enlarging revision (becoming *Le grant routier*). No charts are in sight, but simple woodcut images pepper the text, showing the outline of snapshots of the coast as they would look to the mariner

Figure 1.7: A page from Garcie's *Grant routier*, in its 1525 edition. Throughout the volume, the shapes of numerous coastal outlines were reproduced as a guide to pilots.

approaching from the sea (Figure 1.7). 'The great rutter' exploded into a myriad of editions, over many decades. The first ever printed pilot book in the English language, in fact, was a translation based on Garcie's text. It was produced in 1528 by Robert Copland, a London printer – who sheepishly declared in the preface that he had never seen the sea! The market for nautical instruction manuals boomed across Europe for centuries to follow.[68]

The use of itinerary-thinking for wayfinding, then, survived as the dominant system well into the early modern period, over and above the emerging notions of 'geometrical space' that dominate modern mapping.[69] European pilots, most of the time, sailed with their nose in the wind and their eyes peeled on the coastline, rather than on a chart, remembering a sequence of instructions and the peculiar shapes of cliffs and promontories emerging from the mist.[70] The mariner's worldview was visual, mnemonic and personal, akin to that of the nuns circling their cloister. He fully inhabited the landscape and the seascape. We then need to stop and look at how maritime mapping came into being, in the first place – for we are, in our story so far, still in a world that apparently knew no such thing.

In the late thirteenth century, just as the Hereford Map with the Exodus was being made, a new, intriguing type of document appeared, seemingly out of nowhere: the so-called 'portolan chart'. Portolan charts are the first known European attempts at maritime mapping, and they are pretty extraordinary. They were normally drawn on dried sheepskins or goatskins. On what had been the neck of the poor beast, usually pointing east or west, the artist often painted the committent's coat of arms, or later a small Virgin Mary with baby Jesus. Different schools produced different levels of decoration, but a common trait was a thick list of place names, written perpendicularly to the coasts, and lining them all the way through. This format, we can see, is a legacy of verbal itinerary lists, and hybrid graphic and textual itineraries like the Dura-Europos shield (Plate 8).

On portolan charts, however, something entirely new makes its appearance: each of them looks as if a pack of raw spaghetti had been scattered on top of it. Portolan charts are the archetypal images that you encounter when someone (generally from Hollywood) wants to portray an 'old' map – criss-crossed by seemingly random diagonal lines. On closer inspection, these lines are not random at all: they originate from the sixteen (later thirty-two) points of the compass rose, and represent the directions in which one could sail. They are known as 'rhumb lines'.[71]

Portolan charts have one great fault: they have catalysed an avalanche of pseudo-historical nonsense. Their origin, in particular, remains a topic of heated debate, in academia and well beyond. To the delight of mystery-hunters, these charts' technical accuracy seems unusual for their times, and their appearance is somewhat abrupt. All the usual suspects have featured in this dispute: the ancient Egyptians, the Phoenicians, the Greeks, the Romans, the Arabs, lost Ice Age civilisations, Atlantis, the Templars – and aliens, of course.[72]

What is true in all of this is that we aren't fully familiar with the knowledge behind portolan charts' production and use. Unfortunately, maps that are deployed as tools, especially in the wet, enjoy a short life: the examples that have survived seem to be mainly ornamented display copies, from which little can be learned of real navigation. Still, most historians believe that the lines were designed to facilitate the practical process of setting a course. Armed with a compass, navigators tended to proceed by 'dead reckoning', estimating their position on the basis of direction, speed, wind and currents; by following the direction of one of the diagonals on the portolan chart, they could be more easily 'channelled' into the next leg of their journey.[73]

Rhumb lines on late-medieval portolan charts aren't quite ship tracks yet. They have been compared to 'networks' of roads, which is possibly the best simile.[74] And, as we said above, roads are fixed features of the territory, rather than marks explicitly left by individuals. They are nothing like the blazing, idiosyncratic path of our modernly recast Odysseus, carving up water into a bold, personal, one-off story. They are, to borrow a distinction drawn by Tim Ingold, 'guidelines' rather than 'plotlines'.[75]

Apart from the Exodus, then, the Voyage of Voyages, Western antiquity and the Middle Ages only produced descriptions and representations of routes that were either hodological or structural. The modern journey track is neither: it's too sanitised to be a genuine experience, and too arrogantly lively to accept generic anonymity. But by 1300, while still distinct, two key seeds of tracks were in place: a chart had been used to sail at sea, and a map had been used for telling a specific – if exceptional – tale. By the time portolan charts ruled the Mediterranean, tracks weren't far behind.

2

TRAILBLAZERS

As far as we know, a group of humans first went all the way around the world 500 years ago. The slow journey took almost exactly three years, and was largely unplanned. The expedition commanded by Ferdinand Magellan and Juan Sebastián Elcano, a small squadron of five ocean-going ships, had set sail from the bustling Spanish port of Seville in September 1519. Magellan was an experienced navigator, with years of imperial campaigns in the Indian Ocean behind him. Those campaigns, however, had been fought on behalf of his mother country – Portugal. When he sailed from Seville, he did so as a traitor, who had just defected to the enemy, the King of Spain. It was in this king's name that Magellan offered to reach the wealthy 'Spice Islands' by heading west, and claim them for Castile, before (in theory) returning to Europe the same way he'd come. The Spice Islands, or 'Moluccas', in present-day Indonesia, promised fabled resources by comparison with which gold and gems glowed dull: cloves, mace and nutmeg, luxury products so rare and in demand that just a few bags were worth fortunes. The expedition was a disaster, beset by miscalculation, mutiny, hunger and madness; along the way, it lost four ships, the vast majority of the crews, and Magellan himself, killed in April 1521. But when Elcano and his seventeen remaining men dragged themselves into port in September 1522, penitent and browbeaten, they had indeed circled the world, if only accidentally.[1]

Magellan and Elcano's was the first route track that ever streaked European maritime maps – or so is often assumed. In particular, these innovative Magellanic tracks have been called the 'trademark' of one specific mapmaker: the Genoese artist Battista Agnese, who spent most of his career churning out splendid manuscript atlases from his Venetian atelier. The earliest atlas in his name bears the date of 1536, and the latest that of 1564, but many other copies have been attributed to him. Of his life, we know nothing else.[2]

Agnese's atlases consisted of various folios, each showing an exquisitely painted map. One of these maps, a 'planisphere', depicted the whole known world, surrounded by the heads of the blowing winds. In most versions of the atlas, the centrepiece of this image is the westward route to the Moluccas – sometimes, a neat black line; sometimes, a blazing path of silver. In a few copies, this line is joined by others: the golden route from Spain to Peru, and the imaginary Arctic *'viazo di Fransa'* (Plate 9).[3]

Agnese's planisphere, in its multiple versions, is one of the most famous cartographical images in history. It's a guaranteed presence in any coffee-table tome on antique maps, and in 2022, on the quincentenary of the voyage, it even featured in the video-game-inspired blockbuster *Uncharted*.[4] Part of its fame has certainly to do with numbers. So far, scholars have discovered nearly eighty illuminated atlases that may have stemmed from Agnese's prolific shop. Luxury objects stand a better chance of survival than most, because they tend to be carefully kept. And these painstakingly painted codices were luxury objects indeed: they were designed as gifts for many of the most powerful rulers and clergymen of Europe. From Charles V of Spain to Henry VIII of England, the list of original owners is a *Who's Who* of sixteenth-century Europe. The extant copies are now scattered all over the world, from the most ancient example in the vaults of the Vatican to dozens of others peppered across Spain and Portugal, Italy, Germany and Austria, France, the Netherlands, Britain, Sweden and Switzerland – plus a spate in the rich university and research libraries across the United States.[5] Many more may be hidden away in private hands. One copy, once belonging to the Prince Elector of Westphalia and Archbishop of Cologne, fetched nearly $2.8 million in a 2012 sale at Christie's in New York.[6] Agnese's routes have firmly embedded themselves in our collective imagination.

The sheer renown of these atlases, however, makes matters seem slightly neater than they are. Despite their loud claims, these

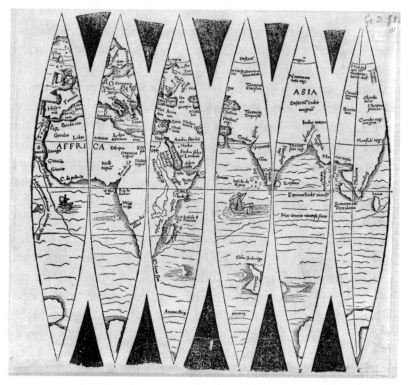

Figure 2.1: Gores for Johannes Schöner's terrestrial globe (1529).
The track line crosses the Indian and Atlantic Oceans.

planispheres aren't actually the earliest European maps to contain
ship tracks. The first confirmed Agnese atlas is from 1536. But a
set of globe gores (printed segments) by the German Johannes
Schöner had reported Magellan's 'series' or 'chain' of navigations
(*'seriem nauigationum'*) a decade before, in 1523, as a way to illustrate the 'wondrous' feat (Figure 2.1).[7] A small gilded globe, made
out of copper either in the late 1520s or around 1535, also bears an
engraved track, with a Latin inscription punched into the metal:
'that line drawn from Seville shows the navigation of the Spanish'.[8]
When a hopeful Magellan himself had his first pre-voyage audience at the Spanish court, some sources say that he brought in a
globe (or a planisphere) and, on the spot, 'traced the course he proposed to take'.[9] Are Magellan's the first European tracks, then, even

if not in Agnese's version? That isn't fully clear, either. In the 1450s and 1460s, two other voyagers, the Portuguese Pedro da Sintra and the Venetian Alvise Ca' da Mosto, undertook expeditions in the Atlantic, sailing along the coast of Africa. Their travels were discussed in a 1508 book entitled the *Itinerarium Portugallensium*. One Latin edition of this work includes maps that show the tracks of these two, together with drawings of a ship. But the maps may be later additions, and their date is uncertain.[10]

These considerations shouldn't invite us to quibble over details, as much as remind us of the sparseness and dubiousness of the material with which we are working. In this context, assigning priority and discovery claims may be an even more questionable activity than usual.[11] The point is not whether Magellan's or da Mosto's tracks came first, whether Agnese developed the idea or simply popularised it. The point is that European ship tracks appear, almost out of nowhere, in conjunction with a specific phase of Iberian maritime expansion.

In the fifteenth and sixteenth centuries, the world suddenly stretched under Europeans' feet. The 'discovery' of the Americas and the great new impulse towards oceanic exploration utterly redrew their image of the Earth. Maps were recruited in understanding and apportioning this novel immense space. Planispheres *created* the world as we know it, skinning the globe and displaying its hide – presenting an overview at a glance that is impossible in reality. The world was a theatre to human action ('*Theatrum*' is the name of a famous sixteenth-century collection of maps by Abraham Ortelius). But now it was also something that humans made, and ruled from above.[12]

Practically, the solid shape of the globe itself became indispensable to make sense of the newly discovered space. With the Treaty of Tordesillas in 1494, Spain and Portugal had sliced up the known world between themselves: everything west of a set mid-Atlantic meridian, they established, belonged to Spain, everything east of it to Portugal. This is why, for example, the bulk of South America became Spanish, but Brazil, protruding eastwards into the Atlantic, turned into a Portuguese colony. This is also why Magellan tried to reach the Indies by heading west, rather than taking the more sensible, well-known route through the Indian Ocean: being labelled as Portuguese, this body of water was off-limits to those serving the Spanish Crown. Yet the flaw in the arrangement is quite apparent: this neat cross-Atlantic division implied a *flat* map, with external edges vanishing into a little-known and still contestable blur. When Magellan's expedition tied together these edges, the issue arose of where the boundary would fall on the *other side*. The question wasn't merely an academic one: such a boundary happened to run pretty close to the Moluccas, which both countries wanted for themselves. In 1529, the Treaty of Zaragoza put a temporary and precarious end to the debate, giving the 'Spice Islands' to Portugal. The meridian of Tordesillas now acquired a quasi-symmetrical 'antimeridian' on the back of the globe: it became a ring (sort of – the Portuguese part was a bit more than a hemisphere), rather than a simple line.[13]

The 'Age of Discovery', however, didn't simply precipitate a global view; it also required an enormous shift in Europeans' conceptions of their relationship to the sea. For the first time, Iberian ships were heading out into endless, empty, indefinite blue oceans, with no visual landmarks or referents that could be grasped, let alone described. For thousands of square miles, for months on end, all was water and sky, and nothing more. Oceanic travel requires some level of abstraction; as contemporary cosmographer Pedro de Medina put it, 'not only industry and spirit but the skill of finding one's way on water where nature has denied it to us'.[14] For the seas bear 'neither path nor trace', and a ship, as the biblical Book of Wisdom wisely pointed out, 'follows no path, and leaves no signs'.[15] A suitable path-finding and path-building abstraction was provided by new navigational methods. When there is nothing around, the last resort is looking up. So it was that European oceanic navigators increasingly came to rely on the only referents they could see: the Sun and stars. But because the Sun and stars aren't on the surface of the world, your own position in its blankness suddenly matters a lot more, if you intend to plan, monitor or recount your journey.[16] Suddenly, that evanescent wake is worth holding onto.

*

In time, as transoceanic trade and travel intensified, maritime routes curdled into fixed notions. Like clockwork, nearly each year for 250 years, the Spanish 'Manila Galleons', or 'China Ships', sailed from Acapulco in Mexico loaded with silver, and returned from the Philippines loaded with porcelain, silk and spices. They always went more or less the same way, aside from some changes in the eighteenth century – a clear oval loop that used winds and season to advantage. This simple shuttling route outlived centuries and dynasties, global wars and local concerns: it lasted from 1565, the moment the Spanish established a foothold in the Philippines, until the end of the Napoleonic Wars in 1815. It fed Spain's American colonies with a constant stream of Asian luxury products, long before Europe could regularly access them, and worked as an early harbinger of 'globalisation' when other oceanic paths remained sparsely beaten.[17] Spanish navigators trod and retrod this loop, learning it in minute detail even as the rest of the immense Pacific Ocean lay utterly unknown. In 1743, the British Commodore George Anson caused furore by finally managing to snatch one of these glittering galleons. Next to 1.3 million golden 'pieces of eight' coins, and nearly a ton of silver, he captured a set of invaluable charts. Within a century or two of its establishment, the Manila Galleon's route had come to life in the visual imagination of European elites: a map of it would adorn Anson's bestselling voyage account, published in 1748 and translated into various languages (Figure 2.2).[18]

Meanwhile, other set routes were developed. The most infamous is the Atlantic 'triangular trade' between Europe, West Africa and the Americas. Even the concept itself of a 'triangular trade' is only made possible by a track-based visualisation. More generally, as historian Gabriel Paquette puts it, the 'fortunes' of Europe's five largest global empires (the Spanish, Portuguese, Dutch, British and French) 'hinged on the density and constancy of maritime links conveying people and commodities from continent to continent'.[19] Tracks were powerful tools for imagining these links – the 'sea lanes' or 'ocean corridors' that environmental constraints and efficiency requirements often turned into forced

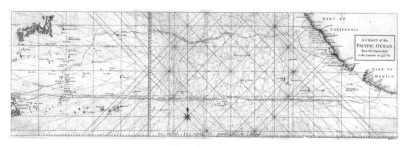

Figure 2.2: Chart showing the route of Anson and
of the Manila Galleon he captured in 1743.

passages. Virtual corridors quickly acquired legal value, as European polities attempted to claim jurisdiction and establish control
over them. The oceanic world, in the words of scholar Lauren
Benton, became 'tubulous', strewn with route claims.[20]

We return to this tubulous sea in Chapter 6. For now, however,
we should note how it bore a peculiar, almost personal quality.
Roads on maps tend to lie within national territory, and just *be*.
But the oceans are different from national territory, and in the
early modern period a hot debate raged on whether they could
be owned and enclosed by states. (The legacy today is the notion
of 'territorial waters'.)[21] Is the sea inevitably 'boundless'? The
seventeenth-century English jurist John Selden, for one, strongly
rebutted this idea: even aside from physical features, boundaries
could be established by measurements and 'imaginarie Line[s]';
'instruments called Thalassodometrae, for measuring of Sea-
voiages', were apparently devised as far back as ancient Greece.[22]
On the other side of the debate, the Dutch Hugo Grotius,
defender of the freedom of the seas, had decried the Iberian notion
that being the first (or supposed first) to navigate certain waters
equalled legal 'occupancy'. He echoed the biblical trope that is by
now a familiar refrain for us: 'no one is ignorant of the fact that a
ship sailing over the sea no more leaves behind itself a legal right
than it leaves a permanent track'.[23] Travel wasn't the only way to
pin lines on the sea, but it was certainly a key method. The legal
value of ocean corridors rested on claims of ownership, or at least

of jurisdiction, and such claims ultimately rested on tales of who came first, who dug the path on the water. What's at stake here is the very existence of the track, in space as opposed to ephemerally in time. To understand this point better, we need to explore how the track actually came to be.

The practical realities of oceanic travel catalysed the emergence of tracks. But ideas never appear out of nowhere. From what sources might European mapmakers have derived the original inspiration?

Ship tracks, we can suggest, have four distinctive roots. We have already encountered the first and most basic: it's planted on firm land. Humans began to represent paths and roads nearly as soon as they began to draw maps, because paths and roads *are there*. They can be seen very neatly, as lines on the territory, from any hilltop or roof. From that, the hybrid notion of line-itinerary, as in the Peutinger Table, was a short step away. This was a step also taken by cultures other than the European. For example, indigenous Mexican painters drew small lines of footprints to mark journeys and pathways, conveying an element of 'embodied' individuality that was lacking in ancient Mediterranean land route maps. As a visual device, these feet pre-dated Christopher Columbus's arrival. Under Spanish occupation, they became embedded into the new, culturally hybrid maps produced by native painter-scribes as administrative and legal aids. A widespread convention, the little feet filled the space between parallel lines, signposting them as walkable roads (Plate 10). Next to footprints, Mexican mapmakers now drew hoofprints, too: the crushing, stamping traces of the animals that the Spaniards had introduced.[24]

But footprints and hoofprints, like dug paths, are real and visible artefacts. Earth is a different medium from water. All tracks, we shall see, run the risk of eventually calcifying into infrastructure. Some, however, do so naturally and almost from the outset. Others, instead – especially watery ones – can only congeal onto this level via storytelling, embalmed and glorified by cartography.

The next two roots of ship tracks, one practical and one pictorial, are firmly ensconced within European culture. Practically, we

need to have another look at portolan charts. We saw in the last
chapter that the lines on them didn't indicate courses as such, but
directions that were used to set them. We don't know exactly how
this worked, as we said, because the surviving portolan charts
aren't the copies that were carted around the wet seas by rough
mariners. Yet one theory is that pilots would repeatedly mark
their position by 'pricking' a sequence of points on the chart. They
would either poke pin holes into the vellum, or stick wax droplets
across its surface.[25] Either way, this reminds us of a large class of
tracks – those marked by a dotted, rather than a continuous line.
A significant proportion of early tracks followed this format, and
many still do today (think of the blue Google Maps dots for walking
journeys). The choice of dotting a track rather than stretching it
out as an unbroken line is partially aesthetic, but it also reflects its
construction: a track is nothing but a chronological and spatial
sequence of discrete positional measurements. Even as they stray
into art and imagination, ship tracks are never too detached from
a navigational 'mode'.[26] This twin nature is at the core of what we'll
discuss over the following pages.

The third branch of tracks' pedigree stretches back to an ancient
pictorial tradition in mapmaking, which had little to do with nautical uses: inserting the drawing of a ship in the middle of the sea.
These little ships were rather ubiquitous; historians have even used
them to reconstruct technological information on lost typologies
of vessels, and particularly on their rigging, which doesn't survive
in many underwater archaeological sites.[27] An image of a ship filled
up blank space when the mapmaker was out of ideas, and (together
with the sea monsters that also infested early modern maps) it provided quaint decoration. But the main function that these ships
served was to mark the territory, showing where Europeans had
been. By the fifteenth century, the miniature vessels had started to
perform this marking in fairly eloquent and sophisticated ways.[28]

The Portuguese mapmaker Diogo Ribeiro was a contemporary
of Agnese. Like Magellan, he had defected to the Spanish court,
and had been appointed as royal cosmographer and master chart-
maker at the Casa de la Contratación in Seville – the official body
in charge of Spain's overseas trade, navigation and cartography.

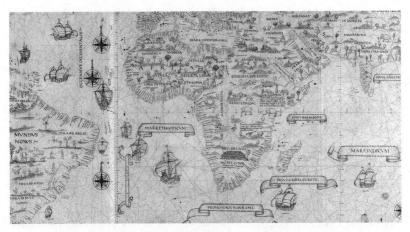

Figure 2.3: Sequence of ships returning up the Atlantic, from a facsimile of Ribeiro's planisphere (original date 1529).

After Elcano's return, he also drew the newly discovered route to the Moluccas, in two 1529 versions of his famous planisphere. However, rather than marking it through a blazing track, he deployed a sequence of ships, clearly turned in one direction of travel, and with little captions next to them for added exposition:

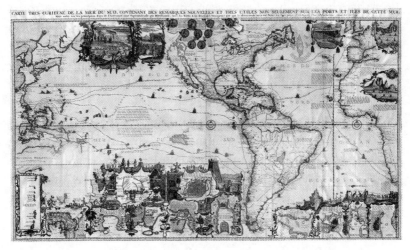

Figure 2.4: A fairly late (1719) example of a map illustrating exploration voyages through both tracks and ship drawings.

'I'm going to the Moluccas' or 'I'm coming back from the Moluccas' (Figure 2.3). In the Pacific, another ship declares, 'I'm returning to the Moluccas': an extra caption explains that this is the *Trinidad*, forced to turn back by contrary winds and the need for repairs. In the more extensive version of the planisphere, known as 'the Weimar copy', the direction tags multiply to indicate journeys to and from the Indies and Flanders, as well.[29] Compared to a line, this seems a slightly clumsy (and certainly, for us, less legible) way of depicting a journey on a map. However, we can tie the two devices together because for many centuries afterwards we see track lines *accompanied* by little ships (as in Figure 2.4). In the sixteenth century, the triumph of tracks as a visual and narrative solution was by no means guaranteed.

So we have roads, pricked courses and the drawings of ships. For the most powerful, and possibly decisive, source of inspiration, however, we must look further afield.

The northern Indian Ocean stretches east to west for over 6,000 kilometres, from the crumbling edges of Indonesia to the eastern coast of Africa. During the Middle Ages, large and sturdy ships crossed it all. Between 1405 and 1433, perhaps the greatest naval fleet that the world had ever seen completed seven voyages to its furthest waters. The enormous vessels, manned by up to 28,000 men, navigated by wind and compass, by careful watching of the monsoon and of the starry sky above. They bore names like *Pure Harmony*, *Lasting Tranquillity* and *Peaceful Crossing*, and visited an estimated thirty-seven countries.[30]

In charge of most of these expeditions was the eunuch Zheng He, China's most famous admiral. The emperors of the Ming Dynasty had tasked him and other eunuchs with a range of diplomatic, commercial, military and tributary missions, and with stretching the broad hand of the Middle Kingdom across the 'Western Ocean'. When he first set sail, Zheng He was in his early thirties; he probably died either during or immediately after the seventh and final voyage, aged well over sixty. His one- or two-year-long missions wove a thick net of contacts across the sea basin, a display of soft and hard power with long-lasting implications. He encountered, intimidated and impressed, kidnapped, slaughtered and subdued, and came home with ships filled to the brim with treasure, tribute, exotic products and plants and animals straight out of the wildest fables. One of the expedition members describes a few of these wonders, which they encountered in Aden: 'the patterned *fu-lu*' that 'resembles a mule', white with black stripes (a zebra); 'the white "camel-fowl"' (ostrich); the giraffe, that strange composite of parts that 'eats unhusked rice, beans, and flour-cakes'; and the lion, shaped like a tiger, 'indeed the king among the beasts': 'All the beasts, when they see it, fall down and dare not rise'.[31] These expeditions, however, were dreadfully costly, and loathed by the landward-looking Confucian faction of the imperial palace. After Zheng He's death, the colossal ships were left to decay, and the curtain fell for good on China's age of monumental maritime endeavours.[32]

Zheng He's voyages have left us one of the oldest known track charts (Figure 2.5). It was published about two centuries later, in a military treatise called *Wubei zhi* ('Treatise on Armament Preparations'), but historians tend to believe that its original drafting was contemporary to the expeditions. A series of short parallel tracts runs across the ocean, like stitches on the water that Zheng He's ships cut. Thick strings of written sailing directions huddle like wrinkles around these stitched lines. There is something that distinguishes the latter from their younger European cousins: the unit of measurement on which they are built is time, rather than space. The length of a route is expressed in *geng*, watches: there are ten to one twenty-four-hour cycle.[33] The map's construction has nothing to do with Western notions of distance and scale. Space bends around travel, and the track line is the true protagonist, rather than an afterthought. Other contemporary Chinese maps follow similar principles: for example, the famous 'Selden Map', rediscovered in 2008 in an archival collection in Oxford. This map, as its name suggests, belonged to John Selden, the jurist who had been advocating a world of marked and enclosed seas. Barely visible in the murky green China Sea is a thin black cobweb of shipping routes.[34]

The most fundamental difference between Eastern and

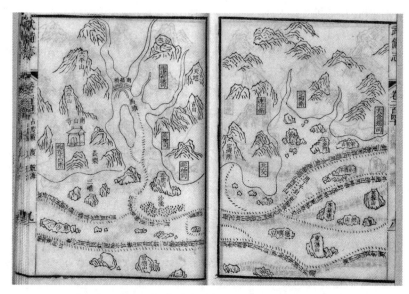

Figure 2.5: One leaf of the map showing the voyages of
Zheng He, in *Wubei zhi* by Mao Yuanyi (1621).

Western tracks, however, is another, identified by historian Elke
Papelitzky. The first Japanese, Chinese and Korean tracks, with
few exceptions, didn't show individual journeys: they showed
networks of connection.[35] The line between the two is blurry:
Agnese's maps, for example, never name Magellan and Elcano –
they officially represent the generic route to the Moluccas. But in
Asia the personalisation of routes never took off at all. Zheng He's
tracks themselves were less about his endeavours – let alone 'discoveries' – than about the structure of common sea routes, some
of them already well practised: what would later become known
as the 'Maritime Silk Road'.[36] In many ways, then, Asian maps and
charts offered oceanic *roads* – not voyage lines. They lacked the
egocentric boastfulness and the storytelling knack of their early
European equivalents. How were the two linked, if at all?

By the end of the sixteenth century, Jesuit missionaries had reached
China. Their cartographical collaboration with local traditions

continued, in hiccups, for centuries. However, historians have shown that these encounters didn't work as unidirectional 'transmission': the resulting maps were complex cultural hybrids.[37] Likewise, we can't simply ascribe Zheng He's tracks and those of the Selden Map to Western influence. For one, there is textual evidence of East Asian sea charts displaying tracks long before Western portolan charts began to display the seas at all.

Even the academics who most doggedly dispute the existence of Graeco-Roman scale maps readily acknowledge that the story was different in China. There, we have incontrovertible evidence of maps made 'to scale', and used for practical purposes, from at least the third century BC.[38] Just as old are references to maritime maps, and from the twelfth or thirteenth centuries written sources begin to mention charts indicating sea routes.[39] In nearby Japan, historians have described the flourishing of so-called 'Japanese portolan charts', heavily influenced by contact with the Portuguese, and how they were grafted onto existing, lively traditions of maritime itinerary cartography; by the early seventeenth century, some of these Japanese charts reported tracks as a double row of pinpricked holes.[40] But already at the beginning of the 1300s, Japan's islands were drawn connected by schematic red lines.[41]

Who influenced whom, then? At present, this question seems difficult to answer. It may well be that the notion of pictorial ship tracks developed in parallel in the East and in the West. It might be that it was transmitted via a chain of intermediaries, in either direction. But the timing is certainly interesting. The Portuguese Vasco da Gama circumnavigated Africa and poked his long nose into the Indian Ocean just as the sand was running out on the fifteenth century, in 1498. Unlike previous European visitors, he brought along a valuable tool: ships.[42] Within a decade, the Portuguese had formed contacts with Chinese merchants in Melaka (present-day Malaysia), within two they had been on diplomatic visits to the great Country itself – from which they were soon kicked out.[43] And in another ten years, by the end of the 1520s, the earliest ship tracks had crawled out of nowhere onto maps of Iberian maritime exploration.

A connection is rather likely, even though we only have hints to work from. On 1 April 1512, Afonso de Albuquerque, Viceroy of Portuguese India, first Duke of Goa, the 'Lion of the Seas', wrote home to King Manuel of Portugal. Among other business, he was sending him a copy of a Javanese pilot map. This map, he announced, showed 'the navigation of the Chinese and the *Gores* [either Ryukyuan Japanese or Koreans], with their rhumbs and direct routes followed by the ships'.

'It seems to me, Sir, that this was the best thing I have ever seen,' the excited commander continued, 'and Your Highness will be very pleased to see it'. In this map,

> Your Highness can truly see where the Chinese and *Gores* come from, and the course your ships must take to the Clove Islands, and where the gold mines lie, and the islands of Java and Banda, of nutmeg and maces, and the land of the king of Siam, *and also the end of the navigation of the Chinese, the direction it takes, and how they do not navigate farther.* The main map was lost in Frol de la Mar. With the pilot and Pero de Alpoim I discussed the meaning of this map, in order that they could explain it to Your Highness; *you can take this piece of map as a very accurate and ascertained thing, because it is the real navigation, whence they come and whither they return.* [my emphases][44]

Now, some historians think that this map is preserved in contemporary sketches by the mapmaker Francisco Rodrigues, who saw and copied it before it was lost at sea.[45] These sketches, disappointingly, don't contain any route tracks. And yet, Albuquerque's description cannot but linger in our ears: 'lynhas e caminhos dereytos', 'rhumbs and direct routes'. '*Caminho*', or in Spanish '*camino*', is, as we'll see, the term that would later become common in several European languages to designate route tracks. Therefore, it seems quite possible that we are dealing with ship tracks, here. And we are also dealing with a very enthusiastic European official, who is not necessarily used to maps that show the 'real navigation', as 'a very accurate and ascertained thing'.[46] The centuries would go by, and this supposed real quality of ship tracks would remain key to the Western obsession with them. But did these tracks, whether originally Asian or European, truly show the 'real navigation'?

It would have been an incautious navigator who set out to use Agnese's route lines as his guide. If we compare any two of the map-maker's planispheres, we immediately see that the track lines don't even match each other. There are two islands that Agnese draws in the Pacific, following direct accounts of the expedition. Magellan and his men called them San Pablo and Tiburones (meaning 'sharks'), and collectively 'Desventuradas', because of their desolation. But historians have no clue as to what they may correspond to in modern geographical terms; there are tens of thousands of islands in the Pacific, including dozens of plausible candidates. Not only do we lack information on where the Desventuradas are: we also don't know where Magellan actually travelled in relation to them. In the various copies of the atlas, the tracks wiggle in different places, slither indifferently either above, below or between these two islands, and share nothing more than a generic shape (Figures 2.6, 2.7, and 2.8).[47]

There is more. Magellan's expedition spent almost a year (from December 1519 to October 1520) on the south-eastern coast of America, between Brazil and Patagonia.[48] But the track on the atlases just flows past, without even brushing the land. Does the line perhaps indicate a generic journey, rather than *that* specific one? It doesn't do that, either. It doesn't represent the real or plausible journey of *any* sixteenth-century ship.

Sailing vessels (any vessel, in fact, but we shall come back to this) couldn't go precisely where they wanted. The Atlantic trade winds dictated one key rule for oceanic travel: when sailing away from Europe, navigators had to stick close to the coast of North Africa; coming back, they had to complete a large C-shaped turn, jutting out towards North America – the so-called *volta do mar*, loop of the sea. There was no other easy way to push a sailing vessel south of the Equator and back up again.[49] Agnese's tracks, instead, rush straight from Portugal to South America, cross the Pacific and Indian Ocean, and pop out again at the Cape of Good Hope,

Figure 2.6: Detail from portolan Atlas of Battista Agnese (n.d.), planisphere.

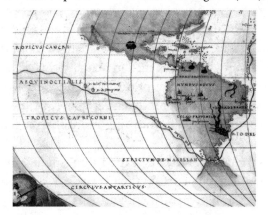

Figure 2.7: Detail from Battista Agnese, *Atlas Universalis* (1542–52), planisphere.

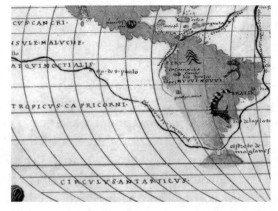

Figure 2.8: Detail from Atlas of Battista Agnese (1544), planisphere.

only to head home vertically. Such a thing could never be done. The journeys on Agnese's maps were journeys of the imagination. No one in his atelier sat down to make this line accurate: it was a free-flowing brush stroke, an idea of a journey more than a real journey – in the words of historian Felipe Fernández-Armesto, 'a cartographic representation of a literary confection'.[50]

To some extent, the discrepancies between one atlas and the other could be traced to the medium – manuscript mapmaking, rather than printing. As William Mills Ivins put it in the 1950s, the spread of print offered something that little else could: 'exactly repeatable pictorial statements'.[51] This isn't the strongest argument, because the discrepancies here are far from minute – the atlas-makers weren't even *trying* to make the copies look similar. Apart from the fact that the supposed intrinsic 'stability' of print is a myth, ignoring the creators' intentions gives too much weight to technology as a causal factor.[52] Still, we must remember that the artists may have painted each set after the previous one had left the atelier. They didn't have any photos of their older work for comparison; once a copy was given away, it was given away for good.

Second, there was the matter of secrecy. For part of the sixteenth century, the *volta do mar* trick was a jealously guarded state secret, because it offered the key to the treasures of the East. Agnese and his atelier may well have been left in the dark, especially if their work was to be gifted to other monarchs and princes. The exquisite craft and the sheer volume of copies give these atlases a veneer of authority: it's easy for us to assume that their authors would have been fully briefed on the facts. But that is a bold assumption to make five centuries later, and in the near-total absence of biographical information on Agnese. It may well be a coincidence, but his first planisphere with a journey line appeared in 1536, which is also the date of the first probable Italian-language edition of two key accounts of the voyage. This edition was likely printed in Venice, of all places, where Agnese himself was based.[53] Was he simply relying on the public press for his news? Over the course of the century, Iberian states desperately tried (and largely failed) to keep geographical information shielded from their competitors. It quickly became clear that this was a doomed attempt, as charts, accounts, pilots and mapmakers slipped through the kings' fingers, crossing borders and spreading information across Europe. A more fundamental problem also plagued any concealing efforts: geographical and cartographical knowledge was only valuable if used in the open air – by navigators, and to back up territorial claims; intrinsically, this meant that it couldn't be kept locked away forever. The initial spirit of secrecy, however, and the enduring obscurity of the most technical navigational details, at least delayed transmission by a few years, or decades.[54]

Lastly, and most importantly, we must be careful not to slip into easy narratives of cartographical 'progress': the intended function of a map conditions its shape and 'accuracy'. We can see this most clearly if we compare Magellan's voyage with its twentieth-century equivalents. In March and April 1927, a crew of four Portuguese military aviators attempted to complete the first aerial circumnavigation of the world, aboard the seaplane *Argos*. They managed the first night-time crossing of the South Atlantic, but not the full spin of the globe: after their successful arrival in Rio de Janeiro, the seaplane was damaged, meaning that they missed the good weather window. The Portuguese authorities decided not to risk a further leg and recalled the *Argos* home. The plane had barely left on its return journey when it went down in the Atlantic, a few miles north of Brazilian Belém and close to the border with French Guyana. The expedition members were rescued from the sea, and that was the end of the story.

Long before this outcome, however, an optimistic propaganda map of the journey had shown the *Argos*'s projected route; the historical imagery was laid on thick, a drawing of a caravel matching that of the seaplane (Figure 2.9).[55] José Manuel Sarmento de Beires, the enthusiastic thirty-four-year-old expedition leader, had drawn explicit inspiration from Magellan's voyage.[56] And his route, as represented on this map, is just as impressionistic and 'unreal' as that of Magellan in Agnese's atlases: direct aerial courses don't follow ruler-straight lines, and the *Argos*'s journey, often using dead reckoning in unfavourable weather, proved more convoluted than planned.

Many of the maps that we shall encounter in the following

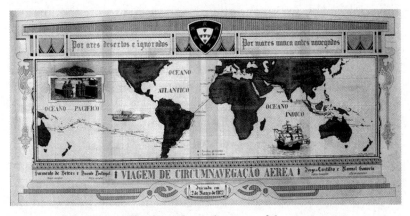

Figure 2.9: Map of the planned voyage of the *Argos* in 1927.

chapters show equally fictional and schematic track routes, regardless of how recently they were produced. You may not be able to use an Agnese atlas to sail the Atlantic, but you wouldn't use an airline poster map to set a course across it, either. Mistaken track representations can be found in the media today even when they genuinely muddle understanding.[57] All the more so, then, are we guilty of 'bad' mapping when there is nothing to be gained from greater accuracy. In the context where they were deployed, it didn't particularly matter if Agnese's route lines were navigationally wrong. These atlases weren't meant to be carried aboard ships: they graced shining palaces and magnificent libraries, as instruments of learning, debate, and, in the case of the Spanish kings, sheer brag.[58]

All this being said, there is also a clear technological reason why Agnese's route tracks *couldn't* be 'accurate'. But first, let's look at another route track, made some twenty years after Agnese's last one.

In the second half of the sixteenth century, relations between Queen Elizabeth I of England and the Spanish continental superpower were fraught. As part of an ongoing exchange of petty provocations, she consented to an outrageous endeavour: a voyage into the little-known seas surrounding South America, then claimed by Spain. The official aim was to explore the area and look for a yet-undiscovered Southern Continent – which, philosophers argued, *must* exist to balance northern land masses.[59] But the foreseeable outcome was also to ransack, harass and annoy the Spaniards. The voyage sailed from Plymouth in December 1577. It was led by a seafarer in his late thirties who had made his fortune through trade, piracy and, at the start of his career, dragging brutally enslaved people across the Atlantic.

Francis Drake has already received abundant historical attention.[60] What interests us here is his track. After crossing the Strait of Magellan, at the bottom of Patagonia, he possibly detected the existence of an alternative opening further south – the modern Cape Horn route. He plundered Spanish ships and settlements up the western coast of South America; then he made landfall in the north, in a place that he bombastically called 'New Albion'.[61] Like many other explorers before and since, he planted a post, and 'also he nayled uppon this post a plate of lead and scratched therein the Queene's name'.[62] Returning home via the Strait of Magellan would have exposed him to unpleasant encounters with his Spanish victims, so after some repairs Drake continued westwards, scratching Queen Elizabeth's name on a far larger canvas: his track became the second ever to wrap fully around the world, nearly sixty years after Magellan's death. Unlike Magellan, he lived to close the loop.

This track certainly did not go unnoticed. It appeared in various map versions, based on the master map that Drake had presented to Elizabeth. Some of these reproductions were not manuscript drawings, but engravings – and as such a product of consumption for a far broader audience than mere princes and bishops. This audience was not simply English: an early engraving, published in Antwerp in 1583, showcased 'The heroic enterprise completed by Mr Draeck of having circled the whole Earth' ('La heroike enterprinse faict par le Signeur Draeck d'avoir cirquit toute la terre') (Figure 2.10). A '*Route de depart*' and a '*Route de retour*', marked by three parallel dotted lines, set off a white corridor across the thickly pointillated seas.[63] If this version was in French, a nearly contemporary watercolour manuscript closely resembles it, but is captioned in Latin, and was possibly drafted by

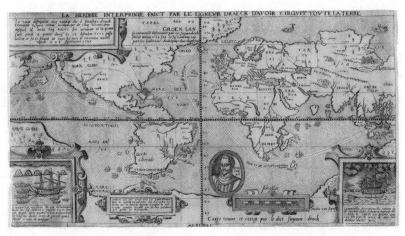

Figure 2.10: Nicola van Sype, 'La heroike enterprinse faict par le Signeur Draeck d'avoir cirquit toute la terre' (*c.*1583).

an Italian cartographer, Baptista Boazio, who lived and worked in England. This is often known as the 'Drake-Mellon' Map, from the US collection that now hosts it (Plate 11). In a fairly faithful graphical retelling of the voyage, five little ships leave England alongside the track, two go up in flames just off the coast of 'Chili' (Drake burned them), three cross through the Strait of Magellan, but only one carries on into the Pacific – now renamed the *Golden Hind*. The *volta do mar*, we should note, is correctly displayed.

Not only do these tracks, at first sight, appear to be faithful retellings: they were explicitly marketed as such. Both the maps we have just considered claimed to be a '*vera descriptio*' or '*vraje description*' (a 'true description') of Drake's expedition. The Antwerp engraving, in fact, boasts a direct line to the original source, claiming to be 'veuee et corige par le dict siegneur drack' ('seen and corrected by the said Mr Drake'). It was as if representing the journey allowed the mapmaker to tap into the seafarers' eyewitness credentials. Through years of fearsome battles with faraway seas, mariners had built unique, vivid expertise.[64] In appropriating the sailors' movement, the track staked a claim to their hard-earned right to spin yarns – and be more or less believed.

But the problem is that in none of these maps did the track

represent Drake's 'real' journey. And, unlike in Agnese's case, this isn't simply a matter of medium, secrecy or function. It isn't a matter of the alleged greater replicability of print over manuscript, because we can see how the Drake-Mellon watercolour is actually more detailed than the Antwerp print: its track is less simplified and vastly more plausible as an 'accurate' journey. The inaccuracy isn't a mere matter of secrecy because, while there were specific aspects of the journey that the English Crown had an interest in keeping hushed – most importantly, the potential discovery of a second route into the Pacific, south of Magellan's Strait – the maps show much of this information in good detail. In the Drake-Mellon Map, a little English flag billows victorious on 'Elizabetha', a spot of land clearly separate from Tierra del Fuego and the South American continent. This island has never been identified.[65] In the Antwerp engraving, the new southern opening couldn't be clearer, and it is, again, well advertised by Elizabeth's arms. Far from hiding the discoveries, these maps trumpet them. Which takes us to the third point: the inaccuracy wasn't a matter of function, either. Like Agnese's, these maps did not have a navigational function. But they did have a political one: they served to make very open territorial claims. By being unreliable, the track spectacularly fails at that.[66]

In fact, as with Magellan's San Paulo and Tiburones Islands, historians have been unsure as to where 'New Albion' exactly was. The 'Drake Navigators Guild' was founded in 1949 to determine this matter. Over the years, it has mobilised geographers, anthropologists, archaeologists, zoologists and sailors, among others. The evidence they present ranges from winds and currents to indigenous feathered baskets, from tiny shards of Ming porcelains to Drake's mentions of 'very large and fat Deere' (elks).[67] Their conclusion seems to be that 'Nova Albion' was in present-day California, some 40 miles north-west of San Francisco. This doesn't matter much per se, but it shows how much Drake's tracks left unsaid. We shall see in the next chapter that within 200 years things would radically change. By the late eighteenth century, explorers planted their tracks like virtual flagpoles. But here we come back to the main question: why, and how, did this transformation occur?

*

Let's look at some seventeenth-century maps that, unlike Agnese's and Drake's, belonged to the navigational 'mode'. In the century and a half following Drake's return, Dutch, French, Portuguese, Spanish and British navigators all increasingly used and drew tracks on their maps and charts. Iberian overseas enterprise had been flanked by the new imperial endeavours of other western European countries, whose navies and commercial companies all vied for seaborne trading supremacy. In this context, across the continent, formal navigational instruction played an important role in quenching the growing demand for maritime expertise.[68] Among other knowledge, manuals systematically taught mariners how to plot their course, marking their estimated position as dots on a line. Ex-pirate Sir Henry Mainwaring's *Sea-mans Dictionary*, published in 1644, described the procedure quite well, using the term 'Plott' as synonym for sea chart (or 'Card'):

> To Pricke a Plott, is to Vote downe the Travers of the Ships way, and so comparing it to your observation, finding where the Ship is, to make a small Prick in the Plot in the Latitude and Longitude, where you suppose the Ship to be, and so still keeping account of the daies, you shall still see how neere, or farre off you are from the place, which you saile to.[69]

By extension, the term 'plot' later came to indicate the line, rather than the chart itself. Magellan and Elcano had not made maps aboard, and it's unclear when the trend changed, but by the early 1600s some pen-sketched examples of navigators' plots begin to surface in the archives. In 1601, for instance, an unknown mariner sailing from Scotland to Norway, via Shetland, drew one such sketch (Figure 2.11). Historians think that he was a pirate, or at best a state-sponsored corsair: on the other side of the sheet, containing the log of a Mediterranean voyage, the author mentions that he captured a Turkish vessel.[70]

These plots crossed back and forth between mapping modes and formats. The demarcation between geographical map (for general, informative purposes) and nautical chart (for technical use by sailors) is well established today. However, as historian

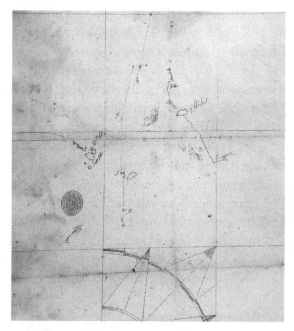

Figure 2.11: Sketched nautical plot (*c.*1600).

Katherine Parker has shown, early modern European navigators couldn't always afford these distinctions, especially when it came to less-known oceanic spaces. Seafarers were forced to use whatever cartographical material was available, however impressionistic; in turn, their charts came to be published in atlases and accounts aimed at non-sailors. In the world of manuscript production, too, the same chart-makers who catered for mariners also made reference copies for a variety of land-bound patrons, academics and officials. Such users dealt with charts as if they were maps, and some seafarers looked at maps to get a general sense of where they were going.[71] In this blurry haze, ships' tracks slithered all over the place.

By the seventeenth century, many of these nautical and geographical map-charts displayed ship tracks, and in a far more 'realistic' way than the Agnese or Drake maps. For example, the published maps of the 1615–16 Pacific expedition by Willem Cornelisz Schouten and Jacob Le Maire were marked with their tracks, duly accompanied by little ship drawings (Figure 2.12). Le

Maire was the son of a wealthy merchant. His aim was to scout out Drake's newly discovered passage at the bottom of South America: this offered a way of bypassing the Strait of Magellan and the monopoly of the powerful Dutch East India Company, which controlled all overseas colonies. Schouten and Le Maire became the first navigators to round what they christened 'Kap Hoorn' and make use of that new route from the Atlantic to the Pacific. They made it all the way to Batavia (today's Jakarta, in Indonesia), only for their surviving ship to be seized by the Company. Le Maire, aged thirty-one, died on the voyage home. After years of legal battles, his father finally obtained reparations. The old Le Maire had desperately tried to keep the lid on publications, but the discovery of a southern passage made for explosive news: already in 1618, circumventing official prohibitions, a map had appeared in Amsterdam, and a voyage account that was attributed to Schouten followed soon after. The book, including various versions of Schouten and Le Maire's route map, was to be reproduced many times in the following years, with booksellers trying to outdo each other in a crowded and cut-throat multilingual market.[72] The two navigators' tracks, reported on relatively large-scale sheets, capture the day-by-day reality of a journey far better than those that we have seen so far. They convey quite vividly the broken and zigzagging pattern of navigation by sail, especially in the rough waters of the Horn. In this period, the tools used by engravers had evolved in ways that made a sheet of copperplate – or even an older-fashioned woodblock – vibrate with fine and ductile lines.[73] But, again, we can't simply wipe away intent and reduce artistic transformations to the automatic offspring of technique: artists *choose* to deploy technologies, for specific reasons – they aren't blindly conditioned by their sheer availability. For maps like this one, the aim was becoming more clearly that of representing an actual journey.

Incidentally, the tracks of this new generation also show us something else. In the earliest editions of Schouten's journal, the trilingual labels, aimed at a pan-European audience, call the line '*wech*' in Dutch, '*Trac ou chemin*' in French and '*ductus*' (literally '[linear] conveyance') in Latin (Figure 2.12).[74] And later on, we know that Russian mapmakers used 'путь' ('*put*', meaning 'path'

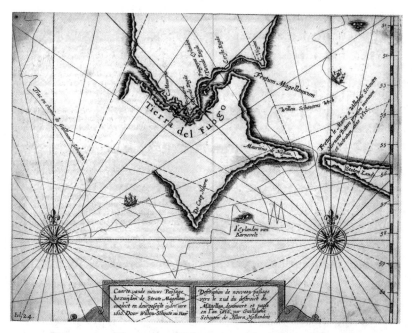

Figure 2.12: The route of Schouten and Le Maire south of the
Strait of Magellan in 1616. The Latin captions are missing in this
specific portion of the map, but the fraught passage through the
Horn is clearly visible, as are the French and Dutch captions.

or 'way') and German ones '*Lauf*' ('run').[75] Spanish had been,
of course, among the first on the scene. Already in 1535, a navigation textbook, the oldest of its kind, contained the definition
of 'route' and 'track': 'by the term *route* ['*derrota*'] is to be understood the track or course ['*camino*'] steered across the sea or that
has to be steered'.[76] In English, still in the middle of the seventeenth century, dictionaries carried no entry for 'track': Edward
Phillips's *General Dictionary* explained the meaning of 'traces',
which, 'among Hunters, signifieth the foot-steeps of wild beasts',
and 'tract', meaning the same in hunting jargon.[77] Fifty years later,
a new edition of that same dictionary now sported 'track, a Footprint or Foot-step, the rut of a Coach-wheel, the run of a Ship, a
Mark that remains of any thing'.[78] An international vocabulary was
beginning to emerge for these new lines treading the seas. They

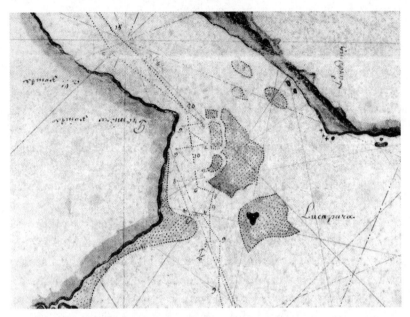

Figure 2.13: Detail from a seventeenth-century manuscript chart of the Straits of Bangka and Sunda (present-day Indonesia), displaying a ship track with what appear to be depth measurement numbers next to it.

were becoming both a named object and a concept, transcending the notions of 'plot' or 'route' and acquiring their specific solidity.

Apart from gaining a deliberate shape and a name, by the mid-seventeenth century many journey lines were also becoming more detailed. In some manuscript charts from those decades the track carries a fine beading of numbers: dates, as in a chart of Dutch navigator Abel Tasman's 'discovery' of New Zealand, or depth measurements, in shallow Indonesian waters well travelled by Dutch East India Company vessels (Figure 2.13).[79] Clear attempts were afoot to anchor this graphic device to the real-world time and space of a voyage. But were they successful?

In the sixteenth and seventeenth centuries, disagreement raged between pilots and what came to be known as 'cosmographers'. The pilots, practical, often illiterate navigators, whose brains were living, encyclopaedic rutters, jealously guarded their ancient trade. All vessels were entrusted to pilots, making them key players in the European maritime enterprise. Up against this professional category went the new academic theorists who wanted to geometrise the globe and the skies: cosmographers aimed to use a mixture of mathematics and empirical data to replace 'hodological' mindsets with a universal view from above. While itineraries were never actually supplanted, and practice and theory eventually converged in chart-making, the tensions between the two kinds of worldview carved a deep, long-lasting rift. Cartometric analysis has shown that the cosmographers' geographical maps were structurally 'incompatible' with navigational charts. The two types of item may look similar at a lay glance, and in fact cosmographers and pilots themselves underestimated their difference. In truth, however, early modern maps and charts were built on radically distinct concepts of space.[80] Track lines criss-crossed from one to the other, but how successfully they did so is another matter.

What was so complicated about drawing a reliable oceanic chart, firmly moored into 'real' space? Fundamentally, two things: the quasi-spherical surface of the Earth can't be automatically represented on a flat support – other than for very small areas, where the approximation may just do; and the compass generally lies. The first point is self-explanatory: squashing the skin of a round shape onto a plane leads to increasing distortion away from the centre of the image. Different cartographical projections solve the problem in different ways, but none can ever offer a perfect reproduction of relative distances. As for the compass, it lies because it dutifully points to the magnetic North; but the Earth's magnetic field isn't perfectly aligned with its shape, so the magnetic North isn't the same as the true 'geographic' North. This phenomenon is known as 'magnetic variation'. Unhelpfully, magnetic variation isn't always constant, either: it changes, quite haphazardly, across places and over time. When the first Iberian caravels set off for the New World, it would still be centuries before the vagaries of the compass could be adequately understood and mapped. In a relatively small area, you can build your charts around the magnetic cardinal directions, follow your compass, and get where you intend to get. This is what the portolan charts of the Mediterranean essentially did. They were further aided by the fact that magnetic variation in the area was, at the time, very low. But if your chart is on a small scale, and includes a series of places where magnetic variation radically differs, a solution of this kind won't work: as your journey progresses, the compass, religiously followed, will literally change the direction in which it sends you.[81] This is even before we begin to consider the magnetic deviation caused by other factors, such as iron in the ship. It can be seen, then, that a chart built around magnetic bearings and distance sailed (the facts that mattered most to practical pilots) ceases to be particularly useful once a voyage embraces half of the globe – or, more accurately, if the ambition is representing half of the globe in 'universal' geometrical terms. What alternative did early modern chart-makers have?

Our position on the surface of the globe can be established by reference to the imaginary grid ('graticule') of parallels and meridians – that is, through latitude and longitude coordinates. This system, or at least its Western version, was invented in the third century BC, in that extraordinary hub of science, mathematics and astronomy that was Alexandria of Egypt under the Ptolemaic Dynasty; it was then fully developed by another Alexandrine, the polymath Claudius Ptolemy, about 400 years later. In the Renaissance, Europeans fell in love with this paradigm, through a rediscovery of Ptolemy's writings.[82] Cosmographers, in particular, became warm proponents of the graticule, especially when Gerardus Mercator's cartographical projection, devised in the 1560s, offered the concrete option of using it for navigation. As a result of these influences, early modern charts acquired a peculiarly hybrid flavour: they often combined a portolan-style skeleton of straight rhumb lines, and a 'plane sailing' framework (assuming that the Earth's surface is flat), to a latitude and sometimes longitude scale.[83] This scale was usually represented through equidistant points, marked on vertical and horizontal bars in the middle of the image. To compensate for magnetic variation, sometimes the bar scales were multiple, or tilted. Various models were trialled for ensuring better navigational usefulness. For example, particularly in the wake of the Mercator projection, latitude scales started to expand as they moved away from the Equator. These innovations met with a carapace of scepticism on the part of the sailors themselves, who were quite wedded to their old ways, and more interested in concrete local detail than in small-scale, broad-sweeping coordinates and projections.[84] More generally, in any case, a fundamental problem persisted. Before the eighteenth century, full navigational use of the graticule remained speculative theory. The main reason was simple: people had no reliable way of finding longitude at sea.

Latitude, an angular value measuring the distance of a point from the Equator, north or south, was relatively simple to calculate, by observing the height of the Sun on the horizon at noon, or that of specific stars at night. Plainly put, the closer to the Poles one goes, the lower will the Sun appear in the sky. This caused issues on a cloudy day, or if the traveller lacked instruments to perform the measurements; but all in all it was an acceptably accurate method, widely used by the end of the fifteenth century.[85] Longitude, however, marking someone's east–west position in relation to a designated meridian, was much harder to figure out.

The Equator does, on some level, *exist*, and its distinctiveness from other lines of latitude is not arbitrary, so it results in observable physical phenomena: longer than any parallel, it marks a continuous string of places where seasons are flattened and day and night always last essentially the same. The mystical uniqueness of the Equator has long fascinated European navigators; line-crossing rituals and ceremonies are documented since at least the early 1500s – that is, more or less as soon as it began to be crossed (1471). Mariners dressed up as the gods of the sea, and the inexperienced sailors received a proper dunking and hazing, in a carnivalesque atmosphere that officers had to tolerate.[86] This one conventional line on the surface of the sea was 'real' and perceptible, both geographically and in seafaring tradition.

A reference meridian, instead, is an entirely arbitrary and artificial construct. Not only does little change when one crosses it, but no meridians have specific properties that make them convenient as a reference. On their charts, the British used Greenwich, the French Paris, and other cartographers the Isle of Ferro in the

Canaries; Americans later insisted on Washington, and in the early 1880s, in an apparent attempt to appease all parties, the Astronomer Royal for Scotland Charles Piazzi Smyth even defended the Great Pyramid of Giza.[87] Everyone wanted their nation to be the centre of the world. Historically, in fact, nearly all civilisations have produced maps that respond to what geographer J. B. Harley called the 'rule of ethnocentricity': us in the middle, everyone else on the periphery. It's a natural cognitive perspective.[88] But it is all wishful thinking: as King Arthur could have explained, a round object intrinsically does away with positions of pre-eminence. This meant that once a voyager had left the shelter of their chosen imaginary meridian, there was no geometrical 'centre' to be found.

On the whole, early modern navigators could know with some certainty how far 'above' or 'below' the Equator they were, but not how far west or east from home. A ship captain might find himself on a straight (imaginary) line, say between Portugal and today's New Jersey, and be none the wiser as to where exactly he was on that line. Constantly measuring the winds, currents, direction and speed could help, but 'dead reckoning' was very uncertain over long distances, as minor errors added up to become huge. As we have seen, before magnetic variation was fully measured and mapped, the direction of travel itself could be ambiguous. In short, the navigator would end up in a situation where *all* relevant elements were mere guesswork. In Portuguese, dead reckoning was called *ponto de fantasia*: imaginary point.[89]

Where does this leave the tidy plots and track charts that we saw above? We can look at this problem from the opposite direction: rather than trying to extract position data from the chart, which appears neat and authoritative, we can take historical position data and see what it looks like once plotted. This is relatively easy to do, because ships' logs, written journals in which officers annotated their position, came into common use from the early modern period.[90]

To drive this point home, let's consider some logs from the late eighteenth and the nineteenth centuries – a period when, according to usual narratives, even the longitude problem had been solved. In the early 2000s, the European Union sponsored a large research project called Climatological Database for the World's Oceans. Researchers extracted data from 1,624 Spanish, British, Dutch and French logbooks of global voyages that had happened between 1750 and 1850. Scientists care about historical logbooks because they report detailed climate observations, multiple times a day: the systematic professionalism of long-dead ship captains and masters can help us map climate change in the past. First, however, one needs to know exactly *where* those observations were made. And this is far from easy. Because most of these journeys used dead reckoning, officers 'reset' the reference meridian every time they bumped into a reliable landmark – meaning that the CLIWOC database contains a stunning 636 zero meridians. This was compounded by the general vagaries of dead reckoning. As a result, a ship track drawn from the numbers in most of those logs, when plotted, does not look like a smooth, sequential line. It's a collection of short chunks of lines, offset from each other and scattered indiscriminately over sea and land.[91] Despite all the time, competence and effort that went into these measurements, and the lives that depended on them, their projection on a chart looks like a sloppy tracing job. Europeans had created an effective system for encasing and labelling the world, but had not yet discovered how to pin it on the world itself, and make it stick.

In many ways, this didn't matter. Lay public opinion, inheriting the cosmographers' enthusiasm, put more store in the value of longitude measurement than most navigators ever did: in known waters, seamen were happy to continue using their time-honoured dead-reckoning and pilotage methods.[92] The imperial sea lanes scarring the oceans had become self-sustaining concepts, and existed in practice even if no one could fix them exactly on a map. However, knowing where you were came to matter more and more for one specific category of person: the 'explorer' straying off the beaten track. Not the amateurish brigand kind, like Magellan or Drake, but the type of man who made it his task to systematically measure, survey, master and claim every corner of the world's oceans, for his own and his country's glory and gain. It is to this kind that we now turn.

WRITING ON WATER

One evening in the winter of 1772, Captain James Cook paid a visit to the famous musician and composer Dr Charles Burney, who lived in a fashionable house in Queen Square, Bloomsbury. Cook had just returned from his first voyage around the world, during which he had observed the transit of Venus over Tahiti, clashed violently with Māori people in New Zealand and staked imperial claims to the eastern coast of Australia. Within a few months, he was to set off on his second voyage, which would take him repeatedly across the Antarctic Circle – the first navigator, it was reckoned, to have gone so far south.[1]

That night he found himself in a far more mundane situation, a dinner party in London's polite society; his travels had made him into a celebrity, which did not especially suit his quiet manner.[2] A copy of rival French navigator Louis-Antoine de Bougainville's *Voyage autour du Monde*, lying on a table, attracted his attention. Bougainville had also sailed around the world, two years before Cook – the first French commander to do so. However, he had behaved in an ungentlemanly manner towards another British officer, Captain Philip Carteret: when the two had met on the high seas, Bougainville had concealed both his identity and the fact that he had just completed a circumnavigation of the globe. 'Voyages of discovery' were tightly bound up with personal competition and with imperial and national expansion. Under a veneer of civility among colleagues, professional and state secrecy obstructed cosmopolitan scientific collaboration.[3]

Cook was not impressed, and said as much, piquing the curiosity of his dining companion. Burney was eager to know about these navigators' tracks, and 'exactly where they had crossed or

approached each other'. There and then, Cook pulled out a pencil
from his pocketbook and marked his own route on Bougainville's
map, 'in so clear and scientific a manner', Burney later commented,
'that I would not take fifty pounds for the book'. The line left by
Cook's expert pencil was later fixed on the page with skimmed
milk (an old artists' trick) and, the enthusiastic host concluded,
'will always be visible'.[4]

Burney's obsession with Pacific voyages did not end there.
Begging and pleading with the Admiralty, he managed to have his
twenty-two-year-old son, James, appointed to HMS *Resolution*.
When Cook sailed again, that summer, the young man went with
him. Less than two years after the Bloomsbury dinner, in December 1773, James Burney was landing his launch in a secluded cove in
New Zealand, in search of ten missing shipmates. He only found,
according to one account, roasted fragments of flesh, a foot, and a
hand tattooed with its owner's name. Nearby, the report alleged,
a group of Māori was feasting on baskets of organs and a Black
ship servant's head. The sketched abstractions of travel narratives
had suddenly acquired a gruesome, unspeakable reality.[5] And yet it
was a reality that was as fluid and unstable as the thin filaments of
journeys stretching across the waves – a reality coloured by expect-
ation and imagination, a shimmering projection onto unknown
and poorly understood seas. When Europeans saw cannibalism,
some scholars have argued, they mainly saw not the 'truth', but the
deepest shadows of their ancestral fears.[6] What did they see when
they saw tracks?

By the eighteenth century, exploration ship tracks were well-de-
veloped technical tools, often drawn in the first person, during a
voyage, rather than by a separate illustrator in the aftermath of it.
The routes that they marked were precisely measured, and meant
to be used as thorough reports. In this chapter, we move more
decidedly from 'maps' to 'charts'. If we look for their initial creation, we need to replace our mental image of a firm table, expensive
colours and a prosperous Renaissance atelier with a tiny, cramped
officer's cabin tossed about by the waves, a blank survey sheet
spread out through most of it. Granted, navigators' tracks and
finds were later redrawn and polished up for publication, by the

officers themselves if they had sufficient competence (and time), or by professional mapmakers if not. Any type of printed map, charts included, has pushed its way through several stages of mediation.[7] The original manuscript line, however, was drawn alongside the voyage – *by* the voyage, we could almost say, as the ship itself turned into a scientific instrument.[8] A route line was no longer just the means of *representing* human dominion over the seas, but the means of *establishing* it, in real time.[9] It fulfilled the function that Hugo Grotius had decried as ludicrous a century and a half before: it documented ownership through presence, and occupation. It was a portal that conjured the ghosts of imagination into the real world. Those ghosts, at times, are not the most pleasant to meet. 'Discovery' claims and territorial marking, deep down, signal a disregard for what lay there before.

The word hydrography comes from Greek, and literally means the marking or inscribing of water. As an applied technology, hydrography boomed in the age of Enlightenment, offering the means to survey and chart the rivers, seas and oceans of the world. The hydrographer is concerned with depths and shallows, coastlines, currents and rocks. Knowing is mastering, which brings prosperity, but most importantly safety. The chart shepherds ships through narrow straits and dangerous sandbanks, dissects the horrifying and the uncertain into mundane routine. However, a more fundamental piece of information is needed for any of this to be useful: navigators must know exactly where on Earth they are.

We have seen how Renaissance navigators already possessed adequate means of establishing latitude. By Cook's time, at least for the 'elite' exploration voyages that could afford the instruments and expertise, longitude, too, had been figured out – by and large. The story is usually told as follows: the British government decided to solve the mystery once and for all, so Parliament passed the Longitude Act in 1714, establishing a scientific body called the Board of Longitude and offering rewards of up to £20,000. In 1720, this would have been the equivalent of £2,965,667 (2023 values), and could have bought you 4,807 cows, or 222,222 days (almost 609

years) off work if you were a skilled tradesman.[10] A 'lone genius'
then emerged, also British: John Harrison was a watchmaker of
modest origins, who came up with a seaclock and then, in 1760,
a seawatch ('H4'), able to function with almost perfect regularity
even when shaken about on the wavy ocean, at varying pressure
and humidity, in the freezing temperatures of Polar seas and in the
merciless heat of the Tropics. Local time, it had long been known,
is the best way to pinpoint longitude, because it varies continuously as we move east or west. So if a clock kept showing, reliably,
what time it was in England, a sailor could simply mark time on
the spot using the Sun and stars, calculate the difference, and thus
deduce longitude at his new location. At the same time as Harrison perfected this invention, astronomers and mathematicians had
devised an alternative method to find longitude at sea, by measuring the angle between the Moon and some given stars. A navigator
who was skilled in trigonometry could extrapolate longitude from
this, with the aid of 'lunar tables' produced by astronomers. A
battle ensued, according to popular accounts, between the proponents of these two methods – the modern engineers and the
backward philosophers – until at long last the clock won and
changed the world.[11]

All of this makes for a riveting tale, but historians are by profession sceptical of riveting tales.[12] A recent project has shown that
reality, as is often the case, was far more complex, and in many ways
more interesting. Britain wasn't the sole hub of innovation: other
European nations also came up with viable solutions, often worked
out transnationally from cumulative research and insights; 'finding
longitude' was not the achievement of a single man, however much
we like heroes; and the timekeeper and lunar methods were not
rivals, but used in a 'complementary' way. Further, dead reckoning,
and navigation based on visual observation and magnetic variation,
were not simply superseded and discarded as outdated methods.
They, too, remained useful tools, in a maritime world where, for the
vast majority of navigators, timekeepers were still too expensive,
and astronomical calculations too complex and time-consuming.[13]
Cook himself, on his first voyage, when he 'discovered' eastern
Australia, carried no timepiece, and calculated all his longitude

fixings using astronomical methods.[14] So Harrison's saga is slightly less central to our story than we are normally led to expect.

Whatever the case may be, a combination of the new longitude methods, together with the development of various hydrographical techniques, allowed seafarers and surveyors to trace more accurate charts. These, in turn, returned images of the world reliable enough to be used for safe navigation. Once the reference grid was solid, route tracks, too, could acquire a new solidity, and clout. 'Accuracy' functions as a powerful 'talisman of authority', supporting any claim the map makes.[15] European Enlightenment culture had become obsessed with measurement, accuracy and precision, particularly when it came to travel accounts, natural histories and maps – an obsession that we have very much inherited in our scientific ethos. Accuracy equalled credibility; it was respectable, truthful and even 'heroic'.[16] Knowing the exact latitude and longitude meant that when navigators drew their track, or indeed the new lands they had 'discovered', they could be increasingly accurate, and less reliant on guesswork. The track then was 'true', at least apparently. Of course, scientists and philosophers know that 'truth' is a nonsensical concept in scientific measurements: we can use more or less precise instruments and be more or less accurate in results, but no measurement *perfectly* reflects reality.[17] The tracks were still, in many ways, a simplification and a story, albeit one couched in technical language. We shall return to this. But even as simplifications, from the eighteenth century onwards, tracks offered a new, extremely powerful tool: they made the experience of movement *portable*, in a creditable and very legible way. Once a narrative is portable, it can be collated, compared and built upon; it can replace reality, as a vivid stand-in, and transform our perception of it.[18]

The most obvious narrative that tracks told was one of empire-building. Even more ambitiously, world-building. As they advanced on the chart, navigators' route lines magically revealed new lands and coastlines, populating areas of the oceans that Europeans had previously seen as blank. Buzzing around islands and continents, the tracks assembled them onto the white sea.[19] They did so quite literally, in fact, because the method of the 'running survey' adopted by hydrographers used the ship itself as anchor point for bearings measurements: the track was the scaffolding on which the coastline drawings were built.[20] By stringing together depth soundings, moreover, the track allowed the mapping of the very shape of the seabed. Its linear structure greatly helped with the task, because it documented the order of proceedings. Near the coast, the tide swells and falls: the water depth is constantly changing. So it's only by knowing the exact timings and sequence of each measurement that the hydrographer can later reduce it to its lowest-ebb, standardised value – which is the one reported on charts.[21] The track is a temporal string that turns into a valuable measurement tool, unrolled behind as the vessel proceeds in its meticulous soundings. It fixes time in space, creating a record of observations.

Even when it led navigators astray, in fact, the track had something to tell them that could be added to the chart. Basil Hall, the son of a Scottish Enlightenment inventor, made his career in the British Navy, reaching the rank of post-captain. Among his varied interests (literature, geology and cookery, to name but a few), he was also an accomplished hydrographer. In a short study published in 1820, he showed how the discrepancy between the track by dead reckoning and that ascertained through measurement isn't simply a dangerous annoyance: it contains invaluable information on the direction and intensity of currents. The navigator's very experience of being pushed off course could be captured on the chart, as an arrow linking the two tracks – the one showing where he *thought* he was and the one showing where he *actually* was.[22] In this way, tracks revealed underlying geographical truths, like a blazing match passed over invisible ink.

However, track lines also dissolved the landmarks they hit, disproving their existence. 'I have been here,' they said, 'and found absolutely nothing.' The most famous example is that of Cook's second voyage, between 1772 and 1775. His tracks on the map wrap around the South Polar Circle, in an apparent stroll into nothing (Figure 3.1). In fact, demonstrating that nothing lay there was his

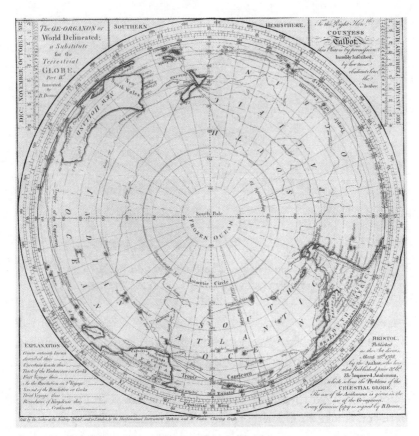

Figure 3.1: Detail from a 1788 map showing Cook's
route around the South Pole in 1775.

very goal.[23] As we saw with Francis Drake, philosophers and arm-
chair geographers across Europe had been arguing for the existence
of a 'Southern Continent' – the globe could not be balanced, they
thought, if all land masses lay in the northern hemisphere. Cook's
chart published what most scientific journals nowadays do not:
negative results.[24] We don't even need to invoke wild theories to
find spectral land masses in the eighteenth-century Pacific. As
Europeans attempted to lay safe itineraries across the ocean, in
the seventeenth and early eighteenth centuries, they had identified and strung together various 'stepping stones', like islands and
harbours. But often, upon further scrutiny, even these empirically

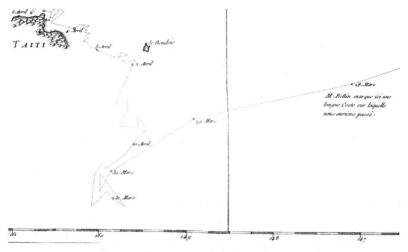

Figure 3.2: Detail of chart 'Seconde division Archipel de
Bourbon', from Bougainville, *Voyage autour du Monde* (1771).

discovered lands proved misplaced or imaginary – a mirage caused
by the technical difficulties of a long knowledge transmission
chain. 'Pepys Island', just off present-day Argentina, lay on British
maps for almost ninety years, and on the sea never.[25] In a contest
between tracks and landmarks, tracks were, surprisingly, the most
resilient: it was always possible for future tracks to be deployed to
check the existence of a landmark; but the tracks themselves, once
laid, were practically unfalsifiable. They were immaterial one-offs,
built on trust and thin water, which was a source of both weakness
and immeasurable strength.

Navigators and cartographers displayed some gusto in the
game of proving their predecessors wrong. Just to the east of Tahiti,
Bougainville, the discourteous Frenchman, leaves a caustic note on
the side of his track: 'Here Monsieur Bellin marks a long Coast,
over which we would have passed' (Figure 3.2).[26] A few years later,
his compatriot Jean-François de Galaup, Comte de La Pérouse,
scathingly wrote that the track of his two ships had passed 'in the
middle of several islands that don't exist, and which idly occupy,
on world maps, spaces where there's never been any land'.[27] One of
the 'Eclipse Isles' discovered by the Briton George Vancouver in

September 1791 proved aptly named when his compatriot Matthew Flinders, ten years later, found no trace of it, 'though it should have lain nearly in our track'.[28] There are countless other examples. At the start of the century, the Pacific was a blurry chaos of imagined islands. By the end of it, it was tidy, and covered in tracks.

In this process of tidying up the world, previous navigators' routes offered a useful record of what was and was not known. In accuracy-obsessed Enlightenment geography, sources and citation practices mattered. A good map had to furnish exact details of how it was constructed – or it would simply be dismissed as uncreditable fantasy.[29] The track did exactly this: it offered a day-by-day record of where a surveyor had been. However, the language that navigators used to discuss tracks went beyond record-keeping: it was strikingly visual and concrete. These phantoms escaped into the real world.

Between 1791 and 1795, Captain George Vancouver led an important diplomatic and surveying mission to the Pacific, producing charts of the north-western American coasts that would be unrivalled for generations. His published account contains many sentences along these lines:

> 'our course was directed between the tracks of Dampier and M. Marion, over a space, I believe, hitherto unfrequented' (September 1791);

> 'This land being at a considerable distance from the tracks of former navigators, I steered for it, in order to be satisfied of its extent, productions, and other circumstances worthy observation' (December 1791);

> 'we passed about 15 leagues to the north-westward of the Resolution's track in the year 1778' (March 1794).[30]

Did Vancouver look out from his quarterdeck and *see* these tracks, painted on the water?

For him and his fellow navigators, the tracks are 'made', carved not only into the virtual representation of the sea on the chart, but into the actual sea.[31] Tracks are treated like features of the seascape, which are near or far from the traveller and can be followed or avoided like paths on land. The space of the chart and the space of the ocean are superimposed and confused with each other, in a human attempt to assert control and ownership over geographical features.

We need to put ourselves in the shoes of these men, travelling in parts of the oceans they knew little or nothing about. Bar the occasional island or incomplete scraps of coastline (which were potentially misplaced anyway), the only elements that existed in this void were the seafarer's own track, and the tracks of those of his predecessors whose reckoning accuracy could be trusted. From these data, he needed to put together a riddle and fill in the blanks, a giant game of Battleships in which the thin virtual line drawn by his ship was the only tool at his disposal. This simple cognitive fact explains why tracks acquired such a vivid reality. They helped navigators deal with the torture of endless, disconcerting, mortifying spaces, which were uniform and non-distinctive to the occasional visitor's eye, and evaded their attempts to turn them into familiar, specific 'places'.[32] Without reference points in the endless blue spread of the ocean, these Europeans' minds naturally ran to mortality and meaninglessness. As Bougainville argued in 1801, the bravery of a soldier was inferior to that of a discoverer. A soldier proved his courage publicly, surrounded and sustained by his own people; if he died, his urn was crowned with laurels. But not so a navigator. A navigator fought his fights 'isolated', 'in the vastest of deserts, between the sky and the waves, often inimical'. And were he to die, 'there will be left no more traces of him than those his vessel leaves on this wave that he has crossed'.[33] The Book of Wisdom echoed in these men's ears even as they drew tracks all over the world's map.

Tracks, then, were not simply tools, but stories that individuals at sea told themselves and about themselves. On voyages of discovery, however, navigators' reliance on their own and their predecessors' tracks did not mean that they were keen to eschew the unknown. Quite the contrary: except for emergencies, tracks were signposts to help them eschew the *known*. In September 1788, seven months before the famous mutiny in his ship the *Bounty*, Lieutenant William Bligh came across a new set of islands at 47°44' S, 179° 7' E. He noted that 'Captain Cook's track, in 1773, was near this spot, but he did not see the islands: he saw seals and penguins hereabouts, but considered New Zealand to be the nearest land'. Bligh thus went on to name them as his own discovery, the 'Bounty Isles'.[34] Discovery was one of his goals, and knowing previous routes was useful for the purpose: he deliberately kept his track 'as distant from any course of former ships as I could conveniently make it', because he knew that, when he sailed close to previously beaten tracks, the chance of new finds was minimal.[35]

The late eighteenth century engendered many of our modern myths concerning knowledge, science and geography. One of these myths, more properly elaborated in the nineteenth century, was that of the 'heroic Explorer', claiming 'proprietary, solitary authorship' over discovery.[36] 'Discovery' can only be a collaborative process: as with Harrison, the idea of the lone genius towering above an army of menial labourers projects a somewhat distorted view of society. *Who* discovered *what* and *when* may fill our school textbooks, but it's ultimately arbitrary: it mostly depends on social acceptance and legitimation. Who 'discovered' oxygen, the natural philosopher who first synthesised it, or the one who recognised that it was a different substance to air? Or the dozens of people whose careers laid the groundwork for these realisations, or confirmed them? Looking at any exciting 'discovery' in this way dissolves it into a long and complicated process.[37] But in the time of Bligh, these subtleties were vanishing from sight. Commercial interests had splintered the scientific world into a constellation of competing jealousies.[38] At the end of the eighteenth century, being able to illustrate the nuts and bolts of a discovery wasn't simply a matter of best academic practice: it was what you had to do to claim a patent. In turn, this *illustration* of an object, rather than an actual invented object, sufficed to give you ownership and original authorship.[39] Competition, intellectual property and individualism in the pursuit of knowledge had broad cultural repercussions, beyond the sphere of trade itself. The notions of priority, novelty and heroic, Great-Man discovery emerged as new clay-footed giants from the bubbling swamp of Enlightenment professional rivalry.[40] National and imperial competition and the rise of Romantic ideals cemented them into idols.

For someone who wished to leave their mark on history and geography, then, the stretches of water crossed by previous navigators were no longer worth visiting: they had ceased to yield the promise of fresh discovery. In 1787, the French commander La Pérouse was happy not to have needed rest on the 'eternal Society Islands', 'on which much more has already been written than on several kingdoms of Europe'. Equally good was that he didn't have to 'speak, neither of Tahiti', nor of its famous and enchanting Queen Oberea, who had become a legend in European narratives. 'I took special care to move away from the routes of the navigators who preceded me', he grumpily concluded.[41] Nine years later, the Englishman William Broughton sailed the same seas in HMS *Providence*, exploring the Chinese and Japanese coasts. He opened the account of his journey on the defensive: his research, he argued, was important, new and filling a knowledge gap, definitely not just replicating La Pérouse's work. Here, tracks became crucial: 'even had the same track been followed entirely', Broughton insisted, 'great advantage might have arisen by it to the interests of science and geography'. The new track could help to correct errors and confirm findings.[42] He raised a valid point, but, again, this was a time when the slow, gradual processes of accretion on which knowledge is based were becoming routinely sidelined by a knack to reward the groundbreaking. The Russian Krusenstern expedition, coming by another few years after the *Providence*, in turn had to face the tough truth that Broughton had just published his book, and thus 'scooped' many of their finds.[43]

Exploration required immense sacrifices and efforts. Yet it is hard to shake the feeling that many of these men regarded the oceans as their ticket to glory. And tracks, in their cartographical permanency and transnational validity, were a way of marking the territory. Like an animal in the wild, the curious and ambitious discoverer shuns the patches that have been trampled on by others. Tracks work like urine trails.

More common, and somewhat complementary, is another horrible metaphor, that of 'virgin' lands or territory, untouched and unsullied by human traces. If we trust our databases of surviving publications, the term 'virgin land' first crops up in English texts precisely in the 1770s, although its proper boom seems to come only around 1850. But analogous uses of the adjective in relation to soil are first attested in the fifteenth century. And in early modern rhetoric, unmapped territory already bore the attributes of femininity.[44] Empire, it goes without saying, bore those of manliness and 'potency'.[45] Much has been written on the imperial practice of appropriating places and landmarks by giving them names.[46] But what of water? That of 'virgin seas' is a less immediate figure, because water does not retain its form. Through the track line on the chart, however, navigators managed to give concreteness to the routes they had opened even on the sea.

So far, we have been discussing relatively abstract matters. But on the ground, they took shapes that were all too real. Track lines do not simply mark fictitious oceanic roads: considered from a different perspective, they are the dark trace of the human impact that these navigators left behind. Complex and violent events often underlay these expeditions' apparently neat and elegant progress across the map.

A caveat is necessary here. It's easy to overemphasise a tale of European agency, of evil 'civilisation' spoiling a timeless Eden.[47] 'Contact' and 'penetration' are terms that make European arrival look like a crucial turning point: they cast anything that came before as a passive prelude.[48] A common prejudice, in the eighteenth century as today, pictures naive and 'primitive' indigenous societies conned into unfair exchanges. But Pacific Islanders were – of course – conscious agents of trade, not malleable, childlike stereotypes.[49] It would also be a gross misconception to imply that they were the simple recipients of European influence, lacking the means to influence a 'superior' civilisation. The impact of Pacific cultures on the travellers, and on the northern hemisphere more generally, was profound. Tattoos and customs, dietary habits, friendships and forms of friendship, languages and worldviews, and images of turquoise seas and immense starry skies imprinted themselves on the bodies and minds of sailors, and in time flooded European lives and dreams. The Pacific bounced back to Europeans as a reflection of their own fears and fantasies, transforming their very shape.[50]

All the same, Western navigators' arrival in the Pacific did have tangible consequences, in the form of economic, epidemiologic and military upheaval, changed local power dynamics, and ultimately occupation and environmental transformation.[51] There are some tracks that we can distinguish quite clearly, and sometimes they were used as evidence by contemporaries, too. Western penetration left Tahiti ravaged by venereal disease, a crime for which officers tried to blame each other. When Cook arrived on the island, in December 1768, he found sexually transmitted infections – otherwise unknown in the South Seas – prevalent among its population. Only two European commanders had touched those shores before: the British Samuel Wallis in the summer of 1767 and the French Bougainville in April the following year. Their journals and track charts documented – in fact, trumpeted – this. In his account, published a few years later, Wallis tried to get himself off the hook. The last venereal case on his ship, if we are to believe him, had been treated six months before their landing at Tahiti:

> the reproach of having contaminated with that dreadful pest, a race of happy people, to whom its miseries had till then been unknown, must be due either to him [Bougainville] or to me, to England or to France; and I think myself happy to be able to exculpate myself and my country beyond the possibility of doubt.[52]

The tracks on the charts could suddenly become evidence of personal and national guilt.

Germs (sexually transmitted and otherwise) weren't the only things that Europeans bestowed on the Pacific, or transported across it from island to island and from shore to shore.[53] Local markets were transformed by the introduction of new trading goods, the beads, clothes, nails and even weapons that changed hands during each expedition. The lingering echo of encounter became visible almost immediately, and remained so. In 1793, the British commander George Vancouver found the Hawai'ian chief Kamehameha wearing a Chinese gown, brought over by Cook years earlier.[54] In that same year, the French navigator Antoine Bruni d'Entrecasteaux thought that he could still see the effects of Cook's second voyage, which had taken place in 1774. The 'New Caledonians', like most islanders, did not originally know iron. However, the ones he met appeared to be aware of it, and could recognise an axe. D'Entrecasteaux found none of the objects that Cook had supposedly left in the village of 'Balade', where he landed, and local habits appeared different from how the Englishman had described them. So he jumped to the conclusion that Cook's gifts had sparked a war, which had resulted in these items being captured by enemy populations, and a radical transformation of New Caledonian society.[55] This example, again, shows the direct blame assigned on the evidence of a voyage, although d'Entrecasteaux's interpretation grants undue weight to European influence.

Even when they weren't discussed by contemporary Europeans, in any case, some of the consequences of these journeys are quite visible to historians and activists looking now. In the Marquesas Islands, for example, US firearms, with their symbolic value, revolutionised indigenous exchange markets. In Fiji, whale teeth brought by Europeans and Americans, seen as extremely precious, shifted political balances and consolidated the power of chiefs.[56] In the nineteenth- and twentieth-century North Pacific, the arrival of foreign whalers spelled disaster and famine for indigenous Yupik, Chukchi and Iñupiat villages. The animals around whom their world – and their energy supplies – revolved became scarce and shy.[57] In Australia and New Zealand, Cook's routes were the heralds of brutal settlement and social and cultural catastrophe, and they remain highly controversial to this day. 'Australia Day', marking the landing of the so-called 'First Fleet' of settler convicts on 26 January 1788, is often confused with Cook's arrival date. Indigenous people call it 'Invasion Day', and in 2017 Cook's statue was graffitied on the anniversary.[58]

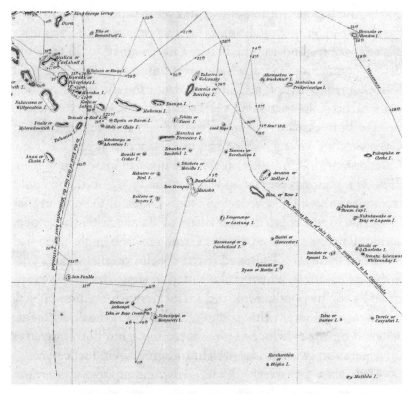

Figure 3.3: Detail from 'Low Archipelago or Paumotu Group',
in Charles Wilkes, *Narrative of the United States Exploring
Expedition During the Years 1838, 1839, 1840, 1841, 1842* (1845).

At times, the legacy of violence from initial 'exploration
voyages' was direct. The tracks of large hydrographic endeavours
like the United States Exploring Expedition of 1838–42 ('U.S.
Ex. Ex.') marked a bloody, deliberate wake of imperial coercion,
intimidation and the massacre of entire indigenous villages.[59] The
attitude of these surveyors is embalmed in the charts they published: next to a tangle of tracks, two lines mark the ocean. One
shows the point past which 'The Natives [...] were supposed to be
Cannibals'; the other, further away, bears a short statement: 'To
the East of this line the Missionaries have not extended' (Figure
3.3) The expedition was set not only on charting the Pacific, but
on changing it.

European visitors certainly left vivid traces of their passage in the memory of Pacific Islanders: when he 'discovered' Tahiti (or 'King George III's Island', as he called it) in 1767, Samuel Wallis became entangled in a chain of mutual misunderstandings. Mistaking derision and challenges to battle for sexual enticements and friendly gifts, he was caught by surprise by the ensuing shower of stones, followed by a full-blown attack. In response, he blasted the Tahitians' canoes out of the water with his nine-pounder guns. It is not surprising that, when Cook arrived there two years later, the islanders – and especially the rivals of the pro-British faction – still talked about the 'terrour' of this encounter.[60] Discovery ships, deliberately or otherwise, dropped behind memories and knowledge, but also disease, fear, war and death.

European expeditions also left their mark on the coastal environment, if not (yet) the sea. They built monuments and laid down plaques, claiming for their nations territories that often belonged to others.[61] More mundanely, they abandoned various objects, which could survive for decades in the wilderness. In February 1793, d'Entrecasteaux came across the cultivations that Bligh had started in Adventure Bay, Tasmania: fruit trees, watercress and cabbage. In a rudimentary replica of a European garden, the Cornishman had carved the names of the plants into the trunks of nearby trees, for the reference of future travellers (although few of the plants had coped well).[62] In 1796, in the Kuril Islands between Japan and Kamchatka, besides indigenous inhabitants wearing Russian-made boots, Broughton found deserted Russian 'settlements', various scattered crosses and 'the Russian arms carved and painted'.[63] The coastline itself was changed by the passage of these spearheads of empire, who planted, hacked, chopped, moved, dug, built, razed and burned in preparation for the colonies that were to come. During the expedition in which he staked the first British claim to the Falklands, in 1764, Commodore John Byron arrived on the coast of Patagonia and found that it was a disappointing place for voyagers seeking wood and water. The grass was 'overgrown', and the soil, 'of a barren sandy nature', needed improvement; so he set it all on fire.

This 'was no sooner done,' one of his officers recounts, 'than the flames ran so fast, that in less than half an hour they spread several miles round'.[64] Perhaps navigators' tracks were concrete marks after all.[65]

The track, however, was not an automatic and docile tool of dominion. It had to be wrangled, and the story it told in its permanence could be one of defeat and powerlessness as much as triumph and control. The track was explicitly deployed to signal success and impact. But the way in which it was constructed, as 'live' process and unbroken presence, meant that it soaked up and fixed onto the chart all sorts of specific information on the voyage that had created it. Most strikingly, it soaked up information on how little the imperial machine actually cared for the individuals who made it tick. Failure makes for gripping tales of Empire as much as success does.

Already in the seventeenth century, charts had begun to show 'failed' tracks. On 28 May 1676, the English navigator John Wood embarked on a voyage that sought to discover a Northeast Passage, crossing the Arctic all the way to Japan. He left an account of the journey, as well as some manuscript charts. One of them, exquisitely painted, shows the track of his vessel, HMS *Speedwell* (Plate 12). A few days after leaving port, Wood was dazzled by the enchanted world of the Arctic:

> In some places found pieces of the Ice driving off a Mile, sometimes more or less from the main body of the Ice; finding it to be in several strange shapes, resembling Trees, Beasts, Fishes, Fowles, &c. The main Body of the Ice being low, but very Craggy, being many pieces lying close together, and some a top of each other, and in some places we saw high hillocks of blue colour, but all the rest of the Ice very white, as though it were Snow.[66]

The idyll was soon over. For several days, the ship's path was blocked, as it 'steered close along the Ice, sailing into every opening, but could not find any Passage through'. It was so cold that the icy fog froze its rigging and sails. If we look at the chart, the dotted track closely follows the blue edge of the ice in all its capricious contortions. And then it ends.

On the night of 28 June, in a thick fog, the *Speedwell* brusquely wore to avoid an ice bank, struck some rocks underwater, and stuck fast. The curtailed track on the map, accompanied by a tiny drawing of a grounded ship, eloquently documents this disaster, while a sharp-toothed walrus and a slightly implausible bear look on indifferently. Most of the shipwrecked men survived, and were later rescued by their support vessel. But on this chart it's the ice that triumphs, not the track.

If tracks are strings of data, their sudden end often betrays tragedy for those who were collecting it. The track of La Pérouse was a well-known example in its day. He had set off from Brest in August 1785, with the two ships *La Boussole* and *L'Astrolabe* ('the Compass' and 'the Astrolabe'). They were, like most other late-eighteenth-century discovery vessels, small, modified merchantmen. The aim of this mission was to follow Cook's tracks and investigate the Pacific further, this time for the benefit of France. In an 1817 painting by Nicolas-André Monsiau, La Pérouse visits Louis XVI, hat in hand, and the king puts his finger on a large chart of the oceans, where he wants the commander to leave France's track (Plate 13).[67]

Via Cape Horn, La Pérouse reached Hawai'i (then known as the Sandwich Islands), zigzagging his way from Alaska to California to the Philippines, the Chinese coast, and back north to Korea and Japan, where he gave his name to the strait between Sakhalin and Hokkaido; thence to Kamchatka, where he sent his Russian interpreter home to Paris via the long Siberian land route, and down south again to Samoa. In one of his letters, he complains of how 'detestable' he found the Spanish chart of the Pacific on which he had traced his route. Knowledge had made 'no progress' over 200 years, because the Manila galleons loaded with spices or silver 'constantly follow the same line, and don't deviate ten leagues from it'.[68] La Pérouse's track, instead, draws two elegant symmetrical loops onto the Pacific, showing the methodical, broad-ranging ambitions of the French empire. Then it suddenly stops, at Botany Bay, on the eastern coast of Australia (Figure 3.4).

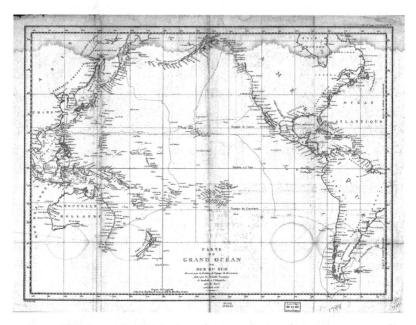

Figure 3.4: La Pérouse's track across the Pacific in 1786–8.

The two ships reached the bay on 26 January 1788, exactly the same day on which the 'First Fleet' moved to nearby Sydney Cove and founded the British Australian colony. La Pérouse had lost over thirty men, drowned at sea or slaughtered in a clash with Samoans; among the casualties was the captain of the *Astrolabe*, his best friend Paul Antoine Fleuriot de Langle. The survivors were, according to La Pérouse's writings, miraculously untouched by scurvy, but exhausted by the fatigue and privations of the journey. There is a passage that the official edition of his letters omitted to print. 'When I return you will take me for a centenarian,' he wrote to his friend Lecoulteux de La Noraye on 7 February, 'I have no teeth and no hair left [...] Tell your wife she will mistake me for my own grandfather'.[69] Three days later, La Pérouse set off to continue his voyage, and was never heard from again.

Another expedition was mounted to look for him: the two ships *La Recherche* and *L'Espérance*, 'Search' and 'Hope', scoured the seas for traces of the lost men, until the *Recherche*'s own commander, d'Entrecasteaux, succumbed to scurvy.[70] It was all in vain. We can truly say, then, that La Pérouse's track ultimately recounts decay, dwindling and disappearance into the blank ocean, ships and men literally consumed by the voyage. Like a radio signal, the line is cut off, and the mariners are swallowed by the wild seas they challenged.

We now know what became of La Pérouse. The remains of his two ships were identified as early as 1827: two wrecks lying on the seabed off Vanikoro, in the Solomon Islands. Oral traditions among the islanders of both Tonga and Vanikoro, together with the iron that the French introduced to these societies, preserved the memory of the passage of the two vessels – again, we may say, an echo of their track.[71] Between the 1960s and the early 2000s, dozens of multinational archaeological expeditions dived into the crocodile-infested waters and retrieved a wealth of items, conclusively proving the identity of each wreck.[72] Australian historian Garrick Hitchcock has gone further, and reconstructed the very last act of the story, thanks to a small column in an Indian newspaper from 1818. According to a sailor who had been stranded for four years on Murray Island, the local inhabitants preserved objects and memories of a vessel that had sunk nearby thirty years earlier. This, according to Hitchcock, may have been the newly built boat in which a few survivors had left Vanikoro. All of them were killed on Murray Island, except for a boy who was adopted by a local family. One night, a few years later, he and his wife ventured out to sea in a canoe, and vanished forever into the ocean.[73] With this young man, the track truly ends.

Today, La Pérouse's home town of Albi, in southern France, remembers its son with a dedicated Musée Lapérouse, in Botany Bay Square. On the wall hangs a large painted map by French artist Jacques Liozu. Like many other maps, this one shows the track of *La Boussole* and *L'Astrolabe* up to Botany Bay. But then it goes further: a new broken line connects the dots, and at last brings the story to its conclusion in the waters off Vanikoro.[74]

Even when they didn't end abruptly, sometimes tracks showed other forms of subtle insubordination. Matthew Flinders, the young British officer who completed the charting of the Australian coastline, was well known for his competence and accuracy as a surveyor.[75] His other defining trait was being one of the most disastrously unlucky navigators of any generation. This misfortune, at times coming close to a curse, is profoundly embedded in his tracks.

When he sailed from England in July 1801, a twenty-seven-year-old lieutenant, Flinders had to abandon his childhood friend and new bride Ann. The Admiralty's regulations were clear in intimating

> that no Women be ever permitted to be on Board, but such as are really the Wives of the Men they come to; and the Ship not to be too much pestered even with them. But this Indulgence is only tolerated while the Ship is in Port, and not under Sailing Orders.[76]

The rule appeared under the article dedicated to 'preserving Cleanliness' aboard, which also banned dirt, stuffy air, fruit and strong liquors, and defecating in the hold of the ship. Gender equality was a long way off in the navy.

It must be said that other officers, in those same years, did manage to smuggle their wives aboard. But Ann would not be permitted to pester a crucial Pacific voyage: her husband, who had originally planned to take her along, was faced with the harsh choice between her and his command. What he chose we may imagine. He would not see her again until he was thirty-six and she thirty-eight. In the letters that he wrote during their nine-year separation, two themes recur, as he begs forgiveness for their pain: financial need, and thirst for scientific knowledge and glory. 'Heaven grant', he wrote in 1804, 'that neither ambition nor necessity may ever again divide us by the intervention of a trackless sea'.[77] Making tracks took a heavy personal toll. But Flinders's track does not simply tell a tale of emotional costs and broken hearts. It also records broken ships.

Not content with wreaking havoc on Flinders's marital life, the Admiralty had also given him a spectacularly ramshackle sloop.

HMS *Investigator* had barely left Britain and it was already leaking. By November 1802, in Torres Strait, this had reached an alarming 14 inches per hour. 'Report after report', Flinders wrote, 'was brought to me of rotten places found in different parts of the ship, – in the planks, bends, timbers, tree-nails, &c., until it became quite alarming'. The carpenter and the master warned him that the ship had six months to live, provided the weather stayed good. Flinders pushed it for as long as he could, but in March 1803, his sloop falling to pieces and his men ravaged by scurvy, he was forced to abandon the mission. He didn't know it yet, but this was the end of his surveying dreams.[78]

Flinders's charting was extraordinarily thorough, and frank. His tracks are a solid line when reported with confidence, but dotted for the sections that he covered in the dark or in bad weather – because he couldn't be absolutely sure of their accuracy (Figure 3.5).[79] He even invented a system of arrows of increasing thickness, indicating the direction and intensity of winds and currents at given points, and how they interfered with the voyage. Flinders's professionalism means that we can use his tracks to reconstruct, day by day, exactly how leaky and slow the *Investigator* was. In May 1803, for example, he was hastening back to Port Jackson (present-day Sydney) to save his very sick crew, yet if we measure the track it shows us that all he could achieve with the best wind was a pithy five and a half knots. In this case, the line is subversive: the story that it actually tells is not the triumphant tale of imperial conquest that it was designed to convey, but a sorry saga of neglect, poor equipment and ultimate defeat.[80]

Flinders's streak of catastrophes had not run out yet. The young, small settlement of Port Jackson was not exactly a throbbing port city, and the few vessels it could offer were barely keeping afloat, let alone in a condition to embark on a surveying journey. So Flinders had to give up completely and return to England. But the ship in which he was travelling struck a reef and was wrecked. In a boat, he made his way back to Port Jackson, where he mounted a rescue expedition for the stranded crew. He then embarked on another ship, which was also badly leaking, and was forced to stop at Mauritius for repair. Mauritius, however, was in the hands of

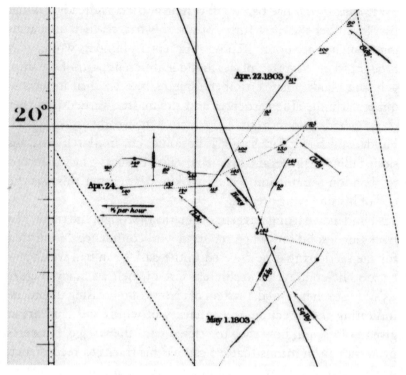

Figure 3.5: Detail from Flinders's *Atlas*, Plate I
(facsimile of an 1822 corrected edition).

the French, and Flinders's passport only granted him protection as long as he travelled in the *Investigator*. He was held prisoner on the island for six and a half years. His loyal cat Trim, who had followed him through all his voyages and shipwrecks, wandered out into the streets one day and was probably eaten. When Flinders finally got back to Britain, he found out that some French navigators he had met along the way had claimed some of his 'discoveries' as theirs, and later published them in a chart with exquisitely French names like 'Gulf Bonaparte', 'Baie Voltaire' and 'Cap Jeanne d'Arc'.[81] At last, in 1814, his great *Atlas* and work of a lifetime was ready for the world. But he died the day after its publication.[82]

The tracks of Wood, La Pérouse and Flinders all show us something important. The great 'discoverers' who laid their paths across the oceans were only marginally less disposable than the blank spaces that they tried to appropriate. As personal records, tracks can vibrate with fragility and anxiety.

Beneath all this lurks one final irony. Even the accuracy of tracks was, ultimately, a story. As much as we tend to perceive the neat ship tracks on exploration charts as drawn in a 'clear and scientific manner', as Charles Burney enthused, they remain the fruits of speculation. This wasn't because of their authors' incompetence, but simply because instrumental measurements could rarely be so precise as to boil down to one single line. The ship track was not the 'true' course, but an average, and a compromise. One navigator in particular reminds us of this detail.

Constantine Phipps was a Royal Navy officer, the future Baron Mulgrave, and the first person to deploy the word 'iceberg' in an English printed text.[83] Between June and September 1773, he led an expedition to the Arctic in HMS *Racehorse* and HMS *Carcass*. These vessels were luckier than the *Speedwell*, as the ice stopped them but didn't sink them. The tracks are a loop rather than a truncated line. Phipps's expedition, while less remarkable than the great Pacific circumnavigation voyages, has remained alive in collective memory partly due to our obsession with individual hagiography: the two crews included a young Horatio Nelson, destined for naval fame, and the African Olaudah Equiano, soon to become a leader of British abolitionism.[84] However, the track of this voyage is more interesting than the sprouts of future heroes.

Phipps is one of the few navigators who openly acknowledge, on the chart, the fallibility of their tracks. Or rather, we may say, who follow a correct lab procedure in laying down the graphic record of their experiments. Next to his route line, he constantly specifies *which* method of measuring longitude he was deploying at any given time. Aboard, he had three timekeepers, two built by watchmaker John Arnold and one by competitor Larcum Kendall on Harrison's design, plus a set of lunar tables. At various moments, he used all of these, and his track boldly shows them – in little stray lines manifesting the width of instrumental uncertainty (Figure 3.6).[85]

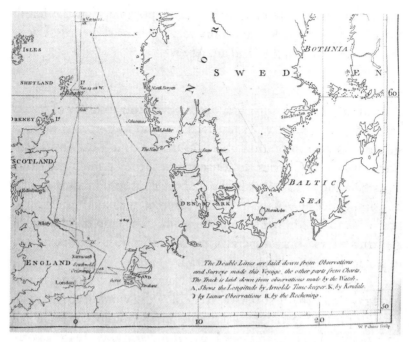

Figure 3.6: Detail of 'Chart Shewing the Track of His Majestys [*sic*] Sloops Racehorse and Carcass during the Expedition towards the North Pole 1773', from Phipps, *Voyage*. The short lines departing from the track show the difference between results obtained with different methods of measurement: 'A' is the Arnold timekeeper, 'K' the Kendall, 'R' dead reckoning, and a little moon crescent indicates lunar observations.

Phipps and his cartographer reveal even to the most casual observer the complex truth behind the scenes: the data that went into the route on the chart was also available in much more thorough form in the position logs that navigators compiled daily, and appended to many of their published accounts.[86] And these data look nothing like a single line, because most exploring officers simultaneously used two or more methods to find longitude (Figure 3.7). The accuracy of timekeepers constantly decreased throughout a voyage, ever so slightly, at a known idiosyncratic rate but also more haphazardly. And even Flinders, the most competent and meticulous of all these navigators, admitted that it would have taken sixty sets of observations, over three or four lunar months,

A P P E N D I X.

No. I.

TABLES of the ROUTE of the PROVIDENCE and her Tender, the Variation of the Compass, and the State of the Barometer and Thermometer, during the Voyage from the Sandwich Islands, July 31st 1796, till our last Arrival at Macao, November 27th 1797.

1796.	Log.	Course.	Distance.	Lat. ob.	Lat. Ac.	Long. Ac.	Long. Watch.	Long. ob.	Mer. Alt.	Variation.	Ther.	Barom.
July 31.		N. 21° W.	78 Miles.	23° 15′ 0″ N.	23° 9′ 0″ N.	199° 20′ 0″ E.	199° 8′ 0″ E.	0° 0′ 0″ E.	24° 45′ 40″	0° 0′ E.	79°	30° 14′
Aug. 1.		W. 8 S.	73	23 6 0	23 4 0	198 0 0	197 52 0		24 40 0		77	30 17
2.		N. 8 W.	103	26 47 0	26 35 0	197 12 0	197 11 0		20 27 30	9 17	78	30 23
3.		N. 14 W.	122	25 3 41	24 54 0	197 28 0	197 29 0		22 26 20		79	30 22
4.		N. 10 W.	89	28 14 0	28 6 0	196 56 0			28 44 30		79	30 24
5.		N. 83 W.	26	28 24 0	28 30 0	195 41 0	195 33 0		28 18 0		80	30 25
6.	81′	W. 4 N.	81	28 25 22	28 23 0	194 8 0	193 52 0		27 59 40	12 18	79½	30 25
7.	61½	W. 10 N.	62	28 36 0	28 26 0	192 57 0	192 22 0		27 32 10		79	30 25
8.	84	W. 4 N.	85	28 41 0	28 36 0	191 21 0	190 36 30		26 54 40	12 31	79	30 25
9.	106	W. 1 N.	6	28 39 0	28 36 0	189 26 0			27 10 25		79	30 24
10.	106	S. 89 W.	126	28 36 8	28 34 0	187 26 0	186 20 0		26 40 5		79½	30 25
11.	107½	N. 87 W.	108	28 41 9	28 30 0	185 22 0	184 9 5	1° 4′ 43″ 27 ⊙ & ☽ ☾ & * Mr. Chapman.	26 16 33	14 4 Amplitude.	79	30 30
12.	100	S. 88 W.	121	28 36 40	28 43 0	183 27 0	182 52 55	182 52 55 ⊙ & ☽ ☾ & * Mr. Chapman.	26 3 30		79	30 25
13.	67	S. 89 W.	67	28 34 32	28 36 0	182 20 0	180 43 30		25 47 5	12 31	79	30 29
14.	43	S. 88 W.	43	28 33 30	28 34 0	181 31 0	179 48 0		25 29 45		80	30 20
15.	26	N. 64 W.	26	28 45 31	28 42 0	181 3 0	179 8 0		24 58 55		81	30 21
16.	2	Calm.	2	28 46 6	28 46 0	181 3 0	179 8 0		24 39 38		81	30 24
17.	9	N. 73 W.	9	28 44 0	28 47 0	180 53 0			24 22 20		80½	30 24
18.	59	N. 73 W.	63	29 2 0	28 53 0	179 42 0	177 29 14	178° 24′ 17″ * E. & W. ☽	23 45 30	13 20	80½	30 21
19.	51	N. 70 W.	52	29 20 19	29 14 0	178 45 0			23 7 8		81	30 20
20.	79	N. 71 W.	83	29 47 6	29 47 0	177 15 0	174 16 20	174 31 27 * E. & W. ☽ Mr. Chapman.	22 20 13		81	30 16
21.	123	N. 78 W.	121	30 11 0	30 16 0	174 55 0			21 36 0 Indifferent.		81½	30 11
22.	130	N. 56 W.	130	31 25 43	31 24 0	171 59 0	170 0 0		70 1 5		81	30 9
23.	142	N. 63 W.	136	32 26 18	32 23 0	169 24 0	167 36 0		68 40 5		81	30 20
24.	122	N. 60 W.	127	33 30 15	33 22 0	167 23 0	165 49 24	166 28 45	67 15 30	9 30	80½	30 24
25.	90	S. 78 W.	92	33 11 0	33 27 0	165 36 0	164 25 25		67 13 55		79½	30 33
26.	125	N. 73 W.	111	33 45 0	33 41 0	163 28 0	162 18 0		66 19 0	9 7	79½	30 28
		Indifferent.										

Figure 3.7: Table of measurements from Broughton, *Voyage* (1804). The various columns show the values of latitude and longitude as 'observed' ('ob.'), 'accounted' ('Ac.'), or derived by the 'Watch'.

to reduce the error in astronomical measurements to less than two minutes of longitude.[87] On the Equator, one minute of longitude equals a mile.[88]

If we were to plot the numbers from these tables onto a large-scale chart, the results would be quite disconcerting. The reality of measurements is not a neat line: it's messy, and it's blurry. It's seeing double and triple and quadruple, depending on how many separate observations are carried out. Perfect precision, stacking all lines into one, is unattainable in science, even with the most sophisticated instruments and the power of information technology.[89] In 2008, artist Jeremy Wood used GPS to record the position of two park benches in Amsterdam; he took six measurements within one minute, with the benches obviously not going anywhere. The result was a stash of *twelve* different benches, all slightly offset from each other, which were later turned into a piece of art

– *Data Cloud.*[90] Precision, then, was all the more unattainable on wooden decks tossed around by the elements, using delicate time-keepers that had been shaken about like stowed casks, or the eyes and minds of weary officers, who every day and every night peered into the sky, put pen to paper, and completed long and difficult calculations. With precision, of course, accuracy also goes out of the window. Which of those lines marks the *real* path of water where the ship passed? Does any?

These new, accurate ship tracks, then, were storytelling in many different ways. They told stories of heroic success and heroic failure, of personal and imperial expansion and violent appropri-ation. But they were also, in their essence, hypotheses, built on probability. And hypotheses are fundamentally akin to fiction.[91]

Saying that tracks were stories doesn't mean that they were weak. On the contrary, their effects were particularly powerful, precisely because they blended the supposed trustworthiness of science with the drama of fiction, the 'objectivity' of instruments with the glitter of personality. Armed with these tools, European empires inscribed the world as if it were theirs.

Charles Burney, in his comfortable Bloomsbury mansion, was not the only landlubber whose eyes sparkled with interest at the mention of adventures on remote seas. These stories of bold exploration were worth a fortune, in terms of political and national propaganda and sheer commercial traction. So were the thin black lines that represented them. The general public did not deal in degrees and minutes of longitude, or the exact differences between a Kendall and an Arnold watch: a list of numbers, precise or imprecise, told them nothing at all. Neither did they have, for remote and 'newly discovered' lands, the geographical reference points that are general knowledge today. Australia was broken, work-in-progress coastline scraps on a mostly blank space, even to those who could place it at all.

To show where exactly he had been, then, a man like Cook had to whip out his pencil and manifest these numbers on a 'user inter-face' – the map, with its track line. Before long, the same line that he had sketched in faint graphite would be printed thousands of times, carved in stone, moulded in bronze, and burnished into the collective European imagination. The unsubtle consumerism of dreams, ruthless imperial self-aggrandisement and the desire to grasp, mark and understand the world meant that ship tracks could be more than a technical tool. They sold, as a product and as a mental framework. Burney was right: these lines would always be visible.

4

STORYTELLING

In 1853, the General Post Office in London attracted a complaint from the other side of the world. An angry reader of the Adelaide *South Australian Register*, signing himself 'A Victim', thundered against the short-sightedness and geographical ignorance of the Postmaster-General: clearly, 'His Mightiness of St. Martin's-le-Grand' was 'under the impression that ships reach Australia by the western or Cape Horn route, or he would never have done so stupid a thing as to send our mails beyond our port'. Adelaide sits about 1,400 kilometres west of Sydney – and many more if one has to travel around the foot of Australia by sea. Why did the post have to go to Sydney first, only to be sent back to Adelaide with a delay of many weeks? This reader's suggestion was that all letters leaving Australia should contain a complaint and, for the instruction of the Postmaster-General, a 'map on which is traced the ships' track to South Australia' (for some reason, in green).[1]

Just two years before, an American sailor-turned-writer had published an enormous and poorly reviewed novel, entitled *Moby-Dick; or, the Whale*. Within a few decades, the book took its rightful place among the classics of English-language literature. In it, Herman Melville recounted a deeply maritime tale of obsession, revenge, death and cetology. His anti-hero, the sulking Captain Ahab, is forever engraved into collective imagination as he stoops over his charts, in the lonely darkness of his cabin, trying to plot the course of his mortal enemy, the white sperm whale Moby Dick. Tracks dominate this vivid image:

> the heavy pewter lamp suspended in chains over his head, continually rocked with the motion of the ship, and for ever

threw shifting gleams and shadows of lines upon his wrinkled brow, till it almost seemed that while he himself was marking outlines and courses on the wrinkled charts, some invisible pencil was also tracing lines and courses upon the deeply marked chart of his forehead.[2]

These two texts – the vexatious newspaper complaint by a snooty member of the public and the immortal words of a great bard of the oceans – came from far-removed corners of the Anglophone world, and seemingly had nothing in common. And yet, they do share one feature. They demonstrate that, by the early 1850s, tracks had firmly colonised the land, and the imagination of the people who inhabited it. No longer did the track necessarily pertain to a specific map or chart: it now lived a life of its own, in language and printed text. It existed as a banal commonplace, a meme, a simile and a metaphor – used to signify specific journeys, yes, but also the idea of journeys, and things that weren't journeys at all, but looked like a track chart. In politics, one would 'steer' one's 'ship' 'through' a predecessor's or a new 'track'.[3] People 'kept track' – or didn't – of days, of milk supplied to their household, of which guard was on watch in a prison, or 'of anything in the shape of a woman'.[4] In metaphorical use, the track as a path on land and the track as an ongoing plot blended and blurred. But water was never too far out of sight. 'I am well aware that your course of reading lies ent[i]rely out of the track of our lighter literature', wrote Edgar Allan Poe in 1844, drafting a letter to a scholar who he hoped would help him get published.[5] A track worked equally well as the simplest geographical diagram to dispel postal misconceptions, and as a literary symbol of a meandering and profoundly scarred soul. How did tracks ensconce themselves so firmly in Western – and particularly English-speaking – culture?

The eighteenth and nineteenth centuries are a time when middle-class mass culture, particularly in oceanic countries like Britain, France and the United States, really turned to the sea – no longer just for work or trade, but also for leisure, and as a boundless source of fancy tales and adventurous, half-dreamed dreams.[6] Melville could assume certain kinds of nautical knowledge – and interest – on the part of his readers. Seafaring terminology and imagery soaked nineteenth-century societies to an extent that our modern, dry world can hardly envisage.[7] We only have faint residuals of this linguistic cosmos in our being taken aback, enjoying 'plain' sailing, giving leeway, and similar.

This deep fascination for all things maritime blended with another, ongoing trend: the slow contagion that, over the course of three centuries, and in parallel with seafaring uses, had taken the convention of route lines from royal manuscripts to public consumption – at times wholly detached from the sea.

This is a book about maritime tracks, but shore-based tracks also contributed to the popularity of journey lines. As lines of movement became more common at sea, they also took hold on land. Some of them were, more properly, fixed landmarks: impersonal roads and routes, in the manner of the Peutinger Table that showed the networks of the Roman Empire. But ashore, as we have already noted, the early modern world had better methods for wayfinding than using tracks – or indeed, with a few sparse exceptions, route maps.[8] In an age of foot and horse, movement still happened over relatively short daily legs, best negotiated through itineraries and landmarks.[9] As a result, most of the tracks that began to appear on land maps had nothing to do with wayfinding: they were there to tell stories.

The greatest story of them all, for early modern Europeans, was the Bible. In the 1450s, it became one of the first books to be printed in a European language, through Johannes Gutenberg's movable-type press. It was also the first non-nautical book to be represented in tracks. This was statistically likely: in the 1500s, the Holy Land featured on European maps more often than any other country.[10] Already in 1300, we saw, the Exodus graced manuscript maps; from the sixteenth century onwards, these were joined by a vast array of printed representations.[11] Tracks, then, reached the land through the power of the Bible, combined with the spatial ambiguity of the pathless 'wilderness', which benefited from clarification and illustration. Printed religious maps didn't stop at the Exodus. By the seventeenth century, they often reported

Figure 4.1: Detail from 'The travels of St Paul and other the Apostles [*sic*] Or, a Geographical Description of those Lands and Countries, where in the Gospel of Christ was first propagated. Being a great help in the reading of the New Testament. Newly Corrected by Joseph Moxon' ([1671]).

miscellaneous other holy trips, both on land and at sea: for example, the travels of the patriarchs, or St Paul's maritime voyage from Jerusalem to Rome (Figure 4.1).[12]

Why did tracks catch on? These track maps, sometimes 'bound up with Bibles', could offer a 'more profitable reading of the Old and New Testament'.[13] This, of course, assumes a specific kind of *direct* reading of Scripture, made accessible to many: the earliest maps bound into Bibles were exclusive to the Protestant world, and most common in vernacular-language editions. Religious authorities demanded 'simplicity' and clarity in the design of these maps, to reflect the simplicity and clarity of the scriptural message.[14] Simplicity and clarity, as we'll see, happened to be tracks' most captivating quality.

This advantage made tracks useful in all sorts of contexts. Next to the footsteps of patriarchs, prophets and evangelists, arm-chair audiences also wanted to follow the footsteps of victorious armies. Maps of battles grew in popularity across the period.[15] They often used tracks to show the manoeuvres of troops. As with biblical travels, these movements were drawn indiscriminately at sea and on land. But many of the most remarkable military tracks remained sea-bound, and, much like navigators' ones, tightly linked to the glory of specific personalities. In 1585–6, Francis Drake led an expedition to the Caribbean and took various Spanish towns. Shortly after, the same Baptista Boazio who may have produced one of his circumnavigation maps brought forth a new one, showing Drake's circular track. The map's key attraction, as announced by the legend, was 'the whole course of the saide Viadge beinge plainlie described by the pricked line' (Plate 14). 'Plainlie' is the operative word: again, the track presented things simply, and clearly. When Drake defeated the Spanish Armada in 1588, some maps depicted the action in a similar style: the opposing fleets of little ships sat on the track like beads on a string.[16] These battle tracks were only the opening shots in a long line, right up to commercial print maps of Admiral Nelson's engagements against Napoleon's fleets, in the late 1790s and early 1800s.[17] Throughout the eighteenth century, all sorts of historical and fictional tracks proliferated, too: from those of Ulysses to the bold voyages of the Argonauts, Julius Caesar, Alexander the Great and Don Quixote.[18] Suffice to say, by then European audiences were quite familiar with narrative tracks on maps. But there is more. They were familiar with narrative tracks on all sorts of objects.

Drake's journey around the world was not only retold in printed and manuscript maps; the *Golden Hind*'s track was also cast in silver. A few years after the expedition, in the 1580s, a grandchild of the Dutch mapmaker Gerardus Mercator designed a commemorative medal. Both faces of this exquisite object, less than 7 centimetres in diameter, are occupied by a map of the voyage – one hemisphere on each side. A little sailing ship is rolled along by the minute hollow dots of a journey track, punched into the metal. Even the *volta do mar* is accurately portrayed (Figure 4.2).[19]

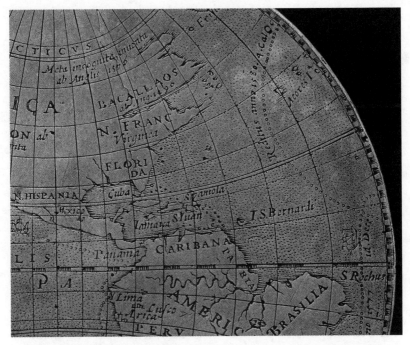

Figure 4.2: Detail from Michael Mercator's silver medal representing Drake's voyage around the world (1589). Drake's return track, including the *volta do mar*, is marked by little dots across the Atlantic (right), and by the string 'Reditus anno 1580. 4. Cal Octobris' ('returned in the year 1580, on the fourth day of the *Calendae* of October', a Latinism meaning 28 September). Note the little ship accompanying the track on the bottom right, just above the Equator.

Another channel through which tracks became objects of consumption was the growing trade in globes. A globe is, first of all, a cartographical solution. If projecting the Earth's surface on a plane causes distortion, why not look at it in its original shape? But a globe of sufficient size to be useful for navigation is a supremely clunky object to carry aboard a ship: we don't know how far this was done. Instead, the fortune of globes stemmed from their teaching, professional, and decorative potential ashore – not to mention their symbolic value. Historians speak of 'the significance of navigation for globemaking rather than the other way around'.[20] Tracks on globes particularly served decorative and symbolic functions.

The voyages of sixteenth- and seventeenth-century navigators, indeed, appear on the very first terrestrial globe made in England, in 1592.[21] Dutch and then English manufacturers sat at the heart of the market, and the tracks they chose often had a national slant. Still in the 1680s, for example, English globe-makers depicted Drake's circumnavigation – by then over a century old – as well as that of his successor Thomas Cavendish (completed in 1586–88) (Plate 15).[22] Globes kept the memory of these voyages alive.[23]

In the eighteenth century, this trend continued. Tracks were printed on the map gores (that is, paper segments) that were pasted onto globes, but users also added their own. The track of Commodore Anson's 1740 circumnavigation is scribbled on a globe once belonging to the Lord Chancellor of England – who, in 1748, became Anson's father-in-law.[24] By the end of the eighteenth century, Cook's tracks were leading the market. They were even inscribed onto very common and portable 'pocket' globes, only a few centimetres in diameter. Many of these globes were in English (Plate 16), but others, popular across central Europe, were made by a German cartographer called Franz Ludwig Güssefeld. His globes were 'silent' – the type without toponyms that is used for teaching children – yet they reported the tracks of Cook, with their dates.[25] Track propaganda travelled transnationally, and across language barriers.

As the track became an article of popular consumption, it slowly turned into a visual refrain almost independent from the map. We witness here the beginning of a process. Endlessly reproduced, the peculiar shape of voyages like Cook's became an object of fetish, a flash left on collective cultural retinas even when the cartographical context around it vanished. His tracks, and those of many other explorer-heroes, have graced stamps and toys, coins, medals, monuments and Hawai'i souvenir shirts – what scholars call 'cartifacts', or map-decorated objects.[26] For example, in the 1780s, the track of Cook's voyages was embroidered by young girls as part of 'world map samplers', which have left us traces of their schooling that weren't as 'ephemeral' and disposable as coursework normally is.[27] In the 1830s, British and then French manufacturers, like the eccentric inventor George Pocock,

Figure 4.3: Captain Cook Memorial, Canberra (1970).

made inflatable balloon-globes that bore the tracks of Cook, La Pérouse and various other explorers – while also pointing out a few historical events and locations. Schoolchildren could assemble these globes themselves, and in the process learn about geography and the history of exploration.[28] In the early twentieth century, imperial and then Soviet Russia awarded colourful 'breast badges', commemorating specific national expeditions. A few of them represented maps with tracks, to be pinned onto veterans' chests.[29] A particularly striking Cook 'tracktifact' is much more modern: a bronze and copper monument next to Lake Burley Griffin, in Canberra. It was opened in 1970, the bicentenary of his visit to 'New South Wales'.[30] The structure represents the world as hollow, a cage of parallels and meridians onto which the land masses are tacked. The track dominates: a blazing, thick, solid line suspended in the air (Figure 4.3).

This might seem quite a smooth linear story, but it is not. There is a gaping abyss between the ways in which a seventeenth-century globe with Drake's track and a nineteenth-century balloon globe were consumed. Truly momentous changes shook European society in the late eighteenth and nineteenth centuries. Tracks, as it happens, were in the right place at the right time.

Across the eighteenth century, both natural philosophy (the precursor of 'science') and geography captivated vast publics of all ages, genders and social positions. Scientific instruments, treatises and lectures held a respectable share of a recent profitable invention – newspaper advertisements.[31] Globes of various sizes, maps and travel accounts sold extremely well, while topics like the quest for longitude engrossed the public in urban coffee houses.[32] In fact, as we have already seen, they possibly engrossed the public more than many actual seafarers, who saw little point in introducing new navigational methods on routes that they knew perfectly well.[33] This was also the era in which periodicals, printed accounts for all pockets, plays, satire, art exhibitions and museum displays first proliferated. They tapped straight into the buzz surrounding overseas 'discovery', and amplified it.[34] By the end of the century, the concepts of latitude and longitude were such common currency that British cartoonists could use them to mock couples mismatched in width and height (Figure 4.4).[35]

Above all, however, this gossipy, information-hungry world incubated a cult of personal celebrity. Celebrity was neither 'glory', admired from a distance, nor narrow 'reputation': it was something new, an obsession both larger than life and grounded in the private and the 'intimate'.[36] In short, people now cared about the details of personal stories, the precise facts that would allow the mediocre observer to *participate*, to *know*, and ultimately to develop a vivid sense of involvement and first-person closeness. We can recognise this very readily: today, we have minute-by-minute reality shows and social media accounts 'keeping up' with celebrities. Two or three hundred years ago, this desire to keep up created a perfect breeding ground for a device like the track. And in turn the track, used in this way, fed its powerful storytelling template deep into European culture – and beyond.

In the fast-paced decades around the turn of the nineteenth century, the new generation of tracks, as devices that allowed the

Figure 4.4: The social currency of geographical concepts,
illustrated in Isaac Cruikshank's *Comic Alphabet* (1836).

public to partake in action and presence and go along on navigational endeavours, had two enormous advantages: they were 'accurate', and, as we have just discussed, they were clear. Let's look at accuracy first, the point where change is most stark.

As shown by Charles Burney's enthusiasm, the supposed accuracy of the track turned it into a relic, to be collected, studied and fetishised. The consumer's interest in purchasing the truth was nothing new, of course; the maps of Drake's circumnavigation made in the 1580s already claimed to be a 'true description' of his expedition.[37] For early modern mapmakers, operating in a world in which the image of the Earth was changing very quickly, accuracy prolonged the 'shelf-life' of a 'product', and could be wielded as a weapon against competitors.[38] However, these descriptions could not be 'true' in the sense that a late-eighteenth-century track could, because in Drake's days the navigators themselves had a limited understanding of where exactly they had been. Two hundred years later, all the meticulous fussing of Broughton or Flinders, their tables of measurements and disquisitions of minutes of longitude, had a powerful (and intended) effect: the European public could begin to really *believe* in tracks.

This faith in the reality of tracks, combined with a desire for participation, made them more real than ever. They became heritage paths, portals to relive the past, time frozen in space. George Vancouver or William Bligh 'saw' the wakes of their colleagues on the ocean in a practical sense, professionally. But through the track, the notion of 'following in the footsteps' of great heroes could be fulfilled, more broadly, as a romantic aspiration. At that point, the track existed in the world quite independently of any map. Even tracks that were in truth irrecoverable came to life in this way. For example, the exact path followed by the Spanish conquistador Hernán Cortés between 1519 and 1521, when he defeated the Aztec empire, is unknowable from the original sources. And yet it was experienced as real by men and women travelling to and across Mexico, from the nineteenth century onwards, in search of meaning for their own small journeys.[39] All the more real, then, were the solid and certified tracks of voyagers who had 'reliably' documented them. As early as the 1790s, American navigators began to 'perform' Cook: repeating his voyages, following his track charts and accounts, imitating his style, and even drawing subtle personal parallels.[40] The same thing happened in Russia in the early 1800s, where Cook became a hero among the nobility. Russian naval officers, often trained in the British Navy, 'worshipped' Cook, and retraced his journeys as many as thirty-six times in the first half of the nineteenth century. They often went along his track stop by stop. They paused at the exact 'memorable spot' where he had been killed, and gawped at details like the mark of the cannonball fired by his officers. Through his track, Cook became the 'immortal Cook.'[41]

Still today, a great fascination buzzes through the general public when expeditions retrace famous tracks. In 2001, for example, a BBC television crew embarked on a journey aboard a replica of Cook's *Endeavour*, with the aim to 'sail in his wake', along a specific leg of his journey. 'History seen from the same ship, the same seas and the same landscape would,' the organisers 'hoped, shed new light on the past and provide fresh insights'. The navigators aboard used eighteenth-century methods and closely followed Cook's track (other than when it would have been too tortuous or dangerous).[42] An account of the 2022 rediscovery of Ernest Shackleton's *Endurance*, buried under Antarctic ice for 107 years, similarly opens with a map of his voyage; every chapter, like a log entry, reports the coordinates of the search. At the end of the trail, the wreck beckoned from the bottom of the sea.[43] Such endeavours, bringing back to life the ephemeral and the long gone, are only possible because the logbooks and tracks of these explorers fossilise their journey for posterity – and for that, tracks are treasured like mortal remains.

We should note here a crucial difference between archaeologists or re-enactors and the nuns whom we met in Chapter 1, walking the Via Dolorosa in their cloisters. Both of their paths are real. But the nuns' one is made real by profound, lived experience and the imagined scenery – which is then transplantable, by sheer emotion and faith, from sun-baked Palestine to a Saxon convent, or an Italian sacred hillock. Cook's and Shackleton's paths, instead, are made real by the fact that they are pinned into an exact *place*. They are just lines: imagining them elsewhere is meaningless, but on the spot they come to life. The hodological Via Dolorosa, grounded in verbal description, travels across time and space, albeit heavily personalised; Cook's path, grounded through the map, travels across time only, like a phantom hovering above the waves.

The fixity of the track's shape, however, also meant that it could travel, relatively unchanged, across languages and cultures. A verbal description of a journey is more vivid, but also more open and interpretable: in some ways, it is less thorough and stable as a package of information. Old tracks were unstable, too. A French mapmaker wishing to copy an English track map of the Exodus, or of Drake's journey, didn't need to see it. Neither the original mapmaker, nor the plagiarist, in reality, had a clue as to *where* exactly the track went. All that mattered was the idea – the fact of the voyage, not its form. Forms *were* commonly copied across languages and editions, but this was usually out of technological and commercial convenience, rather than investment in the specific line.[44] After the big hydrographical voyages of the eighteenth century, this would no longer do. The form was the marvel: its accuracy, precision, and the exact spots brushed and claimed by its loops.

Most of the 'discovery' maps and charts that we encountered in the last chapter travelled across languages, and the tracks on them remained identical: a genuine 'fact'. In Charles Burney's house, Cook could annotate Bougainville's French track chart exactly as he would have its English-language translation. The track chart of Phipps's voyage to the Arctic, showing the discrepancies between various measurements, was reported in an identical sheet at the start of the French translation of his book.[45] Only, all captions and legends were now in French – very accurately reproduced, word for word and down to the font style (the *Racehorse* was called, phonetically, 'Race-horce'). The line, even if closely inspected, is the same.

Cook's charts, too, spread all over Europe. The account of his first voyage, together with those of a few other British circumnavigators, appeared in a book curated by the civilian writer John Hawkesworth – who was heavily criticised for playing fast and loose with the original journals. Still, it sold like wildfire, and libraries couldn't keep it on their shelves for long: in Bristol, it was borrowed an average sixteen or seventeen times a year for the first twelve years.[46] Within four or five years of Cook's first voyage, through various, more or less faithful editions of this text, French, Italian, German and Dutch readers could learn about British navigators' adventures in the Pacific. The German translation was entrusted to a cousin of Friedrich Schiller, the philosopher and playwright.[47] Cook's subsequent travel accounts, too, were widely circulated in many languages, and their meanings wobbled a little. In Russia, translations by a prominent naval officer aimed to spur on Russian emulation.[48] In France, the account of Cook's third journey was translated in a way that amplified the racial and colonial language.[49] Along with these narratives went the maps, also translated.

In context and emphasis, maps, like all texts, never survive translation unchanged. In the United States, Cook was revered almost immediately, as a prototype of the humble self-made hero.[50] What particularly captured Americans' interest were his tracks in the Pacific: an ocean that seemed remote to Europeans was less remote for a country that was beginning to think in terms of 'frontier' and westward expansion.[51] An atlas published in Philadelphia in 1814 gave a whole sheet to Cook's North Pacific tracks, when they were searching for the Northwest Passage. The Philadelphia meridian was used as reference next to Greenwich, just to make a patriotic point (Figure 4.5).[52] In Italy, the Venetian publisher Antonio Zatta produced various cartographical representations of Cook's and Bougainville's voyages. An identical version of Cook's New Zealand, printed in 1778, is especially striking. The legend calls the tracks '*linee puntate*' ('dotted lines'), which 'demonstrate the route of the Vessel' ('dimostrano la strada del Vascello'). The toponyms on the maps of new portions of the world underwent fascinating lexical transpositions. Zatta, for example, used a mixture of the original English or Māori names attributed by Cook, their French translations (showing how the charts had reached Italy via France), and new Italian interpretations. 'Cape Kidnappers', where a group of Māori attempted to kidnap a boy from the crew, becomes 'C. Kidnappers (de ladri de Fanciulli)'. 'Ladri de fanciulli' means 'kidnappers of children': Zatta, or his source, had clearly read the account, and added this detail into the map (Figure 4.6). Other Italian mapmakers, too, took interest in Cook's routes. For example, a 1793 manuscript globe reports little twisting stretches of his second voyage, just when the track peeks below the South Polar Circle: they look like small loops of string tied onto it.[53] This was a very selective (and to my knowledge unique) way of reporting a track. Cook's cartographical voyages eventually bounced back to the seas where they had first arisen: by the turn of the nineteenth century, we come across Chinese and Japanese maps copying English originals, and reporting Cook's tracks – albeit, importantly, not always with attribution (Figure 4.7).[54]

The maps as a whole, then, underwent a process of cultural translation – and mistranslation. But not so much the tracks: within the limits of map resolution, craftsmanship and projection, the tracks stayed unchanged, a sharp black line always in the same

Figure 4.5: 'Map of the Discoveries made by Capts. Cook & Clerke in the Years 1778 & 1779 between the Eastern Coast of Asia and the Western Coast of North America, when they attempted to navigate the North Sea', from *Carey's General Atlas, Improved and Enlarged; Being a Collection of Maps of the World and Quarters, Their Principal Empires, Kingdoms, &c.* (c.1814).

Figure 4.6: Detail from 'La Nuova Zelanda: trascorsa nel 1769 e 1770 dal Cook Comandante dell'Endeavour, Vascello di S.M. Britannica', a plate in the Italian *Atlante novissimo, illustrato ed accresciuto sulle osservazioni, e scoperte fatte dai più celebri e più recenti geografi* (1778).

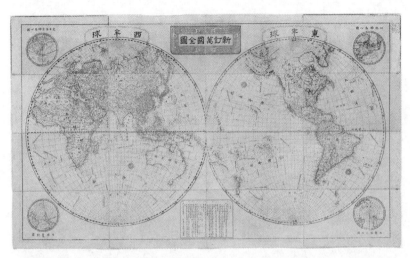

Figure 4.7: Kageyasu Takahashi, 'Shintei bankoku zenzu' ('New Revised Map of All Countries'). This specific map does attribute Cook's tracks.

shape, always in the same place. A sharp black line that was, by now, a culturally universal sign across a large part of the world. We can set details of the American and Japanese maps we have just seen next to each other. The two representations came from the opposite sides of the globe, through different cartographical genealogies and projections, and they were made over thirty years after the original voyages. Yet the tracks agree on nearly everything. They agree on the exact loops and bends drawn by Cook's ships across the sea, they agree on the little southward swirl they made upon touching California, and they agree on precisely where Cook passed in relation to the intricate pack of the Sandwich Islands – today's Hawai'i – when he was killed (Figure 4.8). Parallels and meridians are a bit off, and the coastlines are almost less precise than the track: these are not navigational charts. But the *shape* of the voyage is preserved, transplanted solid. Compare this with the Drake maps, vaguely gesturing in the direction of New Albion, or even the three Agnese atlases in Figures 2.6, 2.7 and 2.8, made in the same decade by the same atelier. Cook's track wields new dignity, and global authority. Every step that preceded and followed his death was permanently fixed on everyone's map.

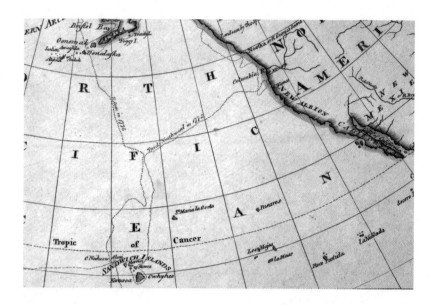

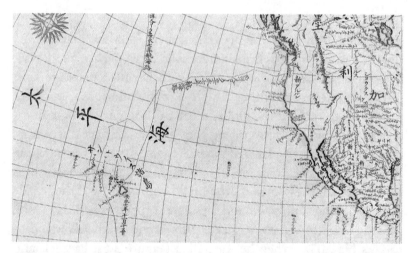

Figure 4.8: Details from an American and a Japanese map of Cook's second voyage to the Pacific, *c*.1810s. It should be noted that the two maps are built on different projections, which accounts for some of the slight rotation and distortion. There is a small mistake in the American map, north of the Sandwich Islands, where the northward and return tracks should cross, but appear only to touch. The engraver here was clearly just reproducing the lines mechanically, without paying attention to their direction and meaning.

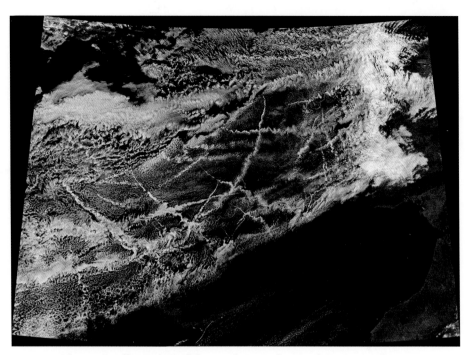

Plate 1: Satellite image of ship tracks over the North-Eastern Atlantic.

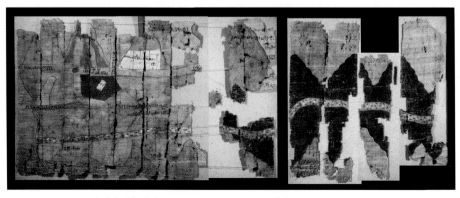

Plate 2: The left half of the Turin Papyrus map of the Wadi Hammamat quarries (c.1150 BC), in one of the possible reconstructed arrangements of its fragments.

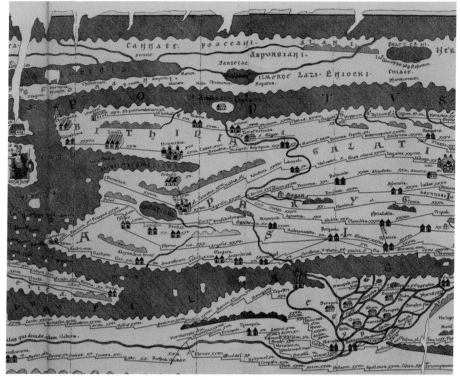

Plate 3: Detail of the Tabula Peutingeriana (nineteenth-century facsimile), showing Anatolia, the Nile Delta and some faint water crossings.

Plate 4: Dura-Europos Map of the Black Sea coastline (third century AD).

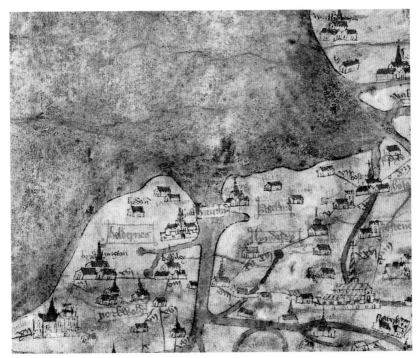

Plate 5: The 'Gough Map' of Great Britain (c.1370 – late fifteenth century): detail of the coast of England around Boston, Lincolnshire (the map is oriented with East on the top). The red lines connecting towns represent routes or distances.

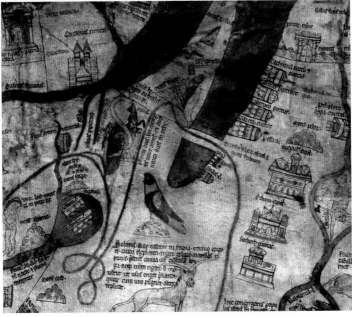

Plate 6: Detail from the Hereford Mappa Mundi (c.1300). The image shows the Exodus route as it crosses the Red Sea.

Plate 7: Italian section of one of Matthew Paris's itinerary maps, which represented the route from London to Palestine (c.1250). The route here starts on the bottom left, at Tortona (*'tortue'*, illustrated by a tortoise), and ends in Apulia (the heel of the Italian peninsula), on the top.

Plate 8: Portolan chart by Luís Teixeira, Lisbon (c.1590–1610).

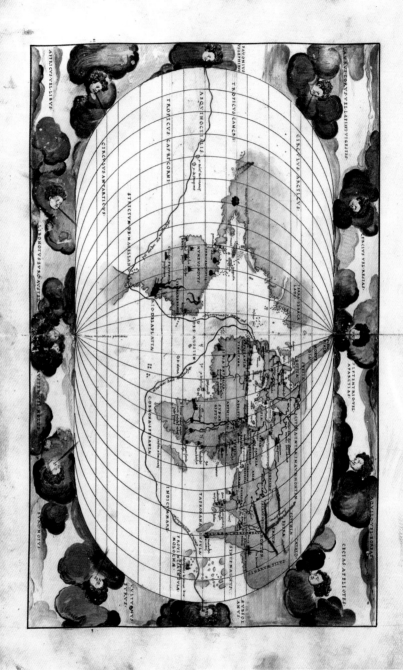

Plate 9: Planisphere from Battista Agnese's *Atlas Universalis* (1542–52).

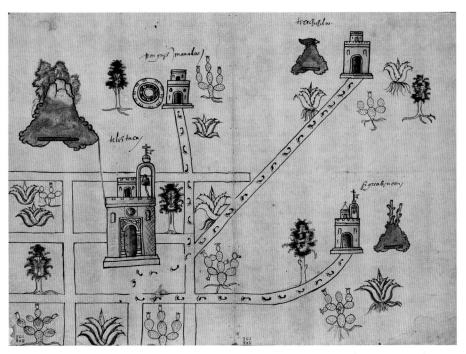

Plate 10: Anonymous indigenous artist, 'Pintura de Tetlistaca' (Mexico, 1580).

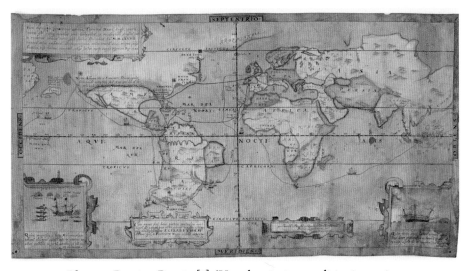

Plate 11: Baptista Boazio [?], 'Vera descriptio expeditionis nauticae Francisci Draci Angli, equitis aurati' (c.1587): pen and ink and watercolour manuscript map of Francis Drake's circumnavigation of the world.

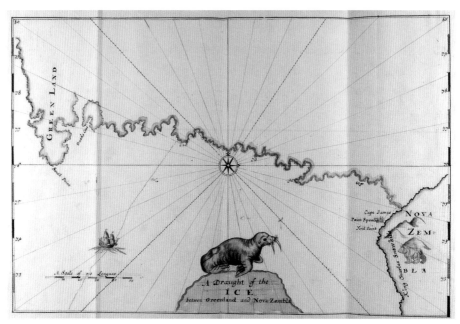

Plate 12: John Wood, 'A Draught of the Ice between Greenland and Nova Zembla' (1676). The site where Wood's vessel was wrecked is on the right.

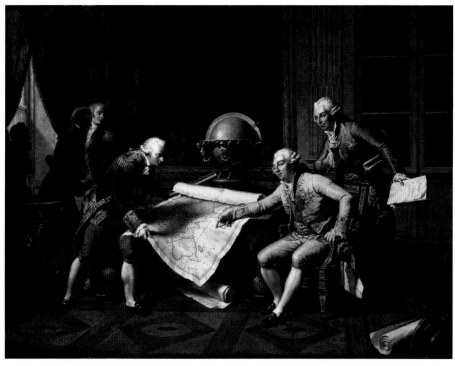

Plate 13: Nicolas-André Monsiau, *Louis XVI donnant des instructions à La Pérouse, 29 juin 1785* (oil on canvas, 1817).

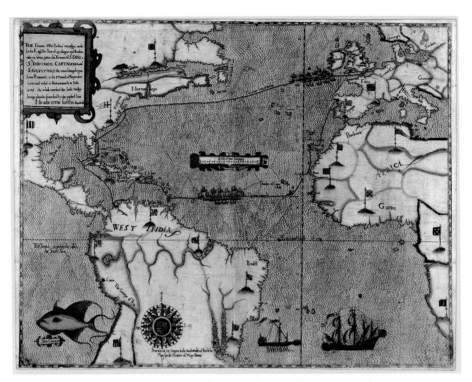

Plate 14: Baptista Boazio, '[Map and views illustrating Sir Francis Drake's West Indian voyage, 1585–6]' ([London?: s.n., 1589]).

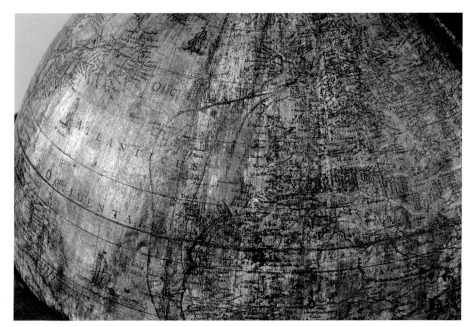

Plate 15: Detail from a 14-inch terrestrial globe made by Robert Morden, William Berry and Philip Lea (London, 1690). The routes of Drake and Cavendish are marked in black, leaving England (easternmost tracks) and returning (westernmost tracks).

Plate 16: 'Cary's Pocket Globe: Agreeable to the Latest Discoveries' (London: J. & W. Cary, c.1791). Cook's and other captains' routes zigzag across the Pacific.

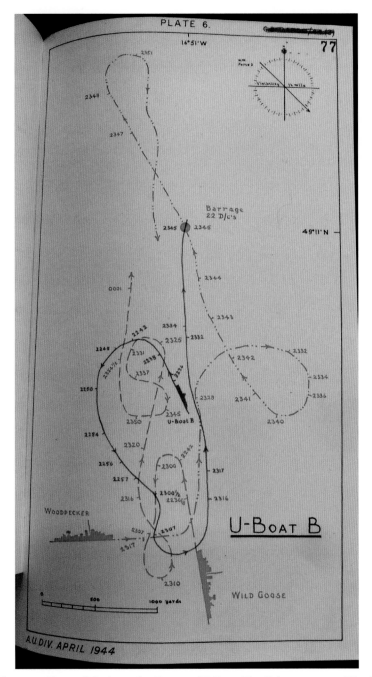

Plate 17: Chart of the hunt for German 'U-Boat B', 9 February 1944, North-Western Atlantic Ocean. Note that the red track of the U-boat contains fewer loops than the green tracks of the two destroyers: this is because it represents more of an approximation and a guess. The submarine's movements are reconstructed on the basis of a few fixings, rather than constantly tracked, and some of these fixings are widely spaced (e.g. between 23.17 and 23.32).

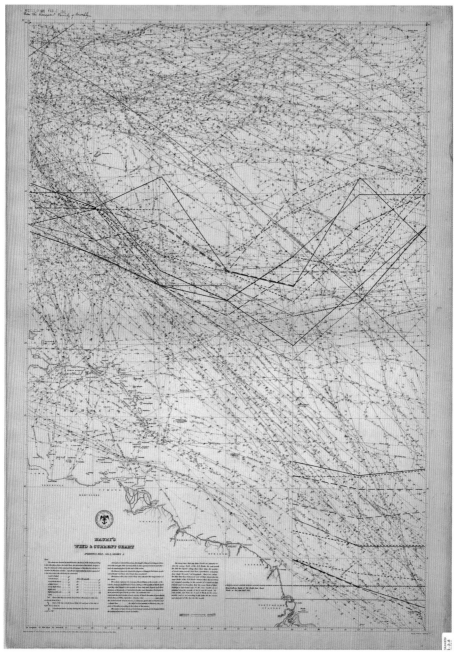

Plate 18: 'Maury's Wind & Current Chart' (1852). Black lines are for journeys completed in winter, green in spring, red in summer, blue in autumn. The pattern of the line (continuous, broken or dotted) indicates the month within each season.

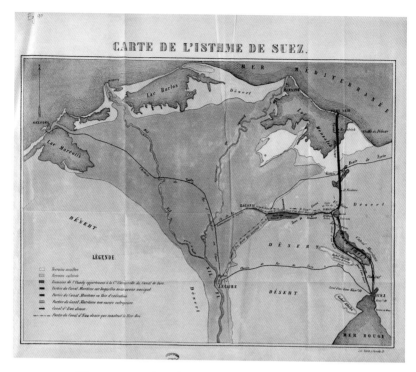

Plate 19: 1865 French map envisaging the final shape
of the Suez Canal (red line on the right).

Plate 20: 1854 French map showing commercial steamliner routes across the
Mediterranean. Blue tracks indicate French ships, red British, orange Austrian, and so on.

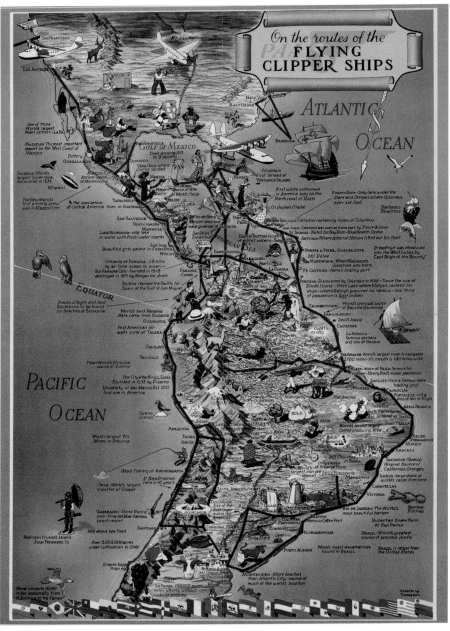

Plate 21: Kenneth W. Thompson, 'On the Routes of the Flying Clipper Ships' (New York: Pan American Airways Corporation, 1941).

OPENING OF THE PANAMA CANAL.

At Which Distant Day Ocean Navigation Will Be a Trifle Out of Date.

Plate 22: J. S. Pughe, 'Opening of the Panama Canal', from *Puck* magazine (1906).

Plate 23: The Suez Canal track cut off by the stranded *Ever Given*, 24 March 2021.

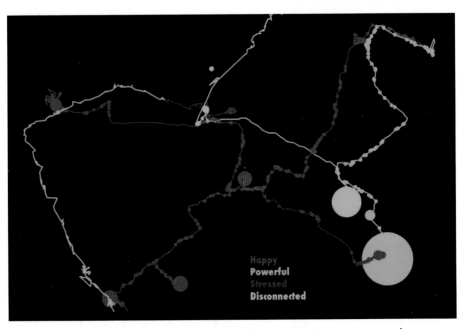

Happy
Powerful
Stressed
Disconnected

Plate 24: 'Mapping Invisibility': undocumented immigrants' movements and emotions across Amsterdam, 2015, as tracked by researchers Naomi Bueno de Mesquita and David Hamers. The thicker lines mark places where the walkers lingered.

So far, in a rhetorical flourish, I have described tracks as if they'd been moving of their own accord, almost by magic. This is, of course, nonsense. National and imperial projection and calculated propaganda also fuelled their global movements. In 1797, the British King George III sent an embassy to the Emperor of China. Along with it went all the finest specimens of British achievement, in the arts, crafts and science – including a globe that showed Cook's tracks. The Emperor was unimpressed: as anthropologist Marshall Sahlins puts it, 'if ever anyone carried coals to Newcastle, it was British people carrying signs of civilization to the Chinese'.[55] Even if not always successfully, tracks were waved as a mark of triumph and accomplishment.

Here we return to the second superpower of the track, next to its new accuracy-powered stability: the track was legible. It was clear, lean, and effective at conveying its message. It was elegant, we may even say. And map-buying customers, after all, valued 'legibility' and elegance even more than they valued truth.[56] In the sixteenth and seventeenth centuries, tracks had conquered the public imagination because they told stories simply enough for religious authorities, and 'plainlie' enough for those wanting to learn about national maritime exploits. But in the eighteenth century, this simplicity, and its aura of universality, came to suit some strands of European visual taste particularly well.[57] The thin black tracks from nautical charts now deserved aesthetic appreciation in their own right – precisely because they were, in their austerity, extraordinarily functional.

To some extent, hydrographical tracks were intentionally 'universal' (at least within the European world, and its narrower Enlightenment definitions of 'universality'). This quality was embedded in them from the moment of their creation, by technical design. Matthew Flinders, for example, in his initial manuscript charts, deliberately used the abbreviation 'Chr' for 'Chronometer', instead of 'T.K.' ('Timekeeper'), to mark his position measurements along the track – 'because it will be understood also by foreigners'.[58] 'Chronometer', unlike 'timekeeper', is a word of Greek origin, with linguistic analogues across Europe. Flinders's original intention was later subverted – the published charts use 'TK' – but

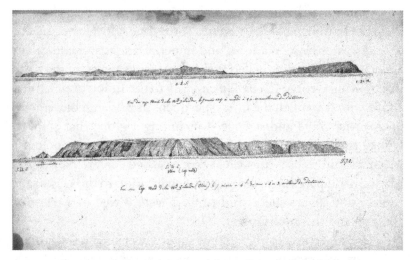

Figure 4.9: Sketch of the coastline of North Cape (Otou),
the northernmost tip of New Zealand, 7 March 1827.

it's the intention that matters here.[59] The implication was that the
only non-universal thing about the track was its accompanying
text, mired in specific national languages and scripts.

Navigation, tracks' primary function, was a naturally cosmopolitan endeavour. However, universality alone doesn't explain their
success. Navigation also relied on other graphical aids, which were
similarly 'universal'. Following a tradition that went back to medieval rutters, eighteenth- and nineteenth-century naval exploration
records still reported illustrated snapshots of coastlines, which the
mariner could compare to what appeared on his horizon. These
'coastal views' crop up all over European hydrographical archives
(Figure 4.9).[60] Clearly, however, such disembodied fragments
of land, no matter how useful to the navigator, failed to capture
the public imagination as incisively as tracks. Their use was more
definitely confined to nautical practice: less transferable, less ambitious and impactful. Tracks, instead, had long outgrown their
navigational roots. They may not have conquered people's minds
entirely by accident, but their clear and comprehensive shape facilitated popularity.

A small caveat is needed here. Not *all* tracks were clear, or popular. In 1845, for example, the geologist Charles Lyell published an account of his travels in North America. This included a colourful and very busy map, in which his route was 'indicated by a double line or road, and by a white streak through the Ohio or Appalachian coal-field, and by a dotted line where I went by water, on the sea or the lakes'.[61] Over the vast splotches of colour, denoting various types of rock, the journey track is an afterthought – and all but impossible to follow (Figure 4.10). Even Charles Darwin, a fellow scientist and Lyell's friend, found little use for this cluttered track map, paired with the lists of toponyms in the text. 'One has no right to expect an author to write down to the zero of geographical ignorance of the reader', he told Lyell;

> but I, not knowing a single place, was occasionally rather plagued in tracing your course. Sometimes in the beginning of a chapter, in one paragraph your course was traced through a half-dozen places; anyone, as ignorant as myself, if he could be found, would prefer such a disturbing paragraph left out. I cut your map loose & I found that a great comfort: I could not follow your engraved track.[62]

Dry itinerary lists of unknown places, as we had occasion to see in Chapter 1, are indeed disturbing. But a track map, if unclearly designed, fares little better. The track has the *potential* to offer clarity: it all depends on how it is drawn.

At this point, we must dig a bit deeper into what 'clarity' actually meant. While their shape and thickness changed, well-designed tracks had been as clear to their viewers in the 1520s as they were in 1800. By then, however, the growth of interest in celebrity, accuracy and scientific knowledge in general had raised the stakes as to how and why audiences consumed 'clarity'. For many decades, 'ordinary' middle-class people had been attending geographical lectures and discussing marine chronometers over coffee. If tracks were real because of the high level of creditable accuracy with which they were drawn, a powerful way for people to partake in navigators' mirages was to grasp that accuracy, to feel that they could understand the deep technical mechanisms behind

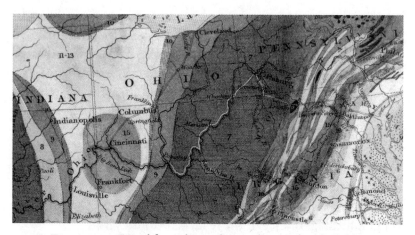

Figure 4.10: Detail from the track map that confused Charles
Darwin: Charles Lyell, 'Geological Map of the United States Canada
&c. Compiled from the State Surveys of the U.S. and Other Sources'
(1845). The white line across the black coalfield is Lyell's track.

the track: the 'scientific manner' in which it was drawn. Fandom
does strange things to people, and one of them is making them
interested in subjects and depths that they would ordinarily find
rather dull.

The first half of the nineteenth century – the decades that led
to *Moby-Dick* and angry enemies of the Post Office – saw other
social processes escalate. This is when mass culture proper, in the
more modern sense, was dawning. Cheap, steam-powered printing
and the acceleration of postal and transport services catered for
new publishing practices and demand, and in turn amplified them.
This meant that an incremental flood of reading and visual material of all sorts reached deep into the crevices of European society.[63]
Nineteenth-century celebrity was all it had been in Cook's time,
and more: both new technologies and the personal emotions of
Romanticism enhanced its power. 'Celebrities'' place in society
would only grow.[64] One of the results was the emergence of a few
modern stock characters.

Cook had never been called an 'explorer' in his lifetime: he
was a navigator, a surveyor and a navy officer. He benefited from

the specific notions of personal discovery and celebrity that we have discussed. But these didn't make *him* an 'Explorer'. The concept of 'explorer' as such, in fact, didn't exist yet, and the word mainly meant a spy. As historian Adriana Craciun aptly puts it, an 'explorer' isn't a universal category that we can take for granted, but rather a nineteenth-century 'consumer product', stemming from the dawning imperial 'tourism and travel industries'.[65] Product is the perfect word here: being a stock character suddenly triggers recognition. 'Surveyor' sounds boring, just a technical job, but 'explorer' makes people interested, and sells field science (one of the most repetitive and painstaking human activities, only possible for the extremely patient) as thrilling adventure.

In the cauldron of themes, stories, news and ideas that whizzed around this enhanced public sphere, the sciences, once again, were one of the topics that attracted much interest. The very terms 'science' (a bit controversially) and 'scientist' (most definitely), much like 'explorer', can only be deployed from this period onwards. By this time, publishers were beginning to identify the non-specialist, 'popular' consumer as a distinct audience (or rather, audiences), explicitly catered for in specific ways. He, or she, was the antithesis of the specialist and of the professional scientist, also newly emerging categories. In the eighteenth century, this dichotomy hadn't existed as such: most men and women of science were what we could call 'amateurs'; scientific publications targeted both those who knew about a topic and those who didn't. In the nineteenth century, instead, scientific communication was not only public, but also, in some of its strands, *designed* to be accessible.[66] The tracks, we said, are perfect communicators. And as such they were employed, and internalised. Via dazzling tales of maritime heroism, the intricacies of navigation captivated common bystanders. The track was there to provide the missing link. One particularly illustrative example comes to us from the bustling public sphere of Victorian Britain.

Commodore John Franklin sailed from England with his two vessels, HMS *Erebus* and HMS *Terror*, in May 1845. His aim was to discover a Northwest Passage, crossing from the Atlantic to the Pacific above the North American continent. Aboard were 129 men. We must remember that in the nineteenth century time spent away at sea acquired a completely different import to how we perceive it today. The two ships had provisions for three years, and were only to be declared dispersed if no communication came by late 1847.[67] Families and friends could only wait, for over two years. No message ever came.

Three initial expeditions were sent out to search for survivors in 1848, from various possible directions. The *Erebus* and *Terror*, it was believed, had got trapped in ice and had to be abandoned. Of course, ice drifts, so the wrecks were a moving target, but the priority was finding the crews, trying to anticipate the decisions they had made as they fought for survival. Dozens of expeditions followed, for decades: British, American, led by the Admiralty or arranged by Franklin's wife Jane, through personal money and vast fundraising.[68] All sorts of ingenious methods were deployed to communicate with the lost seamen. Messages were dispatched by rocket, paper balloons filled with hydrogen, carrier pigeons, and carrier foxes.[69] The sea was searched, along with the Arctic ice and the frozen land: a lethal, barely passable haystack over 1,000 square kilometres wide.

Over frozen surfaces, the expeditions used heavy man-dragged sledges; on lucky days, the tent floors could be mounted as sails, and the sledges would glide along on the ice like 'a fleet of Malay proas, with their dark sails of mat, the snow drift appearing like foam on the water in a fresh breeze'.[70] The men had to run to keep up, but on *very* lucky days one or two of them got to sit on the sledges to slow them down, so that they wouldn't outstrip the runners. In the immense shimmering expanses, the searchers were struck by vicious frostbite and snow-blindness.[71] Ice, in its apparent featurelessness and emptiness, resembles water and deserts: this was a background that required the strangers to draw tracks, lest they got lost. The sledge parties, however, were also making real tracks – carving scudding lines into the frozen surface and building cairns to preserve messages and supplies. All of these became features of the landscape, used by subsequent search parties as reference points (Figure 4.11).[72] When marked on a chart, then, they acquired a

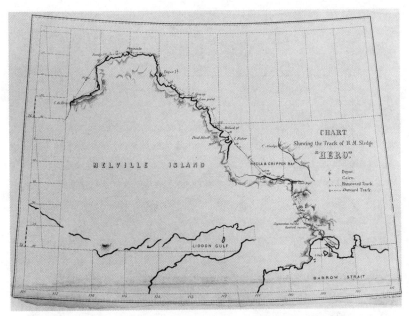

Figure 4.11: 'Track chart of HM Sledge *Hero*, of HMS *Resolute*, on its outward and return routes from Dealy Island to Cape DeBray while engaged in searching for the Franklin Expedition' ([1852]). The cairns are clearly marked.

solidity that oceanic tracks would never achieve.

For coordination at home, too, it remained important to highlight which parts of the land and navigable water had been covered in the search. Tracks on charts did exactly that. In the 1920s, an ex-naval officer called Rupert Gould would eventually collate all this cartographical information into a summary map: the sparse remains of the original expedition, uncovered over the decades, were carefully marked onto it. Speculative dotted tracks signalled various possibilities for the *Erebus*'s and *Terror*'s 'probable drift' (Figure 4.12).[73]

By the 1850s, Franklin remained lost, but disquieting traces had begun to emerge. Objects were found, and human and animal remains. In 1850, one of the expeditions came across three graves. They couldn't open them at the time, but this was done in the twentieth century, and three bodies were found, perfectly

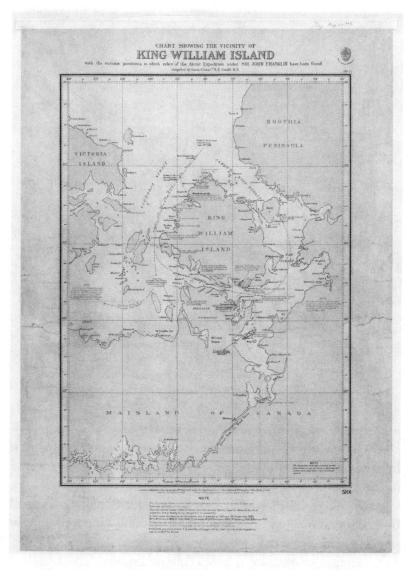

Figure 4.12: Rupert Gould, 'Chart showing the vicinity of King William Island with the various positions in which relics of the Arctic Expedition under Sir John Franklin have been found' (1927).

preserved: morbid, shocking images of the frozen mummies were plastered all over the press, the TV, and even children's books.[74] In 1854, John Rae, a Scottish surveyor working for the Hudson's Bay Company, spoke with Inuit people and discovered the grim fate of the remaining crew members. Back in Britain, his testimony brought horror and sadness. But soon a press campaign, started by Charles Dickens, lambasted his supposed finds. The reason was simple: Rae, and, most outrageously, his non-white informers, had dared to state a distasteful truth. The story of Franklin and his men ended in cannibalism.[75] In 1859, yet another expedition, sponsored by Jane Franklin, closed the search for survivors: Captain Leopold McClintock found a cairn with the first and only official note from the dispersed men. Franklin, it confirmed, was dead. He had been since 11 June 1847. That is, he had been dead since before many people in England had begun to worry, and before the two ships were even abandoned, in April 1848. By the time that year was out, no one had been left alive.[76]

And yet, while the men's end was known, the track remained truncated. A big mystery continued unsolved: where *were* the *Erebus* and *Terror*?

The answer had to wait another century and a half, and it is a rather prosaic one. The *Erebus* was tracked down in 2014 by a Parks Canada expedition. It sits to the west of the Adelaide Peninsula: because the wreck is still a restricted National Historic Site, the coordinates released pertain to a rather wide rectangular area, between 68° 14' 45" N 98° 52' 22" W, 68° 17' 44" N 98° 40' 18" W, 68° 13' 15" N 98° 32' 16" W, and 68° 10' 17" N 98° 44' 19" W. The *Terror* (found in 2016) lies in Terror Bay, by King William Island, between 68° 54' 25" N 98° 59' 42" W, 68° 54' 25" N 98° 51' 29" W, 68° 48' 46" N 98° 51' 31" W, and 68° 48' 46" N 98° 59' 42" W.[77]

These figures, and even the place names, mean very little to people who are not navigators, and not deeply familiar with the rugged and chaotic chart of the Arctic. But here we may pause and consider our own curiosity. Why did we care about the location of the two ships, if the answer could only be something hardly intelligible or relevant to us? Why does the simple question 'where *were* the *Erebus* and *Terror*?', coming after Franklin's dramatic tale, work as a narrative cliffhanger? For a similar reason to why it worked in the nineteenth century, even after human concern was swept off the table by McClintock's sad report. In fact, if we dig a bit more deeply into this sentiment, we can get to the bottom of ship tracks' popular success.

Mystery and horror stimulate public interest like little else. The search for Franklin still made headlines in 2016, when HMS *Terror* was found – remarkably well preserved, and in a rather unexpected location. The discovery of HMS *Erebus*, exactly two years and one day earlier, had been hailed by the press not only as a great Canadian moment, but also as 'the biggest find since the opening of Tutankhamun's Tomb'.[78] This media enthusiasm, however, is but a feeble last echo: in the nineteenth century, the fate of the lost expedition sparked a genuine transnational craze. Particularly in Britain, minute geographical speculation as to where exactly the ships might have gone, and where search parties should look, became a near-universal object of discussion. Newspapers were flooded with letters and suggestions.[79]

In January 1850, for example, naval officer Sherard Osborn, who would later participate in some searches, bombarded *The Times* with anonymous complaints against the 'delay and procrastination' of the Admiralty, dilly-dallying over Christmas celebrations. The first spate of search expeditions had failed; in this correspondent's view, not enough was being done to arrange new endeavours and send them in the right directions. His visualisation of the matter was unambiguously cartographical, and in fact framed in terms of tracks: 'The trail of the murderer skulking from justice was followed with far more skill and ability than the footsteps of those devoted servants of Great Britain', he railed. He suggested the use of auxiliary steam, but then continued: 'I would not be understood as advancing any such mad schemes as those I hear daily proposed over exhilarating club dinners, such as taking a steamer up to Melville Bay, and *slashing* her across to Melville Island, and *slashing* her back again! I know full well that there is no slashing wood or iron through "thick-ribbed ice."'[80]

Cartographical routes became a matter of national pride, even more so than in the days of Cook and Bougainville. Abandoning Franklin and his men, out of concern that more lives might be lost in the attempt, would be 'un-English', mused Osborn; 'let not the United States snatch from us the glory of rescuing the lost Expedition'. This was not to say that the Americans should be barred from contributing: in fact, he laid out detailed plans for what they should do. However, he hoped that they would 'not waste time and money in merely treading over the same ground as ourselves'.[81]

Also in 1850, *The New Monthly Magazine and Humorist* printed an article entitled 'The Track of Sir John Franklin'. 'Having kept our readers *au fait* to the progress of Arctic research and discovery', it opened, 'and to the still more heart-stirring researches now being made after our long-lost countrymen, it behoves us to give some account of the traces that have been met with of Sir John Franklin's expedition, and the deductions to be founded upon this discovery'. Four detailed pages followed, discussing the ins and outs of very specific finds. 'Providence', it was to be hoped, 'may still restore the lost mariners, whose track has at length been struck, to their friends and country'. The track was at the same time a sum of 'traces', Ariadne's thread to bring the lost men home, and a tool to keep the interested public '*au fait*' to 'heart-stirring' developments.[82] The track was a story that kept both those lost in the ice and those curious in their sitting rooms dangling from a thin thread.[83]

Even once people in Europe knew for sure that the expedition had been lost forever, the mystery remained alive, as a rather ghoulish curiosity fully replaced any sense of concerned urgency. Among other initiatives, several public exhibits of Franklin 'relics', retrieved by searchers, entertained English audiences in the 1850s and 1860s. In practice, these were a bizarre blend of holy display and archaeological exhibition, but relating to an episode that had taken place only some ten years before.[84] In 1860, for example, the Museum of the United Service Institution laid out a number of 'relics' 'for the inspection of the public' in Whitehall. The collection ranged from a torn 'fragment' of an ensign, a 'medicine chest' and some religious books and navigational instruments, to a ramshackle series of objects such as 'a piece of white scented soap', 'a seal, with the emblem of Freemasonry', 'a clay pipe bowl', 'a scrap of a coloured cotton shirt', 'two brass hooks and a strap', 'a brass match box', 'a piece of canvas', 'a piece of sealing wax', some leather goggles ('"Goggles"', the guide explained, 'are a species of spectacles like railway spectacles, to protect the eyes in the snow'), and many more treasures along those lines. The dispersed, their bodies, and their daily lives and routines lingered on through these objects. Made of a carefully detailed range of materials, they had all resisted the wear of sea and ice, and were described with narrative gusto. The back of the catalogue pamphlet was well filled with various commercial ads.[85]

Together with the relics, the organisers did not forget to supply two charts: one, an Admiralty chart indicating 'the spots whereon the Boat and Relics were found, with the new land discovered by Captain McClintock'; the other, 'a map by Wild, hydrographer, Charing Cross'. A few years before, James Wyld, Hydrographer to the Queen, had dedicated a Chart of the Arctic Regions to Jane Franklin, and we may assume that this was the one on display. This chart is fairly original, in that it doesn't report ship tracks per se. However, it indicates the Arctic coastlines 'discovered' by each explorer by highlighting them in different colours.[86] The pilgrims who flocked to Whitehall to gaze at the relics were offered a clear backdrop to situate the stories they consumed. 'Relic' itself is an interesting term: in its Latin root, it means something that is 'left behind' ('relinquished'), that 'remains'. The track could take pride of place among the broken tools and holy scraps of civilisation out of which it was built.

Another of James Wyld's endeavours, nine years earlier, had been a 23-metre-tall Monster Globe, installed in the middle of the run-down Leicester Square, in London. This world was concave and hollow; with a one-shilling ticket, people could climb four flights of stairs into its bowels. On every side, they were surrounded by the whole surface of the Earth, womb-like (Figure 4.13).[87] 'The World, as has often been remarked by moralists before, is exceedingly hollow', commented the satirical magazine *Punch*; 'but then, if it were not, we could never have seen it for one shilling'.[88] The Globe was contemporary to the famous Crystal Palace Exhibition of 1851. As one historian puts it, what we witness with the Great Exhibition is 'the broader Victorian obsession with liberating perception from the shackles of time and space'.[89] The world, past and present, supposedly came to London. The inside-out tourist globe wasn't a new invention: it ripped off a French idea from twenty-six years before, called 'georama'. And soon after the first georama, in 1832, a similar sphere in Passage Colbert, in Paris, had surrounded visiting schoolchildren with historical representations of voyages.[90] More commonly, 'panoramas', cylindrical 360-degree painted vistas of a given landscape, were all the rage in nineteenth-century European cities. People liked to travel without travelling, learn and see with minimal effort. Panoramas were the virtual realities of their age.[91]

Wyld's Globe included a 'model of the Arctic regions', on which 'the route of the Franklin missing vessels' was 'laid down with plainness and accuracy, in such a way as to be easily traced and understood'. As some exhibition reviewers concluded, 'the investigation will prove interesting to the inquirer, besides being in itself a work of high art'.[92] The official publication accompanying the Globe offered an even more significant explanation, which is worth reporting in full:

> The spectator, with the polar regions' chart in his hand, will trace on the globe the supposed route of Sir John Franklin, and the routes of the successive expeditions; and, more particularly, the indications which have been found of his earlier progress. He will there be able to form his own judgment as to whether adequate means have been taken to secure the proposed end; and he may arrive at an opinion as to the probability of success, and the expediency of further relief being provided. For such distinct inquiry he will find to his hand all the materials necessary to lead to a conscientious decision.[93]

Of course, whatever they may have felt, it was not up to generic members of the public to *decide* whether to launch Admiralty expeditions – much less on their direction. However, the popular display of ship tracks allowed everyone to play at being

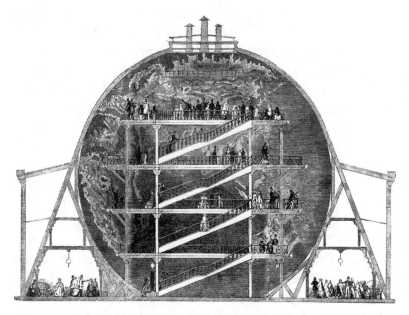

Figure 4.13: Wyld's Great Globe, as pictured in the
Illustrated London News (7 June 1851).

a hydrographer, captain and Explorer. Shown a nautical log, the
average landlubber would have only seen a series of indecipherable
numbers, like those that mark the wreck sites today. But the track
was different: it was clear, and it spoke a plain visual language that
apparently required no further competence. By and large, customers like to think that they are on top of things. Men like Wyld had
perfectly understood this, and what they sold through a line was
the delusion of expertise. And yet, the public was never passive: in
consuming knowledge, audiences always reshape its meaning. They
pick and choose; they dictate what will seep into collective imagination, and how – and what will not. In this public 'marketplace',
an air of 'authority' was a key trait of successful communication.[94]
By being true, and yet simple, the track gained all the authority it
needed. It glowed bright.

In Chapter 6, we will return to the ways in which tracks became
prime technologies to sell customers a sense of control. But before
then, let's see what was happening to the tracks as professional

tools – just as 'professional' people, in the modern sense, were beginning to emerge as a social category. A device that makes the private visible, the ephemeral stable, and the past present holds vast powers of application. Apart from hydrographers and famous explorers, who was using nautical track charts in the nineteenth century – and why?

KEEPING TRACK

Charles Marsden was twenty-one years old when he was shot. The Battle of Jutland, commencing on 31 May 1916, was the biggest naval engagement of the First World War. A shipmate of Marsden's later described the state of their ship, HMS *Southampton*, when the following day dawned: 'The foremast, the rigging, the boats, the signal lockers, the funnel casing, the mainmast, everything was a mass of splinter holes'.[1]

Marsden was a sub-lieutenant, freshly transferred from the Royal Naval Reserve, and in HMS *Southampton* he served as Navigating Plotting Officer. The job required both precision and sangfroid. As shells rained down on the light cruiser, and other warships blew up all around it, he stood on the bridge and marked the ship's position on a track chart, at ten- to fifteen-minute intervals – sooner if the vessel made a rapid tack (Figure 5.1). The track, in sharp pencil lines, begins at 2.35 p.m., around longitude 4° 54' E; after a series of writhing turns, it ends at 10.15 p.m., at 6° 10' E and considerably further south than it had started.[2] It reports minutely details that are confirmed from other sources – for example, the fact that the *Southampton* delayed until 4.45 p.m. before following the rest of the squadron in the 180-degree turn that had been ordered at 4.38 p.m.[3] For about an hour either side of 6.00 p.m., the *Southampton*'s Navigator expertly took it on a zigzagging course to dodge the German fire, as shells splashed in the water all around it.[4] This, too, was religiously recorded in the young Navigating Plotting Officer's pencil track. Shorter tracks, marking the movements of other friendly and enemy vessels, are spattered on the sheet. So is Marsden's blood.

We don't know much about the exact circumstances of his wounding. The *Southampton* had made it into the night seemingly

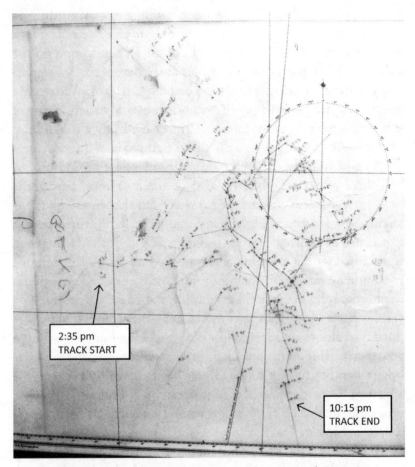

Figure 5.1: Detail from a track chart of HMS *Southampton*'s movements at the Battle of Jutland, on 31 May 1916. The brown blood stains are visible in the middle and in the top-left area of the chart. The track ends at 10.15 p.m. on the bottom right.

unscathed, and was manoeuvring in the dark, when suddenly, just after 10.00 p.m., it fell in with the German line. It exchanged fire with four imperial ships, at close range: in a storm of shrapnel, 75 per cent of the men on the upper deck were 'mowed down' in three and a half minutes, and an officer in another warship 5 miles away was able to 'read a signal on the bridge by the light of [...] [the *Southampton*'s] fires'.[5] Marsden's track ends there.

The young officer lived to fight another day. According to the surgeon's journal, he had been 'struck on the L'[eft] Leg by a piece of shrapnel or exploded shell causing a deep wound on the outer side', but the bone was intact and 'there was no haemorrhage' – even if evidently there was bleeding.[6] The ship's log, amid thirty-four dead and thirty-six wounded, lists Marsden as one of those who were 'Slightly Injured'.[7] The chart, likely a rough draft of the official record eventually submitted to the Admiralty, was donated by Marsden himself to Churchill College in Cambridge, fifty-three years later. The navy also let him take home part of the brass plate that had covered the *Southampton* charthouse: the rectangular tile is astonishingly heavy, and lacerated in three points, like a filmy cashmere devoured by moths (Figure 5.2). Marsden had it inscribed with a few lines and mounted on a wooden support, to commemorate the gruesome event. Lastly, he donated an album of photographs, many of them from the day of the battle, showing various parts of the ship torn to pieces by enemy fire. In one he is portrayed alongside a few fellow officers – a smiling, curly-haired young man slumped on a chair and hatless, while most of the others stand in full uniform. His left leg is raised and covered by a blanket.[8] Marsden was sent to hospital on 3 June, and remained on sick leave until 1 October: his wound was perhaps more severe than the ship's log had recognised.[9]

These artefacts, vivid and shocking, leave us with a strong impression of disciplined duty, and of the pride that Marsden took in this quality. The performance of duty was accurately tracked or, rather, self-tracked, in the striking visual dimension of the chart. The exact movements of the ship had to be documented, nearly minute by minute, quite literally come hell or high water.

The tracks that we have encountered so far in this book served to tell the stories of their makers, but their original purpose had to do with the mapping of territory, rather than the mapping of individual behaviour. They may have made navigators into celebrities, but the spotlight ultimately remained on the seas and lands that they had explored: their novelties, their riches and their dangers – or even just their shape. When tracks became a technical surveying tool, more than ever they mainly served the coastline, brought it

Figure 5.2: Brass plate from the charthouse of HMS *Southampton* (1916).

into existence and hovered around it. At times, they even became implicit, dissolving into a string of soundings (Figure 5.3). The navigator's own presence via the track was still, at that point, somewhat incidental.

Soon, this presence would become a requirement, and in fact, for most naval officers, the very reason why the track must be drawn. The sea slowly blurred into a flat and unimportant background to human action. Over the course of the nineteenth century, we witness a major change in the nature and function of tracks: they evolve from tools of surveying into tools of surveillance. They had started off as a way of indicating *where* seafarers had been, but now they began to be interrogated in a different way: they could show *what* seafarers had done, and *how*.

This shift was rather seamless. While it liked to hide behind instruments, nineteenth-century survey science remained an activity that was strongly dependent on the surveyor's person – on his or her senses, hands, decisions, mental state, strength and physical presence.[10] British colonial officers in the Indian subcontinent even trained indigenous men to use their bodies as instruments: agents like the Bhotiya cousins Nain Singh and Mani Singh learned to set the length of their step so regularly that they could be sent into Tibet, where no Europeans were allowed, and secretly produce accurate maps of the region.[11] In general, as we have seen, much of the individual's own self was contained in the track. This also lent

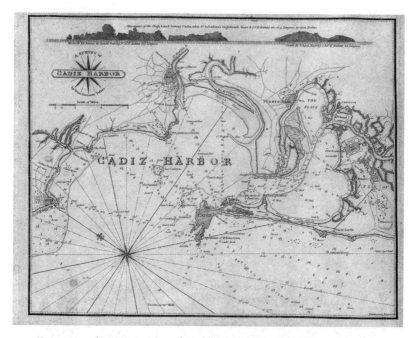

Figure 5.3: '1 A: A Survey of Cadiz Harbor', by Don Vicente Tofiño (1814). The depth soundings are clearly arranged along the course of the vessel that measured them. Tofiño taught mathematics at the Spanish officers' academy in Cádiz, and trained many hydrographers.

the track credibility. A few decades ago, historian Steven Shapin suggested that modern science is founded not on direct experience, as we like to think, but on *trust* in the testimony of others. In the seventeenth century, at the beginning of 'science' as we know it, those worthy of trust fell into two categories: gentlemen, whose word was honourable, or people with first-hand expertise.[12] This matters here because the men who made tracks in the seventeenth, eighteenth and nineteenth centuries belonged to both groups: they were gentleman officers, and professional sailors. In tracks, their own word was at stake.

Once you create such a tight bond between an individual and his output, you have found a perfect way of monitoring his activities – of *judging* him by that output. If the reliability of a survey depended on the reliability of its creator, in some ways the opposite was also true: the survey, in both its form and its content, provided clear evidence of the surveyor's behaviour and conscientiousness. The disciplined environment of European navies offered a perfect terrain for the track to flourish into something else: the great-grandparent of human tracking and geo-surveillance. But how exactly did this happen?

In 1795, Admiral Hugh Cloberry Christian had an appalling Christmas. As the war with France raged, the military situation in the West Indies was rapidly deteriorating. Christian had been tasked with the vital errand of escorting there a large troop convoy, as a matter of urgency. But the weather had different plans.

Very unusually for that season, the Channel and North Atlantic were being hammered by relentless southerly and south-westerly gales. Admiral Christian's convoy sailed from Portsmouth in November, and didn't make it very far; some ships went down, and hundreds of drowned servicemen were washed ashore on the Dorset coast. In December, he tried again. For forty-seven days and nights, Christian's 218 ships fought against the storm, buffeted and tossed around the same stretch of water like scraps of paper in the wind, crashing against each other and battling to keep afloat. The soldiers grew sick and mutinous, and the crews exhausted. Eventually, the sea won the struggle for the second time, and on 25 January 1796 Christian raised the signal for most of his convoy to return to port.[13] 'I cannot write more,' he stated in his report, on 29 January; 'I am now down with anxiety & fatigue. Yet I bear it because I think I have done my Duty'.[14]

Here we have it again – the same sense of duty that kept Marsden occupied in his charthouse under German shelling. Christian, too, produced a track chart of his misadventures – a tangle of desperate zigzags, heading out from Portsmouth for a few miles, before slashing back (Figure 5.4). This chart, however, wasn't necessarily required of him: he spontaneously attached it to his letters to the Under-Secretary of State for War, as evidence to justify his failure. No one, looking at this chart, could say that he hadn't tried. The visual shape of the track holds extraordinary power. Officers themselves intuitively exploited this feature: the track spoke in plain language, as we have seen, and almost begged to be used to inculpate or – from their point of view – exonerate its creators. But, as we shall see, a structural change was needed to make this into a systematic form of top-down control.

Christian, incidentally, wasn't officially blamed for the disaster – in fact, he was made a member of the Order of the Bath – but he inevitably acquired a certain reputation as a Jonah among the most superstitious seamen. He did eventually make it to the West Indies, after another attempt in early spring. The relatively fresh troops swept the French off St Lucia, Grenada and St Vincent, and brutally suppressed the desperate insurrections of local populations, executing, deporting and re-enslaving.[15] None of this would bring an end to the global war, which was to rage, almost uninterruptedly, for another nineteen years. The admiral died of a seizure two years later, aged fifty-one. What he did achieve was the glory of having these freakish midwinter storms named after him: 'Christian's Gales' of 1796 remained famous in the annals of seafaring.[16]

How do we go from a track brandished ad hoc by a worried officer to a tool of surveillance and employee management? At the turn of the nineteenth century, big developments were afoot in European navies. They were fostered by a hundred years or so of on-and-off war, mainly between Britain and France, which culminated in the Revolutionary and Napoleonic Wars of 1793–1815. The most significant shift was a general tightening of bureaucratic rules.

Eighteenth-century fleets had always been astonishingly efficient (all things considered) when it came to detail management and book-keeping. Granted, sailors might not see their pay for months and years, but Admiralties nonetheless kept meticulous lists of their names and demographic details. Hundreds of thousands of seamen's registers, ships' musters, hospital musters, medical journals, lists of ships, victualling contracts and miscellaneous letters, to name but a few items, were painstakingly copied and archived by the quills, elbow grease and overtime of clerks and secretaries. On multiple evenings, John Wilson Croker, the First

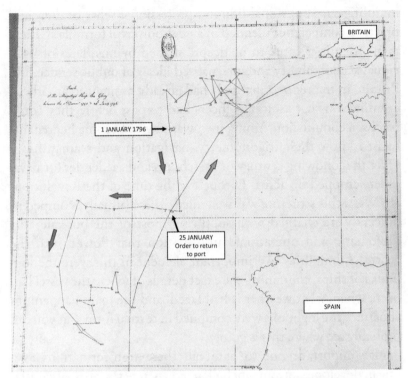

Figure 5.4: 'Chart of the track of the ship HMS *Glory* between 10 December 1795 and 26 January 1796 off the coasts of France and Spain'. The captions and directional arrows are added here for clarity.

Secretary to the British Admiralty between 1809 and 1827, had to apologetically write to his wife from the office, explaining that he hadn't had time to pen a message before.[17]

As navies increased their bureaucratic reach, and stretch, the officer class across Europe had been slowly 'professionalising'. This meant practical seamanship from a young age in Britain, theoretical preparation in Spain, service abroad in Denmark and Sweden, and a whole host of transformations in France – where the navy, like everything else, ended the century turned upside down by the Revolution. Broadly speaking, however, almost everywhere the pattern was the same: out went the untrained noblemen, and in came skilled sailors. Sometimes they still belonged to the aristocracy, but often these new career officers were the children of the middling sorts; personal honour, professional sense of duty and practical competence blended in a new, powerful formula.[18] These men's identities came to be deeply shaped by mandates of individual accountability and internalised ideals of public service.[19] In Britain, in the 1670s, Charles II had already brought in an official examination that aspirant officers had to pass before they could receive a commission. Young men wanting to become lieutenants had to know their trigonometry, navigation and seamanship.[20] Over the following century or so, schools and academies for naval cadets cropped up across Europe. By the time of the Revolutionary Wars, this structure was well oiled. These (usually) competent officers were charged with supplying most of the bureaucratic, diplomatic and operational information that flowed into the central Admiralties. An important element of this were the logbooks of ships, containing the exact details of where the vessel had been, when, what weather it had faced, and the main happenings aboard.[21] The logbooks were compiled in textual form, but you can probably see where this is going.

It's important not to paint all these transformations as a linear development, an unchallenged march towards organised 'modernity'. As always, change was wobbly, and highly dependent on individuals and circumstances. In Britain, for example, the peak of disciplinary tendencies came at the very beginning of the nineteenth century, when John Jervis, Earl of St Vincent, was First Lord of the Admiralty (1801–4). All we need to say about St Vincent is that, when still a humble admiral, he habitually appeared on the main deck at 3 a.m., and used his spyglass to check whether the captains in his squadron were up and at them, or still lazing in bed. Once he was put in charge of the Admiralty, he tried to introduce engineer Samuel Bentham and philosopher Jeremy Bentham's 'panopticon' system in the dockyards, for the total surveillance of employees. The 'panopticon' (literally meaning 'all-viewing') was an architectural model mainly devised for prisons, with a guard in the middle able to keep every inmate within eyesight; in turn, the prisoners would know that the guard was there, even though they could not see him – and this would lead them to regulate their behaviour. Thanks to the philosopher

Michel Foucault, the panopticon has become an emblem of modern surveillance.[22]

In some ways, then, the link between naval management and surveillance begins with an old man and a spyglass. Overall, however, the persecutions of leaders like St Vincent were not necessary: officers had been brought up with sufficient sense of duty and discipline that they could be trusted, most of the time, to keep track of their own behaviour. Young Marsden at Jutland was the culmination of two centuries of training.

Where are the charts in all of this? The venerable written form of the logbook had already evolved into a tool of employer surveillance, in both navies and shipping companies. Many officers baulked at the idea of having to measure and jot down endless columns of useless data, at every hour of the day and night. No one, least of all a ship's captain, likes to be micromanaged, and out on the open seas the only form that micromanagement could take was the injunction to *self*-track – even if nobody ever glanced again at the mountains of logs that accumulated in Admiralty and business warehouses.[23] Like wealth, information can be hoarded far beyond concrete usability. The eighteenth century, indeed, is a period that many historians see as the hatching of the modern 'information state'.[24]

But charts served a specific role in relation to logs. They were the cherry on top of the pile of paperwork that increasingly burdened seafarers. We've seen how the track has a visual readability that appeals to non-experts. This visual readability, in fact, appeals to experts, too. From the 1860s, new rules came in: in the British Navy, officers were explicitly required to keep a track chart, for two main reasons – neither of which had to do with the traditional functions of laying a course or mapping new waters.

First, the track recorded in a stark visual way the resources that an officer had expended. We tend to think of the nineteenth-century introduction of steam as an abrupt revolution in navigation, meaning that ships could travel wherever they wanted, whenever they wanted, and fast. There will be more to say on this in the next chapter. For now, however, we can consider a specific logistical catch: the coal used to produce steam was extremely expensive, and running out of it in the middle of the ocean could cause delays and disasters. Any captain who chose to use steam rather than sail, at any given point of his voyage, had better be sure that this was necessary. The British Admiralty's *Regulations and Instructions* were extremely clear on this point: the 'slightest neglect' of the rule would get an officer into trouble. Of course, exactly when to use steam was up to his 'judgment', but it was nonetheless a choice that he must be ready to 'justify'. Every occasion of travel under steam had to be underlined in red on the logbook, and marked in red on the track chart, for the scrutiny of a senior officer at the earliest available opportunity.[25] The senior officer was generally an admiral, perfectly capable of reading a logbook. But a red-stained track chart was a much quicker way of checking what a subordinate had done.

The second occasion on which track charts came under the spotlight was less pleasant still. Whenever they had to face a court martial for wrecking their own ship, British naval captains were ordered to hand over not only their logbooks, but also a track chart of their journey. All this data was then reworked by an officer who was a neutral party, and another track chart of the hours preceding the accident was presented to the court, so that the events could be discussed and assessed with a clear visual referent.[26]

The track didn't work independently of human interpretation. In October 1867, in a squally sea off the coast of Liguria, in northern Italy, the officers of HMS *Cruizer* mistook a church steeple for a lighthouse, wrongly altered their course, and very nearly grounded the ship. These shores are quaint holiday postcards in the summer, but the Ligurian Sea is fierce and treacherous when in a mood. The *Cruizer* managed to drop anchor just in time, but overnight the cable split in the wind; a second anchor, close to the beach, 'happily held'. The captain set the men to build rafts, but only to keep them distracted: no raft could have survived that sea. The storm washed over the ship, causing its engine furnaces to fail; for a while, the situation looked dire – until, just before dawn, HMS *Arethusa* and HMS *Endymion* appeared on the horizon, and towed the *Cruizer* to safety. This was a lucky rescue: as the storm raged, the locals had spotted a British ship struggling in

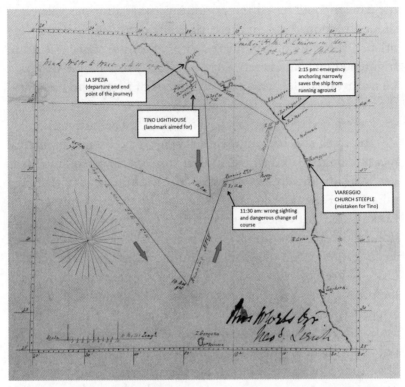

Figure 5.5: Track chart of HMS *Cruiser* in the Ligurian Sea, 7–9 October 1867. The captions and directional arrows are added here for clarity.

the distance, and the authorities telegraphed the Commander-in-Chief in La Spezia just in the nick of time.[27]

A couple of days later, the sloop's erratic track was closely inspected by a court martial, and the officers were made to point out their positions and presumed positions on the chart (Figure 5.5). In many ways, the accident was a failure in pilotage and in the ancient skill of wayfinding by looking around, more than in navigation by chart. However, some neglect was also discovered in the way in which bearings and soundings had been taken and the position of the ship fixed in the preceding days.[28] The commission's report, anyway, concluded on a milder note: 'But it must be borne in mind that although we, sitting quietly around a table with the charts before us, are enabled to indicate the means by which the danger could have been avoided, yet that a furious gale came suddenly upon them, and the time for consideration was very brief'.[29] The reduction of the reality of a storm – angry waves and frightened men and barely floating wood – to a simple pen tract on a chart holds less power on the minds of those who have lived the sea than on the average landlubber. But even for the expert the track remained an effective visual tool, if not a definitive one.

The track also had another advantage over discrete numerical measurements: it conveyed an illusion of *continuous* monitoring. We have already seen how the 'truth' of the lay of a track is a mirage. But the very linear structure of the track is a mirage, too. Let's assume that officers could fix their position with exact precision (which they could not), and that they could do so again and again, every second of a voyage, with no interruption of activity. Once plotted on a 1:1 scale, this set of measurements would still look like a long queue of dots, not an unbroken line. The line is a speculative, at times plainly fictional, joining of points. As an aside, this is true of any line on a map. Coastlines, for example, are notorious for being in the eye of the observer. The only way to plot a coastline is by fixing points along it and linking them with a tract. The more points you measure, the more closely your mapped line follows the actual twists and turns of the real coastline – and the longer this coastline becomes.[30] This is known as the 'Coastline Paradox', and it's the reason why memorising the length of your country's borders down to the metre is a pointless chore.

However, from a practical point of view, an unbroken line serves its illustrative and analytical purpose superbly. Sociologists have argued that modern surveillance 'operates by abstracting human bodies from their territorial settings and separating them into a series of discrete flows', to be analysed in isolation.[31] Your movement is a flow, your credit card transactions are a flow, and so is your streaming history, or your steam consumption when you could have sailed: under surveillance, you are dissected into the single decontextualised strands of your being. What better way, then, to make sense of an individual's movements, than visualising them as a cartographical track line, which is quintessentially unidimensional 'flow'?

*

We are still missing a practical step. How *exactly* did the track chart, a surveying tool, turn into this formidable instrument for monitoring employees? To begin with, navigational charts had to be brought under a common authority. We may think that eighteenth-century cartography already was under the control of the state: after all, nearly all the navigators we have encountered so far were naval officers or government employees. However, things were not so simple.

First, an increasing number of voyages and charts were produced by private shipping businesses, most notable among them the East India Companies of various western European nations. These organisations were generally quicker than navies in realising the value of accumulating cartographical information, and in keeping a tight grip on their captains and voyages. Initially, Britain lagged behind France and the United Provinces: as a 1755 pamphlet put it, by comparison with French materials, the English-language 'Indian Pilot' was 'only fit for the Grocers and Chandlers Shops, or posterior uses'.³² But in the late 1770s, the Scottish hydrographer Alexander Dalrymple spearheaded a revolution. Collecting enough voyage tracks, he thought, would lead to in-depth knowledge of the best routes to follow in all seasons. So he issued blank tabular journals and charts, instructing East India Company officers to mark their track on them. Since he couldn't compel anyone, this didn't quite work, but we see the sprouting of an important idea: requiring officers to track their journeys.³³

There was also the problem that copyright worked differently in the eighteenth century. Today, anything produced by a public servant during the course of their duty belongs to the state, or is exempt from copyright, but back then this didn't apply. When a navy officer drew a chart, it was theirs to republish, and the Admiralty (and, earlier, officers themselves) had to buy copies like any other customer.³⁴ The market for nautical charts was utterly chaotic. In France, the problem was first addressed in October 1773 by a judgment of the Royal Council: from then on, the national *Dépôt des cartes et plans de la Marine* was to hold the official monopoly over the production of marine charts and rutters. The *Dépôt* had existed since 1720, and was the earliest of its kind anywhere. It would have a long history, culminating in today's *Service hydrographique et océanographique de la Marine* (SHOM). The battle to centralise chart production wasn't over in 1773 – it took many years and several further decrees. Yet it was fought, for the sake of consistency and reliability in nautical information. Other countries were slower: the Spanish *Dirección de Trabajos Hidrográficos* appeared in 1797, and in Britain the ancestor of the modern Hydrographic Service was only founded in 1795, again by Alexander Dalrymple. At first, however, his task was mainly collecting existing documentation: the British Board of Longitude had held the monopoly over the printing of almanacs since 1765, but not charts.[35] Voyages of 'discovery' were slightly better monitored, and in the new century their publication was eventually dragged under full Admiralty monopoly. John Hawkesworth's account of the expeditions by Cook and his predecessors offered a precedent. But even these nascent regulations were more concerned with distribution than 'format' or production guidelines.[36]

In the second half of the eighteenth century, then, as they tightened their administrative structures, European navies also started to pay more attention to hydrography. A collective attempt was under way to tame the oceans; the prerequisite for safe and frequent navigation was an exhaustive knowledge of the world's waters and coastlines. Celebrity navigators like Cook or Bougainville led the way, but their tracks were sparse, one-dimensional threads across the immensity of the sea. Surveying could only be a collective endeavour. European and American officers swarmed around the oceans, intent on trade and war; if each of them brought back information on a single bay, a single square mile of shoal, a single depth sounding, the mosaic would be slowly built.

During the early reign of Queen Victoria, the British Admiralty's *Regulations* mentioned this task, but in passing. A captain was to set his officers to surveying if he stumbled onto uncharted – or badly charted – places, but only 'whenever the Service' would 'admit of it'. There was no mention of tracks at all.[37]

By 1862, we find a decided change in tone: captains were now expected to turn in, alongside their various logs and remark books, a track chart of the voyage, complete with the winds they'd encountered. The chart was kept by the master, the navigation officer aboard.[38] While he remained the main expert on the matter, all young gentlemen who aspired to a naval career had to receive navigational training, and they would be preferably adept at drawing.[39] After two and a half years in the service, midshipmen sat an intermediate examination: by that point, they had to be able to indicate the ship's position on a chart, 'and to lay off the True and Compass Courses'.[40] The Commander-in-Chief in the Mediterranean even organised competitions for these boys, recognising the best watercolour sketch of 'places visited by the ship' and 'the best executed and most correct Track Charts of all passages made by the officer's ship'.[41] Officers were systematically schooled in keeping track of themselves.

The same methods were adopted by other navies. We find boys drawing tracks even in countries that were only just building up a substantial fleet. Italy, for example, had a hallowed maritime tradition, but a fragmentary one: before the second half of the nineteenth century, we speak of Italian navies in the plural, belonging to the various states and cities. After unification in 1861, the Savoy dynasty set to bringing its national fleet up to international standards. Officer training was key. This took place on dedicated 'school ships', which travelled around the Mediterranean in 'campaigns of instruction'.

One such campaign has left us a magnificent chart. Yellow and tidy, it was completed by the cadets Bagini and Gozo and signed off by their lieutenant instructor in Naples, on 30 October 1874. Drawn in a long line accompanied by direction arrows is the route followed by their school ship, the *Vittorio Emanuele* – named after the first king of newly formed Italy. The line heads out of Genoa, then continues down the Tyrrhenian Sea, rounds Calabria squeezing through the Strait of Messina, tucks itself into another narrow corridor between Corfu and the Greek mainland, skirts the Peloponnese, cuts across the Greek islands to 'Scalanova' (today's Kuşadası) on the coast of Turkey, and bounces to northern Crete (which Bagini and Gozo call 'Candia' as a whole), touches Valletta in Malta, heads back through the Strait of Messina, and ends in

Naples.[42] We don't know much about the two boys' subsequent careers, but Bagini may well be the Massimiliano Bagini who by the start of the twentieth century was a frigate captain, and held a fairly senior administrative position in the Ministry of the Navy.[43]

The most stunning feature of this chart is that it is entirely hand-drawn, including the finely shaded coastlines and the graticule of parallels and meridians. This fact is given away by the calligraphy of the toponyms, and the note 'Longitudine di Grenwich' scribbled in the bottom left. Even Italian seamen were using Greenwich as their reference point. They also borrowed something else. If we look at the legend, the track takes two different shapes: it's unbroken for tracts covered under steam ('*Tratto fatto a machina* [*sic*]'), and fragmented into short lines when the *Vittorio Emanuele* was under sail – which it was for the vast majority of the time. Chart-drawing conventions were spreading: tracks were a language that every European officer could speak.

There is a paradox here. The track was commissioned both as a little tile of larger national projects, an anonymous contribution to the mosaic of oceanography, and as a personal record, used for individual accountability. This paradox is intrinsic to any form of surveillance: the aim is collective, but the method delves deeply into the personal sphere. Surveillance dances a delicate dance on the line between 'care' and 'control'.[44] More often than not, it slips. Once an officer was good at making a track, and was required to make it, and, given that the track was so tightly associated with his activities and conduct, the geography of the sea itself slowly fell out of focus. We can see how this unfolded during a pretty disastrous year on the British Navy's North-eastern Pacific station, in 1866.

HMS *Sparrowhawk*, commanded by Edwin Augustus Porcher, had been on a tour of the settlements along the coasts of present-day Alaska and British Columbia. The gun vessel had taken the Bishop of Columbia (a fervent colonial missionary from a naval family) to visit his scattered flock, and scouted out a location for a new coal wharf in Skidegate Harbour, Queen Charlotte Islands.[45]

On 16 May, the *Sparrowhawk* was on its way back from Fort (or Port) Simpson (Lax Kw'alaams), heading for Metlakatla across a narrow channel between the mainland and Finlayson Island. The

landscape here is rugged and vertical – thick forests of dark conifers, and the blue snow-capped mountains of the Kitimat Ranges
encroaching upon the sea. Three miles out, the *Sparrowhawk*
struck a submerged rock. After an hour and a half, the rising tide
set it back afloat, and it limped to port with an estimated six weeks
of repairs ahead.

The usual court of inquiry was convened, and Commander
Porcher supplied a 'rough sketch' of the grounding site, made by
his ship's master: this shows the track from the previous day, on
its way into Port Simpson, as well as the place of the accident
on 16 May, but no track for the unfortunate outward journey itself
(Figure 5.6). Admittedly, this isn't a great sketch, which is quite
remarkable, because Porcher is remembered for his fine plans and
watercolours: a few years earlier, when posted in the Mediterranean, he was painting exquisite landscapes and archaeological
finds from Cyrene and Carthage.[46] Perhaps the rocks of British
Columbia didn't quite inspire him, so he didn't intervene on his
master's squiggles.

Once this sketch and the report reached the desk of the Admiralty Hydrographer, in London, the man tore into Porcher. First,
he wrote, 'I donot [*sic*] consider that it was prudent to take the
ship thro a passage so scantily sounded and so partially surveyed'
'for the sake of gaining 2 miles' over the better-known route. But
second, he went on, Porcher 'should be desired to send Correct
Magnetic Bearings' of the rock's position, and mark it properly on
the official chart provided. 'He now sends bearings which will not
shew even approximately where the danger is'.[47] The captain of the
Sparrowhawk was twice at fault: for badly scraping his ship, and
for supplying poor data – that is, for failing in the universal naval
imperative of self-tracking. It might seem that the morphology of
the sea still mattered most in Porcher's case: the Hydrographer's
main aim was, on the face of it, to collect information about the
rock. But in reality the situation was slightly more layered.

George Henry Richards, the Admiralty Hydrographer, was
a severe man. Less than a month after the *Sparrowhawk*, another
ship struck ground in the same station – HMS *Scout*, commanded
by Captain Price, who had sat on Porcher's court martial. As the

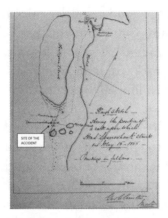

Figure 5.6: Detail of 'Sketch showing the position of a rock at Port Simpson (now Lax Kw'alaams), British Columbia (now in Canada) on which HMS *Sparrowhawk* struck on May 16 1866, with Port Simpson, Finlayson Island and the track of the ship'. The site of the accident is in the bottom-left quarter of the sketch.

Commander-in-Chief noted, the *Scout* was the sixth casualty in two years, and at that rate the Admiralty ought to consider furnishing the station with a repair dock.[48] (You may have noticed the hint of a bias in this chapter towards catastrophes and mishaps: most tracks of successful operations didn't warrant scrutiny, and therefore survival. Glitches quash routine when it comes to archival visibility.) This time, the Hydrographer had nothing to say on the information and track charts supplied. Captain Price was trained in surveying, and enclosed both the master's sketch track of the accident, with notes on the rocks, and a neat chart of his movements for the days before. However, this wasn't enough to satisfy Richards: Price had been imprudent, too. Why on earth had he thought it a good idea to run 'a vessel of 1,500 Tons' through a narrow uncharted channel, 'scarcely 100 yards wide', and without any soundings? Not even sending a boat ahead first? 'The Charts and Sailing Directions are ample for the safe navigation of Ships,' he bluntly concluded, 'but no Charts will suffice unless those who use them can interpret them, and will exercise a proper judgment in navigating H. M. Ships.'[49]

This rebuke contains a slightly defensive undertone. As Hydrographer, Richards was likely concerned with shifting fault away from himself: while Porcher had blamed the pilot of the *Sparrowhawk*, Price's report subtly hints at the fact that the charts available were insufficient – a direct indictment of the Hydrographer and his office. The track, then, became a crucial tool of contention in a struggle to assign guilt. The rocks that actually sank ships were in many ways just a backdrop – even for the Admiralty Hydrographer, the man who should have cared more about rock positioning than anyone else in the Royal Navy. This kind of mechanism explains how surveying gradually left the stage to surveillance: tracks speak more powerfully about people than about geography.

There is a second point to consider. The Hydrographer had taken issue not only with *where* the track of the *Sparrowhawk* went, but also with *how* it was reported. This is yet another example of the shift in focus from the sea to the track. In decades to come, entire courts martial would revolve around the question of how well the track had been made.

About fifty years later, on the evening of 8 April 1917, the British Second Light Cruiser Squadron was sent out to intercept some German mine bumpers, heading west just off the coast of Denmark. The Germans were escorted by two destroyers, and there was a risk of submarines. 'The force should be warned', the orders stated, 'that recent experience shows that enemy destroyers are very handy with their torpedoes.'[50]

The operation was a mess. The British vessels were meant to follow the Germans' projected course backwards, from west to east, until they intercepted them. In reality, they fumbled in the dark and low visibility for over ten hours, and then repaired to Rosyth empty-handed. A small consolation was that 'a strong wind and some sea' would have prevented mine-bumping operations anyway. But a lot of details had gone wrong. The Noord Dogger Light Vessel provided bearings that were utterly at odds with the position as fixed by dead reckoning. The light vessel, it was claimed, had drifted 3 or 4 miles south, and was in the wrong place – but this excuse was later found to be incorrect. All ships in the squadron returned track charts with their reports, but one of them stood out: the Senior Officer, Commodore Cecil Lambert, complained that he was 'unable to understand the courses set by' HMS *Champion*. Its captain, James U. Farie, had committed an egregious misstep: 'The courses stated in his report do not agree with those plotted on his chart'.

A court of inquiry was ordered. The charts don't seem to have survived, but we do have the minutes of the trial proceedings. The court was asked to consider the discrepancies between Farie's report, his track, and the orders he had received, and 'state to whom, if to anyone, blame is attributable, and to what extent'. Blame is the key word here. Explicitly, this was blame for faulty (and therefore, in at least one component, false) reporting, and potential disobedience. But underlying all this was the question of blame for the failed operation. And here we understand why Commodore Lambert was so tenacious in calling for Captain Farie's head. The court exonerated Farie, but Lambert wrote another letter in open disagreement. Farie's actions, he stated, had meant that the squadron missed the interception line and let the Germans slip away. At that point, the Rear-Admiral chipped in: Farie had shown 'lack of initiative', but 'the failure of the operation' was first of all Lambert's fault; he had sent confusing signals and disposed his forces poorly. The Lords of the Admiralty agreed with this assessment, in curt and icy terms: the operation had been 'barren of result', and Lambert and Farie were 'to be informed that the failure is very regrettable'. This judgment didn't seem to cause much damage to Lambert's career, given that halfway through the dossier his title changes from Commodore to Rear-Admiral – he was promoted on 13 April.[51] However, it gives us an insight into the real personal stakes of this dispute.

So, were the supposed discrepancies in the track just a pretext deployed by Lambert? They turned out to be very minor issues. Two of them were 'clerical errors', and two, which had apparently violated orders, had been necessary to avoid breaking other standing orders (and ending up in a minefield past longitude 6° 30′ E), and to obey a signal that Lambert himself had given. But this is not to say that the discrepancies didn't matter. 'Some blame', the court concluded, was 'due' to Lieutenant-Commander Malby D. Brownlow, Farie's Navigating Officer: 'he was inaccurate and lacking in care in making out the track chart and furnishing out details for his Captain's report'. At 3.15 a.m., he had pricked his position on the chart 'incorrectly', and at 4.15 he had pricked it correctly but then had accidentally transcribed the course into the report as N 57 W instead of N 41 W. Brownlow, ten days shy of his thirtieth birthday, was a career officer, who had been in the navy since 1903, his record immaculate then and since, with a long string of captains agreeing that he was 'capable', 'careful' and 'trustworthy'.[52] This was clearly just a glitch. He was pricking his chart, tracking his position, and making his calculations in the dead of the night, on a dark, freezing bridge in the middle of the North Sea; yet, even then, his profession did not admit of typos.

And, just like that, the sea is gone. There is no trace of it in Brownlow's defence, nor on his colleague Marsden's chart, the following month at Jutland; and there is no trace of the sea in most twentieth-century naval track charts, which were, by now, more 'plots' than maps. We have hydrographers squabbling with captains, commodores squabbling with captains, and young subordinates glued to chart and pencil, yawning and bleeding; the sea was set aside.

This impression is conveyed most forcefully by one specific type of track chart. We saw that, when they searched for the missing ships of La Pérouse or Franklin, eighteenth- and nineteenth-century expeditions still had an eye firmly planted on the territories they touched. They looked for lost compatriots, but they also kept 'discovering' and colouring up new coastlines. Some of the big prizes of Western exploration – the Pacific, the Northwest Passage, and so on – remained up for grabs. By the First World War, track charts depicting searches for people were only performing that function, without secondary tasks; the seas were a supposedly known entity, or rather, the craze for discovery had abated, in the mistaken assumption that all that was left to collect were crumbs. In an increasingly compartmentalised professional world, surveying and oceanography more generally had returned to the status of distinct, specialised tasks.[53] What did searches at sea look like, then?

In late September 1942, HMS *Exe* was on routine duty in the North Atlantic. It had just stopped in Reykjavik because one sailor was sick with appendicitis, and another had abdominal pains – a fairly extreme detour for the sake of two men, as the Director of Anti-Submarine Warfare subsequently noted. On the evening of 28 September, the *Exe* had barely rejoined its squadron when a sudden order arrived from the Commander-in-Chief. The destroyer HMS *Veteran* had been sunk by a German U-boat as it attempted to escort a convoy to safety. At the time of the attack, it had just picked up some survivors from one of the convoy ships, SS *New York*, which had also been torpedoed; but those men's bad luck had clearly not run out. Hundreds of people from both ships were now dispersed at sea. The news was already two days old, so there was no time to lose. The *Exe* dashed to the presumed spot, and, with the help of HMS *Gentian*, began a meticulous search, supported by aircraft. At night, they fired illuminating star-shells, scanning the sea for flares.[54]

We have an aerial track plot of that search (Figure 5.7); for three days, the two ships danced a meticulous coil, stretching over tens of square miles. And this coil dominates the chart. Its context is set in wholly human terms: not coastlines or depth measurements, but the arbitrary referents of latitude, longitude, and the defined box of the search area. This was a track deployed to interact with other human activities, rather than the seascape. It marked the presence of mines, the sighting of other vessels ('Spoke S.S. Columbia Star') and the passing of time – tiny, regular figures, in the hhhh/dd format, which counted away the remaining hope for survivors. Like Matthew Flinders's tracks around Australia, this track highlights periods of low visibility or darkness, but it does so to signal that it may have missed other people, rather than a coastline. The representation of time and movement completely overtook concerns with the geographical environment – the same environment that, in its materiality, made the search desperate. The *Exe* and *Gentian* combed the sea between 52° 30' N and 54° 30' N,

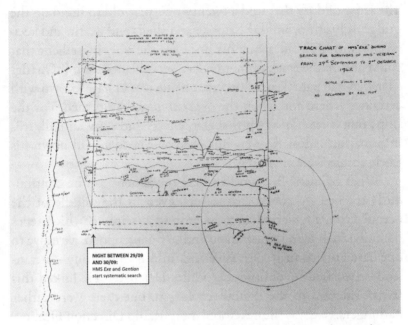

Figure 5.7: Detail of the track chart of HMS *Exe* during the search
for survivors of HMS *Veteran*, 29 September to 2 October 1942.

the latitude of Labrador, and 23° 10' W and 19° W, in the middle
of the North Atlantic. In early autumn, the water and air there
descend into difficult temperatures for castaways in a lifeboat –
assuming that anyone had survived the torpedoing. We will never
know, because nobody was found. The ocean, its winds and currents made the difference between deliverance and disappearance.
But this natural setting was sanitised into emptiness.

There is a facile narrative, here, arguing that nineteenth-century
ship tracks were essentially the same as our present-day 'track and
trace' systems, using lines on digital maps to monitor the movement of people and objects. The image and concept of track
certainly link the two, but there is an important difference: up
until a hundred or so years ago, especially in the vast and remote
space of the sea, all tracking had to be disciplined *self*-tracking.

The sense of duty that told a twenty-one-year-old to stand on the bridge of his ship, amid the smoke and shells and death, and keep on measuring and drawing his line, was the only ingredient that could ensure the track's function as a surveillance tool. If Charles Marsden had panicked at Jutland, no one would have known with certainty where and when the *Southampton* had turned. For the ships that were blown up that day, charts and duty and all, this information is lost forever. But even as Marsden laid down his track, things were changing.

What happens in a world where movement can be continuously tracked by *external* observers, even in the middle of the ocean? From a society structured around 'discipline', which relies on individuals being constrained and self-constrained, we move to one based on 'control', pervasive and unbroken scrutiny – a transition theorised by philosopher Gilles Deleuze.[55] He linked this transformation to the digital revolution, but there were earlier harbingers: one was the development of Radio Direction Finding, used extensively during the First and Second World Wars. RDF allowed the detection of vessels across vast distances, although its exact positioning powers remained limited, and its functioning was tied to the carelessness of its targets: it required their active involvement, as transmitters. Switch off your radio, and you revert to invisibility.[56] Another handmaiden of control societies was the invention of aeroplanes. Aerial surveillance was used quite extensively in the Middle East during and after the First World War. As pointed out by historian Priya Satia, the desert looked like a disorienting, 'unmappable' space to the Western spies filled with romantic dreams of the 'mysterious' Orient: the view from planes, they thought, made sense of that.[57]

As the flight range of aircraft expanded, having wings became useful for looking down at what happened on the sea, as well (another baffling and romanticised space). To Beryl Markham, the first pilot to cross the Atlantic westwards, in one go and solo (in 1936), sea travel compared unfavourably to flight. Ships, she wrote, 'are small and slow. They have no speed, nor any sense of urgency; they do not cross the water, they live on it until the land comes home'.[58] From high above, movement at sea is not even something to be tracked – it doesn't look like movement at all. Planes make the sea into a static map, press the pause button on movement below and give an overview for miles around. They were the dream of anyone intent on surveillance, before being replaced by satellites even further up. However, some devices were developing that could also look at what happened *under* the sea.

By the First World War, a formidable threat had begun to lurk in the depths of the oceans: submarines. Germany in particular made extensive use of them, deploying new forms of indiscriminate warfare that sank military and civilian shipping alike, with no prisoners takeable or taken. As a response, navies began to look for methods of identifying these silent killers. Attempts to use various kinds of 'hydrophones' to detect the sound emitted by U-boats largely failed. Between 1916 and 1917, the British Admiralty was desperate enough to listen to members of the general public. A specially trained music-hall sea lion, it was suggested, could come to see submarines as tasty fish dispensers, and trail them. This wasn't even the most original attempt: at some point, a psychic was invited to track U-boats on a chart with her pendulum.[59] One scientist on the Board of Invention and Research, the eccentric Sir Richard Paget, also tried to measure underwater sound by dunking his head in, and then tapping his skull to compare the note (apparently the skull emits a G-sharp). But what naval scientists increasingly focused on, in the aftermath of the war, was the use of sound waves *actively* sent out by the searching ship. The system was dubbed ASDIC(S), and later SONAR by the Americans ('Sound Navigation and Ranging'). When these waves were reflected against the hull of a hidden enemy, a trained operator could hear the echo in his headset, measure the time lag, and fix a position to blast with a depth charge.[60]

By the Second World War, then, we encounter a new type of track chart, featuring a line of movement that is non-consensual, imposed on the tracked by an external observer. Plots of submarine hunts make a mockery of U-boats' lethal invisibility – they turn it into a red line flitting in circles until it's pinned down by an Allied destroyer. Charts like these appeared regularly in the 'Monthly Anti-Submarine Reports', which were printed by the Anti-U-Boat

Division of the British Naval Staff. These publications offered up-to-date figures on shipping losses, details of innovations, mugshots of German officers and enthusiastic descriptions of 'kills'. The green track of the destroyer follows the red submarine around – the time of the fixing never quite in the right place – until the place *is* right, the two tracks cross each other on the same spot and, in the same moment, the target is aligned, and the green scythes off the red. Then, it leisurely circles back for 'collecting souvenirs' (Plate 17).[61] The submarine has no voice any more, its memories and its logs are debris floating on the water – but the trace of its final movements is *known*, it's there for the rest of the British Navy to peruse and celebrate in next month's report. Craft at sea no longer has to write its own story. And the sea itself – its surface, and even its depths – ceases to be a mystical space where human movement will be inevitably lost from sight.

Active self-tracking didn't instantly vanish from naval practice. Whatever the source of positional data, manual plotting procedures, with pencil and paper charts, proved difficult to supersede. In the late 1980s, an anthropologist filming the chart table on the bridge of a US Navy ship captured gestures, calculations, interactions, and concerns that much resembled what we have discussed so far.[62] As late as 2008, a hand-drawn track chart was responsible for a nasty naval accident. In the Red Sea, a British nuclear submarine smashed into a rocky pillar, at high speed. The obstacle lay just 123 metres under the surface, but the officers had 'misread' this as 723. The reason was simple: when the projected course had been plotted on the chart, the track line had covered up the spot, hiding part of the number. A court martial ensued, during which, much like a century and a half earlier, the chart played a central role; the record it presented was unambiguous, and careers were sadly ruined.[63]

The use of tracks for surveillance, in any case, eventually overflowed the maritime context. The power and clarity of the track, as we have already established, make it an eminently transferable device. And away from professional expertise, automation has to prevail. In today's digital world, each individual can act as a transmitter, their movements easily mappable through this 500-year-old visual convention. However, digital technologies often make the drawing of tracks into less of a conscious and purposeful choice. While nineteenth-century analogic tracks required – and, among navigators, still require – large amounts of effort, constancy and technical skill, digital tracking is automated and apparently painless to the user, as a phone dormant in a pocket draws your movements for you. How conscientiously we track ourselves no longer matters: the tracking is all externally done. But the track is still *our* track. Some people use the information it captures as a form of meditation – a way of turning technology into a powerful tool of self-knowledge.[64] For others, when we accept being tracked for the sake of convenience we succumb to 'a twenty-first-century Faustian compact', feeding ourselves to the monster of 'surveillance capitalism'.[65] Either way, it's difficult to decouple the track from the person to whom it belongs.

Whether made by a conscientious officer or by an enemy destroyer, tracks of the self or tracks of someone else, there is one thing that all tracks have in common: the vulnerability that stems from exposure. John Franklin and Leopold McClintock were celebrities in their day, but this meant that their life-and-death decisions amid the ice were open to the scrutiny of the curious crowd. On a global scale (and on the cartographical globe itself), naval officers engaged in imperial conquest and warfare enjoyed powerful and privileged positions – but their logs and tracks unrolled their every choice on their superiors' desks, ready to be assessed and criticised. Much action and movement at sea was not done and forgotten, because, once marked down, it was there to stay, for better or for worse. It was extracted from its own time and space, and pickled for subsequent analysis. The question, then, is: what do we get if we combine vulnerability, a craving for God-like control and a diminishing interest in the natural environment?

A COMMON HIGHWAY?

In 1916, twenty-two-year-old Gilbert William Smith was a steward aboard a British Royal Mail ship that had been requisitioned into naval service. As the First World War raged in Europe and submarines began to haunt the seas, he travelled far and wide around the world, until he was demobilised in February 1919.[1] He documented much of these voyages in careful journal entries, full of wonder and detail. These weren't technical logs at all, but personal diaries. He recorded key events in his day, and things like the 'thousands (and I mean thousands) of Sea Lions, whose continual roaring sounded like feeding time at 100 Zoos', who kept him awake all night in Chimbote, Peru.[2] But he never bothered with winds, latitude or longitude. His journals were, through and through, those of a landlubber out at sea.

One of the journal volumes, in rough copy, is written on the first notebook that Smith could find: a blank Royal Mail Steam Packet Company 'List of Packages'. This was an oblong rubric-type book with alphabetical letter indentations along the outward right edge.[3] Although the vessel had been poached by the navy, clearly RMSPC stationery was still lying around, and Smith had free access to it. Indeed, he used it for something else, as well.

Filed away in the archives, together with his journals, we find Smith's very own track map. The Royal Mail Steam Packet Company gave out elegant concertina maps to its passengers. The front cover announced their use: 'R.M.S.P. Track Chart'. Inside, colourful paintings showed wonderful exotic landscapes, the Sphynx, and a steamship: 'tours for health or pleasure in luxurious mail steamers'. Fully unfolded, the leaflet revealed a map of the world, onto which passengers were invited to draw their own voyages as they went along. Smith got hold of one of these fancy maps: his track, in crude black and blue pen marks, crosses every sea and touches every continent, sometimes more than once.[4] Much like the journals, this track is a personal sketch, completely shorn of technical details: a million miles from that of the young man – also a twenty-something naval recruit – whom we encountered at the start of the last chapter, bleeding at Jutland. They both went to sea and they both drew tracks, but Marsden, unlike Smith, was trained in navigation: the point of his track was marking exact spots, precisely, for his superior officers. What was the point of Smith's track?

At this time, Smith was not alone in drawing 'non-technical' tracks. Much like the RMSPC, various steamship companies gave away self-tracking materials, to keep their customers amused during long voyages. Cunard, for example, produced quaint little 'Passenger log books', loaded not only with information on the vessels, but also with countless ads for everything from cooking appliances to woollen underwear; only a dwindling couple of blank pages were left in for recording the journey. This probably tells us something about the priorities of the target users of this 'log book'.[5] In other cases, however, people were handed or sold 'Passenger track charts'. Some travellers filled them in quite minutely, bothering to find out the latitude and longitude each day.[6] Others, like Smith, just went for general display value, drawing straight lines from departure to destination.[7] And many, no doubt, will have left their charts perfectly blank, occupying themselves otherwise, or too seasick to face a pen. In short, passengers made of these charts exactly what they wished, drawing – or not drawing – tracks as they pleased, remembered, or could.

This marks a huge step change from the naval uses that we have encountered so far. In navies, the cartographical track had to be rigidly determined, because the journey itself wasn't. Officers were in command of a vessel and exerted some discretion over where they went, so they could only be controlled by their superiors through an accurate track, following set rules. For steamship passengers, it was the opposite: because they weren't in charge of the journey anyway, nor directly accountable to anyone, the track they

Figure 6.1: Detail of a track map belonging to, and perhaps drawn by, 'Miss Young' (*c.*1880). A track can be seen crossing the Mediterranean, Red Sea and Indian Ocean.

drew was entirely up to them. It was perfunctory, but, as a result, uniquely deliberate.

Here, we are dealing with a pretty wide range of users. We can see the name of one of them on the elegant pocket cover of a surviving chart, kept at the British Library in London – whose template was printed by none other than James Wyld, creator of the Monster Globe in Leicester Square. The track on this map is of the type that records a dot each day, for a round journey between Britain and Australia aboard the ships *Almora* and *Parramatta*, in 1880 (Figure 6.1). The name on the cover, written in hasty cursive, is 'Miss Young'.[8] It wasn't just women who dealt in tracks: children did too. This included at least one boy in a desperate position, who chose to fashion his experience as a track. In 1938, the twelve-year-old Jewish refugee Fritz Freudenheim, fleeing his native Germany, drew his journey across the Atlantic to Uruguay: on a red track, the colourful steamer *Jamaïque* conveys him and his family 'From the old home to the new home!' ('Von der alten Heimat zu der neuen Heimat!') – never to return.[9] Fritz wasn't using a template map, but drawing from scratch. The track was, simply, the way in which he visualised his journey.

An important shift in perspective occurred between the second half of the nineteenth century and the first half of the twentieth. Many laypeople – civilians, women and children, mostly from the middle classes – became used to seeing and drawing their *own* tracks: not just those of heroes, explorers and sailors, but their personal ones. It wasn't stern naval mentors who taught them to do so. They learned from maps of the world's routes and from transport companies' advertising campaigns. These campaigns included 'draw-it-yourself' passenger charts, but also, increasingly, and truly booming by 1900, publicity leaflets, posters and journey memorabilia.[10] We saw earlier how the track, in its simplicity, worked well for selling stories and armchair travel. With growing tourism and mass mobility, on land, at sea, and later in the air, European and American companies quickly realised that the track worked well for selling real-life travel, too. Some tracks sold efficiency and directness, a speedy, neat, and hassle-free conveyance to destination. Others sold interesting voyages: 'glowing new luxuries and glittering new routes', or 'storied routes', as a Matson Navigation Company leaflet – complete with track map – put it in 1956.[11] Others still, like the fillable track charts or detailed route networks, served to give the customer the impression of being informed, and in control. Overall, packaged up in those attractively simple lines, was a peculiar way of understanding movement: with a sense of ownership. On land, in private vehicles, owning movement signified freedom and (gently nudged) choice, as shown by the personalised uses of early motoring or cycling route maps.[12] At sea, it signified something else.

The nineteenth century marked an apparent conquest of the seas. In rhetoric if not in fact, every man, woman and child – or, more accurately, every paying customer – was invited to partake in this conquest. The new type of commercial track line, popular and widely available, conferred importance, power and self-realisation. Like all improbably well-spun tales, it also concealed something: the dark underbelly of modernity.

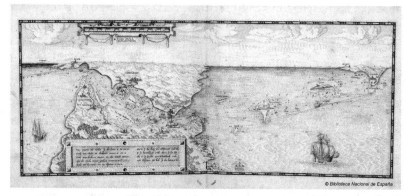

© Biblioteca Nacional de España

Figure 6.2: Dutch chart showing the course through the straits between Denmark and Sweden (1586). The chart is oriented with west on the top.

*

The notion of 'sea lanes' had developed almost as soon as the first Iberian navigators started leaving tracks behind. The transformation of the oceans into spaces marked by paths was well under way by the end of the early modern period, as individual wakes ossified into highways.[13] When referring to set routes, tracks could be used by hydrographers just like trails and roads on maps – to mark an anonymous line of travel. In the 1580s, for example, a Dutch manuscript chart used schematic track lines to show mariners which courses to follow in the narrow channel separating Denmark from Sweden, or in the shallows between Holland, Texel and Friesland (Figure 6.2).[14] There are other instances, too. In extremely familiar waters, around European coasts and estuaries, it made no sense to attribute authorship to tracks, but they worked well to illustrate the optimal path to be trodden, lest a vessel run aground on deceitful shallows.[15]

Even at their most impersonal, however, many tracks still contained a glint of individuality: they witnessed a journey that had been verified as possible, or expedient, *on a specific occasion.* They witnessed, more precisely, a journey that had been *recognised* as possible. The words 'reconnaissance' and 'recognition' share a root, which implies a personal intermediary.[16] The boom in oceanic highway construction came when navies and commercial companies realised that there was value in such specific occasions: we have already discussed this growing thirst for charts and logs. In the campaign to understand the oceans and turn them into an efficient network, one man went further than most.

Matthew Fontaine Maury is often hailed as a founding father of American oceanography. He was for the US Navy what Alexander Dalrymple had been for the British. His career spanned a commission as lieutenant and superintendence of the Depot of Charts and Instruments; he was eventually put in charge of the Naval Observatory in Washington. In 1861, when the Civil War broke out, he defected to the Confederacy, and his fortunes embarked on a downwards spiral. But in the decade or so before that, from his perch at the Observatory, he had directed a titanic and unprecedented concert: thousands of vessels, from multiple nations, collecting data about the oceans through their journeys. Maury produced over a hundred thematic charts, dissecting marine depths and temperatures, seasonal winds and whale migration patterns. One of these charts is even referenced in *Moby-Dick*, in a last-minute footnote, as fiction blurred into reality. Out of this vast output, what is of particular interest to us here is an astonishing series of track charts, patiently teased out of logbooks by his team of young officers.[17]

Like a spider, Maury wove together thousands of tracks and turned the oceans into a web of voyages, coded by month and season through different patterns and colours (Plate 18): 'a common highway', as he put it. Some of these charts are so complex that they are all but indecipherable. Yet, for him, tracks were 'full of meaning', and they showed the personality of the sea and of their makers alike: 'a crazy fellow always makes a crooked track'.[18] On his charts, then, each line embodies an experience, a course that worked, or didn't, at a specific time of year; each journey recounts, through its very shape, the bend of the currents, the force of the winds and the mariners' beliefs and decisions. Cautionary tales and success stories mark the water for future travellers, and they instantly made voyages safer and faster. The sea was described for universal use, but through individual accounts. These thin, personal lines are the infrastructure of all universal knowledge:

normally, we hide them away like a skeleton in the closet, but here they are, uniquely, naked.

Maury was a religious man. He believed that the sea had patterns, a rational balance ordained by God's providence.[19] So we could say that for him human journeys were akin to dustings on a fingerprint, revealing the underlying structure. But not everyone in the nineteenth century thought in the same way, and this is key to understanding how tracks evolved.

The term *trackless*, in English, seems to be first attested in the middle of the seventeenth century; *pathless*, an equivalent, had appeared at the end of the sixteenth.[20] By the nineteenth century, they had become rather ubiquitous, and a staple of romantic poetry. One morning in September 1811, fifteen-year-old Robert Ritchie woke up at home in Edinburgh and contemplated his new uniform. He was about to fulfil his dream of becoming a naval trainee officer, and his thoughts were cheerful: 'A sailor's is a noble profession; he defends his country when in danger, he undergoes toil & hardships for it, & by a grateful country he is rewarded with honours & applause; he travels into all countreis [*sic*], wanders over the pathless ocean; sees all nations: & where are people so happy to be found?'[21] Seven decades later, in 1883, lower-deck sailor Richard Cotten spent his free time on HMS *Comus* writing verses: 'I am a man before the mast / I plough the trackless sea', he began his book of poems.[22] The American whaling captain William George Bailey, in the 1840s, also scribbled poetry in his log: 'This book contains the story of its life / And journeys made upon the trackless seas / I tell of calms and elemental strife / Of rushing winds and of the foaming breeze'.[23] And we have seen Matthew Flinders writing of 'a trackless sea' to the wife he had abandoned in Britain to go and map the other side of the world. When trite tropes are repeated even by people with direct experience of their subject, we know how powerful they have become. The image of tracks – and the lack thereof – didn't only permeate bright-eyed landlubber romance: it fed back into seafarers' own understanding of what they were doing out there on the 'empty' main.

Being trackless (as opposed to pathless) is, of course, the default state for the oceans. But the very fortune of this word alerts us to the fact that, in the nineteenth century, the world was changing. Supposedly empty nature – 'wilderness' – slowly floated to the fore of Westerners' concerns, because it now seemed so scarce and threatened. By the turn of the twentieth century, American conservationists were particularly vocal in this fetish of wilderness, which even assumed imperialistic dimensions.[24] Sometimes, however, the worry had nothing to do with preservation: it was a sense of urgency, an awareness that the window of opportunity to prove oneself in nature was fast evaporating. The blank surfaces onto which one might carve their own path, through perils and the unknown, were now part of the suffocated urban bourgeois's most intimate aspirations: their dangers meant adventure, and their tracklessness was an opportunity for greatness.[25] The same mindset that exalted the untrodden sea from the nineteenth century onwards led to the boom in sports like mountaineering and rock climbing. It nurtured a specific aesthetic: that of the 'first ascent', the heroic, manly individual 'opening', conquering and claiming routes on increasingly sheer rock faces, steeper glaciers, venturing where nobody had supposedly gone before – or in fact was meant to go.[26] The imaginary lines that had long marked the oceans would soon appear in the mountains, too. To this day, they are used in guidebooks to illustrate a known 'route': personally and sometimes meaningfully named, graded and often signed, with a date and the first climber's name.[27] At sea and on land, the spaces available to draw routes were constantly shrinking, but this only made the race hotter. If leaving a track was the ultimate goal, the antidote to banality and mortality, the precondition was, paradoxically, finding a trackless slate of one's own. This is the other face of control – boredom.

If Western tracks had started like East Asian ones – as anonymous networks of sea paths – none of this would have happened. But by the nineteenth century, the idea of the individual building their personal trail was too powerful, gorged on three centuries of imperial exploration and a newly developed fascination with heroic 'Authorship'. The Cunard or P&O first-class passenger needed to know that they would travel safely and in a timely manner, on a well-tested route. But many of them also wanted to retrace that route on their personal map, day by day. Tolstoy has a wonderful image in *War and Peace*: Napoleon is 'like a child who, holding a couple of strings inside a carriage, thinks he is driving it'.[28] He was making a point about history, human agency and divine providence, but the allegory works equally well on a more mundane level. Passenger tracks are, after all, just like those strings. To return to the two terms used by anthropologist Tim Ingold, the nineteenth-century traveller drawing tracks on his chart uses 'transport', but still pretends to be a 'wayfarer'.[29] Just as he rejoices at human technological mastery and carves deeper into the trafficked highways of the oceans, demanding good service, he stares at the foam in awe, and calls it a trackless adventure. While hydrographers like Maury tried to turn the individual into collective, making the seas legible in their own terms, individuals often fought to retain control over their track. Understanding and using the sea was almost beside the point: the process of *taming* it was what mattered. And so it was that, even in the era of oceanic highways, Western tracks never fully lost their personality. In fact, new technological changes were afoot that made them more vocal and prepotent than ever. The nineteenth century was, apparently, the age of steam, the age of ships 'fed on fire and water, breathing black smoke into the air, pulsating, throbbing, shouldering' their 'arrogant way against the great rollers in blind disdain of winds and sea'.[30]

The sun-baked promenade, the colourful fish restaurants and souvenir shops, and the rubbish floating on the water alongside small sailing boats make the seafront of Toulon, on the southern coast of France, look like any other Mediterranean resort. But there is one peculiarity. The restaurants' clientele, the people striding around the promenade, even the odd runner – many of them are men, and they wear identical dark clothes. A stone's throw away, tightly gated up, is the stronghold of the French Navy, the largest naval base in the entire Mediterranean.[31] From here, in 1850, France launched the first ever screw-propelled steam warship, the

Figure 6.3: Steam trampling the waves. Louis-Joseph Daumas,
Le Génie de la Navigation (1847), Toulon seafront.

Napoléon.[32] A tall bronze monument towers over the waterfront.
Made by the sculptor Louis-Joseph Daumas, and inaugurated in
May 1847, it represents 'The Genius of Navigation': a classically
shaped, all but naked man holds a tiller and points out to sea. Rectangular friezes decorate each side of the pedestal. In the frontal
one, an angel holds up two enormous books, which contain a list
of great European explorers: from the ancient Greek Pythias to
the French Jules Dumont d'Urville, via all the usual suspects.[33] On
another side, we meet a truculent female incarnation of Steam. The
base of her throne bears a potted (and patchy) genealogy of the
steam engine, listing the names of various inventors and engineers:
'Papin' (Denis Papin), 'S.on Decaus' (Salomon de Caus), 'Watt'
and 'Fulton' (Figure 6.3). Fist raised in the air, Steam stamps down,
barefoot, onto the neck of a human-shaped wave.

Steamships transformed people's relationship with the sea.
But, most importantly, they transformed their *perception* of their

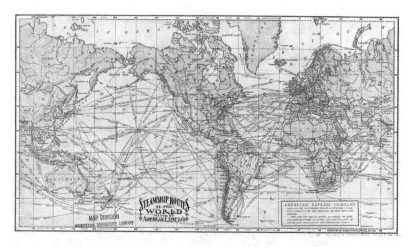

Figure 6.4: A symbolic representation of full-powered steamship routes (*c.*1900).

relationship with the sea.[34] For one thing, steam travel was much quicker. In the 1870s, for example, a steamer could whizz from the Black Sea to Marseille three to six times faster than a sailing vessel, depending on the season: in winter, navigation under sail is particularly slow. Sea and winds forced sailers to take cautious and convoluted courses that could vary by hundreds of kilometres, deferring to circumstances and the time of year. If you wanted to get from the Aegean Sea to France in winter, you went through the Strait of Messina, sheltered between Italy and its islands; in summer, you had to sail around the whole of Sicily, on the outside: the winter route would have got you becalmed. Steamers, instead, or so the story goes, were able to tread and retread the same efficient paths, like clockwork. Steamers feared no calms, and few winds. They could travel back and forth following the same route: in the Atlantic, they could happily dismiss the *volta do mar* of Magellan's days, and just power through in a straight line home (Figure 6.4).[35] As always, there was some friction between theory and practice, imagination and reality. But let's look at the imagination first.

The nineteenth century is often pictured as the age when steam took over – on land and at sea. At sea, as always, the story is slow and complicated. The first paddle steamers had short range, precarious balance, fragile structures and appalling manoeuvrability. They devoured fuel, needing constant resupply, and they relied on what is known as 'sail-assist' to keep on a steady course. It wasn't until the perfectioning of the modern underwater propeller (the 'screw'), in the 1850s, that anything even resembling the myth of steam trampling the oceans came true. Nonetheless, a steam-powered vessel first crossed the Channel as early as 1816. By the 1830s, light paddle steam packets trod up and down the Red Sea and the Arabian Sea, ferrying news between Europe and India in the face of sluggish winds and the unsailable seasonal monsoon. In 1838, the mighty *Great Western*, a 212-foot-long passenger ship built by Isambard Kingdom Brunel, and hours before it the slower and smaller *Sirius*, carved the first two steam-only tracks across the Atlantic – although sail-assist was still required. The winds were not quite disposable yet. But in that same year, the British Navy began trials with screw propellers, soon to be followed by other countries' fleets.[36] Brunel struck again, with an even bigger, if ultimately ill-fated, monster: the iron screw SS *Great Britain*. In January 1845, its trials bedazzled the Admiralty observers aboard; it was stable, perfectly responsive even in choppy seas – '*one* Man was sufficient to Steer her' – and, most importantly, *fast*. The only problem were the engineers and stokers, so horrifically seasick that, by the end of the cruise, sailing was the only option.[37]

Steam revolutionised the structures and fighting doctrines of navies. As *The Times* put it in 1853, it presented 'the sublime idea fully realized of man controlling the sea and subjecting the winds by a mechanical power'.[38] By then, commercial steamers were crossing the oceans, too; at first, they drew most of their revenue from mail-carrying, but with the rise of iron screw vessels, more capacious than wooden paddle steamers, passengers and migrants became a lucrative commodity, especially in the Atlantic.[39] Steam enterprise, even when not directly engaged in warship construction, was deeply intertwined with empires: it could only really take off thanks to the subsidies that states pumped into it. Public contracts were often granted as monopolies, consolidating official and set routes across all the oceans of the world.[40]

The establishment of regular transoceanic services, contractu-
ally defined, made tracks in a frequent and reliable way. The term
that had come into common use at this point was cartographically
inspired: these weren't simply shipping lanes, but shipping *lines*.[41]
And let's look at the verbs summoned up in relation to these lines.
In British parliamentary debates, speakers would freely refer to 'the
line which the East India Company *had* from Suez to Bombay'; 'the
importance of *establishing* a line of steam communication with our
Australian possessions'; or, most strikingly, 'the strides taken by the
United States in *occupying* seas with regular and rapid lines of steam
navigation to our prejudice' (emphases added).[42] In the nineteenth
century, European and American liners *owned* lines on the sea, *established* them onto thin foam, and in so doing *occupied* the main for
themselves. These lines were seen as both property and a concrete
presence on the oceans, contested and farmed out by imperial states
to private companies. From the middle of the century onwards, they
began to appear on maps of the world as set features – each with a tag
showing distance and promising an exact duration in days.[43]

This supposed solidity of lines also pervaded the imagination
of navigators. At this point, even pilotage instruction books offering textual descriptions of routes not only used an indiscriminate
mixture of conventional and 'real' reference points (rocks and
parallels, shallows and meridians), but also deployed the vivid language of precise, almost surgical incision: the route line should
'slice' ('*couper*') a given parallel at a given place.[44] This slicing was
soon to transcend its metaphorical import.

'The Northwest Passage!', railed the *New York Times* in 1869,
two months before the opening of the Suez Canal; 'does any one
believe that it could ever be useful to man? It would be almost as
reasonable for us to set to work again trying to discover the philosopher's stone, or the *elixir vitæ*'. The era of Franklin and bold
Arctic ventures was over: 'the time has gone by when nations or
governments will consent to help men to throw away their lives in
the pursuit of phantoms'.[45] Even two decades earlier, as the search
for the Passage was in full swing, articles in periodicals had started

to frame it as a waste of time and life, by comparison with the canal that Americans were looking to build across Panama. Franklin's had been the fifty-eighth Arctic attempt, and this wild goose chase (a 'Quixotic' 'crusade') was costing Britain national prestige and geopolitical control: as a British essayist mused in 1850, '*they*, and not *we*, will have the high credit of having opened a passage by sea from the western to the eastern world'.[46] The Panama Canal, despite the huge engineering challenges it posed (it would take until 1914 for it to come into being), could be visualised readily on a map: a short track, cutting across a flimsy strand of land. The Northwest Passage, on the other hand, remained an unclear possibility, in a blurry chaos of splintered peninsulas and shifting, unmapped ice. Real passages across the continents, still unfound, were deemed phantoms. Phantoms, on the other hand, became real.

Carving out a passage between the Mediterranean and the Red Sea wasn't a new idea. It had been contemplated, with partial success, since the times of the pharaohs.[47] It wasn't until 1869, however, that the full cut was completed. This had started as a French initiative, against British resistance. Once built, however, the canal had a game-changing impact particularly on the British empire; it afforded a quick, straighter line to India, and changed the very way in which British authorities saw the Mediterranean: no longer a cul-de-sac 'lake', but a 'lane'.[48] The Suez Canal was the new wonder of the world, 164 kilometres in length and 8 metres in depth, with edges straighter than any river (Plate 19, Figure 6.5).[49] It joined two seas and effectively turned Africa into a massive island. More importantly, it linked the West to the East, rhetorically and financially. In the run-up to its construction, the French thinker Barthélemy-Prosper Enfantin referred to it in sexually explicit language: 'There we will commit the act / That the world is waiting for / To confess that we are / Male'. In true track style, here was the West penetrating the feminine Orient.[50] If we wanted to be rude, we could even say 'screwing it over': the construction of the canal contributed to bankrupting Egypt. Within six years, the country was forced to sell all its Suez shares (44 per cent) to Britons, for a measly £4 million. Within thirteen, it was a de facto British protectorate.[51]

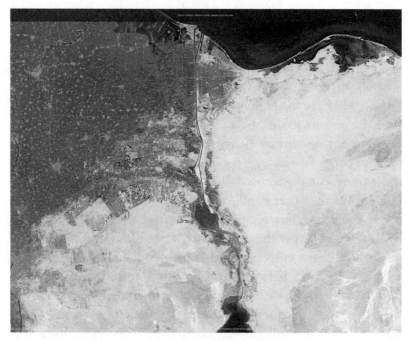

Figure 6.5: The actual line that did cut the isthmus of Suez: satellite image of the Suez Canal, January 2023.

With the carving of the Suez Canal, the term 'highway' of the sea ceased to be a metaphor. Maritime paths were no longer just hidden currents, or virtual lines on maps, but gashes through solid sand and rock. At this point in time, the lines left by ships began, quite literally, to cement themselves onto the seascape and the human societies they touched.

The first real human line across the sea, however, was older than the Suez Canal, and it wasn't a ship track: it was a telegraph cable track – a journey line for electricity and news, rather than people. In 1851, a 25-mile copper cable successfully joined Dover and Calais.[52] This line sat on the sea in maps, but *under* it in reality, buried beneath tens of metres and an enormous volume of water. Seven years later, in August 1858, an electric message buzzed along 2,000 miles of line, joining the two sides of the Atlantic – this time 2 miles deep, in spaces then unreachable for humans. It had taken six attempts, and the cable broke within about a month. Another cable, set out in the Red Sea, went the same way. A better scientific understanding of electricity was needed, and particularly of underwater induction and conduction. But the idea was in place: the imaginary line linking the ocean's shores had suddenly ceased to be imaginary; it had mobilised mass enthusiasm. And, much like the carcass of the unfortunate cable, buried in the submarine depths, it could not be easily withdrawn. Demand for a solution pulled forward research into electrical physics.[53] In 1864, a cable waded the Persian Gulf, linking Britain to India.[54] By 1866, the Atlantic was successfully bridged, and all other oceans would follow.[55] The rainforests of South-East Asia were scoured to extract 'gutta-percha', the solid gum material that safely insulated submarine cables. The rare trees producing it were all but driven to extinction: around 88 million of them were killed in the nineteenth century alone.[56] Nested on the sea floor, telegraph lines were faithful copies of their mapped images: the British Empire spreading its rubbery and metallic branches, its orders and its news across the globe. When the new century dawned, 210,000 miles of cables ran through the watery expanses of the Earth – most owned, and nearly all made, by British companies (Figure 6.6).[57] The ships laying these cables, then, had become the first in history to physically drop behind real, fixed tracks: hundreds of thousands of solid tons of them.[58] Some were later retrieved, some sit there still.[59]

As steam routes and cables were tangled around the world, they acquired powerful symbolism. Here we might recycle the image used by novelist Frank Norris in 1901 to describe railways: wrapping the territory like greedy octopuses – 'a plexus of red, a veritable system of blood circulation, complicated, dividing, and reuniting, branching, splitting, extending, throwing out feelers, offshoots, taproots, feeders.'[60]

In the following century, air travel would adopt the same visual language, through advertising materials that showed the world strewn with blazing lines. Some of the early examples, like Pan American's 'Clipper' 'Flying Boats' (1931–46), explicitly smacked of nostalgia for a mythical age of sail (Plate 21).[61] But, symbolically, flying tracks were all that steamship and cable tracks had been, and

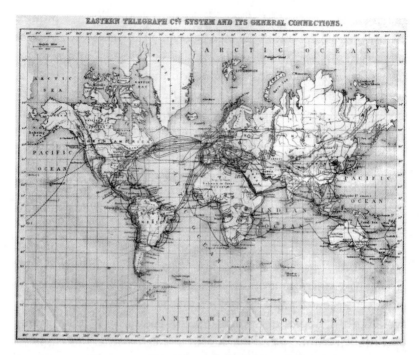

Figure 6.6: 'The Eastern Telegraph C°'s: System
and Its General Connections' (1901).

more: unlike the meandering tracks of sailing ships, they were
direct, modern and triumphant. The Panama Canal was proving so
difficult to build that some joked it would soon be superseded: in
an American satirical cartoon from 1906, the channel line is shown
from above, but as an empty backwater now bypassed by aerial
balloons (Plate 22). Desperate signs along it try to lure customers,
through souvenirs and 'special inducements'. The occupation of the
waters is derided ('This ocean for sale cheap', reads a sign planted
into the Pacific), and a balloon overhead promises 'all the bird's-eye
views of the world'. The cartoon is entitled 'Opening of the Panama
Canal', but a smaller subtitle scornfully adds: 'At Which Distant
Day Ocean Navigation Will Be a Trifle Out of Date'.

    The point here isn't that oceanic navigation had genuinely
become out of date. It hadn't (commercial air travel was decades
away), and it still hasn't today: the vast majority of the world's trade

continues to flow on water. The point is that, at the turn of the century, many in the Western world saw (or satirised) the exhilarating speed of modernity as an unstoppable barrelling force – an inevitable, ongoing stream of progress. Between the nineteenth and the twentieth centuries, networks became fashionable images of this new era. They showed disciplined, accelerating connection, the direct shooting for targets through capillary and unhindered structure, rationality and technology.[62] The new modern world was mobile, straight and fast, network lines seemed to say. It ran like clockwork, and waited for no one. It is here that tracks apparently lose their 'personal' quality, and come to resemble roads. However, this was in itself a trick. Some of that individuality clung on: oceanic tracks weren't *everyone's* tracks. They belonged to specific groups of people.

Indeed, sea lines weren't always a diffuse network, with all parts of it equally well served: rather, they displayed geopolitical and economic power, radiating from a clear centre. A propaganda map published in Britain in 1927 bore the title 'Highways of Empire'. In it, pervasive lines of transoceanic communication flowed in and out of Britain and imperial nodes like Australia, while bright-red splotches, that familiar representation of colonial extension, stained large swathes of most continents. These transoceanic lines may have been infrastructure, but they were still grounded in personal tracks: a caption referred to 'the Englishmen, who blazed the first trails along the highways of Empire'.[63] Meanwhile, across the Pacific, the marine highways linking Australia and North America were used as a striking symbol in political discourse – they signalled the ethnic and imperial ties between white Anglo-Saxon countries.[64] Social power and physical power are one and the same: empire and environmental impact, the ruling of water and of people.[65]

A wide-ranging atlas published in Paris in 1854 contained a 'Map of Steam Navigation in the Mediterranean Basin' (Plate 20). This map provides extremely dense topographic, orographic and hydrographic details of inland Europe, North Africa and the Near East. However, there is no doubt that ship tracks are the centrepiece.

The gently curved filaments of various routes, highlighted in different colours, are elegantly draped around the Mediterranean and Black Sea, some stretching out to skirt the Atlantic coasts of Europe. The colours indicate national shipping lines – the British are red, the French blue, the Austrian orange, and so on: together with the heavy shade of the land masses, they encroach onto the Mediterranean, pull it tight, and dye it in an extraneous rainbow. The track lines are also accompanied by strings of text. Along with the main places touched by the journeys, these captions offer a combination of descriptive information that would be of no direct use to the traveller (the distance in leagues, rather than travelling time), and – occasionally – more practical detail ('1 fois par mois', 'once a month', we are told next to the Gibraltar–Smyrna–Constantinople line). Departure dates and the duration of voyages are reported in a more systematic way in a table alongside the map: the line linking Southampton with Alexandria of Egypt, 1,050 leagues long, represents fifteen days of travel. Although sailing vessels are still clinging on (the Alexandria–Beirut voyage, the table tells us, is 'under sail' or 'à voiles'), this map celebrates the triumph of commercial steamers, supposedly making the world a little bit more manageable, reachable and reliable. But there are quite a few things that the map does not show us.

Historians of the Mediterranean have long stressed how historically interconnected this sea is: an area of flourishing inward interaction and exchange.[66] Yet these long-standing connections were very different from the stark modern tracks that sewed it together in set ways.[67] The connectivity of steamer tracks wasn't as flexible, uniform and universal as the map would make out. Stressing connectivity, while 'mesmerizing', papers over 'hinterlands, the confined, the subjugated and the particular'.[68] Even when no obvious 'fountainheads' are in sight, centres of power from which routes radiate, it can be an intrinsically imperialistic endeavour.[69] The networked linkages of the modern world imply subjection and imposition behind a mask of friendly egalitarianism: they forget the nooks and crannies, the gaps in the shiny net of modernity, in which large numbers of people and local cultures live, or (barely) survive.

In 1859, a steamer passage from Marseille to Naples cost 181 francs in first class and 50 even in fourth. Travelling all the way to Alexandria cost 469 francs in first class and 105 in fourth. A ticket to Rhodes was a whopping 697 and 147 francs respectively.[70] In 1853, on average, a French carpenter or mason – a skilled worker – made slightly less than 2 francs a day.[71] Getting to Egypt on that neat and simple line would have taken him almost two months' salary each way, even travelling in the most squalid conditions. To go on the same journey, a field labourer from Tunis would have needed to save his entire salary for the best part of a year.[72] Thirty-five million migrants traversed the Atlantic from Europe to America between the early nineteenth century and the First World War; the convenience of steam did make migration 'less permanent', but, for most of them, this remained a once- or twice-in-a-lifetime passage, paid for through loans and great sacrifices – not the regular open route that maps may suggest.[73] And even such travellers only constituted a small proportion of the population. These elegant filaments on water were still, for the vast majority of people, mirages.

In some cases, they were worse than mirages. Around the world, local communities that drew their livelihood from the sea occasionally benefited from the new highways. Yet, all too often, they were suffocated by them. The world of steam was one of brutal competition, efficient and relentless, in which only those controlling high concentrations of capital could thrive. In Sri Lanka, fishermen were pushed away from the main 'modern' harbour of Colombo; in Naples, the fishing industry struggled to survive in the new, fast-moving maritime world.[74] Sailing companies and seafarers were remarkably resilient, picking up routes that steamers wouldn't or couldn't, and adapting to a shifting market. But eventually the profession became untenable, and local labour dynamics collapsed, taking entire communities with them: mariners either made the transition to steamship personnel, if they could, or they simply quit the seas. Families split, workers relocated, and ancient economies were swept into global channels of waged labour.[75]

These channels, in turn, took lives. To procure gutta-percha for telegraph cables, Chinese, Dayak and Malay labourers had to wade deep into dangerous forests, the home of tigers and lethal vipers;

Figure 6.7: A track line of human labour, installing
the Persian Gulf cable in 1864.

later on, Arab and European workers also waded up to their chests
in the waters of the Persian Gulf, to install the cables on the sea floor
(Figure 6.7).[76] In ship-coaling stations around the world, the dirty,
dusty tons of coal devoured by steamers were shifted and loaded by
indigenous labourers: non-unionised and heavily underpaid men,
women and children, racialised in turn as lazy or hardened to the
climate, and despised even by the white common sailors.[77] Aboard
the steamers, the furnaces were powered by men who toiled shovel-
ling coal in unbearable noise and at unbearable temperatures, up to
60 degrees. This inferno was often reserved to non-white seamen,
on the pseudo-biological assumption that their bodies could handle
it better. As a stoker later recalled, coal dust burrowed deep: 'when
we spat it was black. When we blew our noses it was black. Even our
excrement was black.'[78] Over 5,600 workers also died in the jungles
of Panama, struck by disease and landslides while digging the new
sea route across the isthmus: about 10 per cent of the workforce
employed. At least 20,000 more had perished during a previous
French attempt to build the canal, in the 1880s.[79] Death rates of
this sort had little to envy compared to those of Ramesses IV's

quarrying expeditions. Drawing modern tracks, which they would never be able to use, cost some people everything.

In the nineteenth century, in short, the new super-powered tracks also accentuated social inequality and segregation. At the same time, their stark, neat shapes made the poverty that multiplied and festered in their shadow utterly invisible. The local and the disconnected were simply a void, lacking their own fancy cartographical symbols. Tracks didn't give voice to humans: they gave voice to *some* humans. Even these straight, apparently neutral transport tracks were still telling particular stories. And this takes us to the next problem with their supposed universality: unlike roads, they remained in the eye of the beholder.

The first issue with a narrative that presents steam blasting on stage and overcoming all maritime transportation issues is that this didn't happen. For the first three-quarters of the nineteenth century, despite the flashy innovations in iron hulls and screw propellers, the bulk of global trade remained firmly in the hands of the old sailers. The sailing vessel was cheaper, and sometimes quite fast in its own right: detailed route charts like Maury's had provided it with invaluable global shortcuts, and its predominantly wooden bottoms were less susceptible than iron ones to barnacles and fouling by marine creatures, which slow ships down. As late as the 1880s, and until the invention of truly efficient high-pressure engines, sailing ships were still useful – not least to ferry the coal guzzled down by steamers. From the 1850s, moreover, their design improved, resulting in fantastically elegant and efficient shapes. For all these reasons, some historians have gone so far as to suggest that the 'great age of sail' actually came in the 1860s and 1870s.[80]

We can see here, once again, how deceptive 'simple' portrayals of discovery and innovation can be. Exactly as the twentieth century dawned, a ship braving the angry waters of the Horn still drew tracks that looked just as tousled and disarrayed as those of the British Commodore Anson in 1741, or of the Dutch Schouten and Le Maire when they had first completed the passage in 1616 (see Figure 2.12).[81] Between 1899 and 1900, the three-masted, steel-built sailing vessel *Blackbraes*, headed from Newcastle-on-Tyne to San Francisco, had a nightmarish experience in trying to get into the Pacific. The whole journey 'took 10 days short of a year', partly because months were spent battling Cape Horn. The first attempt went on from 1 September to 20 October, after which the ship retreated to the Falklands for repairs, its sails in shreds. The second attempt began on 10 February, and it was only on 5 March that the *Blackbraes* finally made it through. All of this can be reconstructed, day by day, from a track chart made by a boy who joined the vessel shortly afterwards. It takes some patience, however, because the sea tangled these tracks almost beyond legibility.[82]

For most of the nineteenth century, then, the majority of ships still ran on wind, and drew tracks accordingly. But could steam vessels, with their straight courses, laugh off all natural obstacles? Steam allegedly gave the sea an entirely new quality – a compliant flatness that turned it into a mute background to human activities. As the British Foreign Secretary Lord Palmerston complained in 1846, dreading a French invasion, the English Channel was 'no longer a barrier', but now 'nothing more than a river passable by a steam bridge.'[83] However, naval men with technical experience were more sceptical: 'a steamer in a rolling sea', one allegedly quipped, was like 'a cat in walnut shells on ice.'[84]

Steamers, whether powered by paddle or screw, weren't immune from angry seas. Cargos were still jettisoned, ships still broke, and men still died, as under sail. One of the very same steamers that could cut a straight line from South America to the Channel, ignoring the *volta do mar* and trade winds, as late as 1926 had to have 400 tons of ballast seawater pumped into its hold to get stabilised in a North Sea storm.[85] Interviewed in 1989 about their careers in steamships, a series of Canadian seamen were very clear on the dangers of underestimating the sea, and human fallibility in the face of natural hazards: 'There were certain ship's masters who didn't learn their ship construction well enough,' recalled one of them, 'and they drive ships bang! Crash! And all of a sudden they're in trouble, the ship's splitting, they come to realize it's a manmade thing and it's being destroyed by man, and he becomes a great respecter of the sea'. In a hurricane, you simply do not venture out.[86]

There were other issues, too. Unruly seas are the domain of wind and water, and wind and water put out fire. When HMS *Cruizer* barely escaped being smashed to pieces on the Ligurian coast, in 1867, this was because the current-beating steam 'was of very little service': 'owing to the ship being battened down, it was most difficult to keep the fires burning'. Later that night, after masses of water poured into the stokehole and defeated the pumps, the furnaces were quenched altogether.[87] More generally, steam relied on energy that is not readily on supply in an aqueous world. Steamers could only go as far as the coal that they could carry. Coaling stations flourished all over the world, but their coverage was never exhaustive. Joseph Conrad, master mariner and master writer, and admittedly no friend of steam, profoundly captured this truth: 'The efficiency of a steamship consists not so much in her courage as in the power she carries within herself. It beats and throbs like a pulsating heart within her iron ribs, and when it stops, the steamer, whose life is not so much a contest as the disdainful ignoring of the sea, sickens and dies upon the waves.'[88]

Very little was needed, in fact, to turn a steam-straightened line back into a curly mess: some technical malfunction, or a little bit of rain. And here is Conrad again, writing about the track of a broken-down steamship:

> The track she had made when drifting while her heart stood still within her iron ribs looked like a tangled thread on the white paper of the chart. It was shown to me by a friend, her second officer. In that surprising tangle there were words in minute letters – 'gales,' 'thick fog,' 'ice' – written by him here and there as memoranda of the weather. She had interminably turned upon her tracks, she had crossed and recrossed her hap-hazard path till it resembled nothing so much as a puzzling maze of pencilled lines without a meaning. But in that maze there lurked all the romance of the 'overdue' and a menacing hint of 'missing.'[89]

Even the most solidly carved track can easily be chopped in two. In the previous chapter, we met George Henry Richards, the stern Hydrographer of the Admiralty, who chastised gung-ho British captains running their ships aground. Richards was sent to Suez in 1869 to appraise the new wonder of the world. Like many of their enthralled contemporaries, he and his colleague, Andrew Clarke, mentioned in their report the canal's potential 'as the grand highway for the naval and mercantile marine of Europe to the East'. However, their enthusiasm was hardly unbounded. The canal may have been a new highway, but it was only suited to certain types of trade, and certain types of vessel (steamers). Most importantly, in their view, it was much too narrow.[90] The canal was substantially improved in the following century and a half, and it looks rather different today. Yet their fears remain justified.

There have been many accidents in the Suez, including in very recent times as freight vessels keep growing in size. But the most famous grounding took place on 23 March 2021, when the enormous container carrier *Ever Given*, 400 metres in length, got stuck right across it, blocking travel in both directions (Plate 23).[91] The vessel defeated attempts at dislodging it for about a week, while hundreds of other ships piled into the queue; since around 12 per cent of global trade today flows through the canal, this interruption had universal ripple effects for at least two months: the maritime industry was swept by a tidal wave of delayed schedules, monstrous port congestion and container shortages.[92] Supply chains were disrupted, and this also affected medical and pharmaceutical products, something that the world could ill afford in the middle of the COVID-19 pandemic.[93] News websites showed the alternative route that ships were forced to redraw around the Cape of Good Hope – about 6,500 kilometres and eight and a half days longer, on average speed.[94] The fragility of shipping lines endures, even long after they have reached full maturity.

Looking at engine-powered tracks a bit more closely, then, beyond generic representations, confirms an important truth. Science and empire are not cause and effect, at the snap of a finger. This simple unidirectional narrative enthralled nineteenth-century Europeans, but, beneath the neat lines that they drew across the globe, the environment broke cables and broke ships, conditioned technologies and rerouted them.[95]

Still, for all these contradictions, the mindset that drew tracks had effects that were all too real. This wasn't despite the tracks' slightly delusional nature, but, in good measure, *because* of it. The ostensible links of globalisation not only leave out entire swathes of the world, but also represent thin, sketchy, shadow-like connections between faraway places, which aren't necessarily joined by real human ties. This type of association is dangerous. As political scientist Peter Jacques puts it, globalisation has 'changed the human–ocean relationship by distancing affecters from effects'.[96] For most of the last couple of centuries, audiences in industrialised countries only saw gleaming tracks, impressive networks steaming into a bright future. What happened to distant oceans and distant people happened off the map. Or rather, it happened behind the storied curtain that the map conveniently provided.

Unlike resource extraction, for most of human history seaborne travel and transportation didn't leave any *actual* traces on the oceans – bar the odd shipwreck. Tracks were solely human hallucinations. But over the last century or so, this has changed.[97] In some senses, the new modern tracks did mark the seas. Under steam, for example, fishing vessels magnified their footprint. Since the late twentieth century, this footprint has ceased to be just a metaphor: studies of their tracks have demonstrated that bottom-trawling 'ploughs' the sea floor, radically levelling and transforming its shape.[98] Power and telecommunications cables also clearly mark the oceans, whether they are simply deposited on or near their bottoms or fully buried into the seabed. Their laying, their presence and their maintenance and retrieval cause a degree of disturbance to marine life. Some studies suggest that the overall impact may be more limited than one could fear. Still, habitats can take a few years to recover from disruption, depending on location and soil type; whales occasionally became entangled in older-generation cables, where their bodies lay mangled and decomposing until the tract was pulled up for repairs; and the electromagnetic field of power cables potentially affects various animals, even though research remains scarce.[99]

The story we are telling here could easily become one of crude causality, or even merely crude correspondence. But it is, in fact, far more interesting than that. Human impact on the oceans takes many forms; relatively few of those are strictly track-shaped, or even directly linked to shipping.[100] Aside from alterations of temperature and chemistry, the greatest harms are caused by microplastics, which most often stem from land-based waste, and are difficult to 'spot' in the first place. Plastic in the seas floats, sinks, breaks up into nanoparticles and is eaten and excreted by various organisms, in patterns that scientists cannot fully map. Studies produce track-shaped graphs only because the ship with a measuring net has to proceed along a single line. But the plastic lies in blotches, not tracks.[101] Massive-scale container shipping results in massive-scale disasters. But, again, 61,280 Nike shoes, or 5 million Lego pieces, or unspecified numbers of Garfield plastic phones, lost off the French coast in the 1980s, don't just line up in an orderly way: they scatter all over the world's shores, following non-human currents and tides. (Or, in the case of the Garfield phones, haunt Brittany's beaches in a slow, thirty-five-year invasion).[102] Even where impact does manifest itself as a direct track, the visible shape is only part of what is going on.

Artificial canals are impressive gashes: anyone flying over the Suez *sees* a ship track, as clear as a line on a map, but fully realised in sand and stone. However, the tracks drawn through isthmus-digging run deeper still. Marine biologists view canals like the Suez or the Panama as 'invasion corridors'. Through these open gaps, extraneous species move from one sea to the other, either by autonomous drift (at times across multiple generations) or by hitching a lift: for example, they cling on to ships' hulls or float in ballast tank water.[103] These human-made tracks, then, don't just mark the isthmic land: they mark the sea, as well, and change it in profound ways to which we may even be visually oblivious. This is the same thing that happens with 'ship track' clouds produced by vessel pollution: they streak the skies, but only a tiny portion of exhaust emissions form a detectable ship track. The rest just melts into the atmosphere, with unknown effects.[104]

*

Where does all this leave us? Over the course of the nineteenth century, well-beaten tracks became 'common highways'. But here we must take 'common' to mean non-extraordinary, rather than universally shared. These tracks belonged to some humans, excluding and even harming the majority of others. When seen up close, they remained lively, idiosyncratic and haphazard stories.

In some senses, both social and environmental, maritime tracks had become real. Yet reality is messier than a map, and more difficult to control. The idea that sea journeys were lines facilitated the establishment of actual lines, with a tangible presence in the world, but the link between culture and reality was far from perfect. No matter how powerful the technologies behind steamships, telegraph cables or isthmic canals, tracks remained, to a large extent, made-up notions: the visual shape of the modern track told a story of speed and mastery that concealed complexity and breakage. At the same time, maritime endeavours began to leave marks that transcended that visual shape; no track could have sufficed to represent the multidimensional effects of human impact on the oceans, and of the environmental catastrophe that was beginning to unfold. The track wasn't just truth, and the truth wasn't just a track. But the track was a powerful glueing symbol in this chaotic interface between ideas and reality, precisely because of its key property: displaying agency. Whether it was accurate or delusional, whether it was infrastructure, storytelling or a blend of both, the question of *who* was drawing it and using it, and why, somehow continued to matter. As more and more people came to make and question tracks, then, something interesting began to brew.

COUNTERTRACKS

T. E. Lawrence, Odysseus, Magellan, Cook, Captain Ahab, a British officer at the Battle of Jutland: almost every chapter of this book has begun with powerful, often famous, sometimes fictional European or North American men. All chapters also continued more or less in the same vein. This is not accidental; for most of their history, maritime tracks have been tools for the personal, narrative expression of relatively powerful white men.

While 'exploration' can be seen as a feature of any human society, the term acquired specific meaning with European imperial expansion.[1] The modern stock character of the Explorer was usually white and quintessentially male, and he represented the pioneering arm of Western science and civilisation.[2] In the preceding centuries, even if this mythical figure had not yet evolved, imperial expeditions were also led – and recounted – by elite white men. Once these successes (or indeed failures) were reported at home, the common sailors and indigenous people who communicated knowledge and actively collaborated in 'exploration' faded into mute side-characters. So did the women – the indispensable wives, companions and labourers who were largely left behind, lest they 'pester' a ship.

Here, however, we must resist the persuasiveness of the track, and look at the discrepancies between truth and representation. It's in those discrepancies that its proper meaning lies. What remains for us to do is put the track into its context: historically, who got to claim tracks, who didn't, and why? Which alternative ways of viewing human movement in the world continued to coexist with the track? And which other stories can tracks be made to tell? Answering these questions means inviting in a new set of protagonists, rather different from most of those whom we have encountered so far.

So let's start this chapter in a different way.

In March 1856, fifteen-year-old Emma Hotchkiss, of Gloucester, Massachusetts, was on her way from Calcutta to Bordeaux in her father's merchant vessel the *Harvard*. Captain Levi Hotchkiss had been suffering from headaches, fever and painful sores on his face. The lively young lady didn't idle about: her tasks ran the gamut from 'mending, serving, washing', to tidying up, reading and studying. However, that was not all. On 29 March, her journal reads: 'been employed by helping father mark off our track of this voyage on another one'.[3]

Emma was wary of stepping out of line in a world to which she didn't belong. When 'Charley', possibly a young relative of hers, was sent to complete some task in the rigging aloft, her writing became reticent: 'as I do not understand what it is, I will not put it down, for if I should make a mistake, there will be a laugh at my expense'.[4] But her embarrassed reservations do her little justice; the journal bursts with nautical knowledge and terminology and reference to winds, weather and speed. She even reports daily latitude and longitude measurements. Had she been a boy, her professional future would have been straightforward. For a girl, the options were limited. Still, on that voyage in the *Harvard*, the first mate was a twenty-seven-year-old man bearing the bizarre name of Horatio Nelson Gray. Six years later, Emma married him, and she spent the rest of her life around ships anyway. By the time she was twenty-seven herself, she was living on the Yangtze River, ferrying passengers and goods on her husband's steamer, the *Fire Queen*.[5]

Why did Emma feel that meddling too far into nautical matters would make her a laughing stock? The mechanisms whereby tracks and exploration shut out femininity were, and are, extremely deep-rooted. We can understand them more readily if we look at present-day debates on wayfinding and spatial cognition. Parts of those debates have inherited, wholesale, centuries' worth of ideas about sex and gender. Some psychologists and neuroscientists argue that, in their experiments, male subjects performed better when using 'absolute' or 'allocentric' orientation systems, such as 2D maps and cardinal points. Women, instead, supposedly thought more in terms of routes and sequences of landmarks, from their own ('egocentric') point of view.[6] In short, men thought by tracks, while women used a 'hodological' or path-shaped vision. The inference is often that such differences are evolutionary and biologically ingrained.

Digging a little more into the literature, however, reveals interesting caveats that undermine this kind of generalisation. For example, a recent survey of the sprawling research on gender and spatial navigation found that, while men did perform better at wayfinding, there were smaller differences between young boys and girls.[7] A navigational experiment during which testosterone was administered to women showed that this had 'a limited effect on spatial cognition' and none on actual 'navigation success'.[8] Instead, there is strong evidence that spatial cognition skills can be trained, and experience can almost wipe out the gender gap.[9] In another study, 518 West Point cadets were given navigational tasks in a forest: women did worse than men because they were 'pausing and revisiting' their direction more often.[10] Women, overall, appear more anxious about getting lost in unfamiliar environments, and this, it has been shown, is linked to the fact that they are socialised to feel less safe in general. In turn, these worries may lead some of them to think in terms of known routes, rather than abstract shortcuts through unexplored areas.[11] So, even if in Western cultures cartographical track-thinking turns out to be a 'male' trait (and the jury is out on that), there is no need to explain this pattern through problematic biological and evolutionary notions.

Instead, the masculinity of tracks is fundamentally linked to the fact that tracks had *voices*. Feminist scholarship on the history of European science has been tackling very similar problems. Why have women's contributions to science generally been forgotten? Perhaps, some researchers propose, it's because the very ideals of 'objectivity' and detachment that seem to govern modern science are essentially male. Psychoanalytic theories of human upbringing suggest that female children, on the contrary, learn attachment, empathy and 'concern for context' from a young age. But Naomi Oreskes has put forward a very convincing counterargument: even when women *did* do objective work, and were fully capable of it, they remained sidelined. The problem, then, is not cognitive, but social and cultural, and grounded in a specific historical context: in a patriarchal society, women are expected to shoulder care tasks and be responsible for others. This automatically excluded them from the heroic posturing and reckless behaviours that made for 'great' science.[12] Caring duties leave no flashy tracks. And if perchance you leave tracks when you should have been home with the children, you are a selfish aberration, whose tracks are, somehow, less valid: a matter of shame, rather than pride.

The great age of the Explorer also coincided with a hardening of gender divides. Female 'explorers' regularly saw their accomplishments doubted, ascribed to men, tinged with scandal and sexual insinuations, or outright prevented. In 1905, Mina Benson Hubbard, a widowed Canadian nurse, travelled by canoe deep into Labrador, accompanied only by four indigenous men: she produced photographs, a book, an excellent map, and a track. Meanwhile, in the newspapers, this successful expedition (unusually respectful of local culture and advice) was reduced to a 'strange visit', 'sentimentally inspired' by the death of her husband on a previous attempt.[13] In the first half of the twentieth century, all the numerous women who applied to join Antarctic expeditions were rejected. And, not coincidentally, confusion reigned until a few years ago as to *who* exactly was the first Western woman to have set foot on the continent. The name of the first reputed to have spotted it, in 1835, was never recorded. Somehow, these facts didn't matter: the very language of records, primacy and exploration didn't seem to mix well with women. They were, in the words of novelist Jesse Blackadder, 'not only physically but narratively excluded'.[14] We know who the first six women to reach the South Pole were, but only because they were deposited there by a US Navy plane in 1969, simultaneously and, by institutional design, unheroically. One of them later recalled the bathos of the occasion: the 'striped pole' that marked the Pole was 'so exactly like a pedestrian crossing marker that I simply couldn't think of the spot as that solemn goal to which Scott and Amundsen had toiled. Indeed, it seemed just the sort of Pole that Pooh and Piglet might have set out to find'.[15]

To these women, constrained, policed, and taken to the Pole as a publicity stunt, the heroism of trailblazers' marks rang hollow. The track as a masculine construct was backed by a whole ideological arsenal, which defined its very essence as the *opposite* of how it defined womanhood: bold, active, daring and powerful.[16] The track, then, was a symbol of the right to express oneself: a competitive freedom of speech, which only some could wield.

While tracks were wielded by few, they were *made* by many, regardless of gender. Young Emma Hotchkiss wasn't a lone example: in the nineteenth century, captains' female family members would regularly trace courses, keep nautical logs and even complete shipboard astronomical observations.[17] If not always as literally as that, there were armies of women behind the tracks of navigators. Of course, we have the supportive wives, like Ann Flinders and Jane Franklin, and many more equivalents lower down the social ranks, who ran the show at home while the men sailed the seven seas. Prostitutes, traders, innkeepers, navy contractors all contributed to keep the system running, as well. And we shouldn't forget the women who worked as sailors themselves, or even shipwrights.[18] But some also had a hand in the very navigational developments onto which tracks were built.

Astronomy is fundamental for both charting and navigation, and women played an important part in it. In the late seventeenth and early eighteenth centuries, for example, within German territories, about one-seventh of astronomers were female.[19] Until less than a hundred years ago, a 'computer' was an individual who performed complex calculations – like those on whose basis nautical almanacs were drawn up and observatories functioned. From the nineteenth century, a growing number of computers were women, and in fact in the United States the job ended up labelled as a menial feminine task.[20] But precedents existed, too: in 1784, Mary Edwards had spent over a decade completing calculations for the British *Nautical Almanac* on behalf of her husband; when she became a homeless, widowed single mother, she took over the job officially. She trained her daughters, as well, and one of them succeeded her.[21] In the 1790s, Marie-Jeanne de Lalande produced an award-winning set of astronomical timetables for the French Navy.[22] A few decades later, the English navigation teacher Janet Taylor published a large number of manuals, including a guide to Matthew Fontaine Maury's charts of winds, currents and oceanic routes. She invented instruments, manufactured them, fixed compasses, assisted the Hydrographic Office with chart-making and ran a nautical school in London. She also received awards from the Admiralty and the East India Company, as well as medals from various European kings, for inventing a simplification of the lunar distances method.[23] When navigation shaded into route infrastructure, women were on the scene, too. Until well into the twentieth century, they were a key workforce at coaling stations in the Caribbean, in the Indian Ocean and in Japan.[24] Many thousands of Black female labourers also supported the construction of the Panama Canal. Historian Joan-Flores Villalobos calls them 'silver women', a reference to the fact that 'unskilled' West Indians were paid in silver, while the white Americans who worked alongside them received gold. The Black women at times transcended these structural barriers, demanding payment in gold. They could do this, however, precisely because their work was unofficial and outside codified contracts.[25] Again, we see a pattern here: invisibility.

Women have always been everywhere in, around and behind the maritime world. Yet the tracks never bear their names. Femininity was excluded a priori, but in this it wasn't alone. In the new models of 'heroic' 'discovery' that arose in the second half of the eighteenth century, the awards podium couldn't be too crowded.[26] The vast networks of labour, thought and creation underlying any 'discovery' were chopped out of the spotlight. Discovery was, like a track line, unidimensional.

A very similar story, in fact, can be told for non-white or non-elite male labourers –sharpened with brutality, enslavement and death. We saw in Chapter 6 how their toil sustained the slick steamship and cable lines in the nineteenth century. However, the same patterns of hidden work stretch right back to the origins of the age of sail and 'discovery', buried underneath name-tagged tracks. Magellan, Drake or Cook didn't travel the world alone on a raft. Some captains were more 'enlightened' than others, but life on the decks of European sailing vessels was hard and dangerous. While circumnavigating the world, Anson lost the majority of his men to sickness and scurvy, their flesh rotting away from vitamin C deficiency; Magellan lost almost everyone, himself included, and never finished his journey.[27] All the while, seamen were harshly disciplined: even the comparatively mild Cook had dozens of sailors violently flogged for shipboard infractions.[28] Yet the track lines on luxury globes, fancy quarto volumes and Hawai'ian shirts bear the captains' names alone. Even when violence and death were not directly involved, the knowledge and work that made tracks never belonged to a single man. It didn't just belong to Europeans, either: in the Pacific, for example, Cook was shown around by the Ra'iātean priest and navigator Tupaia, who even drew a map for him.[29]

Like gender, class and race increasingly came to define who was excluded from the club of legitimate track-makers.[30] Many 'ordinary' seafarers mattered little to their employers, and as a result have left scanty records: what historian Gopalan Balachandran calls 'footprints on water'.[31] But to us this is bitterly ironic – because we have just seen how even footprints on water are actually more enduring than the subaltern voices that the maritime enterprise silenced.

What are we to make of these silences? The crucial thing here is, again, not to take the tracks on their own terms. If we can take away one point from this book, it is that tracks are historically and culturally contingent: they express a specific point of view. We saw earlier how the language of tracks and priority territorial claims resembled that of virginity and penetration. As such, it clashed with other ways of seeing the world, based on the idea that water, space and bodies shouldn't be framed as objects of occupation.

In nineteenth-century Europe and North America, even in the heyday of 'exploration', this idea still circulated. Here, we might refer to long-standing traditions of radicalism and social justice that came to a head in Marxist and feminist movements; but instead, let's look at a comic poem entitled 'My Aunt', which was reproduced many times in American periodicals between the late 1820s and the early 1850s. It opens thus: 'My Aunt has many queer notions – / She never butters her bread'. The whole piece is a playful derision of a stuffy relative who has outdated ideas of sin and impropriety. The aunt censors, among other things, 'youth' kissing, 'opera dancing', drinking, and various works of literature. But here is the final stanza of the poem:

> She thinks she can tell the mark that's left,
> On my cousin's lip, by a kiss;
> And of all her antiquate theories
> I'm sure not to meddle with this.
> She might tell the track of a bird thro' the air,
> Or the track of a ship in the sea; –
> On the viewless heart – not the visible lip –
> The stamp of a kiss will be![32]

The view of tracks as ephemeral and non-marking, suggested in the Book of Wisdom and repurposed in various ways, was never entirely superseded. Some elite men claimed tracks, but other models of living in the world were possible – and they never fully disappeared. If we leave modern Europe for a moment, this becomes especially clear.

Until the second half of the twentieth century, Western scholars thought that 'the Pacific' was a Western construct. Europeans, so the story went, stitched it together with their exploration and colonisation journeys. However, the Pacific was stitched together long before that.[33] The story is almost the opposite, in fact: as argued by Epeli Hau'ofa, the modern anthropologist and bard of that ocean, islander cultures' current, internalised state of 'belittlement' and fragmentation, of smallness, isolation and impotence, is a direct result of colonialism. It is the direct result of a perspective that stresses the land and its narrow economic and productive value, rather than the sea – an immense, aquatic world of contact and exchange that had known few boundaries before.[34] Indigenous traditions of seafaring, or 'voyages', stretch back thousands of years. The old story went that the earliest Pacific settlers merely 'drifted' to their islands – for how could uncivilised populations achieve something as complex as deliberate and accurate long-distance sea travel? In fact, seafaring masters, historians and anthropologists have proved that these voyagers, much of the time, knew exactly where they were going. 'Traditional' navigation methods and craft are absolutely capable of carrying people across immense expanses of water.[35] In many ways, indeed, they may be better suited to movement through tightly packed archipelagos and shallow reefs, which were the curse of clunky-bottomed European vessels and their methods of navigation by coordinates.[36]

If indigenous Pacific seafarers crossed such distances, where are their tracks? The answer is, in their minds, in the sky and in the sea, but not as lines inked onto it. There were many methods for creating and preserving routes. First, 'sea routes were mapped on chants', as Epeli Hau'ofa puts it: 'songlines', verbal lists of stops that remind us of the ancient Western 'itinerary vision'.[37] Sea routes were also mapped as mental frameworks, just as 'portable' as European paper devices. On a clear night, the sky above the ocean sparkles in a dazzling jangle of stars. These voyagers knew vast numbers of them, and their rising and setting directions offered a mental immersive compass somewhat analogous to the Mediterranean wind rose (although in the Pacific a 'wind' as opposed to 'star' compass was specific to Polynesia alone).[38] The star compass used in the Micronesian Caroline Islands bears some striking similarities to that of Arab navigators, and there is a slight chance that contacts across the Indian Ocean led the one to influence the other: both systems use the rising and setting points of the star Altair as their central axis. This doesn't make much sense from the Arabic peninsula, but the long string of the Caroline Islands happens to lie directly under Altair's heavenly path.[39]

In these mental maps, the traveller didn't move: it was the islands that moved around her. The European sailor imagined himself as a dot or a line advancing across a passive, immobile seascape; the Carolinian, instead, sat still, as islands drew near or dropped behind, in sight or in the hidden expanses beyond the horizon.[40] As in Homer's *Odyssey*, or in the Chinese maps of 'Zheng He''s expeditions, a voyage was measured by how long it took, not by the ground it covered.[41]

Pacific seafarers didn't carry charts aboard: all the information they needed was in their memory, although they sometimes made charts to be learned while still ashore. These objects contained lines, but of a radically different kind to those developed in European mapping. The rhumb lines on European portolan charts nominally marked courses according to the 'winds', yet in practice they utterly disregarded the features of sea and currents, slashing all as they went. The modern graticule of parallels and meridians is an even more abstract caging of the world, a convention making itself into fixed landmark. In the Pacific, instead, charts pulled their structural lines directly from the sea.

The Marshall Islands are two parallel chains of islands and atolls, running south-east to north-west and stretching nearly a million square kilometres. In this place, lying at a latitude untouched by the gales of trade winds, local navigators carried their art to the highest level: they learned to read not only the starry sky above, but the sea below as well. For them, the apparently formless and endless expanse – which puzzled and haunted European voyagers – was a familiar territory, with its visible landmarks and morphology: no longer just space, but a *place*, displaying its own recognisable character, and intimately known to the people who spent their whole lives a few metres (or centimetres) from it. When deep oceanic swells hit an island, they are refracted, reflected and diffracted into patterns. The skilled canoe navigator could spot these patterns, even from very far away, and in fact *feel* them through his or her own body, gently rocked by the pitch and roll of the canoe. These swells were cast into what we now call 'stick charts', made of midribs from palm leaves firmly tied together. In the chart varieties known as *meddo* and *rebbelith*, possibly slightly influenced by Western mapping, these midribs reproduced the specific patterns of a given group of islands; *mattang* charts, instead, displayed more general models (Figure 7.1).[42]

For the Marshall Islanders who had learned navigation, the sea was not pathless. It was a bumpy, predictable surface that

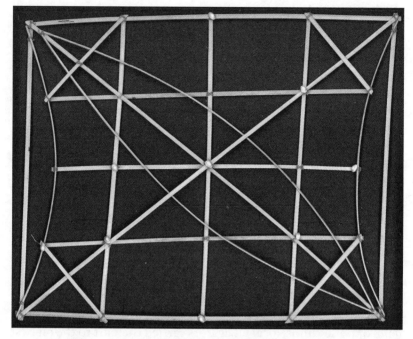

Figure 7.1: Marshall Islands *mattang* stick chart (Majuro, Marshall Islands, 1920s?), wood and shells, 74 × 91 cm.

constantly gave away the shape of what lay beyond the horizon. The lines on the water weren't those left by their journeys; they were the very structure of the ocean.

　　Here we ought to be careful. We cannot draw a sharp distinction between 'indigenous' and 'Western' knowledge systems, the former 'local' and empirical and the latter 'universal' and theoretical. This sort of 'block' thinking would erase myriad differences, similarities and historical connections. It would also perpetuate the racist classification of people into nature-dwelling and 'primitive' on the one hand, sophisticated and 'civilised' on the other.[43] To pick two examples among many: we saw that *mattang* stick charts offered generic, potentially universal models of the sea; conversely, Western imperialism could itself function through supposed local 'intimacy' with a place – for instance, men like Lawrence claimed in-depth, personal knowledge of 'Arabia'.[44]

What we can say, however, is that an important perspective, among those adopted during European imperial endeavours, was the pursuit of universal laws: principles that could be transferable and relevant everywhere, as a blanket method. At the same time, alternative knowledge systems do exist, in Europe and beyond, even if we don't want to flatten them under the label of 'indigenous'. They are *specific*, contextual and grounded. They may have wider applicability, in a narrow utilitarian sense, but this doesn't matter per se, and in fact can pervert their meaning. Instead, they develop in a deep dialogue with local place, community, nature and – crucially – 'obligations' to each of those.[45] This is one key difference between the track and other systems for wayfinding and journey-telling: the track is highly unspecific. How do you represent your journey home from the shops? The voyage of ninety-four men across the world in a wooden ship 250 years ago? The meanderings of the Hebrews in the Sinai Desert? The answer is always a line. In some cases, you could literally cut the line out of one map and paste it onto another, regardless of scale, time and place. I could take segments of Cook's track across the North Pacific and stick them onto a plan of the city of Cambridge, where I work, showing my walk from College to the department. It would look odd, but it would convey the idea of my movements. The track reduces the experience of motion in the world to a shape, and one that isn't even readily available to the traveller through her unmediated senses. In the process, it both gains huge power and erases, or at least upstages, the world itself.[46] In 2024 Europe or North America, journey lines look natural and obvious. But this process of erasure of the world is far from obvious. Tracks are mainly needed, as storytelling systems, when you are overstretching, in a place that isn't your home and that you haven't taken the time to understand on its own terms.

Our final task is to look at the ways in which tracks have been shifting in ownership and significance. There was always resistance on the part of the excluded, but it is perhaps most meaningful for us to conclude by looking at the specific forms this resistance has developed in our century. The rise of modern surveillance has gradually broadened the ranks of who draws tracks. The track, then, has also become a tool of *dis*empowerment and control. However, the track per se is only a tool; its aspecificity means that it can be wielded in many different ways. It's just 'waiting to be unleashed'.[47] Once unleashed, it works very well to expose the constituents of power, and to empower unexpected constituencies.

At some point in *Mission Impossible 6*, the protagonist Ethan Hunt, played by Tom Cruise, is chasing a villain across London. His IT technician Benji follows his progress from a van, on a screen map with moving dots and a track route. He gives Hunt directions over the radio: 'You need to cross the street on your left as soon as you can'; 'Ethan, you're gaining on him, go straight!'; 'OK now turn right!' However, Benji is baffled when the hero starts running in circles, or when he hesitates before following simple indications: what *is* he doing? Hunt, it turns out, is running up the spiral staircase into the dome of St Paul's Cathedral, crossing streets by leaping from roof to roof, and taking the required turns by jumping out of windows. 'Oh, sorry, I had it in 2D,' says Benji.

The relationship between tracks and surveillance shows two main cracks. The first is that, as we have just seen, there are limits to what a track can say. Benji might be able to switch his geo-software to 3D, but he still won't see the faces of the office staff whose day has been interrupted by a maniac jumping out of windows. Tracks are simplifications of life. Power needs to make social phenomena 'legible' in order to monitor and direct them, but in doing so it loses bits of information.[48] This paradox comes inbuilt in any attempt to achieve overview and oversight. Lines, tracks and arrows sanitise life, but they can also sanitise death and displacement; the implications of this were discussed, for example, during Russia's 2022 attack on Ukraine, which prompted a profusion of illustrative maps in the media. How can we flatten the suffering of millions of refugees into an arrow, the same sign we use to represent invasion?[49] Where are bodies, values and emotions in conventional mapping?[50]

Here we go back to the distinction between immersive ancient itineraries and superficial modern maps. In the third quarter of the twentieth century, 'Situationist' thinkers described the aimless

wandering of a man lost in a city, perhaps under the effect of intox-
icants, as an act of freedom. They called this 'psychogeography',
or 'drifting' as one pleases in an apparently set and restrictive
urban environment. The Situationists themselves are somewhat
over-glorified: mostly men, they framed what they were doing
as resistance to rationalist architecture and to the objective map,
yet they practised drift with sexualised and predatory attitudes
towards the 'feminine' city, which they hoped to dominate and
possess at will.[51] In any case, this type of freedom, bypassing structures and impositions and 'making one's own path', also has much
broader and more positive potential. A person practising parkour,
the physical discipline that involves running, climbing and vaulting across urban architecture, is known as a *traceur* – someone
who traces a route. As philosopher Michel de Certeau puts it,
walking is a 'speech act', a form of personal, discerning expression.
In his view, the *graphical* representations of those living tracks are
nothing but a dead 'relic', 'procedures for forgetting' that 'only
refer [...] to the absence of what has passed by'.[52] The graphic track
is, admittedly, dead, by comparison with a person vaulting over
roofs, or drifting in a drunken haze, or marvelling at the Holy
Places in 333 AD. But here, perhaps, we can also slightly disagree
with de Certeau.

The second problem with tracks, indeed, is in some ways the
opposite of the first: they may not say everything, but they say
a lot. The track speaks. Denying that it does would be akin to
denying all the stories of empire, occupation and oppression that
we have encountered so far. Worse, it would mean detaching those
stories from the individuals who drew them. But if tracks can
speak, what are the implications? A tool that speaks is inherently
double-edged. It can give voice to those who have none, and frame
even the powerful, when they are out of line.

Technologies like the Global Positioning System, with some
important limitations, democratise geographical knowledge:
they allow anyone with an electronic device to make maps and re-
define space.[53] I would further say that it isn't just GPS that allows
that. The track does, and always did. Already in 1938, we saw, all a
refugee child needed to recount his story on the world's map was a

piece of paper and some coloured inks.[54] But modern technologies certainly enhance that power.

There is a whole branch of mapping today that is known as 'performative mapping', attempting to shift attention to the processes and gestures through which mapping is made: the idea is to try to bring in feeling and sensory experience, breaking beyond the traditional, codified forms of representation.[55] Here, suddenly, tracks can become very handy, because their key property is exactly the ability to capture the process of their creation. What if 'ordinary' people used the track to convey a message? Speaking with their feet, with their life and movement? Through digital mapping tools, the land, the water and the sky are a canvas available to many.

Some artists use pre-existing network route maps, rejigging them to convey alternative messages. The iconic London Underground diagram has been an especially popular target. In 2006, a website collecting unofficial reworkings of it received a takedown injunction, on the grounds of intellectual property infringement. They reacted by posting another Tube map. The names of the 'stations' spelled out the following message: 'in March 2006 Transport for London's lawyers suddenly took offence to tube maps designed in the style of the Great Bear by Turner Prize nominated artist Simon Patterson being hosted by world record holding tube enthusiast Geoff Marshall and used legal bullying to force their removal. We think the people responsible for this decision are'. The segments of routes, tastefully arranged, formed a big, colourful 'wankers'.[56] Like parrots, these 'transport' route lines may seem to be confined to repeating things, but in fact they are fiercely independent: they can speak in unintended (and at times impolite) ways.

These, of course, are still set networks, however reframed. But other forms of 'counter-mapping' are more directly related to personal experiences of movement. From 1968 to 1979, every single day, artist On Kawara marked his track on a fresh black and white photocopied map, in 'red ballpoint pen'; he stored these thousands of maps in binders – a sequence of his moving life, both more and less than a diary.[57] Over the last twenty years or so, another artist, Jeremy Wood, has completed a series of stunning projects using

GPS tracks. In one, titled *Meridians*, he wrote a quote from *Moby-Dick* over a broad stretch of London: 458.6 miles of travelled path spelling out, in thick capital letters, 'It is not down in any map; true places never are'. Each word fell onto a meaningfully chosen location: for example, 'NOT' straddled a park and a schoolyard, and 'DOWN' was walked in a cemetery.[58] Wood is a firm believer in the lively potential of the track, its 'rhythms and patterns', which are like 'seeing your own ghost': 'The speed of travel', he points out, 'can also be coloured to indicate the cold blues of slow dithering to red hot top speeds, and the altitude of tracks can add pressure and depth of line'.[59] These are still culturally defined conventions, but powerful insofar as they are understood.

Beyond individual artistic expressions, all this potential has been mustered by activists. Movement, feminist scholars have argued, *is* a form of identity. It's a 'signature'. As media researcher Lisa Parks observes, her 'GPS map of California would look quite different from that of a migrant worker, a Chinese pharmacist, a high-tech executive or a groaning seal for that matter.'[60] We can think again of the American hydrographer Maury, here, although he put it rather dismissively: 'a crazy fellow always makes a crooked track'.[61] A woman feeling unsafe, or self-doubting, an individual pressed by circumstances, a child or an elderly person all draw distinctive lines. Undocumented immigrants in European cities walk the streets every day, socially and legally invisible. In 2015, as part of an ethnographic project, some of them inscribed their digital paths through Amsterdam, colour-coded for emotion: their favourite places to go, their daily struggles to survive (Plate 24). These paths are very different from those of documented citizens. They show the forced, constant motion of people who can't work, lack money for shopping, can't spend the day in the overnight shelters where they sleep, and can't stay still without attracting unwanted attention. As they walked along, these immigrants recounted their lives and experiences, which were recorded as audio files. Through an app, anyone could follow their story – as a track line, but also as a trail of sound: if the user stepped off the route, the recording faded away. This is an example of 'surveillance art': of an alternative and defiant use of surveillance technologies by people whom the system forces into marginality, and who make the decision of 'not wanting to hide any longer'.[62] Visibility is dangerous, but it can also be a first step towards raising awareness, and challenging hierarchies of silence. The hodological marries the track, and the two, literally, speak.

At sea, too, the track has been adopted as a means to give new voices to indigenous cultures of navigation. For almost fifty years, for instance, the Polynesian Voyaging Society has sailed around the Pacific, using re-elaborated traditional navigation methods and the reconstructed canoe *Hōkūle'a* ('Star of Gladness', that is, Arcturus). In 2017, *Hōkūle'a* completed Mālama Honua ('to care for our Earth'), a worldwide voyage. In press releases, this voyage is depicted as a colourful track that wraps across the globe: a stark display of the knowledge and value of cultures that modernity would claim to have 'left behind', but which can, in fact, coexist and cooperate with it in a new harmony.[63] This programme, as the Society's website puts it, 'ultimately [...] is a story of survival, rediscovery, and the restoration of pride and dignity'.[64]

Of course, we must not be naive. Structural constraints remain: inequality of technological access and prejudice determine who gets believed, or whose tracks are deemed worth considering. There is also a more fundamental problem. Speaking in tracks, or speaking in modern maps, still requires a distortion of different worldviews, squeezed into overarching conformity with one model. It requires playing by at least some of the rules of the game.[65] None of this can disappear with the wave of a magic wand. But, even if from within the system, the potential to draw alternatives and challenges is there. Again, the track holds an important key. Because movement is often so fundamental to human life and knowledge, it offers a powerful bridge between people, cultures and 'incommensurable' worldviews: a bridge made of 'songs, stories and narratives' – however communicated.[66]

Tracks can be 'countertracks' in a second sense: not only can they be made by new, unintended users, but they can also be *read* by unintended users. If they have the power to give visibility to those who are deprived of it, what else do they make visible to a fresh eye? And now we come to the engine-propelled craft scarring the seas with foul tracks of oil, exhaust fuel and passenger faeces. People's relationship with the environment is perhaps the context in which the notion of 'footprint' is most used today.

The climate crisis is often framed as a 'global' problem: we are all in it together, and we all need to adopt emergency measures. And yet, as activists and intellectuals from the Global South point out, that is a profoundly unjust way of framing matters. It artfully skates over questions of 'environmental debt' – the decades and centuries of ecological damage caused by specific actors and countries.[67] In this light, tracks do act as individual signatures, but as individual signatures on a crippling loan.

This isn't just a fancy metaphor. Nowadays, tracks are used to point to environmental responsibilities in a specific way. The ethical double edge of surveillance is especially sharp here.

In 2022, 15,000 tons of oil were spilled into the oceans through shipping accidents.[68] But much of the oil that has ended up in the sea to date hasn't done so by accident. In 2020, the total yearly average stood at an estimate of around 457,000 tons.[69] Some captains discharge their dirty bilge or ballast water, deliberately offloading pollutants into the marine environment. Out at sea, oil leaves a *real* track: a so-called 'oil slick', often line-shaped (Figure 7.2). Oil flattens the waves with a smooth film that is detectable by various instruments – for example, satellite-controlled radar. This visible track is how offenders get caught. Within a few hours, the data may be available to law enforcement; particularly in conjunction with electronic Vessel Monitoring Systems – the descendants of logs and track charts – the 'rogue vessels' can be identified quite efficiently.[70] Vicinity to the site of a spill – that is, having been in the wrong place at the wrong time – makes a vessel a prime suspect. And its having been in the wrong place at the wrong time is established through the *virtual* track, recorded by its navigation logs. International conventions explicitly rule that, when oil spills are observed, the investigation of responsibilities should take into account 'the wind and sea conditions, the track and speed of the ship, other possible sources of visible traces in the vicinity, and any

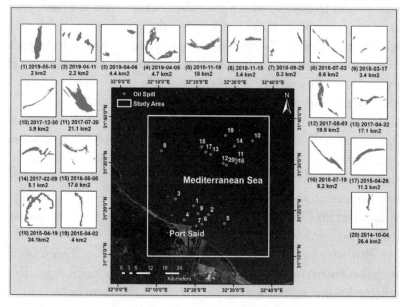

Figure 7.2: Shapes of radar-detected oil spills near the entrance of the Suez Canal in 2014–2019, as reported in a 2020 scientific article by Islam Abou El-Magd et al.

relevant oil discharge records'.[71] But there is more: the oily track has a unique 'fingerprint'. Through analysis of its chemical components, and comparison with samples drawn from the tanks of suspected offenders, forensic analysts can trace the oil itself to its source.[72] A track pins down the culprit precisely because it is permanent, virtually *and* physically, even a while after the ship has passed.

There are a few elements that complicate this picture. First, theory is always neater than practice. Particularly away from coastal waters, on the high seas, governmental enforcement powers are limited, and detection technologies can be, as well. Blanket surveillance and prosecution are often unrealistic, so authorities have experimented with alternatives – reducing the financial incentives of pollution, rather than punishing it after the fact. Intentional ('operational') pollution is usually committed as a way of avoiding the cost of port services, so a few states in the Baltic, by way of experiment, have supplied vessels with free or all-inclusive in-port tank cleaning and waste-disposal facilities. This 'No-Special-Fee' system doesn't seem to work fully, but the readiness to proffer such an expensive carrot speaks volumes as to the impracticality of tracking.[73] The fact that ships are leaving behind a foul track doesn't mean that someone will be there to pick up the scent. Still, it's important that the potential exists.

Second, who is tracking down and policing whom? Precisely because surveillance is costly and technology-intensive, might this just be a continuation of imperialism, with powerful states hunting down less well-equipped tankers from poorer countries, and punishing them through rules that were established, in practice, almost unilaterally? Here the postcolonial critique of environmentalism makes itself felt. The situation is certainly complex, and the ethical implications of automated surveillance troubling. However, we should note that national ownership is very muddled at sea. Companies from wealthy countries regularly register their vessels under 'flags of convenience' – that is, the flag of a foreign state where fiscal, labour and safety regulations are laxer. Indeed, many flags that are commonly used as flags of convenience (for instance, Panama or Malta) in the past have also fallen under the category of 'flag of non-compliance', meaning that they didn't comply with international technical requirements. Flag-of-non-compliance vessels, historically, have been key culprits at least of accidental oil spills (on which we have better data than for intentional ones).[74] Crews get drawn into these legal cases, but so do the owners – wherever they are based. Exactly who draws and who checks tracks at sea, and who holds whom accountable, isn't a straightforward matter.

In 2016, a junior engineer, working for one of the most powerful corporations in the cruise-line sector, discovered that his ship seemed to be covertly disposing of oily waste at sea. This spiralled into a high-profile court case that uncovered a great deal of abuse, and culminated in a record-breaking fine of $40 million.[75] Prosecutions across the sector aren't especially frequent, but have resulted in large fines and prison time for both shipboard officers and company executives ashore; the clinching evidence is often in the logbooks, which, even if tampered with, tell eloquent stories of *where* a vessel was when waste was disposed of.[76] Negative publicity is an extremely powerful tool, because, fines aside, it can affect customer uptake. Environmental activists, indeed, use interactive track websites to reveal the impact of the sector on marine ecosystems, and point the finger at specific offenders.[77] Regardless of who is using it, the track carries with itself all the limitations, practical and ethical, that we have discussed so far. However, it is quite good at keeping records – because that is what it was designed for. With all due caveats, the track *can* work in subversive ways.

There is one last point worth noting. The acts of using one's own track and assessing others' tracks can combine their radical potential at the point where we admit to shared responsibilities. The track can speak of our *own* positionality, impact, and even guilt. The Ocean Cleanup foundation, which works to combat the issue of plastic pollution at sea, grasps this idea perfectly. Its 'plastic tracker' website feature allows you to input your location, and generate a random model visualisation of where the plastic you throw away ends up. The bottle of sparkling water that sits on the desk by my laptop has a 'medium' chance of reaching the sea. Over the next twenty years, it will cross the same endangered Arctic habitats as cruise ships, before drawing a zigzagging blue course around the North Atlantic rim and bouncing, like Magellan's ships, off the Iberian coast, only to end its journey in the Caribbean 63,304 kilometres later.[78] If I 'try again from the same location', the track wanders around the Bay of Biscay until it's coloured it full, or it disappears into the Arctic. We have seen enough of tracks not to take this as 'truth', but it is certainly food for thought.

If only partially, then, each track can be matched by a countertrack. To the imperial tales of Magellan, Cook or Drake, we can oppose *Hōkūleʻa*, and the wide-ranging tracks of modern Polynesian voyagers; to military surveillance, the deliberate tracks drawn by practitioners of counter-surveillance and surveillance art; to the global statements of nineteenth-century steamliners, environmentalist mapping and anti-pollution legislation. Tracks and their power to shape reality have started to be reclaimed by previously silenced agents. Their genealogy, however, remains grounded in specific historical uses. Born of imperial arrogance, solidified through colonial technology, and manifested through environmental pollution: both precarious and violent, tracks embody many of the contradictions inherent to modern mobility. A route line on a map gave some humans the illusion that their small journeys left a significant track on Earth – and on the pathless sea.

CODA

'For Celsus saith that planks or piles laid in the sea are his who laid them, but that is not to be granted if the use of the sea by that means shall become worse.'

Grotius, *Mare Liberum*[1]

Ship tracks are a form of territorial occupation. This much was already clear to the Dutch jurist Hugo Grotius in the early seventeenth century. Where occupation impinges on pre-existing rights, or causes damage, it becomes pernicious. Pollution, much like colonialism, stems from a sense of 'entitlement'.[2] We can see the 'world as property', generic, flat, inanimate, or we can see it 'as lasting home', a place that we inhabit, a place that surrounds us in its specificity, rather than being encircled and marked by *our own* prepotent specificity.[3]

This is the bottom line. But the historian looks for change and cause, not for bottom lines. Different worldviews don't necessarily lead to 'bad' or 'good' actions; they merely influence individuals' choices and attitudes, amid a swarm of changing variables. In the process of telling a story like that of tracks, the apparent explanatory power of technology can easily tempt us astray. There is no clear trajectory from the *periploi* of the ancients to GPS devices. And yet, 'How did we get here?' is a pressing question. Patterns are dangerous, but we can spot some.

In every chapter of this book, the track seems powerful. However, there is always a catch. The blazing trails of Renaissance navigators were impressive, but ultimately groundless. Instrumental accuracy and precision, in the hands of trained Enlightenment hydrographers, gave the track enormous power, but also contained the seeds of its dissolution into an infinity of irreconcilable measurements. And the more realistic it became, the more did the track show exactly how the hydrographers themselves straggled, failed, and died. The Victorian customer enthralled by tales of global adventure enthusiastically bought into the clear 'truth' of the track, yet all they were buying was a pre-packaged simplification. Through the track that he left behind, the naval officer who was a surveyor seamlessly turned into a target of surveillance. The roaring steamer carved its track into the environment, yet in so doing it provided ready-made evidence of guilt, where it did have a real impact – and of vanity where it had none. Tracks signal colonial appropriation, but can in turn be re-appropriated to give a voice to the weak. The track marks the seas, in godlike fashion, but its shape always belies the proud little human, battered and contradictory.

Perhaps, then, we have been talking about mortality all along. Disappearing at sea, being lost without a trace, is the alternative, unspeakable fate that drives any modern plot – on the chart, and otherwise. The body claimed by the deep haunts Western nautical fiction as an omnipresent cliché. At the start of *Moby-Dick*, the sailor Ishmael visits a Whaleman's Chapel in New Bedford, Massachusetts, and is deeply affected by the plaques commemorating men lost at sea: 'the beings who have placelessly perished without a grave' leave their loved ones uniquely inconsolable.[4] Let's look at another of the earliest instances of a maritime novel, James Fenimore Cooper's *The Pilot* (1823). The American ship carrying the main characters has just fought a bloody engagement against three British vessels. The people killed in action are 'committed to the deep', in naval fashion, 'when the yards of the ship were again braced by the wind, and she glided along the track-less waste, leaving no memorial in the midst of the ever-rolling waters, to mark the place of their sepulture'.[5] Here it is again, the spectre of the Book of Wisdom, which has chased us through every chapter. Here it lurks at the very heart of modernity: the shadow of a doubt that tracks may just be, after all, shadows.

No historical account can ever turn a blind eye to mortality. Yet even mortality is too generic a concept. What we have been talking about in this book is a *specific* way of imagining life and death, a specific model of mortality that the track seeks, in vain, to exorcise. This is the model of the French navigator Bougainville, for whom the soldier, buried with all honours, has an easier fate than the discoverer unceremoniously swallowed by the oblivion of the seas. Schematisation, occupation and personal priority claims, the key uses that some Europeans found for the track, are all tools for ensuring one's persistence. Not even fearing death is universal, however: it's historically, culturally, and indeed personally contingent. Leaving a mark on the world is only one possible way of confronting existential problems. The fact that a ship glides across the waves without leaving traces needn't be lived as a waste, a tragedy, or a challenge. The historical processes we have discussed, perhaps, help us explore the particular contours of the modern Western conviction that it does.

'I loved you, so I drew these tides of men into my hands / and wrote my will across the sky in stars'. These are the powerful words with which Lawrence 'of Arabia', a stark emblem of brutal colonial delusions and of the modern self-tormented individuality, opened his memoir *Seven Pillars of Wisdom*.[6] In those lines, just as he spoke of inscribing the firmament, he was mourning the death of his lover. Lawrence and his modernly reframed Odysseus, with whom we began this book, are fitting characters with which to end it as well.

The maps of the *Odyssey* are, in many ways, the least 'accurate' or 'real' of all the maps we have encountered. Not only do they depict an imaginary line, but they depict a most likely imaginary voyage, on an imaginary sea. Still, in many other ways, Odysseus' track is one of the most realistic. It embeds the material and environmental realities of sea travel, the resistance that the 'will of the gods' poses to human pathways and technologies, better than the neat line on any Agnese atlas or cruise ship brochure. In a Victorian translation of the poem, Odysseus and his men recall 'the wanderings to and fro and the long-lost homeward track'.[7] Thinking about these wanderings, after they have subdued the witch Circe and settled in the haven of her palace, the traumatised heroes burst into tears. By now, we can readily see that the word 'track' is an anachronistic interpolation on the part of the English translator. The Greek original has the weary men simply recalling 'áles khalepês (ἄλης χαλεπῆς)', their 'harsh wanderings'.[8] This nineteenth-century flourish, then, speaks of a powerful cultural analogy: the harshness of life is a lost track. John Finley, the historian who wrote an Introduction to Lawrence's *Odyssey*, claimed that 'Homer mirrors above all man's relation to nature and to himself'.[9] In our modern, visually oriented culture, Odysseus' haphazard tracks on the pathless ocean serve this same purpose excellently. But if we approach the track as a mirror, the image we see in it, however schematic, can be startlingly honest. What was said of Lawrence in his day holds for imperial visions more generally: 'the dream and the business did not march together'.[10] Tying internal ideals and struggles to one's ability to master the world out there is a fraught and often intrinsically violent endeavour. Its results, accordingly, can be disconcerting. The tracks left behind are never as clean and sharp as their authors should like them. We might be tempted to confine this truth to the Mediterranean craft of 3,000 years ago, if we hadn't seen the track of the *Blackbraes* writhing around Cape Horn as the twentieth century was born, or the *Ever Given* rammed into the Suez by the wind. The resistance crumpling up the track doesn't just come from the sea, either: in each imperial ship's wake, suppressed voices gather.

The fact that they are conventional, delusional, conditioned shadows doesn't make our chaotic tracks any less real. People's trails in the oceans and across the land and skies have made themselves unerasable: we have crossed a climatic point of non-return. The traffic of tracks has indeed mowed down the sea monsters, choking them in shit, oil and plastic. Billions of us buzz across space leaving tracks, planning tracks, drawing and redrawing well-worn tangles of apparently free and personal movement – which is, in truth, largely guided and intimately channelled. We aspire to individuality by slotting into subtly and less subtly prescribed tracks, and in so doing we carve them deeper.

The ocean isn't, and never was, pathless: some Europeans just wiped it blank so that they could pretend to build their own stories on it. But something is worth bearing in mind: stories, even skinned to their bones, are powerful, double-edged, and can have unwieldy and unsavoury consequences. We should care about what stories we tell, why, and how.

ACKNOWLEDGEMENTS

Researching and writing this book was a wonderful and strenuous journey. To tell its story, I'll use the joyous task of thanking the unthankably numerous people who fuelled me along the way.

A book is, in its materiality, a collaborative project. My agent, Chris Wellbelove, Ed Lake and Andrew Franklin at Profile Books, and the Ideas Prize committee believed it into existence; Nick Humphrey, my editor, patiently and competently walked it to press; Jon Petre tolerated with astonishingly good cheer my chaotic, ever-shifting image permissions spreadsheet, as I pestered dozens of librarians and licence managers around the world; Linden Lawson copy-edited the manuscript with care; Anna Howarth expertly checked the quality of images; and Sarah Kennedy oversaw the book's production.

Intellectually, my debts are innumerable. Many are in the endnotes, of course, but others vastly overflow them.

Dániel Margócsy has been an extraordinary mentor. He replies almost instantly to any email, big and small, and his patient and wise guidance shepherded me through this whole process. He has taught me that crises are opportunities and that the apparently weirdest ideas always need to be given a chance, because they are where things get really interesting. He also read, chapter after chapter, the whole first draft – fresh off the oven, bloated, patchy and unevenly shaped – and offered invaluable suggestions to squeeze it into presentability.

Nick Guyatt is another of those senior colleagues whom high rank leaves completely untouched. He always has time for students and junior scholars, even if that involves last-minute reading of book proposals. His own work is ultimate proof of the fact that there are ways to talk to non-historians that don't betray the essence of what we do, and don't simply switch back to jargon past the book cover. Whether I have managed to tread this fine path is a different matter, but knowing it was there helped me to venture out in the first place. After I had done so, he read the whole manuscript so thoroughly and carefully that he knew how many times I had used the word 'sailer' in it. His suggestions were detailed, generous and important, and made for a much better text.

Renaud Morieux, who was my PhD supervisor, still finds time to read my work several years after being rid of me. As ever, his comments on a few chapters of this book made me think much more deeply about what I was writing, and hugely improved it. It's impossible to overstate the extent of his kind and wise guidance over the years. When my previous book was published, I wanted to give him a copy, and wrote a dedication in it: 'Thank you for everything you taught me. A tiny fraction of that is in here.' Then I realised that this might not come across quite as I meant it, as that book stemmed from my PhD thesis – so he received a fresh copy instead. But the point still stands, and I'll make sure I write in pencil this time.

Jake Dyble's near-daily WhatsApp audio bulletins, as he progressed from chapter to chapter, became real highlights for me. They were invariably replete with wisdom, expertise and wit. His subtle eye caught issues with pace and style as well as maritime historical points. He also saved me from accidentally implying that naval cadets 'grew thicker than ever' throughout the eighteenth century.

When I asked Christina Faraday whether she would read some of my manuscript, I said that if she had to choose between that and writing a speech for my wedding she should read the manuscript. In the end, she actually did both things. Her list of notes on Chapter 2 ran to several pages, and her advice was as clever as it was learned – which describes her perfectly.

I had given a copy of the first draft to Cath Holloway, to read if she felt like it. She returned it carefully annotated and accompanied by a wealth of good points and kind words. Katie Parker is the nicest and most knowledgeable historian of cartography in our generation, and I was extremely keen to hear her thoughts on the manuscript; she found the time to read it in a particularly busy year, and her encouragement was genuinely invaluable to me. Elke Papelitzky is the leading expert on East Asian tracks; she read the relevant sections of the manuscript with her usual keen and generous eye, helping me to get things right in an area where I am very much an outsider. Remaining mistakes are, naturally, my own. Gianamar Giovannetti-Singh read two chapters, one of which I sent him the day before my final deadline: within one hour and thirty-nine minutes he had returned it with truly useful comments, which must set some kind of record of kindness. Anna-Luna Post also gave me valuable feedback on two chapters, raising expert and perceptive points. Elisa Ercolin, with her profound expertise in classical archaeology, was the perfect person to read Chapter 1, which she kindly did. Craig Holloway, Teresa Birch and Ray Healy helpfully read and commented on the chapter from which it all began, and their enthusiasm made the difference. The entire Early Science and Medicine Work-in-Progress Group, at the Cambridge Department of History and Philosophy of Science, also read a chapter, and gave me substantial and important feedback over panini and iced tea. Audiences at various seminars and conferences and three sets of anonymous journal article reviewers offered precious comments and suggestions on the project as a whole.

Further insight, enthusiasm and support came from a very large number of people, friends, colleagues, scholars and administrators, at all stages of this work. I'm sure I must be forgetting someone (sorry), but here are a few of them, alphabetically: Sally Archer, Mary Brazelton, Pippa Carter, Lorenzo Ciardo, Marlon Crispatzu, Silvia De Renzi, Jordana Dym, Amy Erickson, Fernanda Gallo, Anna Groundwater, John Jarman, James Kirkham, Sebastian Kroupa, Bobby Lee, Emily Manson, Josh Nall, Annja Neumann, Nathan Procter, Olesya Razuvayevskaya, Sujit Sivasundaram, Christina Skott, Alexander van Dijke, Louis Volkmer, Vitali Vitaliev, Paul Webster, Alice Zanghi.

My time at the Deutsches Schifffahrtsmuseum in Bremerhaven, in autumn 2019, was crucial to the development of this project, and I remember colleagues there very fondly: Ruth

Schilling, Frederic Theis, Florian Tüchert, Helga Berendsen and the helpful library and conservation staff. Equally brilliant was the support I received during my connected visit to the archives of the Gotha Perthes Collection, where I was allowed to call up an outrageous number of folders over the space of a handful of days. For two and a half, rather dreamlike weeks – abruptly cut off by the first lockdown – the Huntington Library in San Marino, California, offered me a fantastic environment where my ideas could brew, and a large archive and library on maritime history. At the National Archives in Kew and Caird Library of the National Maritime Museum in Greenwich, archivists put up with all my map and chart requests and provided me with enormous table-kingdoms of my own, where I could spread them out at leisure. Staff at the British Library, and particularly Jeff Kattenhorn and Fiona McHenry, helped me with the most specific queries – like that time when, during lockdown I had to ask them whether one of their Agnese Atlases bore a specific inscription (they ordered it and sent me a reference photo), or that other time when I called up all their 1771 French copies of Bougainville's *Voyages* to try to find Cook's pencil annotation (I didn't). The staff at the Archivio di Stato di Alessandria made my day with courtesy and professionality, producing some of the most exciting tracks I've found. At the Archives Nationales in Paris, Service Historique de la Défense archives in Toulon, National Library of Scotland in Edinburgh and Biblioteca della Fondazione Federico Zeri at the University of Bologna, among other places, tiles came into place in ways that they couldn't have otherwise. Dozens of other collections I visited digitally, and they immensely enriched the project during the long pandemic months when we were all home-bound – and beyond. Only a small proportion of the total of material I saw made its way into this book, but the whole mattered.

The libraries of the University of Cambridge have been, as always, the most mind-boggling resource: as I raided the catalogue across periods and themes, and went down shadowy historiographical rabbit holes, there was hardly ever a book or an article that I couldn't instantly access, no matter the language or obscurity of topic. This is what academic privilege looks like, or probably privilege full stop. Click and Collect and Scan and Deliver were vital services during the various lockdowns, and the staff displayed their usual, utterly humbling efficiency. The University Library, Whipple Library, Seeley Library and Magdalene College Library certainly deserve individual thanks. Half of their collections are currently on my shelves: I promise that, as soon as I've checked the proofs, I will return *everything*. Catherine Sutherland at the Pepys Library of Magdalene College let me consult rare seventeenth-century tomes and archival materials even in the middle of the pandemic, as soon as rules permitted it, and provided impeccable and friendly assistance. Mark Hurn, of the Institute of Astronomy Library, kindly allowed me to come and have a look at the 1914 edition of the Admiralty's *Manual of Navigation*. The University Library Map Room and the Scott Polar Research Institute Library, with its ship bell announcing morning coffee, were unfailingly welcoming places. The staff at the Churchill Archives Centre deserve an award for their friendliness; it's not every day that someone patiently helps you ferry a brass plate all over the room to try to capture a reflection-free photo.

Behind nearly every image in this book is an email thread with helpful archivists, librarians and administrators all over the world: corresponding with each of them made the Sisyphean task of requesting image permissions as smooth as can be. Special thanks go to the Whipple Museum and Magdalene College, both institutions to which I am affiliated, for their courtesy in waiving permission fees.

Teaching, as always, pumps stagnant ideas into a flow, and it offered me crucial opportunities to road-test, read and reflect on some of the key topics in this book. I am grateful to my brilliant students and colleagues, for inspiring me each day. At Cambridge, various institutions sheltered and nurtured me while I wrote this book. The first mention must go to Magdalene College, which has been a warm home for over four years. It's a fantastic intellectual community, built on kindness and tolerance. Every time I go in for lunch I learn something interesting. Second is the Faculty of History, a sprawling powerhouse of ideas. After more than eight years, I'm still meeting new colleagues at each event, but the many dozens I know are lovely people. Lastly, but only in chronological order, in October 2022 I had the privilege of joining the Department of History and Philosophy of Science, which is an amazing creative environment, bubbling with ideas, projects and events. My continued work as an academic was made possible, in all these places, first by a Magdalene College Lumley Research Fellowship, and then, from 2022, by a British Academy Postdoctoral Research Fellowship (PF22\220060). I began to research ship tracks much earlier, when I was a Master's student at the University of Edinburgh, and later a PhD student at the wonderful Robinson College: so both places deserve a warm mention on this list, too.

The final paragraph must go to family. My parents and my sister have always been staunch supporters, and I owe them all I am. Very often, in their acknowledgements, colleagues mention how their non-academic spouses graciously put up with their work, yet wouldn't touch it with a bargepole. Cameron certainly tolerated, nourished and encouraged. He bore with mounting piles of books and notes, until there was no floorspace left in the house. But, he also read, re-read and commented; he absorbed a semi-constant, detailed, live commentary on my 'discoveries', insights, blunders and failures: for years now we have shared a desk, a deal that my oceans of paper and mugs win about 60:40. He said 'Don't blame me!', but this book is for him.

ILLUSTRATION CREDITS

Figure 0.1: Image by Dieter Martin from Pixabay https://pixabay.com/photos/flight-route-advertisement-plane-888686/; David Rumsey Historical Map Collection, 3404.063m, 'Chart of the Discoveries made in the South Atlantic Ocean, in His Majestys [*sic*] ship Resolution, under the Command of Captain Cook, in Jany. 1775', in James Cook, *A Voyage towards the South Pole, and Round the World ...*, 2 vols, 2nd edn (London: W. Strahan and T. Cadell, 1777), II, facing p. 210 https://www.davidrumsey.com/luna/servlet/detail/RUMSEY ~8~1~24116~870130

Figure 0.2: Library of Congress, Washington DC, Rare Book and Special Collections Division, Jay I. Kislak Collection & Hans and Hanni Kraus Sir Francis Drake Collection, G3934.S2 1589 .B6, Baptista Boazio, '[Map and views illustrating Sir Francis Drake's West Indian voyage, 1585–6]' (London?: s.n., 1589) http://hdl.loc.gov/loc.gmd/g3291sm.grb00002; Image 2 https://www.loc.gov/resource/g3291sm.grb00002/?sp=2

Figure 0.3: Rijksmuseum, Amsterdam, NG-800, New Hollstein Dutch 983, Willem Barendsz., 'Kaart van het Noordpoolgebied' (Amsterdam: Cornelis Claesz., 1598), public domain http://hdl.handle.net/10934/RM0001.COLLECT.303715

Figure 0.4: https://www.pxfuel.com/en/free-photo-xgoll

Figure 1.1: T. E. Shaw (Lawrence of Arabia), *The Odyssey of Homer: Newly Translated into English Prose* (New York: Oxford University Press, 1932, 9th popular impression, 1947), front endpaper

Figure 1.2: Sächsische Landesbibliothek – Staats- und Universitätsbibliothek Dresden (Deutsche Digitale Bibliothek), *Homers Odyssee von Iohann Heinrich Voss*, 3rd edn (Tübingen: J. G. Cotta, 1806), II, CC BY-SA 4.0 http://www.deutsche-digitale-bibliothek.de/item/AS43LYSWDQ2QBE7PFZPNTF7EDFBQMIHD

Figure 1.3: David Rumsey Historical Map Collection, 11713.068, 'Geografia Primitiva de Greci Secondo Esiodo ed Omero – Viaggi d'Ulisse e degli Argonauti', in F. C. Marmocchi, *Atlante di geografia universale ...* (Florence: V. Batelli e Compagni, 1842), Plate xxiv (B) https://www.davidrumsey.com/luna/servlet/detail/RUMSEY~8~1~304641~90075129:Geografia-Primitiva-de-Greci-Second?

Figure 1.4: mharrsch at https://flickr.com/photos/44124324682@N01/19212374832, CC BY 2.0 https://commons.wikimedia.org/wiki/

Figure 1.5: Giovanni Battista Piranesi, *Le antichità Romane, Opere di Giovanni Battista Piranesi, Francesco Piranesi e d'altri* (Paris: Firmin Didot Freres, 1835–9 [1756]), Vol. I, Plate IV. Scans from www.coe.l.u-tokyo.ac.jp, Wikimedia Commons, public domain https://commons.wikimedia.org/w/index.php?curid=8259688

Figure 1.6: Marco Ansaloni / Science Photo Library, C047/7365 https://www.sciencephoto.com/media/1066145/view/artemidorus-papyrus

Figure 1.7: Bibliothèque nationale de France, Paris (Gallica), Département Réserve des livres rares, SMITH LESOUEF R-198, Pierre Garcie dit Ferrande, *Le Grant routier et pilotage et enseignement pour ancrer tant es portz, havres que autres lieux de la mer* (Rouen: Jean Burges le Jeune, 1525), [p. 18v], public domain https://gallica.bnf.fr/ark:/12148/bpt6k316736z/f44.item.zoom#

Figure 2.1: Bibliothèque nationale de France, Paris (Gallica), GED-582, 'Globe terrestre / de Johannes Schöner, accompagnant l'ouvrage qui a pour titre: "De nuper sub Castiliae ac Portugaliae regibus sereniss, repertis insulis ac regionibus [...] epistola et globus geographicus Timiripae, 1523 ... "' (1529), public domain https://gallica.bnf.fr/ark:/12148/btv1b84394929/f1.item

Figure 2.2: Birmingham Public Library, G9236.P54 1748 .S43, Richard William Seale, 'A Chart of the Pacific Ocean from the Equinoctial to the Latitude of 39 ½ᵈ. No.', from George Anson, *A Voyage Round the World, in the Years MDCCXL, I, II, III, IV* (London: John and Paul Knapton, 1748) https://bplonline.contentdm.oclc.org/digital/collection/p15099coll3/id/1225

Figure 2.3: Library of Congress, Washington DC, Geography and Map Division, G3200 1529 .R5 1887 MLC, Diego Ribero, 'Carta universal en que se contiene todo lo que del mundo se ha descubierto fasta agora' (London: W. Griggs, [1887?]) http://hdl.loc.gov/loc.gmd/g3200.ct002450

Figure 2.4: Norman B. Leventhal Map & Education Center, 06_01_000091, Henri Abraham Chatelain, 'Carte tres [*sic*] curieuse de la Mer du Sud, contenant des remarques nouvelles et tres [*sic*] utiles non seulement sur les ports et iles de cette mer: mais aussy [*sic*] sur les principaux pays de l'Amerique [*sic*] tant Septentrionale que Meridionale [*sic*], avec les noms & la route des voyageurs par qui la decouverte [*sic*] en a été [*sic*] faite' (Amsterdam, [1719]), CC BY-NC-SA https://collections.leventhalmap.org/search/commonwealth:3f462t25d. Reproduction from the Mapping Boston Collection, imagery courtesy of the Norman B. Leventhal Map & Education Center at the Boston Public Library.

Figure 2.5: Library of Congress, Washington DC, Asian Division, E701.M32.1, 2004633695, 'Wu bei zhi / Mao Yuanyi zuan' http://hdl.loc.gov/loc.gmd/g7821rm.gct00058; Image 7 https://www.loc.gov/resource/g7821rm.gct00058/?sp=7

Figure 2.6: Library of Congress, Washington DC, World Digital Library (from Biblioteca Reale di Torino), 2021668747 ((WDL)19478), 'Portolan Atlas of Battista Agnese' ([1536–64]) https://hdl.loc.gov/loc.wdl/wdl.19478; Image 17 https://www.loc.gov/resource/gdcwdl.wdl_19478/?sp=17

Figure 2.7: Ludwig-Maximilians-Universität München, Cim. 18 (= 2° Cod. ms.

337a), Battista Agnese, 'Atlas Universalis' (1542–52), f. 17. Available at *Open Access LMU* https://epub.ub.uni-muenchen.de/10934

Figure 2.8: Library of Congress, Washington DC, World Digital Library (from Biblioteca Nacional De España – Biblioteca Digital Hispánica), 2021668456 ((WDL)07336), 'Atlas of Battista Agnese' (1544) https://hdl.loc.gov/loc.wdl/wdl.7336; Image 3 https://www.loc.gov/resource/gdcwdl.wdl_07336/?sp=3&st=image

Figure 2.9: Arquivo Nacional Torre do Tombo, Lisbon, PT/TT/EPJS/SF/001-001/0195/0272, Mapa das etapas da viagem do Argos http://digitarq.arquivos.pt/details?id=1206810

Figure 2.10: Sidney R. Knafel Map Collection, Phillips Academy, Andover, Mass. USA, n. 1355, Nicola van Sype, 'La heroike enterprinse faict par le Signeur Draeck d'avoir cirquit toute la terre' ([Antwerp]: [s.n.], [*c.*1583]) https://collections.leventhalmap.org/search/commonwealth:hq37vv605. Imagery courtesy of the Norman B. Leventhal Map & Education Center at the Boston Public Library, Digital Collections.

Figure 2.11: The National Archives, Kew, EXT 6/98, 'Formerly E 163/28/12. Map of northern waters. No scale shown. Compass rose. Indication of [?] latitude or longitude', *c.*1600.

Figure 2.12: Library of Congress, Washington DC, World Digital Library (National Library of Chile), 2021668424 ((WDL)03970), 'Description of the New Route to the South of the Strait of Magellan Discovered and Set in the Year 1616 by Dutchman Willem Schouten de Hoorn', from *Journal ou description du merveillevx voyage de Guillaume Schovten, hollandois natif de Hoorn, fait en années 1615, 1616 & 1617* (Amsterdam: Harman Lanfon, 1619), p. 88 https://hdl.loc.gov/loc.wdl/wdl.3970

Figure 2.13: Bibliothèque nationale de France, Paris (Gallica), Département Cartes et plans, CPL GE SH 18E PF 197 DIV 3 P 7 RES, Saillot, '[Carte française des Détroits de Banca et de la Sonde]' (seventeenth century), public domain https://gallica.bnf.fr/ark:/12148/btv1b5905717w/f1.item.r=SH%2018e%20pf%20197%20div%203%20p%207#

Figure 3.1: David Rumsey Historical Map Collection, 15401.002, Benjamin Donn, *The Ge-Organon or World Delineated; a Substitute for the Terrestrial Globe. Part. IId Invented by B. Donne* (1788) https://www.davidrumsey.com/luna/servlet/detail/RUMSEY~8~1~348419~90116275:The-Ge-Organon-or-World-Delineated-

Figure 3.2: Smithsonian Libraries and Archives via Biodiversity Heritage Library, [Louis-Antoine de Bougainville], *Voyage autour du monde, par la frégate du roi La Boudeuse, et la flûte L'Étoile; en 1766, 1767, 1768 & 1769* (Paris: Saillant & Nyon, 1771), opposite p. 185 https://www.biodiversitylibrary.org/page/41034521

Figure 3.3: David Rumsey Historical Map Collection, 4442014, 'Low Archipelago or Paumotu Group by the U.S. Ex. Ex. 1839', in Charles Wilkes, *Narrative of the United States Exploring Expedition During the Years 1838, 1839, 1840, 1841, 1842*, 5 vols and Atlas (Philadelphia: Lea & Blanchard, 1845), I, facing p. 307 https://www.davidrumsey.com/luna/servlet/detail/RUMSEY~8~1~32583~1151954

Figure 3.4: Library of Congress, Washington DC, Geography and Map Division,

G9230 1788 .C3 TIL, 'Carte de Grand Océan ou Mer du Sud' (1788) http://hdl. loc.gov/loc.gmd/g9230.ct000022

Figure 3.5: State Library of South Australia, M. Flinders, 'General Chart of Terra Australis or Australia: Showing the Parts Explored between 1798 and 1803' (facsimile ed., Bathurst: Central Mapping Authority of New South Wales, 1981) https://www.catalog.slsa.sa.gov.au/record=b1509035~S1

Figure 3.6: British Library, London, Rb.31.b.117, Constantine John Phipps, *A Voyage towards the North Pole undertaken by His Majesty's Command, 1773* (London: J. Nourse, 1774), front map. From the British Library archive.

Figure 3.7: William Robert Broughton, *A Voyage of Discovery to the North Pacific Ocean* (London: T. Cadell and W. Davies, 1804), p. 382. Courtesy of Canadiana https://www.canadiana.ca/view/oocihm.28207/463

Figure 4.1: Pepys Library, Magdalene College, Cambridge, PL 2636, Joseph Moxon, 'Sacred Geographie. Or Scriptural Mapps' (London: at the sign of the Atlas, [1671]), n. 5. By permission of the Pepys Library, Magdalene College, Cambridge.

Figure 4.2: © The Trustees of the British Museum. All rights reserved. British Museum, London, object no. 1882,0507.1, Michael Mercator, 'Medal' (1589) https://www.britishmuseum.org/collection/object/C_1882-0507-1

Figure 4.3: Bidgee, 'Captain Cook Memorial located on the banks of Lake Burley Griffin in Canberra, Australian Capital Territory' (8 January 2009), Wikimedia Commons, CC BY-SA 3.0 https://commons.wikimedia.org/wiki/File:Captain_Cook_Memorial.jpg

Figure 4.4: Beinecke Rare Book and Manuscript Library, Yale University, 1978 1351, Isaac Cruikshank, 'L, Latitude & Longitude', from *A Comic Alphabet, Designed, Etched & Published by George Cruikshank, No. 23 Myddelton Terrace, Pentonville* (1836) https://collections.library.yale.edu/catalog/16414889

Figure 4.5: Andrew McCormick Maps and Prints, Rare Books and Special Collections, University of British Columbia Library, G9235 1796 C37, *Carey's General Atlas, Improved And Enlarged; Being A Collection Of Maps Of The World And Quarters, Their Principal Empires, Kingdoms, &c.* (Philadelphia: M. Carey, c.1814) https://open.library.ubc.ca/collections/mccormick/items/1.0023193

Figure 4.6: David Rumsey Historical Map Collection, 11598.000, *Atlante novissimo, illustrato ed accresciuto sulle osservazioni, e scoperte fatte dai piu* [sic] *celebri e piu* [sic] *recenti geografi* (Venice: Antonio Zatta, 1778), Vol. III https://www. davidrumsey.com/luna/servlet/detail/RUMSEY~8~1~295495~90066638

Figure 4.7: National Archives of Japan Digital Archive, 186-0759, 'Keiyasu Takahashi, *Xīn dìng wànguó quán tú* ('New Revised Universal Map')', CC0 https://www.digital.archives.go.jp/file/1795284.html

Figure 4.8: Andrew McCormick Maps and Prints, Rare Books and Special Collections, University of British Columbia Library, G9235 1796 C37 https:// open.library.ubc.ca/collections/mccormick/items/1.0023193; National Archives of Japan Digital Archive, 186-0759, CC0 https://www.digital.archives.go.jp/ file/1795284.html

Figure 4.9: Archives Nationales, Paris, MAR/5JJ/102/A, Voyages de circumnavigation et de découvertes: Voyage de Dumont d'Urville sur l'"Astrolabe" – Vues des côtes et dessins à la mine de plomb [par Louis-Auguste de Sainson, dessinateur sur l'Astrolabe], f. 9 https://www.siv.archives-nationales. culture.gouv.fr/siv/media/FRAN_IR_054071/c-3xnaconq9-7z1d955vkek4/ FRAN_0044_02425_L

Figure 4.10: University of North Texas Libraries, UNT Digital Library, 917 L986, Charles Lyell, *Travels in North America, in the Years 1841–2; with Geological Observations on the United States, Canada, and Nova Scotia* (New York: Wiley and Putnam, 1845) https://digital.library.unt.edu/ark:/67531/metadc29428

Figure 4.11: The National Archives, Kew, MPII 1/18/4, 'Track chart of HM Sledge Hero, of HMS Resolute, on its outward and return routes from Dealy Island to Cape DeBray while engaged in searching for the Franklin Expedition' ([1852]).

Figure 4.12: Map: Chart showing the vicinity of King William Island [cartographic material] with the various positions in which relics of the Arctic expedition under Sir John Franklin have been found / compiled by Lieut.-Commdr. R. T. Gould, R.N. Source: Library and Archives Canada/Admiralty fonds/ e010761879 https://recherche-collection-search.bac-lac.gc.ca/eng/home/ record?app=fonandcol&IdNumber=3674742

Figure 4.13: Unknown author, from the *Illustrated London News* (7 June 1851), Wikimedia Commons, public domain https://commons.wikimedia.org/w/ index.php?curid=10666732

Figure 5.1: Churchill Archives Centre, Cambridge, MRDN 1/1, The Papers of Captain Charles Marsden, 'Track chart showing the positions of HMS Southampton at the Battle of Jutland, 1916-05-31'.

Figure 5.2: Churchill Archives Centre, Cambridge, MRDN 1/4, The Papers of Captain Charles Marsden, 'Brass plate from the charthouse of HMS Southampton, 1916'.

Figure 5.3: David Rumsey Historical Map Collection, 13404.004, William Heather, *The New Mediterranean Harbour Pilot* (London: J. W. Norie, 1814) https:// www.davidrumsey.com/luna/servlet/s/4xe565

Figure 5.4: The National Archives, Kew, MPG 1/569, 'Chart of the track of the ship HMS Glory between 10 December 1795 and 26 January 1796 off the coasts of France and Spain'.

Figure 5.5: The National Archives, Kew, MPI 1/652/2, 'Italy: Ligurian Sea. Track chart of HMS Cruiser 7–9 October [1867]'.

Figure 5.6: The National Archives, Kew, MFQ 1/632/6, 'Sketch showing the position of a rock at Port Simpson (now Lax Kw'alaams), British Columbia (now in Canada) on which HMS Sparrowhawk struck on May 16 1866, with Port Simpson, Finlayson Island and the track of the ship'.

Figure 5.7: The National Archives, Kew, MPI 1/689 (2), 'Track Chart of HMS "Exe" during search for survivors of HMS "Veteran" from 29th September to 2nd October 1942'.

Figure 6.1: British Library, London, Cartographic Items Maps C.44.d.58, 'Wyld's outline chart from England to Australia & China for the purpose of pricking off a ships track' ([*c*.1880]). From the British Library archive.

Figure 6.2: Imágenes procedentes de los fondos de la Biblioteca Nacional de España.

Biblioteca Nacional de España, Madrid, RES/237, 'Recueil et pourtraict d'aulcunes villes maritimes et plus memorables ports et leurs advenves et marcques servantes a la navigation en la mer oceane [Manuscrito]', 1586, f. 34, available at Biblioteca Digital Hispánica, CC BY http://bdh-rd.bne.es/viewer. vm?id=0000135241&page=34

Figure 6.3: Photograph by Sara Caputo.

Figure 6.4: Princeton University Library, Map Division, 'Steamship Routes of the World Issued by American Express Co.' (*c*.1900) https://commons.princeton. edu/mg/steamship-routes-of-the-world-circa-1900

Figure 6.5: European Union, contains modified Copernicus Sentinel data 2024.

Figure 6.6: Unknown author, 'The Eastern Telegraph Co.: System and its general connections' (1901), Wikimedia Commons, public domain https://commons. wikimedia.org/wiki/File:1901_Eastern_Telegraph_cables.png

Figure 6.7: 'The Indo-European Telegraph: Landing the Cable in the Mud at Fāo, Persian Gulf'. From Charles Bright, *Submarine Telegraphs: Their History, Construction, and Working* (London: Crosby Lockwood and Son, 1898), p. 73. Courtesy of Canadiana https://www.canadiana.ca/view/oocihm.00867/142

Figure 7.1: Library of Congress, Washington DC, Geography and Map Division, G9461.P5 1920 .M2, '[Marshall Islands stick chart, Mattang type]' ([Majuro, Marshall Islands, 1920s?]) http://hdl.loc.gov/loc.gmd/g9461p.ct003133

Figure 7.2: Islam Abou El-Magd, Mohamed Zakzouk, Abdulaziz M. Abdulaziz and Elham M. Ali, 'The Potentiality of Operational Mapping of Oil Pollution in the Mediterranean Sea near the Entrance of the Suez Canal Using Sentinel-1 SAR Data', *Remote Sensing* 12:8 (2020), 1352, p. 9, 'Figure 7. Oil spill accidents within the period 2014–2019', CC BY (https://creativecommons.org/licenses/ by/4.0/) https://mdpi-res.com/remotesensing/remotesensing-12-01352/ article_deploy/remotesensing-12-01352-v2.pdf?version=1587893312

Plate 1: 'Signs of Ships in the Clouds', *NASA Earth Observatory* (16 January 2018) (NASA image by Jeff Schmaltz, LANCE/EOSDIS Rapid Response) https:// earthobservatory.nasa.gov/images/91608/signs-of-ships-in-the-clouds

Plate 2: Zyzzy, 'Fragments of Turin Papyrus', photograph at the Turin Museum courtesy of J. Harrell, Wikimedia Commons, public domain https://commons. wikimedia.org/w/index.php?curid=359165

Plate 3: Tabula Peutingeriana, first to fourth century CE, facsimile edition by Konrad Miller, 1887/1888, Ulrich Harsch Bibliotheca Augustana, Wikimedia Commons, public domain https://upload.wikimedia.org/wikipedia/ commons/5/50/TabulaPeutingeriana.jpg

Plate 4: Bibliothèque nationale de France, Paris (Gallica), Département des manuscrits, Supplément grec 1354 (2) V, 'Fragments de parchemin trouvés à Sâlihiyed (anc. Doura-Europos)', public domain https://gallica.bnf.fr/ ark:/12148/btv1b105388698#

Plate 5: Unknown author, 'The Gough Map', Wikimedia Commons, public domain https://commons.wikimedia.org/w/index.php?curid=3499458

Plate 6: Unknown author, 'Hereford Mappa Mundi', Wikimedia Commons, public domain https://commons.wikimedia.org/wiki/File:Hereford-Karte.jpg

Plate 7: British Library, London, Royal MS 14 C VII, ff. 4r–5r, 'Matthew Paris's Itinerary Maps from London to Palestine', public domain https://www.bl.uk/collection-items/matthew-paris-itinerary-map. From the British Library archive.

Plate 8: Huntington Library, San Marino, CA, mssHM 1549, Portolan chart by Luís Teixeira ([1590–1610]) https://hdl.huntington.org/digital/collection/p15150coll7/id/48058/rec/5

Plate 9: Ludwig-Maximilians-Universität München, Cim. 18 (= 2° Cod. ms. 337a), Battista Agnese, 'Atlas Universalis' (1542–52), f. 17. Available at *Open Access LMU* https://epub.ub.uni-muenchen.de/10934/

Plate 10: Benson Latin American Collection, LLILAS Benson Latin American Studies and Collections, the University of Texas at Austin, Joaquín García Icazbalceta Manuscript Collection, Relaciones Geográficas of Mexico and Guatemala, JGI XXV-12, 'Pintura de Tetlistaca' (1580), public domain https://collections.lib.utexas.edu/catalogutblac:6f42ff06-ff73-4471-9454-d3a264276d67

Plate 11: Yale Center for British Art, Paul Mellon Collection, Rare Books and Manuscripts, Folio C 2009 2, Baptista Boazio (?), 'Vera descriptio expeditionis nauticae Francisci Draci Angli, equitis aurati' (*c*.1587), public domain https://collections.britishart.yale.edu/catalog/orbis:9579023

Plate 12: Pepys Library, Magdalene College, Cambridge, PL 2542, John Wood, 'A Draught of the Ice between Greenland and Nova Zembla' (*c*.1676). By permission of the Pepys Library, Magdalene College.

Plate 13: Nicolas-André Monsiau, *Louis XVI donnant des instructions à La Pérouse, 29 juin 1785*, Wikimedia Commons, public domain https://commons.wikimedia.org/wiki/File:Louis_XVI_et_La_P%C3%A9rouse.jpg?uselang=fr

Plate 14: Library of Congress, Washington DC, Rare Book and Special Collections Division, Jay I. Kislak Collection & Hans and Hanni Kraus Sir Francis Drake Collection, G3934.S2 1589 .B6, Baptista Boazio, '[Map and views illustrating Sir Francis Drake's West Indian voyage, 1585–6]' ([London?: s.n., 1589]) http://hdl.loc.gov/loc.gmd/g3291sm.grb00002; Image 2 https://www.loc.gov/resource/g3291sm.grb00002/?sp=2

Plate 15: Whipple Museum of the History of Science, University of Cambridge, Wh.2691, '14-inch terrestrial globe by Robert Morden, William Berry and Philip Lea, London, 1690' https://collections.whipplemuseum.cam.ac.uk/objects/12045

Plate 16: State Library of South Australia, 912 C332 d, 'Cary's Pocket Globe: Agreeable to the Latest Discoveries' (London: J. & W. Cary, *c*.1791) https://digital.collections.slsa.sa.gov.au/nodes/view/2618#idx18787

Plate 17: The National Archives, Kew, ADM 199/2061, Admiralty: War History Cases and Papers, Second World War – Monthly Anti-Submarine Reports Vol. 5, 1944, *Monthly Anti-Submarine Report – March 1944* (Anti-U-Boat Division of the Naval Staff, 15 April 1944), Plate 6, f. 77.

Plate 18: From the American Geographical Society Library, University of Wisconsin-Milwaukee Libraries. (AGS) (RARE) 700 A-Var Maury Charts (am003564), 'Maury's Wind & Current Chart, 3d. edition 1852, no. 2, series A' https://collections.lib.uwm.edu/digital/collection/agdm/id/1717

Plate 19: The National Library of Israel, Eg 90, אוסף המפות ע"ש ערן לאור, 'Carte de l'isthme de Suez', in S. Berteaut and J. Roux, *Rapport sur l'entreprise du Percement de l'isthme de Suez adressé a* [sic] *la chambre de commerce de Marseille* (Marseille: Imprimerie et lithographe de Jules Barile, 1865) https://www.nli.org.il/en/maps/NNL_ALEPH990033734430205171//NLI#$FL155340111

Plate 20: David Rumsey Historical Map Collection, 12050.057, 'Carte de la Navigation à Vapeur dans le Bassin de la Méditerranée', in *Atlas de choix, ou Recueil des meilleures cartes de géographie ancienne et moderne dressées par divers auteurs* (Paris: Chez J. Andriveau-Goujon, 1854), p. 48 https://www.davidrumsey.com/luna/servlet/detail/RUMSEY~8~1~284521~90057063

Plate 21: David Rumsey Historical Map Collection, 11146.001, Kenneth W. Thompson, 'On the Routes of the Flying Clipper Ships' (New York: Pan American Airways Corporation, 1941) https://www.davidrumsey.com/luna/servlet/detail/RUMSEY~8~1~289765~90061373:On-the-routes-of-the-flying-clipper

Plate 22: Library of Congress, Washington DC, Prints and Photographs Division, AP101.P7 1906 (Case X) [P&P], J. S. Pughe, 'Opening of the Panama Canal', *Puck* 59:1509 (New York: J. Ottmann Lith. Co., 31 January 1906), centrefold https://www.loc.gov/pictures/item/2011645812

Plate 23: European Union, contains modified Copernicus Sentinel data 2024.

Plate 24: Naomi Bueno de Mesquita and David Hamers, 'Mapping Invisibility', in *Proceedings of the 3rd Biennial Research Through Design Conference, 22–24 March 2017, Edinburgh, UK*, Article 27 (2017), 423–37, at 429 (Figure 2), CC BY 4.0 https://figshare.com/articles/journal_contribution/Mapping_Invisibility/4747015

NOTES

1   Translation from the King James Version, via *King James Bible Online* https://
www.kingjamesbibleonline.org/Wisdom-of-Solomon-Chapter-5.

2   Earlier drafts of some sections of this book have appeared in two academic
articles, authored by myself; I have substantially rewritten, expanded and
reorganised the contents for a broader audience. See: Sara Caputo, 'Human
Tales on the Pathless Sea?: Imperial Subjectivities and Exploration Ship Tracks
in European Maritime Mapping, c.1500–c.1800', *The English Historical Review*;
Sara Caputo, 'From Surveying to Surveillance: Maritime Cartography and Naval
(Self-)Tracking in the Long Nineteenth Century', *Past and Present* (ahead-of-
print 2024). This book was also discussed in an article recently published in a
journal forum: Sara Caputo, 'Trailblazers' Wakes: Ship Tracks in Western
Imperial Mapping', *Imago Mundi* 75:2 (2023), 288–93.

3   In a book that questions the origin and power of priority claims, I make none:
other scholars have researched 'journey lines' before me (independently using
the same term), and many others, I hope, will do so in future. Just as I was
finishing this manuscript, I became aware of Jordana Dym's excellent *Mapping
Travel: The Origins and Conventions of Western Journey Maps* (Leiden: Brill,
2021). Her book approaches the topic from a different angle: she is a historian of
cartography and travel, whereas I am a historian of empire and maritime spaces;
the stories we tell seem to me beautifully complementary yet distinct.

4   For this distinction, see also Elke Papelitzky, 'Red Lines in the Ocean: Sea
Routes on Early Modern East Asian Maps', unpublished paper from the
workshop *Mapping Practices and Transpacific Transfers of Geographic Knowledge,
Sixteenth to Early Nineteenth Centuries*, 19–20 May 2022. For an alternative
taxonomy of itinerary mapping, not distinguishing between set itineraries and
personal journeys, but between 'exploration-based, commemorative, and
proposals for possible routes', see Quentin Morcrette, 'L'espace récité de la carte
d'itinéraire: exemples français et américains',
M@ppemonde 118 (2016) http://mappemonde.mgm.fr/118as5. Among
wayfinding maps, one can also distinguish between single 'itinerary' and
'network' maps: James R. Akerman, 'Finding Our Way', in James R. Akerman
and Robert W. Karrow Jr. (eds), *Maps: Finding Our Place in the World* (Chicago
IL and London: University of Chicago Press, 2007), 19–63, at 39–47.

5   Not coincidentally, we'll see how the only exceptional track pre-dating those on
water crossed an equally 'pathless' desert, the biblical Wilderness. The
comparison between seas and deserts has been made very often for the
Mediterranean and the Sahara, e.g.: David Abulafia, 'Mediterraneans', in W. V.

Harris (ed.), *Rethinking the Mediterranean* (Oxford: Oxford University Press, 2005), 64–93; Achim Lichtenberger, '"Sea without Water": Conceptualizing the Sahara and the Mediterranean', in Mihran Dabag et al. (eds), *New Horizons: Mediterranean Research in the 21st Century* (Paderborn: Ferdinand Schöningh, 2016), 267–83; Peregrine Horden and Nicholas Purcell, 'Situations Both Alike?: Connectivity, the Mediterranean, the Sahara', in Peregrine Horden and Nicholas Purcell, *The Boundless Sea: Writing Mediterranean History* (Abingdon and New York: Routledge, 2020), 191–205 (stressing elements of difference more than comparison). On the representational problems raised by the Arctic for European visitors see also Christopher P. Heuer, *Into the White: The Renaissance Arctic and the End of the Image* (New York: Zone Books, 2019).

6   Margaret Cohen, *The Novel and the Sea* (Princeton NJ: Princeton University Press, 2010).

7   These three concepts are quite key to Cohen's theory of the novel.

8   Kapil Raj, *Relocating Modern Science: Circulation and the Construction of Knowledge in South Asia and Europe, 1650–1900* (Basingstoke and New York: Palgrave Macmillan, 2007), 60–94; Kapil Raj, 'Networks of Knowledge, or Spaces of Circulation? The Birth of British Cartography in Colonial South Asia in the Late Eighteenth Century', *Global Intellectual History* 2:1 (2017), 49–66; Bronwen Douglas, 'Naming Places: Voyagers, Toponyms, and Local Presence in the Fifth Part of the World, 1500–1700', *Journal of Historical Geography* 45 (2014), 12–24; Sujit Sivasundaram, *Waves across the South: A New History of Revolution and Empire* (London and Dublin: William Collins, 2020), 255–9, 264; Joy Slappnig, 'The Indigenous Map: Native Information, Ethnographic Object, Artefact of Encounter' (unpublished PhD thesis, Royal Holloway, University of London, 2021) https://pure.royalholloway.ac.uk/en/publications/the-indigenous-map-native-information-ethnographic-object-artefac.

9   Bruno Latour, 'Drawing Things Together', in Michael Lynch and Steve Woolgar (eds), *Representation in Scientific Practice* (Cambridge MA and London: MIT Press, 1988), 19–68, quote at 21.

10 Latour, 'Drawing Things Together', 26. See also the definitions of 'epistemic image' in Alexander Marr, 'Knowing Images', *Renaissance Quarterly* 69:3 (2016), 1000–13, at 1005–8, and 'working object' in Lorraine Daston and Peter Galison, *Objectivity* (Brooklyn NY: Zone Books, 2007), 19–22 and Lorraine Daston and Peter Galison, 'The Image of Objectivity', *Representations* 40:40 (1992), 81–128, at 85–6. I am very grateful to Dr Christina Faraday for suggesting Marr's piece to me. For an example of application of these notions to the history of cartography see e.g. David Turnbull, 'Cartography and Science in Early Modern Europe: Mapping the Construction of Knowledge Spaces', *Imago Mundi* 48 (1996), 5–24.

11 They serve as tools of 'virtual witnessing', to use Steven Shapin and Simon Schaffer's term. As they point out, even far more detailed and 'prolix' forms of virtual witnessing fail at conveying exactly lifelike meaning. But the point here isn't exact conveyance, as much as *credible* conveyance: Steven Shapin and Simon Schaffer, *Leviathan and the Air-Pump: Hobbes, Boyle, and the Experimental Life*, new edn (Princeton NJ and Oxford: Princeton University

Press, 2011), 60–65, 262. On the pedagogical use of diagrams, and, crucially, the *process* of making them, as simple means to convey information, see also, e.g., Renée Raphael, 'Teaching through Diagrams: Galileo's *Dialogo* and *Discorsi* and His Pisan Readers', in Nicholas Jardine and Isla Fay (eds), *Observing the World through Images: Diagrams and Figures in the Early-Modern Arts and Sciences* (Leiden and Boston MA: Brill, 2014), 201–30.

12 James C. Scott, *Seeing Like a State: How Certain Schemes to Improve the Human Condition Have Failed* (New Haven CT and London: Yale University Press, 1998); Denis Wood, *Rethinking the Power of Maps* (New York: Guilford Press, 2010).

13 Richard Sorrenson, 'The Ship as a Scientific Instrument in the Eighteenth Century', *Osiris* 11 (1996), 221–36.

14 *Wisdom of Solomon*, 5:10. Translation from the King James Version, via *King James Bible Online* https://www.kingjamesbibleonline.org/ Wisdom-of-Solomon-5-10.

15 For a brilliant elucidation of the shape of water, see Tristan Gooley, *How to Read Water: Clues & Patterns from Puddles to the Sea* (London: Sceptre, 2016).

16 David H. Lewis, 'Ara Moana: Stars of the Sea Road', *The Journal of Navigation* 17:3 (1964), 278–88, at 282.

17 On this subdivision see Fernand Braudel, *The Mediterranean and the Mediterranean World in the Age of Philip II*, 2 vols, 2nd edn, trans. Siân Reynolds (London: Collins, 1972–3).

18 Tricia Cusack, 'Looking over the Ship Railings: The Colonial Voyage and the Empty Ocean in Empire Marketing Board Posters', in Courtney J. Campbell, Allegra Giovine and Jennifer Keating (eds), *Empty Spaces: Perspectives on Emptiness in Modern History* (London: University of London Press, 2019), 87–110. On notions of emptiness and empire see also, more generally, Siobhan Carroll, *An Empire of Air and Water: Uncolonizable Space in the British Imagination, 1750–1850* (Philadelphia PA: University of Pennsylvania Press, 2015) (Ch. 2 on the sea).

19 Paul J. Crutzen, 'Geology of Mankind', *Nature* 415 (2002), 23. While this book was in press, the international Subcommission on Quaternary Stratigraphy ruled against granting the Anthropocene the status of an official 'epoch'. The decision has been challenged.

20 John H. Conover, 'Anomalous Cloud Lines', *Journal of Atmospheric Sciences* 23:6 (1966), 778–85; Philip A. Durkee, Kevin J. Noone and Robert T. Bluth, 'The Monterey Area Ship Track Experiment', *Journal of Atmospheric Sciences* 57:16 (2000), 2523–41; Edward Gryspeerdt et al., 'The Impact of Ship Emission Controls Recorded by Cloud Properties', *Geophysical Research Letters* 46 (2019), 12,547–55; Veronika Eyring et al., 'Transport Impacts on Atmosphere and Climate: Shipping', *Atmospheric Environment* 44:37 (2010), 4735–71, esp. at 4736 (for the statistics on global sulphur oxide emissions), 4754–5 (on ship tracks). Engines emit SO_2, which then oxidates to H_2SO_4. More images are viewable at 'Ship Tracks off the Kamchatka Peninsula', *NASA Earth Observatory* (27 July 2015) (NASA image courtesy of LANCE/EOSDIS Rapid Response) https://earthobservatory.nasa.gov/images/86499/

ship-tracks-off-the-kamchatka-peninsula; 'Ship Tracks over the Atlantic', *NASA Earth Observatory* (11 May 2005) (NASA image courtesy of Liam Gumley, Space Science and Engineering Center, University of Wisconsin-Madison) https://earthobservatory.nasa.gov/images/5488/ship-tracks-over-the-atlantic. These ship tracks are the superficial manifestation of profound (and as yet poorly understood) environmental mechanisms, triggered by some humans and now grafted deep into the planet's skin. Even their sudden reduction, at this point, may be the dying coal-mine canary heralding a climatic planetary shock: international regulations have recently clamped down on sulphur emissions, but sulphate particles in the atmosphere reflect the sun away from Earth, and potentially have a cooling effect. See: Leon Simons, James E. Hansen and Yann duFournet, 'Climate Impact of Decreasing Atmospheric Sulphate Aerosols and the Risk of a Termination Shock', *Annual Aerosol Science Conference 2021* (November 2021) http://dx.doi.org/10.13140/RG.2.2.22778.62408; Haakon Lindstad et al., 'Maritime Shipping and Emissions: A Three-Layered, Damage-Based Approach', *Ocean Engineering* 110 (2015), 94–101. There is a considerable amount of debate on this point, and various models and datasets don't always agree with each other. 'Ship tracks' specifically, some scholars have argued, have a 'negligible' cooling effect (as opposed to sulphate aerosols more generally): Mathias Schreier et al., 'Global Ship Track Distribution and Radiative Forcing from 1 Year of AATSR Data', *Geophysical Research Letters* 34:17 (2007), L17814; Eyring et al., 'Transport Impacts', 4755–9, 4766. Other studies are even more conservative, questioning the role of aerosols altogether: Franziska Glassmeier et al., 'Aerosol-Cloud-Climate Cooling Overestimated by Ship-Track Data', *Science* 371:6528 (2021), 485–9; Velle Toll, Matthew Christensen, Santiago Gassó and Nicolas Bellouin, 'Volcano and Ship Tracks Indicate Excessive Aerosol-Induced Cloud Water Increases in a Climate Model', *Geophysical Research Letters* 44:24 (2017), 12,492–500. For a positive assessment of ship tracks' role, on the other hand, see Michael S. Diamond et al., 'Substantial Cloud Brightening from Shipping in Subtropical Low Clouds', *AGU Advances* 1:1 (2020), 1–28. More decisive conclusions may be possible soon, as a few years of data become available to assess whether the 2020 sulphur regulations had a significant impact on global cooling processes (Diamond et al. 'Substantial Cloud Brightening', 15).

21 Jesse Oak Taylor, 'Globalize', in Jeffrey Jerome Cohen and Lowell Duckert (eds), *Veer Ecology: A Companion for Environmental Thinking* (Minneapolis and London: University of Minnesota Press, 2017), 30–43, at 35–6. For more on this new global vision see Chapter 2.

22 See e.g.: Michael Simpson, 'The Anthropocene as Colonial Discourse', *Environment and Planning. D, Society & Space* 38:1 (2020), 53–71; Kyle Whyte, 'Indigenous Climate Change Studies: Indigenizing Futures, Decolonizing the Anthropocene', *English Language Notes* 55:1–2 (2017), 153–62; William Cronon, 'Modes of Prophecy and Production: Placing Nature in History', *Journal of American History* 76:4 (1990), 1122–31, at 1128–9; Gabrielle Hecht, 'The African Anthropocene', *Aeon* (6 February 2018) https://aeon.co/essays/if-we-talk-about-hurting-our-planet-who-exactly-is-the-we; Andreas Malm and Alf Hornborg,

'The Geology of Mankind? A Critique of the Anthropocene Narrative', *The Anthropocene Review* 1:1 (2014), 62–9.

23 Tim Ingold, *Lines: A Brief History*, 2nd edn (London and New York: Routledge, 2016).

24 For a sociological analysis of the wide range of ways in which maritime spaces can be constructed see Philip Steinberg, *The Social Construction of the Ocean* (Cambridge: Cambridge University Press, 2001). Some scholars have devised a concept that is quite useful here – what they term 'modernity/coloniality': Walter D. Mignolo and Catherine E. Walsh, *On Decoloniality: Concepts, Analytics, Praxis* (Durham NC: Duke University Press, 2018), esp. 139–40, 150–51. On the situatedness of apparently 'universal' science see also Steven Shapin, 'Placing the View from Nowhere: Historical and Sociological Problems in the Location of Science', *Transactions of the Institute of British Geographers* 23:1 (1998), 5–12.

25 Wood, *Rethinking the Power of Maps*.

26 In this, the track is efficient, but not alone: maps have a long and varied history of representing temporal phenomena. See: Kären Wigen and Caroline Winterer (eds), *Time in Maps: From the Age of Discovery to Our Digital Era* (Chicago IL and London: University of Chicago Press, 2020); D. Dransch, 'Dynamic Mapping in Geography', in Neil J. Smelser and Paul B. Baltes (eds), *International Encyclopedia of the Social & Behavioral Sciences*, online edn (Saint Louis MO: Elsevier, 2001), 3908–11; Mark Monmonier, 'Strategies for the Visualization of Geographic Time-Series Data', *Cartographica* 27:1 (1990), 30–45, reproduced in Martin Dodge (ed.), *Classics in Cartography: Reflections on Influential Articles from Cartographica* (Chichester: John Wiley & Sons Ltd, 2011), 55–72. Tracks fit somewhat imperfectly in Monmonier's taxonomy, but they would most likely fall under the category of 'dance maps', with 'map symbols describing a transition from one place to another' (62–3, 71). On maps representing mobility, specifically for wayfinding, see also James R. Akerman (ed.), *Cartographies of Travel and Navigation* (Chicago IL and London: University of Chicago Press, 2006). For a critical reflection on what the track leaves untold, and possible alternatives, see Margaret Wickens Pearce, 'Framing the Days: Place and Narrative in Cartography', *Cartography and Geographic Information Science* 35:1 (2008), 17–32.

27 J. B. Harley, 'Deconstructing the Map', in Trevor J. Barnes and James S. Duncan (eds), *Writing Worlds: Discourse, Text, and Metaphor in the Representation of Landscape* (London: Routledge, 1992), 231–47.

28 On the arbitrariness of imagining borders as lines see e.g. Sarah Green, 'Lines, Traces, and Tidemarks: Further Reflections on Forms of Border', in Olga Demetriou and Rozita Dimova (eds), *The Political Materialities of Borders: New Theoretical Directions* (Manchester: Manchester University Press, 2019), 67–83.

29 John K. Wright, 'Map Makers Are Human: Comments on the Subjective in Maps', *Geographical Review* 32:4 (1942), 527–44.

30 David Harvey, *The Condition of Postmodernity* (Oxford: Basil Blackwell, 1989), 240–59. For a discussion of this narrative see: Denis Cosgrove, 'Introduction: Mapping Meaning', in Denis Cosgrove (ed.), *Mappings* (London: Reaktion

Books, 1999), 1–23, at 4, 18–19; Ricardo Padrón, 'Mapping Plus Ultra: Cartography, Space, and Hispanic Modernity', *Representations* 79:1 (2002), 28–60, at 28–31, 42–3.

31 Scientific hypotheses, as they developed in the Enlightenment, have a lot in common with fiction: John Bender, 'Enlightenment Fiction and the Scientific Hypothesis', *Representations* 61 (1998), 6–28. For more on how the track is a form of hypothesis see Chapters 3 and 5.

32 Richard W. Unger, *Ships on Maps: Pictures of Power in Renaissance Europe* (Basingstoke and New York: Palgrave Macmillan, 2010), 177–9; Chet Van Duzer, *Sea Monsters on Medieval and Renaissance Maps* (London: British Library, 2013), 118–19; Michel de Certeau, *The Practice of Everyday Life*, trans. Steven Rendall (Berkeley CA: University of California Press, 1984), 121 (he terms these images 'tour describers'). For different accounts stressing the persistence of ornamentation and narrative in modern cartographical and visual representations see: Alistair S. Maeer, 'The Cartography of the Sea: Mapping England's "Mastery of the Oceans"', in Claire Jowitt, Craig Lambert and Steve Mentz (eds), *The Routledge Companion to Marine and Maritime Words, 1400–1800* (Abingdon and New York: Routledge, 2020), 67–94; Martin Jay, *Force Fields: Between Intellectual History and Cultural Critique* (New York and London: Routledge, 1993), 114–20. On the shift from the 'narrative' to the 'cartographic' see also Denis Cosgrove, *Geography and Vision: Seeing, Imagining and Representing the World* (London and New York: I. B. Tauris, 2008), 6–7.

33 Daston and Galison, 'Image of Objectivity'; Daston and Galison, *Objectivity*. On the uses of quantification see also Theodore M. Porter, *Trust in Numbers: The Pursuit of Objectivity in Science and Public Life*, new edn (Princeton NJ: Princeton University Press, 2020).

34 William Rankin, *After the Map: Cartography, Navigation, and the Transformation of Territory in the Twentieth Century* (Chicago IL and London: University of Chicago Press, 2016); Lisa Parks, 'Plotting the Personal: Global Positioning Satellites and Interactive Media', *Ecumene* 8:2 (2001), 209–22; Mei-Po Kwan, 'Affecting Geospatial Technologies: Toward a Feminist Politics of Emotion', *The Professional Geographer* 59:1 (2007), 22–34. This is only one strand of evolution that we are considering in isolation: there are, of course, many more aspects in which ancient itineraries, graphical maps and contemporary digital systems differ from each other – although there is no space to discuss them here.

35 David Woodward's and Ricardo Padrón's work already takes us halfway along in this argument, showing that the 'itinerary mode' of mapping survived into the early modern period, flanking the supposed 'geometrisation' of the globe: David Woodward, 'Cartography and the Renaissance: Continuity and Change', in David Woodward (ed.), *The History of Cartography – Volume III: Cartography in the European Renaissance*, Pt. i (Chicago IL: University of Chicago Press, 2007), 3–14, at 7–8, 11–12, 23; Padrón, 'Mapping Plus Ultra'.

36 Simon Schaffer, 'Scientific Discoveries and the End of Natural Philosophy', *Social Studies of Science* 16:3 (1986), 387–420; Thomas S. Kuhn, 'Historical Structure of Scientific Discovery', *Science*, New Series, 136:3518 (1962), 760–64;

Matthew H. Edney, 'Creating "Discovery": The Myth of Columbus, 1777–1828', *Terrae Incognitae* 52: 2 (2020), 195–213, esp. 206–7. 'Discovery', as a term, also conceals the role of preconceptions: Richard White, 'Discovering Nature in North America', *Journal of American History* 79:3 (1992), 874–91. On how 'heroism' sometimes even trumps 'objectivity' as an ideal in science see Naomi Oreskes, 'Objectivity or Heroism? On the Invisibility of Women in Science', *Osiris* 11 (1996), 87–113.

37 Ingold, *Lines*, 74–106.

38 Ibid., 83–7.

39 Matthew H. Edney, *Cartography: The Ideal and Its History* (Chicago IL and London: University of Chicago Press, 2019).

40 See e.g.: Mark D. Hersey and Jeremy Vetter, 'Shared Ground: Between Environmental History and the History of Science', *History of Science* 57:4 (2019), 403–40; Cronon, 'Modes of Prophecy'; Donald Worster, 'Seeing beyond Culture', *Journal of American History* 76:4 (1990), 1142–7; Richard White, 'Environmental History, Ecology, and Meaning', *Journal of American History* 76:4 (1990), 1111–16; Gregg Mitman, 'Living in a Material World', *Journal of American History* 100:1 (2013), 128–30; Paul S. Sutter, 'Nature Is History', *Journal of American History* 100:1 (2013), 145–8; Sverker Sörlin and Paul Warde, 'The Problem of the Problem of Environmental History: A Re-Reading of the Field', *Environmental History* 12:1 (2007), 107–30; White, 'Discovering Nature'.

41 James Corner, 'The Agency of Mapping: Speculation, Critique and Invention', in Cosgrove (ed.), *Mappings*, 213–52. See also Wood, *Rethinking the Power of Maps*, esp. Ch. 2.

Chapter 1: The Trackless World

1 *The Odyssey of Homer Newly Translated into English Prose*, trans. T. E. Lawrence (New York: Oxford University Press, 1932).

2 Priya Satia, *Spies in Arabia: The Great War and the Cultural Foundations of Britain's Covert Empire in the Middle East* (New York: Oxford University Press, 2008), Ch. 2, quote at 59, 75 on Lawrence carrying the *Odyssey* around, 80 on Edwardian agents and the *Odyssey*; B. M. W. Knox, 'Lawrence's Odyssey', *Arion: A Journal of Humanities and the Classics*, Third Series, 1:3 (1991), 17–28.

3 Knox, 'Lawrence's Odyssey', 17.

4 I managed to check several impressions, as physical copies in libraries or as online sale listings: the latest American copy that I could find bearing no map was the third impression, of December 1932 (blue cover binding), and the earliest in which the map appeared was the 'popular impression' of 1934 (red cover binding, available here: https://archive.org/details/ odysseyofhomerneoooohome/page/n7/mode/2up). However, I wasn't able to track down any of the intermediate ones. The first British edition, published in 1935 (London: Humphrey Milford, Oxford University Press), still bore no map, and appeared with a blue cover.

5 This was in a second edition, which classicist Johann Heinrich Voss published together with the *Iliad*, in 1793, as *Homers Werke*. More easily accessible today is

a subsequent one: Johannn Heinrich Voss, *Homers Werke*, 2nd improved edn, 4 vols[?] (Königsberg: Friedrich Nicolovius, 1802), III, facing the Odyssey title. See https://archive.org/details/bub_gb_xvAGAAAAYAAJ/page/n13/mode/2up.

6   Bibliothèque nationale de France, Paris, Département Cartes et plans, GE D-12440, Hellwag and Carl Jäck, 'Homerische Welt-Tafel' (1793) https://gallica.bnf.fr/ark:/12148/btv1b8490975c#. For a colour version see Bibliothèque nationale de France, Département Cartes et plans, GE D-12443, 'Homerische Welt-Tafel' (n.d.) https://gallica.bnf.fr/ark:/12148/btv1b8490285b. On the geography of the *Odyssey* and its limited match with 'real' places, see e.g.: Irad Malkin and Arie Fichman, 'Homer, *Odyssey* III.153–85: A Maritime Commentary', *Mediterranean Historical Review* 2:2 (1987), 250–58, at 251–2; Elizabeth Della Zazzera, 'Roundtable: The Geography of the *Odyssey* – Or How to Map a Myth', *Lapham's Quarterly* (27 February 2019) https://www.laphamsquarterly.org/roundtable/geography-odyssey; Peter T. Struck, 'Map of Odysseus' Journey', *Greek & Roman Mythology* (2000–20) https://www2.classics.upenn.edu/myth/php/homer/index.php?page=odymap.

7   See also Gotha Perthes Collection, SPK-10-V.A A-05, 'Géographie primitive des Grecs' – 'Hésiode, Homère, Orphée, neuf siècles avant notre ère. Voyages des Argonautes et d'Ulysse' (Brussels: Th. Lejeune, 1832).

8   Alex. Keith Johnston, *School Atlas of Classical Geography*, new and enlarged edn (Edinburgh and London: William Blackwood and Sons, 1867), Plate 3. Examples of citations: 'The West wind. Ten days sail Od. X. 26'; 'Seven days rowing Od. X. 78:81'; 'Od. X. 1 Time undefined'. This map originally comes from W. E. Gladstone, *Studies on Homer and the Homeric Age*, 3 vols (Oxford: Oxford University Press, 1858), III, Plate, viewable at https://www.gutenberg.org/cache/epub/53004/pg53004-images.html. On the issues with mapping the classics of the ancient world see Kai Brodersen, *Terra Cognita: Studien zur römischen Raumerfassung* (Hildesheim: Georg Olms Verlag, 1995), 11–13.

9   This passage is quoted and the geographical routes fully analysed in Malkin and Fichman, 'Homer, *Odyssey* III.153–85'.

10   *Odyssey*, 3.169. The Greek text of this verse, in the edition curated by A. T. Murray, is most readily available in the 'Explore Homer' section of the Scaife Viewer platform (https://scaife-viewer.org/): https://explorehomer.scaife-viewer.org/reader/urn:cts:greekLit:tlg0012.tlg002.perseus-grc2:3.169; for the nuances in the meaning of the term πλόος, see its entry in this fantastic online resource, which combines several ancient Greek dictionaries in various languages: Philippe Verkerk, *Eulexis-web – Lemmatiseur de grec ancien (version en ligne)* (2020) https://outils.biblissima.fr/fr/eulexis-web/?lemma=%CF%80%CE%BB%CE1%BD%B9%CE%BF%CF%82. For a similar example of 'modern' translation, see also how Murray himself translates verse 3.168 just above: 'μετὰ νῶϊ' ('metà nōi', 'after us') becomes 'upon our track' ('late upon our track came fair-haired Menelaus') https://explorehomer.scaife-viewer.org/reader/urn:cts:greekLit:tlg0012.tlg002.perseus-grc2:3.168 and https://explorehomer.scaife-viewer.org/reader/urn:cts:greekLit:tlg0012.tlg002.perseus-eng3:3.141.

11   Otto Cuntz (ed.), *Itineraria romana – Vol. I: Itineraria Antonini Augusti et*

Burdigalense (Stuttgart: B. G. Teubner, 1990), 83–4, ll. 517:5–519:2, 523:3–525:2 (my translation). '*ITEM INTER SICILIAM ET AFRICAM: insula Cossura a Lilibeo de Sicilia sunt stadia CLXXX, a Clipea ex Africa stadia DXC, insule Malta Ciefesta et Falacron, insula Cercena, haec a Tacapis distat stadia DCXXII, insula Girba a Gitti de Tripoli stadia XC. Insula Traieia Syrota Cephallania Asteris Itaca Paxos Propaxos Oxia.*'; '*Insule Strophades, que ante Plote dicte sunt, in Ionio mari, quo Grecia alluitur, in hac Arpiae morabantur; insule Cephalanie Zacinthos et Dulcia, hic est mons Itacus, ubi est patria Ulixis;*'. On the question of dates see Benet Salway, 'Sea and River Travel in the Roman Itinerary Literature', in Richard Talbert and Kai Brodersen (eds), *Space in the Roman World: Its Perception and Presentation* (Münster: Lit Verlag, 2004), 43–96, at 68–9.

12 Matthew Maher, 'Fall of Troy VII: New Archaeological Interpretations and Considerations', *TOTEM: The UWO Journal of Anthropology* 11 (2002–3), 58–66. For an accessible overview of Trojan history see Alexandra Villing, 'The Search for the Lost City of Troy', *The British Museum Blog* (2019) https://blog. britishmuseum.org/the-search-for-the-lost-city-of-troy.

13 Pietro Janni, *La mappa e il periplo: Cartografia antica e spazio odologico* (Rome: Bretschneider, 1984); Brodersen, *Terra Cognita*; Kai Brodersen, 'The Presentation of Geographical Knowledge for Travel and Transport in the Roman World: *Itineraria non tantum Adnotata sed etiam Picta*', in Colin Adams and Ray Laurence (eds), *Travel and Geography in the Roman Empire* (London and New York: Routledge, 2001), 7–21; Kai Brodersen, 'Mapping (in) the Ancient World', *The Journal of Roman Studies* 94 (2004), 183–90; Wood, *Rethinking the Power of Maps*, 17–27.

14 Janni, *Mappa*, 79–82. He does refer to 'evolution', though.

15 A. R. Millard, 'Cartography in the Ancient Near East', in J. B. Harley and David Woodward (eds), *The History of Cartography – Volume I: Cartography in Prehistoric, Ancient, and Medieval Europe and the Mediterranean* (Chicago IL and London: University of Chicago Press, 1987), 107–16, at 107–8. On itineraries in general see Benet Salway, 'Travel, *Itineraria* and *Tabellaria*', in Adams and Laurence (eds), *Travel and Geography*, 22–66; Catherine Delano-Smith, 'Milieus of Mobility: Itineraries, Route Maps, and Road Maps', in Akerman (ed.), *Cartographies of Travel*, 16–68.

16 *Numbers* 33:1. The translation 'stages in the journey' is from the *New International Version* (https://www.biblegateway.com/ passage/?search=Numbers%2033&version=NIV), whereas we read 'journeys', e.g., in the *King James Version* (https://www.biblegateway.com/ passage/?search=Numbers+33&version=KJV). To find the original, I consulted the Hebrew version of the text in תֹרָה – *Bibbia ebraica: Pentateuco e Haftaroth*, ed. Dario Disegni (Florence: La Giuntina, 1998), 282. '*Mas'ei*' is in fact the title of the whole chapter, because it's the first significant word in it. For the meaning of the word *mas'ei* see the entry for the verb נסע ('*nasa*') in Francis Brown, William Gesenius and Edward Robinson, *A Hebrew and English Lexicon of the Old Testament with an Appendix Containing the Biblical Aramaic* (Oxford: Clarendon Press, 1906 [1939]), 588, 652.

17 Tomislav Bilić, 'The Myth of Alpheus and Arethusa and Open-Sea Voyages on

the Mediterranean – Stellar Navigation in Antiquity', *The International Journal of Nautical Archaeology* 38:1 (2009), 116–32; Pietro Janni, 'The Sea of the Greeks and Romans', in Serena Bianchetti, Michele R. Cataudella and Hans-Joachim Gehrke (eds), *Brill's Companion to Ancient Geography: The Inhabited World in Greek and Roman Tradition* (Leiden and Boston: Brill, 2016), 21–42.

18 Salway, 'Sea and River Travel', esp. at 46–52.

19 Or, in cartographer Margaret Wickens Pearce's words, 'a sense of enclosure by a moving landscape': Pearce, 'Framing the Days', 25.

20 Pascal Arnaud, 'A propos d'un prétendu itinéraire de Caracalla dans l'Itinéraire d'Antonin: les sources tardives de l'itinéraire de Rome à Hierasycaminos', *Bulletin de la Société Nationale des Antiquaires de France* 1992 (1994), 374–80. For the opposite argument, see Denis Van Berchem, 'L'itinéraire Antonin et le voyage en Orient de Caracalla (214–215)', *Comptes rendus des séances de l'Académie des Inscriptions et Belles-Lettres* 117:1 (1973), 123–6.

21 The way these matters are established is interesting in itself: from other surviving texts, we know roughly when given localities began to be called in certain ways – so we can theoretically compare the forms used here to the existing record, and in that way date the source. Yet all these itineraries only survive as later copies, rather than originals, often at the end of a centuries-long chain. Did the copyists stick to the original names, or modernise them? See: Pascal Arnaud, 'Entre Antiquité et Moyen-Âge: l'Itinéraire Maritime d'Antonin', in Lorenza de Maria and Rita Turchetti (eds), *Rotte e porti del Mediterraneo dopo la caduta dell'Impero Romano d'Occidente: Continuità e innovazioni tecnologiche e funzionali – IV seminario: Genova, 18–19 giugno 2004* (Soveria Mannelli: Rubbettino, 2004), 3–19; Giovanni Uggeri, 'Portolani romani e carte nautiche: Problemi e incognite', in Giovanni Laudizi and Cesare Marangio (eds), *Porti, approdi e linee di rotta nel Mediterraneo antico – Atti del seminario di studi Lecce, 29–30 novembre 1996* (Galatina: Congedo editore, 1998), 31–78, at 52–9 (for a datation of the maritime itinerary between 450 and 535 AD). On the two parts of the itinerary, disproving some of Uggeri's points, see also Salway, 'Sea and River Travel', 68–85.

22 R. J. A. Talbert, 'Author, Audience and the Roman Empire in the *Antonine Itinerary*', in Rudolf Haensch and Johannes Heinrichs (eds), *Herrschen und Verwalten: Der Alltag der römischen Administration in der Hohen Kaiserzeit* (Köln: Böhlau Verlag, 2007), 256–70, esp. at 263–5.

23 Cuntz (ed.), *Itineraria romana*, 79, ll. 498:2–4.

24 Lionel Casson, *The Periplus Maris Erythraei: Text with Introduction, Translation, and Commentary* (Princeton NJ: Princeton University Press, 2012), 90–91, 238–41, ll. 64:11–20.

25 Casson, *Periplus*, 92–3, ll. 66:7–9.

26 Didier Marcotte, 'The Indian Ocean from Agatharchides of Cnidus to the Periplus Maris Erythraei', in Bianchetti et al. (eds), *Brill's Companion to Ancient Geography*, 163–83, esp. 174–83.

27 Casson, *Periplus*, 78–81, ll. 46:28–33.

28 Ibid., 74–5, 195–7, ll. 40:29–32; 188 for more on the snakes.

29 On the gender point see Laurie Douglass, 'A New Look at the Itinerarium

Burdigalense', *Journal of Early Christian Studies* 4:3 (1996), 313–33, although her deductions possibly went too far: Susan Weingarten, 'Was the Pilgrim from Bordeaux a Woman? A Reply to Laurie Douglass', *Journal of Early Christian Studies* 7:2 (1999), 291–7.

30 Cuntz, *Itineraria romana – Vol. I*, parts cited here are from 88, 94–9. On this itinerary see: Douglass, 'New Look'; Jaś Elsner, 'The Itinerarium Burdigalense: Politics and Salvation in the Geography of Constantine's Empire', *The Journal of Roman Studies* 90 (2000), 181–95 (189–90 on the 'rising pattern of description' as the Holy Land is approached).

31 Eugenio Alliata, 'The Anonymous Pilgrim of Bordeaux (333 A.D.): The Earliest Christian Description of the Holy Places – Map I: Europe', *Early Christian Pilgrimage to the Holy Land, Franciscan Cyberspot* (1999) https://web.archive. org/web/20110604105814/http://www.christusrex.org/www1/ofm/pilgr/ bord/10Bord01MapEur.html.

32 Unlike in some nautical itineraries, natural landmarks are strikingly absent from the text, but historical and emotional ones are not.

33 See e.g. Janni, *Mappa*, 31–2; Salway, 'Travel, *Itineraria* and *Tabellaria*', 31.

34 This debate is summarised well in Edney, *Cartography*, 69–71 and John Krygier, 'Cartocacoethes: Why the World's Oldest Map Isn't a Map', *Making Maps: DIY Cartography* (13 October 2008) https://makingmaps.net/2008/10/13/ cartocacoethes-why-the-worlds-oldest-map-isnt-a-map. For the initial identification and images see James Mellaart, 'Excavations at Çatal Hüyük, 1963: Third Preliminary Report', *Anatolian Studies* 14 (1964), 39–119, at 55 and Plates V and VI. On this and other less ancient examples (although the captions appear to have been swapped) see also David Turnbull, *Maps Are Territories: Science is an Atlas* (online edn, 2008) http://territories.indigenousknowledge.org/ exhibit-3.html.

35 For an image and explanation of the tablet see Olof Pedersén, Paul J. J. Sinclair, Irmgard Hein and Jakob Andersson, 'Cities and Urban Landscapes in the Ancient Near East and Egypt with Special Focus on the City of Babylon', in Paul J. J. Sinclair, Gullög Nordquist, Frands Herschend and Christian Isendahl (eds), *The Urban Mind: Cultural and Environmental Dynamics* (Uppsala: African and Comparative Archaeology, Department of Archaeology and Ancient History, Uppsala University, 2010), 113–47, at 131; Turnbull, *Maps Are Territories* http:// territories.indigenousknowledge.org/exhibit-3/2.html.

36 Daniel Weiss, 'Nippur Map Tablet', in 'Mapping the Past', *Archaeology* 72:3 (2019), 26–33, at 27, available at https://www.archaeology.org/issues/338- features/maps/7544-maps-iraq-babylonian-nippur-map-tablet. On both Nippur tablets see Millard, 'Cartography in the Ancient Near East', 110–13.

37 *The Stanford Digital Forma Urbis Romae Project* (2002–16) http://formaurbis. stanford.edu/; Tina Najbjerg, 'The Severan Marble Plan of Rome (Forma Urbis Romae)', *Stanford Digital Forma Urbis Romae Project* http://formaurbis. stanford.edu/docs/FURmap.html; Charles Davoine, 'La Forma Urbis Romae: Bilan de vingt-cinq années de recherches', *Histoire urbaine* 20:3 (2007), 133–52; Lluís Casas et al., 'Exploring New Ways to Reconstruct the *Forma Urbis Romae*:

An Archaeometric Approach (CL Color and Stable Isotope Analyses)', *Minerals* 11:12 (2021), 1400ss.

38 A. J. Peden, *The Reign of Ramesses IV* (Warminster: Aris & Phillips Ltd, 1994), 1–24; Zahi Hawass et al., 'Revisiting the Harem Conspiracy and Death of Ramesses III: Anthropological, Forensic, Radiological, and Genetic Study', *British Medical Journal* 345:7888 (2012), e8268ss; Sahar N. Saleem and Zahi Hawass, 'Computed Tomography Study of the Feet of Mummy of Ramesses III: New Insights on the Harem Conspiracy', *J Comput Assist Tomogr* 41:1 (2017), 15–17; Barbara Mertz, *Temples, Tombs and Hieroglyphs: A Brief History of Ancient Egypt* (London: Constable & Robinson Ltd, 2010), 262–5 (on Ramesses III).

39 Peden, *Reign of Ramesses IV*, 24–32. For a sample of Bekhen-stone see 'Wadi Hammamat – Eastern Quarry (#28a): green graywacke sandstone', in James A. Harrell, 'Ancient Egyptian Quarries and Mines', *University of Toledo* (2016) http://www.eeescience.utoledo.edu/Faculty/Harrell/Egypt/Quarries/Stones_List.html.

40 James A. Harrell and V. Max Brown, 'The Oldest Surviving Topographical Map from Ancient Egypt: (Turin Papyri 1879, 1899, and 1969)', *Journal of the American Research Center in Egypt* 29 (1992), 81–105; David M. McMahon, 'The Turin Papyrus Map: The Oldest Known Map with Geological Significance', *Earth Sciences History* 11:1 (1992), 9–12; James A. Harrell and V. Max Brown, 'The World's Oldest Surviving Geological Map: The 1150 B.C. Turin Papyrus from Egypt', *The Journal of Geology* 100:1 (1992), 3–18; A. F. Shore, 'Egyptian Cartography', in Harley and Woodward (eds), *History of Cartography – Volume I*, 117–29, at 121–4.

41 Giambattista D'Alessio, 'On the "Artemidorus" Papyrus', *Zeitschrift für Papyrologie und Epigraphik* 171 (2009), 27–43, at 27–8.

42 Richard Talbert, 'P.Artemid.: The Map', in Kai Brodersen and Jaś Elsner (eds), *Images and Texts on the 'Artemidorus Papyrus': Working Papers on P.Artemid. (St John's College Oxford, 2008)* (Stuttgart: Franz Steiner Verlag, 2009), 57–64, at 59–62; Bärbel Kramer, 'The Earliest Known Map of Spain (?) and the Geography of Artemidorus of Ephesus on Papyrus', *Imago Mundi* 53 (2001), 115–20, at 117–19; Salway, 'Travel, *Itineraria* and *Tabellaria*', 29–30.

43 Barbara Capone et al., 'Does the Artemidorus Papyrus Have Multiple Lives? Seeking for the Answer in the Inks through a Raman and PCA Analysis', *Journal of Cultural Heritage* 48 (2021), 1–10; Richard Janko, 'Review: The Artemidorus Papyrus', *The Classical Review*, New Series, 59:2 (2009), 403–10. In favour of the forgery hypothesis, see e.g.: Luciano Canfora, 'The So-Called Artemidorus Papyrus: A Reconsideration', *Museum Helveticum* 70:2 (2013), 157–79; Luciano Bossina, 'Il cosiddetto "papiro di artemidoro". Dalla parte degli scettici', in Isabel Velázquez and Javier Martínez (eds), *Realidad, ficción y autenticidad en el Mundo Antiguo: La investigación ante documentos sospechosos – Antigüedad y Cristianismo xxix* (Universidad de Murcia, 2012), 285–320; Luciano Canfora, 'Comment Simonidès s'est fait Artémidore', *Revue d'Histoire des Textes* 6 (2011), 377–97; Luciano Canfora, 'Dietro la maschera di Artemidoro', *Il Corriere della Sera* (20 March 2008) https://www.corriere.it/spettacoli/08_marzo_20/

dietro_la_maschera_di_artemidoro_1baaa79e-f651-11dc-a713-0003ba99c667.
shtml. Against the forgery hypothesis: Salvatore Settis, 'Artemidoro, ecco perché
quel papiro è autentico', *La Repubblica* (13 March 2008) https://ricerca.
repubblica.it/repubblica/archivio/repubblica/2008/03/13/artemidoro-ecco-
perche-quel-papiro-autentico.html; Salvatore Settis, 'Papiro di Artemidoro,
dichiarato falso ignorando la comunità scientifica. Spataro ha sentito solo il
parere di Canfora', *Il Fatto Quotidiano* (15 December 2018) https://www.
ilfattoquotidiano.it/in-edicola/articoli/2018/12/15/il-vero-papiro-e-i-falsi-
esperti/4837713; Jürgen Hammerstaedt, 'Come fa ad essere un papiro falsato?',
Atti Acc. Rov. Agiati Series viii, 9(A):2 (2009), 83–103; D'Alessio, 'On the
"Artemidorus" Papyrus'.

44 See e.g. Ottavia Giustetti, 'Il Papiro di Artemidoro è un falso. Venne pagato
quasi tre milioni di euro', *La Repubblica* (10 December 2018) https://torino.
repubblica.it/cronaca/2018/12/10/news/
il_papiro_di_artemidoro_e_un_falso_venne_pagato_quasi_tre_milioni_di_
euro-213885644.

45 Richard Talbert, 'Greek and Roman Mapping: Twenty-First Century
Perspectives', in Richard J. A. Talbert and Richard W. Unger (eds), *Cartography
in Antiquity and the Middle Ages: Fresh Perspectives, New Methods* (Leiden and
Boston: Brill, 2008), 9–27, at 21–2.

46 Emily Albu, 'Rethinking the Peutinger Map', in Talbert and Unger (eds),
Cartography in Antiquity, 111–19; Emily Albu, *The Medieval Peutinger Map:
Imperial Roman Revival in a German Empire* (Cambridge: Cambridge
University Press, 2014).

47 Annalina Levi and Mario Levi, *Itineraria picta: Contributo allo studio della
Tabula Peutingeriana* (Rome: 'L'Erma' di Bretschneider, 1967), 26–7. On this
map see also: Benet Salway, 'The Nature and Genesis of the Peutinger Map',
Imago Mundi 57:2 (2005), 119–35; 'Explore Peutinger's Roman Map', *Institute for
the Study of the Ancient World* https://isaw.nyu.edu/exhibitions/space/tpeut.
html; Richard J. A. Talbert, *Rome's World: The Peutinger Map Reconsidered*
(Cambridge: Cambridge University Press, 2010): 'Peutinger Map Resources'
(2010) https://peutinger.atlantides.org.

48 Salway, 'Travel, *Itineraria* and *Tabellaria*', 30–31; Talbert, *Rome's World*, 109.

49 Delano-Smith, 'Milieus of Mobility', 29–33, 58–9.

50 Salway, 'Sea and River Travel', 86–92; Talbert, *Rome's World*, 116. The point on
interrupted lines also comes from Salway.

51 Simon James, *The Roman Military Base at Dura-Europos, Syria: An
Archaeological Visualization* (Oxford: Oxford University Press, 2019); J. Baird,
'The Ruination of Dura-Europos', *Theoretical Roman Archaeology Journal* 3:1
(2020), 1–20; Deborah Amos and Alison Meuse, 'Via Satellite, Tracking the
Plunder of Middle East Cultural History', *National Public Radio* (10 March 2015)
https://www.npr.org/sections/parallels/2015/03/10/392077801/
via-satellite-tracking-the-plunder-of-middle-east-cultural-
history?t=1661364210201.

52 Franz Cumont, 'Fragment de bouclier portant une liste d'étapes', *Syria* 6:1
(1925), 1–15.

53 Salway, 'Sea and River Travel', 92–5; Cumont, 'Fragment', 5–8. On the history of the garrison see James, *Roman Military Base*.

54 Janni, 'Sea of the Greeks and Romans', 25.

55 Uggeri, 'Portolani romani', 64–78.

56 *The Gough Map of Great Britain*, Bodleian Libraries (2021) http://www.goughmap.org; Brian Paul Hindle, 'The Road Network of Medieval England and Wales', *Journal of Historical Geography* 2:3 (1976), 207–21; Delano-Smith, 'Milieus of Mobility', 16–27. On bishops' itineraries and the historical evidence available to attempt their reconstruction see: Philippa M. Hoskin, 'How to Travel with a Bishop: Thirteenth-Century Episcopal Itineraries', in D. W. Rollason (ed.), *Princes of the Church: Bishops and Their Palaces* (London: Routledge, 2015), 169–78, and Julia Barrow, 'English Bishops' Itineraries, *c.*700–*c.*1200', ibid., 161–8.

57 Dym, *Mapping Travel*, 37–8.

58 Jocelyn Wogan-Browne, 'Reading the World: The Hereford *Mappa Mundi*', *Parergon* 9:1 (1991), 117–35, esp. 131–3; Thomas de Wesselow, 'Locating the Hereford *Mappamundi*', *Imago Mundi* 65:2 (2013), 180–206, esp. 196–7 (see also here for the Exodus as symbolising salvation).

59 See Chapter 4.

60 'The Largest Medieval Map – Mappa Mundi Hereford' (2023) https://www.themappamundi.co.uk/mappa-mundi. I am very grateful to Professor Jordana Dym for suggesting that I look at what happens to Exodus maps on the Red Sea.

61 Richard Vaughan, *Matthew Paris* (Cambridge: Cambridge University Press, 1979 [1958]), here esp. 16.

62 Daniel K. Connolly, 'Imagined Pilgrimage in the Itinerary Maps of Matthew Paris', *The Art Bulletin* 81:4 (1999), 598–622; Michael Gaudio, 'Matthew Paris and the Cartography of the Margins', *Gesta* 39:1 (2000), 50–57. On these itinerary maps, and the rest of Paris's cartographical production, see also Suzanne Lewis, *The Art of Matthew Paris in the* Chronica Majora (Aldershot: Scolar Press, 1987), 321–76; Vaughan, *Matthew Paris*, 235–50.

63 See e.g., on some Italian and Spanish examples: Centro di Documentazione dei Sacri Monti, Calvari e Complessi devozionali europei, *1° Convegno Internazionale sui Sacri Monti – Varallo, 14–20 aprile 1980* (Quarona: Tipolitografia Delos, 2009); Amilcare Barbero and Giuseppe Roma (eds), *Di ritorno dal pellegrinaggio a Gerusalemme: Riproposizione degli avvenimenti e dei luoghi di Terra Santa nell'immaginario religioso fra XV e XVI secolo – Atti delle Giornate di Studio 12–13 maggio 2005 Università della Calabria* (Ponzano Monferrato: Centro di Documentazione dei Sacri Monti, Calvari e Complessi devozionali europei, [2008]).

64 June L. Mecham, 'A Northern Jerusalem: Transforming the Spatial Geography of the Convent of Wienhausen', in Andrew Spicer and Sarah Hamilton (eds), *Defining the Holy: Sacred Space in Medieval and Early Modern Europe* (Aldershot and Burlington VT: Ashgate, 2005 and Abingdon and New York: Routledge, 2016), 139–60.

65 Connolly, 'Imagined Pilgrimage', 617–18; Lewis, *Art of Matthew Paris*, 325. The article and the book cite the version kept at Corpus Christi College, University

of Cambridge, but the British Library version in Plate 7 also reports similar instructions (see the top-left corner). Earlier in the journey, in another version of the itinerary, the Channel is just a perpendicular rivulet briefly interrupting the road line: Matthew Paris, *Liber additamentorum*, British Library, ms Cotton Nero D i, ff. 183v–184r. The image is reproduced in Connolly, 'Imagined Pilgrimage', 609.

66 British Library, London, Sloane MS. 683, f. 42, fifteenth century. I found this document thanks to a reference in Delano-Smith, 'Milieus of Mobility', 35.

67 D. W. Waters, *Science and the Techniques of Navigation in the Renaissance – National Maritime Museum Maritime Monographs and Reports n. 19* (London, 1976), 6.

68 Pierre Garcie, *Le Routier de la mer jusques au fleuve de Jourdain* (Rouen: Jacques Le Forestier, 1502–9). As a modern critical edition of the various versions, I also consulted D. W. Waters (ed.), *The Rutters of the Sea: The Sailing Directions of Pierre Garcie – A Study of the First English and French Printed Sailing Directions with Facsimile Reproductions* (New Haven CT and London: Yale University Press, 1967), (see 53 (5) for the statement in Copland's prologue: 'for I never came on the see, nor by no cost therof.'). On rutters see also Sarah Tyacke, 'Chartmaking in England and Its Context, 1500–1660', in David Woodward (ed.), *The History of Cartography – Volume III: Cartography in the European Renaissance,* Pt. ii (Chicago IL: University of Chicago Press, 2007), 1722–53, at 1726–7.

69 Padrón, 'Mapping Plus Ultra'.

70 Matthew Boyd Goldie, 'An Early English Rutter: The Sea and Spatial Hermeneutics in the Fourteenth and Fifteenth Centuries', *Speculum* 90:3 (2015), 701–27, at 702–3, 721–7.

71 For the details on portolan charts in this and the previous paragraph see Tony Campbell, 'Portolan Charts from the Late Thirteenth Century to 1500', in Harley and Woodward (eds), *History of Cartography – Volume I*, 371–463; Ramon J. Pujades I Bataller, *Les cartes portolanes: La representació medieval d'una mar solcada* (Barcelona: Institut Cartogràfic de Catalunya, 2007).

72 For a summary see Campbell, 'Portolan Charts', 380–84. For a sample of the academic debate (between those who argue that portolan charts could not have been built on magnetic bearings and distances, and those who rebut this point) see: Roel Nicolai, 'How Old are Portolan Charts Really?', *Maps in History* 52 (2015), 16–24; Joaquim Alves Gaspar, 'Dead Reckoning and Magnetic Declination: Unveiling the Mystery of Portolan Charts', *e-Perimetron* 3:4 (2008), 191–203; Joaquim Alves Gaspar, 'How Old Are Portolan Charts Really?: Review of Roel Nicolai's Article by Joaquim Alves Gaspar', *Maps in History* 53 (2015), 20–24; Tony Campbell, 'How Old Are Portolan Charts Really?: Review of Roel Nicolai's Article by Tony Campbell', *Maps in History* 53 (2015), 25–7.

73 For an interpretation downplaying the navigational usefulness of these charts vis-à-vis pilotage skills see Patrick Gautier Dalché, 'La carte marine au Moyen Âge: outil technique, objet symbolique', in Michel Balard and Christian Buchet (eds), *The Sea in History – The Medieval World* (Woodbridge: The Boydell Press, 2017), 101–14.

74　Akerman, 'Finding Our Way', 51–3.

75　Ingold, *Lines*, 160–65.

Chapter 2: Trailblazers

1　The best and most recent English-language account of this expedition and its context is Felipe Fernández-Armesto, *Straits: Beyond the Myth of Magellan* (London: Bloomsbury Publishing, 2022), (21–2 on spices). See also A. Teixeira da Mota (ed.), *A viagem de Fernão de Magalhães e a questão das Molucas: Actas do II colóquio Luso-Espanhol de história ultramarina* (Lisbon: Junta de investigações científicas do ultramar, 1975).

2　Most controversially, some scholars backdate the start of Agnese's map production to as early as 1514. On the 'trademark' attribution see e.g. Peter Whitfield, *New Found Lands: Maps in the History of Exploration* (London: Routledge, 1998), 96. On Agnese and his atlases see: Alberto Magnaghi, 'Agnese, Battista', *Enciclopedia Italiana Treccani* (1929) https://www.treccani.it/enciclopedia/battista-agnese_%28Enciclopedia-Italiana%29; Francesco Cagnetti, 'Agnese, Battista', *Dizionario Biografico degli Italiani – Volume I* (1960) https://www.treccani.it/enciclopedia/battista-agnese_%28Dizionario-Biografico%29; H. R. Wagner, 'The Manuscript Atlases of Battista Agnese', *The Papers of the Bibliographical Society of America* 25 (1931), 1–110; Alberto Magnaghi, 'L'atlante manoscritto di Battista Agnese della Biblioteca Reale di Torino', *Rivista Geografica Italiana* 15:2 (1908), 65–77, 135–48; Ingrid Baumgärtner, 'Battista Agnese e l'atlante di Kassel. La cartografia del mondo nel Cinquecento', in Ingrid Baumgärtner and Piero Falchetta (eds), *Venezia e la nuova* oikoumene: *Cartografia del Quattrocento* (Rome and Venice: Viella, 2016), 245–70; Henry Harrisse, *The Discovery of North America: A Critical, Documentary, and Historic Investigation* ... (London: H. Stevens, 1892), 626–30; Corradino Astengo, 'The Renaissance Chart Tradition in the Mediterranean', in Woodward (ed.), *History of Cartography – Volume III*, Pt. i, 174–262, at 213–16.

3　The odd copy, especially from early on in Agnese's assumed production, bears no track lines at all – for example, the one kept at the University of Pennsylvania: Penn Libraries, University of Pennsylvania, Philadelphia, LJS 28, '7 double-page navigational maps marked with place names and rhumblines, probably from the workshop of Battista Agnese' ([Venice], [between 1535 and 1538]) http://hdl.library.upenn.edu/1017/d/medren/9948452623503681.

4　*Uncharted* (2022) https://www.imdb.com/title/tt1464335.

5　For a full list to date see Corradino Astengo, 'Agnese, Battista (GE)', in Annalisa D'Ascenzo (ed.), *Digital DISCI. Il Portale del Dizionario storico dei cartografi italiani* (Rome: Labgeo Caraci, 2018) https://www.digitaldisci.it/agnese-battista-2.

6　Sale 2622 (New York, 10 April 2012), Lot 159, *Christie's* https://www.christies.com/lotfinder/books-manuscripts/agnese-battista-5546150-details.aspx?intobjectid=5546150&fbclid=IwAR2ZBwrVdzvplAheKHy2X_po6mnRf782Tv_tfL4kxer6Wb3bYeZTaSOYylw.

7　Johannes Schöner, *De nuper sub Castiliae ac Portugaliae Regibus Serenissimis repertis Insulis ac Regionibus, Ioannis Schöner Charolipolitani epistola & Globus*

Geographicus, seriem nauigationum annotantibus (Timiripae, 1523). The facsimile is reproduced in *Reimpression fidèle d'une Lettre de Jean Schöner à propos de son globe, Écrite en 1523* (St Petersburg: Röttger & Schneider, 1872). For the gores that were enclosed, with the route marked on them, see Bibliothèque nationale de France, GED-582, 'Globe terrestre / de Johannes Schöner, accompagnant l'ouvrage qui a pour titre: "De nuper sub Castiliae ac Portugaliae regibus ...", 1529 https://gallica.bnf.fr/ark:/12148/btv1b84394929/f1.item. See also, in passing: Unger, *Ships on Maps*, 160; Jerry Brotton, 'Terrestrial Globalism: Mapping the Globe in Early Modern Europe', in Cosgrove (ed.), *Mappings*, 71–89, at 83.

8 Bibliothèque nationale de France, Département Cartes et plans, GE A-333 (RES), *Nova et integra universi orbs (sic) descripsio*, [*c*.1527] https://gallica.bnf.fr/ark:/12148/btv1b55008739c/f2.item.zoom# (catalogue entry: http://catalogue.bnf.fr/ark:/12148/cb406736699). Wagner, 'Manuscript Atlases', 26; Harrisse, *Discovery of North America*, 562–8; Jan Mokre, 'Globen als Repräsentationen des Zeitalters der europäischen Expansion', in Michael Bischoff, Vera Lüpkes and Wolfgang Crom (eds), *Kartographie der Frühen Neuzeit: Weltbilder und Wirkungen* (Marburg: Jonas Verlag, 2015), 51–66, at 56; Jim Siebold, '*Nova et integra universi orbis descripsio* [Paris Gilt or De Bure Globe] (n. 344)' (1527), in *Renaissance Maps: 1490–1800* (2015) https://myoldmaps.com/renaissance-maps-1490-1800/344-the-paris-gilt-or-de/344-gilt-globe.pdf. The inscription reads: '*Illa linea ex Sibilla dvcta hispanorvm navigationem ostendit*'. The BNF catalogue gives the date of 1527, but elsewhere scholars have attributed different dates. For example, *c*.1528 (Gabrielle Duprat, 'Les globes terrestres et célestes en France', *Der Globusfreund* 21/23 (1973), 198–225, at 211) or *c*.1535 (Elly Dekker, 'Globes in Renaissance Europe', in Woodward (ed.), *History of Cartography – Volume III*, Pt. i, 135–73, at 161; 'Globe terrestre, dit "Globe doré": *Nova et integra universi orbis descripsio*', *Bibliothèque nationale de France – Le monde en sphères* http://expositions.bnf.fr/monde-en-spheres/grand/mes_077.php).

9 Brotton, 'Terrestrial Globalism', 82; Fernández-Armesto, *Straits*, 81–5. On the possibility that this wasn't a globe but a planisphere (map) see Marcel Destombes, 'The Chart of Magellan', *Imago Mundi* 12 (1955), 65–88, at 68, 77.

10 René Tebel, *Das Schiff im Kartenbild des Mittelalters und der Frühen Neuzeit: Kartographische Zeugnisse aus sieben Jahrhunderten als maritimhistorische Bildquellen* (Bremerhaven: Deutsches Schiffahrtsmuseum, 2012), 102–5.

11 For more on why priority and discovery claims are dubious, see Chapters 3 and 7.

12 On this creation of the world, and the triumph of 'Atlas' over '*Theatrum*', see Ayesha Ramachandran, *The Worldmakers: Global Imagining in Early Modern Europe* (Chicago IL and London: University of Chicago Press, 2015), Ch. 1. On the Renaissance redrawing of the world see also: Ricardo Padrón, *The Spacious Word: Cartography, Literature, and Empire in Early Modern Spain* (Chicago IL and London: University of Chicago Press, 2004); Frank Lestringant, *Mapping the Renaissance World: The Geographical Imagination in the Age of Discovery* (Cambridge: Polity Press, 1994); Denis E. Cosgrove, *Apollo's Eye: A Cartographic*

Genealogy of the Earth in the Western Imagination (Baltimore MD and London: Johns Hopkins University Press, 2001), esp. Chs 4–5.

13 Brotton, 'Terrestrial Globalism'.

14 Cited in Padrón, *Spacious Word*, 13–14.

15 Pedro de Medina, *L'art de naviguer de Maistre Pierre de Medine* ... (Lyon: G. Rouillé, 1561), f. 3r, as cited in Lestringant, *Mapping the Renaissance World*, 15.

16 Astengo, 'Renaissance Chart Tradition', 174; Christoffer H. Ericsson, 'Seafaring, Hydrography and Chart Making in the Baltic Sea', in Christoffer H. Ericsson, Leena Miekkavaara, Juha Nurminen and Nils-Erik Raurala (eds), *The Routes of the Sea: Sea Chart from the 16th Century to Present Times* (Helsinki: John Nurminen Oy, 1988), 9–40, especially 10–17; Janni, *La mappa e il periplo*, 58–9; Padrón, 'Mapping Plus Ultra', 48–51. For a useful summary of the development of astronomic navigation, and its general impact on mapping, see also Joaquim Alves Gaspar, 'From the Portolan Chart to the Latitude Chart: The Silent Cartographic Revolution', *Cartes & Géomatique: Revue du Comité français de cartographie* 216 (2013), 67–77.

17 José L. Gasch-Tomás, *The Atlantic World and the Manila Galleons: Circulation, Market, and Consumption of Asian Goods in the Spanish Empire, 1565–1650* (Leiden and Boston MA: Brill, 2019); Manuel Carrera Stampa, 'La Nao de la China', *Historia Mexicana* 9:1 (1959), 97–118.

18 On Anson's voyage and his subsequent fame see: N. A. M. Rodger, 'Anson, George, Baron Anson (1697–1762)', *Oxford Dictionary of National Biography* (Oxford: Oxford University Press, 2004) https://doi.org/10.1093/ref:odnb/574; Katherine Parker, 'Memorialising Anson, the Fighting Explorer: A Case Study in Eighteenth-Century Naval Commemoration and Material Culture', in Quintin Colville and James Davey (eds), *A New Naval History* (Manchester: Manchester University Press, 2019), 133–50.

19 Gabriel Paquette, *The European Seaborne Empires: From the Thirty Years' War to the Age of Revolutions* (New Haven CT and London: Yale University Press, 2019), 7.

20 Lauren Benton, *A Search for Sovereignty: Law and Geography in European Empires, 1400–1900* (Cambridge: Cambridge University Press, 2009), 104–11.

21 Thomas Wemyss Fulton, *The Sovereignty of the Sea: An Historical Account of the Claims of England to the Dominion of the British Seas, and of the Evolution of the Territorial Waters: With Special Reference to the Rights of Fishing and the Naval Salute* (Edinburgh and London: William Blackwood and Sons, 1911), esp. Ch. 9; Edward Gordon, 'Grotius and the Freedom of the Seas in the Seventeenth Century', *Willamette Journal of International Law and Dispute Resolution* 16:2 (2008), 252–69; Monica Brito Vieira, 'Mare Liberum vs. Mare Clausum: Grotius, Freitas, and Selden's Debate on Dominion over the Seas', *Journal of the History of Ideas* 64:3 (2003), 361–77; Philippa Hellawell, 'Systematizing the Sea: Knowledge, Power and Maritime Sovereignty in Late Seventeenth-Century Science', in Richard J. Blakemore and James Davey (eds), *The Maritime World of Early Modern Britain* (Amsterdam: Amsterdam University Press, 2020), 257–82; Renaud Morieux, *The Channel: England, France and the Construction of a Maritime Border in the Eighteenth Century* (Cambridge: Cambridge

University Press, 2016), Ch. 4; Timothy Brook, *Mr Selden's Map of China: The Spice Trade, a Lost Chart and the South China Sea* (London: Profile Books, 2015), 27–39.

22 John Selden, *Of the Dominion or Ownership of the Sea Two Books*, trans. Marchamont Nedham, 2 vols (London: Printed by William Du-Gard ..., 1652), quotes at I, 139, 141.

23 Hugo Grotius, *Commentary on the Law of Prize and Booty*, ed. Martine Julia van Ittersum, trans. Gwladys L. Williams (Indianapolis IN: Liberty Fund, 2006 [1950]), 334. In the original Latin the term used is '*vestigium*', meaning 'trace' ('*Sed nemo nescit navem per mare transeuntem non plus juris quam vestigii relinquere.*'): *Hugonis Grotii De Jure Praedae Commentarius*, ed. H. G. Hamaker (The Hague: Martinus Nijhoff, 1868), 228. This chapter was the only part of the treatise published by Grotius in his lifetime (anonymously), in the pamphlet *Mare Liberum*. The contemporary English translation there is slightly different ('a ship passing the seas leaveth no more right than the way thereof'): Hugo Grotius, *The Free Sea*, trans. Richard Hakluyt, ed. David Armitage (Indianapolis IN: Liberty Fund, 2004 [1609]), 34. For more on the etymology of 'track' across languages see below.

24 Alex Hidalgo, *Trail of Footprints: A History of Indigenous Maps from Viceregal Mexico* (Austin TX: University of Texas Press, 2019), (42–5, 48 for hoofprints examples); Serge Gruzinski, 'Colonial Indian Maps in Sixteenth-Century Mexico: An Essay in Mixed Cartography', *RES: Anthropology and Aesthetics* 13 (1987), 46–61. I am very grateful to Dr Sebastian Kroupa for recommending Hidalgo's book to me. For an example with hoofprints see also Benson Latin American Collection, LLILAS Benson Latin American Studies and Collections, the University of Texas at Austin, Relaciones Geográficas of Mexico and Guatemala, JGI XXIII-15, 'Pintura de Cuzcatlan' (1580) https://collections.lib. utexas.edu/catalog/utblac:e38f8f71-f967-46fb-9493-1edec8cbc1b3.

25 Campbell, 'Portolan Charts', 443–4; Bataller, *Cartes portolanes*, 166–7, 462.

26 I use this term in the sense in which it's deployed in Edney, *Cartography*, 33–4, 100. An important confirmation of the role of navigational pricking in this story is that Jordana Dym also hypothesises that early modern pilgrims' itinerary maps drew inspiration from the chart plotting that they had witnessed during their sea passage: Dym, *Mapping Travel*, 28–9.

27 Unger, *Ships on Maps*, 12.

28 Unger, *Ships on Maps*; Van Duzer, *Sea Monsters*; Tebel, *Das Schiff*. Other iconographic elements had sophisticated symbolic meanings – for example, images of navigational instruments: Surekha Davies, 'The Navigational Iconography of Diogo Ribeiro's 1529 Vatican Planisphere', *Imago Mundi* 55 (2003), 103–12.

29 Armando Cortesão, *Cartografia e cartógrafos portugueses dos séculos XV e XVI (Contribuição para um estudo completo)*, 2 vols (Lisbon: Edição da "Seara nova", 1935), II, 130–67. In a 1527 version of the Planisphere the ships are oriented in the right directions but bear no captions (142, 146, 148, 152, 155, 161). See also: Richard W. Unger, 'Ships, Routes and the Discovery of the Sea in the Renaissance', in Nicole Hegener and Lars Ulrich Scholl (eds), *Vom Anker zu*

Krähennest: Nautische Bildwelten von der Renaissance bis zum Zeitalter der Fotografie / From the Anchor to the Crow's Nest: Naval Imagery from the Renaissance to the Age of Photography (Bremen: H. M. Hauschild, 2011), 60–73, at 67–8; Unger, *Ships on Maps*, 87–90, 160; Wagner, 'Manuscript Atlases', 26.

30 J. V. G. Mills, 'Introduction', in Ma Huan, *Ying-yai sheng-lan: 'The Overall Survey of the Ocean's Shores' [1433]*, ed. J. V. G. Mills and Feng Ch'eng-Chün (Cambridge: Cambridge University Press for the Hakluyt Society, 1970), 18–22. On the question of whether Australia was visited, see also Roderich Ptak, 'Selected Problems Concerning the "Zheng He Map": Questions without Answers', *Journal of Asian History* 53:2 (2019), 179–219, at 195–6. On the controversy surrounding the size of these vessels, see Sally K. Church, 'Zheng He: An Investigation into the Plausibility of 450-Ft Treasure Ships', *Monumenta Serica* 53 (2005), 1–43.

31 Ma Huan, *Ying-yai sheng-lan*, 158–9.

32 For an overview of the expeditions, as discussed in this paragraph, see: Geoff Wade, 'The Zheng He Voyages: A Reassessment', *Journal of the Malaysian Branch of the Royal Asiatic Society* 78:1(288) (2005), 37–58; Angela Schottenhammer, 'Consolidating Southeast Asia and the Meaning of Force in History: Pax Ming and the Case of Chen Zuyi 陳祖義', *China and Asia* 3 (2021), 130–68; Deng Hui and Li Xin, 'The Asian Monsoons and Zheng He's Voyages to the Western Ocean', *The Journal of Navigation* 64 (2011), 207–18; Robert Finlay, 'The Treasure-Ships of Zheng He: Chinese Maritime Imperialism in the Age of Discovery', *Terrae Incognitae* 23 (1991), 1–12; Sally Church, 'Zheng He', in Helaine Selin (ed.), *Encyclopedia of the History of Science, Technology, and Medicine in Non-Western Cultures*, 2 vols (Berlin: Springer-Verlag, 2008), II, 2354–7; José Eugenio Borao Mateo, 'Las crónicas de los viajes de Zheng He y de Magallanes-Elcano', in *V Centenario de la primera vuelta al mundo: Congreso Internacional de Historia "Primus Circumdedisti Me" – Valladolid, 20–22 marzo 2018* ([Madrid]: Ministerio de Defensa, 2018), 51–63. On Chinese medieval maritime endeavours in general see: Angela Schottenhammer, 'Maritime Relations between the Indian Ocean and the China Sea in the Middle Ages', in Balard and Buchet (eds), *The Sea in History– The Medieval World* , 794–807; Qu Jinliang, 'The Chinese Fleets in the Indian Ocean (13th–15th Centuries)', in ibid., 822–36. On how Chinese maritime endeavours continued in different forms in subsequent centuries, see Ronald C. Po, *The Blue Frontier: Maritime Vision and Power in the Qing Empire* (Cambridge: Cambridge University Press, 2018); Zheng Yangwen, *China on the Sea: How the Maritime World Shaped Modern China* (Leiden and Boston: Brill, 2012); Gang Zhao, *The Qing Opening to the Ocean: Chinese Maritime Policies, 1684–1757* (Honolulu HI: University of Hawai'i Press, 2013).

33 Mei-Ling Hsu, 'Chinese Marine Cartography: Sea Charts of Pre-Modern China', *Imago Mundi* 40:1 (1988), 96–112, at 97–104.

34 Stephen Davies, 'The Construction of the Selden Map: Some Conjectures', *Imago Mundi* 65:1 (2013), 97–105; Robert Batchelor, 'The Selden Map Rediscovered: A Chinese Map of East Asian Shipping Routes, c.1619', *Imago Mundi* 65:1 (2013), 37–63; Brook, *Mr Selden's Map of China*, 109–128. For the

map itself see Bodleian Library, Oxford, MS.Selden supra 105, 'The Selden Map of China' https://iiif.bodleian.ox.ac.uk/iiif/viewer/?iiif-content=https://iiif.bodleian.ox.ac.uk/iiif/manifest/58b9518f-d5ea-4cb3-aa15-f42640c50ef3.json#?c=0&m=0&s=0&cv=0&r=0&xywh=-7070%2C-579%2C21029%2C11561.

35 Papelitzky, 'Red Lines in the Ocean'; Elke Papelitzky, 'Making a Case for Trade: Shi Shipiao's Map of the Eastern and Southern Oceans', *East Asian Science, Technology, and Medicine* 55:2 (forthcoming). My heartfelt thanks to Dr Papelitzky for sharing her work with me, and for her cheerful and generous support.

36 Ptak, 'Selected Problems'.

37 For the evolutions of this collaboration over the centuries, see e.g.: Mario Cams, *Companions in Geography: East-West Collaboration in the Mapping of Qing China (c.1685–1735)* (Leiden and Boston MA: Brill, 2017); Richard J. Smith, *Mapping China and Managing the World: Culture, Cartography and Cosmology in Late Imperial Times* (Abingdon and New York: Routledge, 2013), 62–70.

38 Brodersen, 'Mapping (in) the Ancient World', 183.

39 Hsu, 'Chinese Marine Cartography', 96–7.

40 Hirosi Nakamura, 'The Japanese Portolanos of Portuguese Origin of the XVIth and XVIIth Centuries', *Imago Mundi* 18 (1964), 24–44, at 30, 33; Peter D. Shapinsky, 'Polyvocal Portolans: Nautical Charts and Hybrid Maritime Cultures in Early Modern East Asia', *Early Modern Japan* 14 (2006), 4–26, esp. at 12–14.

41 Papelitzky, 'Red Lines in the Ocean'.

42 Fernández-Armesto, *Straits*, 10–15; Finlay, 'Treasure-Ships', 1–2, 8.

43 For a good summary see John E. Wills, Jr., 'Maritime Europe and the Ming', in John E. Wills, Jr. (ed.), *China and Maritime Europe, 1500–1800: Trade, Settlement, Diplomacy, and Missions* (Cambridge: Cambridge University Press, 2011), 24–77, esp. 24–32.

44 This translation of the letter comes from Armando Cortesão (ed.), *The Suma Oriental of Tomé Pires: An Account of the East, from the Red Sea to Japan, Written in Malacca and India in 1512–1515; and The Book of Francisco Rodrigues: Rutter of a Voyage in the Red Sea, Nautical Rules, Almanack and Maps, Written and Drawn in the East before 1515* (London: Hakluyt Society, 1944), lxxviii–lxxix. For the original Portuguese see Raymundo Antonio de Bulhão Pato (ed.), *Cartas de Affonso de Albuquerque seguidas de documentos que as elucidam*, 7 vols (Lisbon: Typographia da Academia Real das Sciencias, 1884), I, 64–5. See also Cortesão, *Cartografia e cartógrafos portugueses*, II, 125–9. In Portuguese, 'rhumbs and direct routes' is 'lynhas e caminhos dereytos'. On the term '*Gores*' see Jaime Ramalhete Neves, 'The Portuguese in the Im-Jim War?', *Review of Culture*, 2nd Series, 18 (2006), 20–24 http://www.icm.gov.mo/rc/viewer/20018/990. On Albuquerque himself see Alexandra Pelúcia, *Afonso de Albuquerque: Corte, Cruzada e Império* (Lisbon: Temas e Debates – Círculo de Leitores, 2016), (32 on his nicknames).

45 J. H. F. Sollewijn Gelpke, 'Afonso de Albuquerque's Pre-Portuguese "Javanese" Map, Partially Reconstructed from Francisco Rodrigues' *Book*', *Bijdragen tot de Taal-, Land- en Volkenkunde* 151:1 (1995), 76–99.

46 In the original, 'cousa muyto certa e muyto sabida'.

47 Antonio Pigafetta's account of Magellan's expedition does not specify where the ships passed in relation to these islands: Antonio Pigafetta, *Pigafetta's Account of Magellan's Voyage*, ed. Henry Edward John Stanley (Cambridge: Cambridge University Press, 2010 [1874]), 65–66. Neither does Francisco Albo's journal: José Luís Morales, 'Las derrotas de Magallanes y de Elcano en el primer viaje de circunnavegación', in Teixeira da Mota (ed.), *Viagem de Fernão de Magalhães*, 343–60, at 352, entries for 24 January and 4 February 1521. On the identification of these islands see Magnaghi, 'Atlante manoscritto', 139; Fernández-Armesto, *Straits*, 217–21. These are not the same as the homonymous 'Islas Desventuradas' just off the coast of Chile: Jaime Rivera Marfán, 'Islas Desventuradas', *Revista de Marina* 116:850 (3/99) (1999), 268–78. For other examples showing the tracks below the island see John Carter Brown Library, Providence, Codex Z 3 / 2-SIZE, '[Atlas of Portolan Charts – Map of the World]', [1543–1545?] https://jcb.lunaimaging.com/luna/servlet/s/o3bnmm; Huntington Library, San Marino, CA, mssHM 26, Battista Agnese, 'Portolan atlas', *c*.1544 https://hdl.huntington.org/digital/collection/p15150coll7/id/46133/rec/3.

48 Max Justo Guedes, 'A armada de Fernão de Magalhães e o Brasil', in Teixeira da Mota (ed.), *Viagem de Fernão de Magalhães*, 361–77; Pigafetta, *Pigafetta's Account*, 43–57; Morales, 'Derrotas de Magallanes', 349–51.

49 John Law, 'Technology and Heterogeneous Engineering: The Case of Portuguese Expansion', in Wiebe E. Bijker et al. (eds), *The Social Construction of Technological Systems: New Directions in the Sociology and History of Technology* (Cambridge MA and London: MIT Press, 2012), 105–27, at 113–14; Alfred W. Crosby, *Ecological Imperialism: The Biological Expansion of Europe, 900–1900*, 2nd edn (Cambridge: Cambridge University Press, 2004), 104–31.

50 Felipe Fernández-Armesto, 'Maps and Exploration in the Sixteenth and Early Seventeenth Centuries', in Woodward (ed.), *History of Cartography – Volume III*, Pt. i, 738–59, at 757.

51 William M. Ivins, *Prints and Visual Communication* (Cambridge MA: MIT Press, 1969), 2. See also Elizabeth L. Eisenstein, *The Printing Press as an Agent of Change: Communications and Cultural Transformations in Early-Modern Europe*, 2 vols (Cambridge: Cambridge University Press, 1979), esp. 46–7, 51–5. As she puts it (p. 9), 'Schoolchildren who are asked to trace early overseas voyages on identical outline maps are likely to become absent-minded about the fact that there were no uniform world maps in the era when the voyages were made'.

52 Eisenstein's work has sparked a large debate, including on this point; for a useful summary and rejoinder (albeit referring to the type press rather than image reproduction) see Harold Love, 'Fixity versus Flexibility in "A Song on Tom of Danby" and Dryden's *Absalom and Achitophel*', in Sabrina Alcorn Baron, Eric N. Lindquist and Eleanor F. Shevlin (eds), *Agent of Change: Print Culture Studies after Elizabeth L. Eisenstein* (Amherst and Boston MA: University of Massachusetts Press, 2007), 140–55. On printing as 'unstable' see also David McKitterick, *Print, Manuscript and the Search for Order, 1450–1830* (Cambridge: Cambridge University Press, 2003), esp. Chs 4 and 5.

53 It's possible that this was preceded by another Venetian edition, in 1534, but the
    matter remains uncertain: Francisco Leite de Faria, 'As primeiras relações
    impressas sobre a viagem de Fernão de Magalhães', in Teixeira da Mota (ed.),
    Viagem de Fernão de Magalhães, 471–518, at 494–8, 507, 510–12.

54 Alison Sandman, 'Controlling Knowledge: Navigation, Cartography, and
    Secrecy in the Early Modern Spanish Atlantic', in James Delbourgo and
    Nicholas Dew (eds), *Science and Empire in the Atlantic World* (New York and
    London: Routledge, 2008), 31–51; J. B. Harley, 'Silences and Secrecy: The
    Hidden Agenda of Cartography in Early Modern Europe', *Imago Mundi* 40
    (1988), 57–76, at 59–65; María M. Portuondo, *Secret Science: Spanish
    Cosmography and the New World* (Chicago IL and London: University of
    Chicago Press, 2009).

55 Arquivo Nacional Torre do Tombo, Lisbon, PT/TT/EPJS/SF/001-
    001/0195/0272, Mapa das etapas da viagem do Argos http://digitarq.arquivos.
    pt/details?id=1206810.

56 On this point, and on the expedition details recounted above, see: Isabel
    Morujão, '*Asas que naufragam*: narrativa de viagens aéreas em Portugal na obra
    de Sarmento de Beires', in Isabel Morujão and Zulmira Santos (eds), *Literatura
    culta e popular em Portugal e no Brasil – homenagem a Arnaldo Saraiva* (Porto:
    CITCEM-Centro de Investigação Transdisciplinar Cultura, Espaço e Memória:
    Afrontamento, 2011), 392–411; Fernando Neves, Jorge Barata and André Silva,
    'First Aerial South Atlantic Night Crossing', *Advances in Historical Studies* 5:1
    (2016). Beires's own 1927 book, *Asas que naufragam*, is extremely rare, and it
    proved impossible for me to access a copy.

57 For example, if the route depicted misrepresents the trajectory of planes that
    were shot down for violating territorial boundaries, or the range of ballistic
    threats. These case studies are described in Peter Vujakovic, 'Cartography and
    the News', in Alexander J. Kent and Peter Vujakovic (eds), *The Routledge
    Handbook of Mapping and Cartography* (London and New York: Routledge,
    2018), 462–74, at 466–8.

58 For more on the atlases' uses, see: Magnaghi, 'Atlante manoscritto';
    Baumgärtner, 'Battista Agnese'. On the importance of distinguishing between
    mapping 'modes' (e.g., here, the geographical and the navigational), see Edney,
    Cartography, 33–4.

59 Avan Judd Stallard, *Antipodes: In Search of the Southern Continent* (Clayton:
    Monash University Publishing, 2016); Mike A. Zuber, 'The Armchair Discovery
    of the Unknown Southern Continent: Gerardus Mercator, Philosophical
    Pretensions and a Competitive Trade', *Early Science and Medicine* 16 (2011),
    505–41.

60 For an excellent overview, see: Harry Kelsey, 'Drake, Sir Francis (1540–1596)',
    Oxford Dictionary of National Biography (2009) https://doi.org/10.1093/
    ref:odnb/8022; Norman J. W. Thrower (ed.), *Sir Francis Drake and the Famous
    Voyage, 1577–1580: Essays Commemorating the Quadricentennial of Drake's
    Circumnavigation of the Earth* (Berkeley CA: University of California Press,
    1984).

61 Sir Simon Cassels, 'Where Did Drake Careen the *Golden Hind* in June/July 1579? A Mariner's Assessment', *The Mariner's Mirror* 89:3 (2003), 260–71.

62 British Library, London, Harley MS. 280, quoted in John Evans, 'The Silver Medal or Map of Sir Francis Drake: Supplemental Remarks', *The Numismatic Chronicle and Journal of the Royal Numismatic Society*, 4th Series, 6 (1906), 77–89 and 348–50, at 85.

63 Phillips Academy Andover, MA, Sidney R. Knafel Map Collection, n. 1355, Nicola van Sype, 'La heroike enterprinse faict par le Signeur Draeck d'avoir cirquit toute la terre', [*c.*1583] https://collections.leventhalmap.org/search/commonwealth:hq37vv605.

64 On seafarers' expertise and early modern knowledge see Philippa Hellawell, '"The Best and Most Practical Philosophers": Seamen and the Authority of Experience in Early Modern Science', *History of Science* 58:1 (2020), 28–50. On how their direct, embodied knowledge was appropriated and reshaped into abstraction see Elin Jones, 'Stratifying Seamanship: Sailors' Knowledge and the Mechanical Arts in Eighteenth-Century Britain', *The British Journal for the History of Science* 56:1 (2023), 45–63. For more on tracks and first-hand, eyewitness trust see Chapter 5.

65 Mateo Martinic, 'Entre el mito y la realidad. La situación de la misteriosa Isla Elizabeth de Francis Drake', *Magallania* 47:1 (2019), 5–14.

66 For more on the Drake maps and the initial secrecy surrounding the expedition see Helen Wallis, 'The Cartography of Drake's Voyage', in Thrower (ed.), *Sir Francis Drake and the Famous Voyage*, 121–63, esp. 122–3 on the maps' international use to stake territorial claims, and 157–9 on Nova Albion.

67 'Drake Navigators Guild' https://drakenavigatorsguild.squarespace.com; Cassels, 'Where Did Drake Careen the *Golden Hind*?'.

68 Margaret E. Schotte, *Sailing School: Navigating Science and Skill, 1550–1800* (Baltimore MD: Johns Hopkins University Press, 2019).

69 Henry Manwayring, *The Sea-mans Dictionary: or, An Exposition and Demonstration of All the Parts and Things Belonging to a Shippe: Together with an Explanation of All the Termes and Phrases Used in the Practique of Navigation* (London: John Bellamy, 1644), viewable at Early English Books Online Text Creation Partnership https://quod.lib.umich.edu/e/eebo2/A51871.0001.001/1:19.15?rgn=div2;view=fulltext.

70 On the pirate log (whose date isn't fully certain) see: N. A. M. Rodger, 'A Pirate's Log?', *The Mariner's Mirror* 67 (1981), 201–4; Sarah Tyacke, 'All at Sea: Some Cartographical Problems in the North 1500–1700', *Imcos Journal* 111 (2007), 38–41, at [5–7] in the version available at https://www.academia.edu/38142804/All_at_Sea_some_cartographic_problems_in_the_north_1500_1700; Tyacke, 'Chartmaking', 1733–4. On chart-making and plotting aboard see: Fernández-Armesto, 'Maps and Exploration', 752; Sarah Toulouse, 'Marine Cartography and Navigation in Renaissance France', in Woodward (ed.), *History of Cartography – Volume III*, Pt. ii, 1550–68, esp. 1558–61; Tyacke, 'Chartmaking', 1735–7.

71 Katie Parker, 'The Ship, the Map, the Chart, and the Book: The Role of the Royal Navy in the Publication of Pacific Geographic Knowledge in the

Long-Eighteenth Century', *Revue de la Société d'études anglo-américaines des XVIIe et XVIIIe siècles* 78 (2021) https://doi.org/10.4000/1718.6939; Katherine Parker, 'Pepys Island as a Pacific Stepping Stone: The Struggle to Capture Islands on Early Modern Maps', *The British Journal for the History of Science* 51:4 (2018), 659–77, at 664, 668; Joaquim Alves Gaspar and Henrique Leitão, 'Early Modern Nautical Charts and Maps: Working Through Different Cartographic Paradigms', *Journal of Early Modern History* 23 (2019), 1–28, esp. 3–4; Tyacke, 'Chartmaking', 1746–7.

72 On the expedition and on the extremely complex publication history of its accounts see: Herman de la Fontaine Verwey, 'Willem Jansz Blaeu and the Voyage of Le Maire and Schouten', *Quaerendo* 3:2 (1973), 87–105; Michiel Van Groesen, 'Changing the Image of the Southern Pacific: Willem Schouten, His Circumnavigation, and the De Bry Collection of Voyages', *The Journal of Pacific History* 44:1 (2009), 77–87. For an example of reproduction see Rijksmuseum, Amsterdam, RP-P-OB-75.472, FMH 1055-AII(5)/1, Atlas van Stolk 982, 'Kaart van de wereld met de reizen van Joris van Spilbergen en Jacob le Maire om de wereld, 1614–1617' http://hdl.handle.net/10934/RM0001.COLLECT.450618.

73 David Woodward, 'Techniques of Map Engraving, Printing, and Coloring in the European Renaissance', in Woodward (ed.), *History of Cartography – Volume III*, Pt. i, 591–610, esp. 599–600.

74 This is the same sense of '*ductus*' found in the Paris Gilt Globe ('*linea [...] ducta*'). See endnote 8 above. For more on the term '*ductus*' see Ingold, *Lines*, 16–17, 95–6, 98–9. Later reproductions of the Le Maire journey also use the term '*navigationis ductus*': Rijksmuseum, Amsterdam, RP-P-OB-75.472.

75 Gotha Perthes Collection, Gotha, SPK-80-3 B-01, 'Пути Беринга и Чирикова 1741 года'; 'Charte von einem Theile des SÜD=MEERES, darinnen die verschiedenen Farthen und Entdeckungen angezeigt sind, welche von nachstehenden, auf S.ʳ Gros=Britt. Maj. Befehl ausgesandten Schiffen gemacht worden sind' (n.d., 1770s?).

76 'Quando se dize derrota, se entiende el camino que por la mar se hazer o deue hazer': quote and translation from Waters, *Science and the Techniques of Navigation*, 17.

77 Edward Phillips, *The New World of English Words: Or, a General Dictionary* (London: Nath. Brooke, 1658).

78 Edward Phillips and J[ohn] K[ersey], *The New World of Words: Or, Universal English Dictionary*, 6th edn (London: J. Phillips, 1706). The fifth edition, which came out in 1696, was still missing 'track'.

79 For the Tasman chart see Österreichische Nationalbibliothek, Vienna, KAR AB 311, Johannes de Vingboons, 'Staeten Landt bescijlt en ondeckt anno 1642 den 13 december met het Jacht Heemskerck on de Zeehaen, ende met groote vlijt seer neersticht ont worpen, door franchoys Jacobse Stierman', [c.1665], which I consulted online on Joaquim Alves Gaspar's wonderful *MEDEA-CHART Database* https://medea.fc.ul.pt/view/chart/5431. This chart represents the western coast of North Island, New Zealand. A modern printed reproduction is viewable at National Library of Australia, Canberra, MAP Ra 265 Vol. 4, Plate 99, 'Franchoys Jacobse, Staeten Landt beseijlt ende ondeckt anno 1642 den 13

December met het jacht Heemskerck ende Zeehaen' (The Hague: Martinus Nijhoff, [1925–33]) https://catalogue.nla.gov.au/Record/4228881.

80 Gaspar and Leitão, 'Early Modern Nautical Charts and Maps'. On the new geometrical models of the world see: Sandman, 'Controlling Knowledge'; Vladimiro Valerio, 'La *Geografia* di Tolemeo e la nascita della moderna rappresentazione dello spazio', in Vanna Maraglino (ed.), *Scienza antica in età moderna: Teoria e immagini* (Bari: Cacucci Editore, 2012), 215–32; Trevor Barnes and Carl Christian Abrahamsson, 'The Imprecise Wanderings of a Precise Idea: The Travels of Spatial Analysis', in Heike Jöns, Peter Meusburger and Michael Heffernan (eds), *Mobilities of Knowledge* (Cham: Springer, 2017), 105–21, at 110–12. Cosmography, as a totalising project, also embraced descriptions of the world. See: Portuondo, *Secret Science*, here especially Chs 1 and 7; Lestringant, *Mapping the Renaissance World*. On the conflict with pilotage see Davies, 'Navigational Iconography', 108–9. On the survival of the itinerary view see Padrón, 'Mapping Plus Ultra'.

81 For some particularly good historical explanations of these concepts see Waters, *Science and the Techniques of Navigation*; Gaspar, 'From the Portolan Chart', 69, 73–4.

82 Janni, 'Sea of the Greeks and Romans', 21–2; Portuondo, *Secret Science*, 20–26. Alexandrine astronomers also used equatorial coordinates to chart stars on the celestial sphere: Victor Gysembergh, Peter J. Williams and Emanuel Zingg, 'New Evidence for Hipparchus' Star Catalogue Revealed by Multispectral Imaging', *Journal for the History of Astronomy* 53:4 (2022), 383–93. In China, separate grid systems were also developed in aid of mapping: for a twelfth-century example, and its contested genealogy, see Cordell D. K. Yee, 'Reinterpreting Traditional Chinese Geographical Maps', in J. B. Harley and David Woodward (eds), *The History of Cartography – Volume II, Book II: Cartography in the Traditional East and Southeast Asian Societies* (Chicago IL and London: University of Chicago Press, 1994), 35–70, at 47–50, 59–60. I am very grateful to Dr Gianamar Giovannetti-Singh for suggesting this chapter to me.

83 For an example see Bibliothèque de l'Institut de France, Paris, Ms. 1288/3, 'Routes du Cap de Bonne-Espérance' ([Joan Blaeu], Chart of the South Atlantic Ocean from the Cabo Verde islands to the Cape of Good Hope, *c.*1650), consulted at *MEDEA-CHART Database* https://medea.fc.ul.pt/view/chart/3873.

84 Gaspar and Leitão, 'Early Modern Nautical Charts'; Waters, *Science and the Techniques of Navigation*; Sandman, 'Controlling Knowledge'; Turnbull, 'Cartography and Science', 9–14; Toulouse, 'Marine Cartography'; Tyacke, 'Chartmaking', 1743–5; Destombes, 'Chart of Magellan', 76.

85 Waters, *Science and the Techniques of Navigation*, esp. 7–15; Richard Dunn, *Navigational Instruments* (Oxford: Shire Publications Ltd, 2016), 23–33.

86 Harry Miller Lydenberg (ed.), *Crossing the Line: Tales of the Ceremony during Four Centuries* (New York: New York Public Library, 1957); Jaime Rodrigues, 'A New World in the Atlantic: Sailors and Rites of Passage Crossing the Equator, from the 15th to the 20th Century', *Revista Brasileira de História* 33:65 (2013),

233–75; Simon J. Bronner, *Crossing the Line: Violence, Play, and Drama in Naval Equator Traditions* (Amsterdam: Amsterdam University Press, 2006); Carie Little Hersh, 'Crossing the Line: Sex, Power, Justice, and the U.S. Navy at the Equator', *Duke Journal of Gender Law & Policy* 9:277 (2002), 277–324; Keith P. Richardson, 'Pollywogs and Shellbacks: An Analysis of the Equator Crossing Ritual', *Western Folklore* 36:2 (1977), 154–9. On the date of the earliest Equator crossing see Waters, *Science and the Techniques of Navigation*, 10.

87 Charles W. J. Withers, *Zero Degrees: Geographies of the Prime Meridian* (Cambridge MA and London: Harvard University Press, 2017), 130–37.

88 Harley, 'Deconstructing', 236.

89 Gaspar and Leitão, 'Early Modern Nautical Charts', 6. The term 'point of imagination' also occasionally features in sixteenth-century English; 'dead reckoning' may have derived from 'ded[uced] reckoning': Charles H. Cotter, 'Early Dead Reckoning Navigation', *The Journal of Navigation* 31:1 (1978), 20–28, at 21–2.

90 Margaret Schotte, 'Expert Records: Nautical Logbooks from Columbus to Cook', *Information & Culture* 48:3 (2013), 281–322. Spanish pilots had been required to return voyage records to the Casa de la Contratación in Seville since at least the first half of the sixteenth century: Portuondo, *Secret Science*, 270.

91 Ricardo García Herrera et al., *CLIWOC Final Report* (2003), 9, 11–13 https://epic.awi.de/id/eprint/17063/1/Gar2003a.pdf.

92 Alison Sandman, 'Longitude and Latitude', in Matthew H. Edney and Mary Sponberg Pedley (eds), *The History of Cartography – Volume IV: Cartography in the European Enlightenment* (Chicago IL: University of Chicago Press, 2019), 735–50, at 738–40; Morieux, *Channel*, 98–104.

Chapter 3: Writing on Water

1 The classic edition of Cook's voyage journals is J. C. Beaglehole, *The Journals of Captain James Cook on His Voyages of Discovery*, 5 vols (Cambridge: Cambridge University Press for the Hakluyt Society, 1955–74).

2 On Cook's celebrity see Chapter 4.

3 Out of a vast literature, see e.g. John Gascoigne, *Science in the Service of Empire: Joseph Banks, the British State and the Uses of Science in the Age of Revolution* (Cambridge: Cambridge University Press, 1998); Katherine Parker, 'Charting and Knowledge in Enlightened Empires: The Case of Tierra del Fuego in Anson's *Voyage Round the World* (1748)', *The Cartographic Journal* 57:4 (2020), 353–65. For a slightly different interpretation, stressing the prevalence of scientific goals, see Jean Fornasiero and John West-Sooby, 'The Acquisitive Eye? French Observations in the Pacific from Bougainville to Baudin', in John West-Sooby (ed.), *Discovery and Empire: The French in the South Seas* (Adelaide: University of Adelaide Press, 2013), 69–97. On the economic goals of eighteenth-century mapping more generally, see Julian Hoppit and Renaud Morieux, 'Cartography and the Economy', in Edney and Pedley (eds), *History of Cartography – Volume IV*, 360–67.

4 Madame d'Arblay [Frances Burney], *Memoirs of Doctor Burney, Arranged from His Own Manuscripts, from Family Papers, and from Personal Recollections*, 3 vols

(London: Edward Moxon, 1832), I, 270–71; Helen Wallis (ed.), *Carteret's Voyage round the World, 1766–1769*, 2 vols (Cambridge: Cambridge University Press, 1965), I, 94–5.

5 Royal Greenwich Observatory Archives, Papers of the Board of Longitude, RGO 14/56, Log book of HMS *Adventure*, by William Bayly (ed. Alexi Baker), 1772–4, f. 100v https://cudl.lib.cam.ac.uk/view/MS-RGO-00014-00056/206; Ruth Scobie, '"Bunny! O! Bunny!": The Burney Family in Oceania', *Eighteenth-Century Life* 42:2 (2018), 56–72, at 60–61.

6 Gananath Obeyesekere, *Cannibal Talk: The Man-Eating Myth and Human Sacrifice in the South Seas* (Berkeley CA: University of California Press, 2005), (32–4 on the details of the Burney episode as reported in various accounts).

7 On this see e.g. Parker, 'Pepys Island', 664.

8 Sorrenson, 'Ship as a Scientific Instrument'.

9 Ibid.

10 'Currency Converter: 1270–2017', *The National Archives* https://www. nationalarchives.gov.uk/currency-converter/#. This returns a value of £2,322,150 for 2017, which is £2,965,667 in October 2023 terms, according to the Bank of England's Inflation Calculator (https://www.bankofengland.co.uk/monetary-policy/inflation/inflation-calculator).

11 The most famous rehearsal of this story is Dava Sobel, *Longitude: The True Story of a Lone Genius Who Solved the Greatest Scientific Problem of His Time* (London: Fourth Estate, 1996).

12 David Philip Miller, 'The "Sobel Effect"', *Metascience* 11 (2002), 185–200.

13 Richard Dunn and Rebekah Higgitt (eds), *Navigational Enterprises in Europe and Its Empires, 1730–1850* (Basingstoke: Palgrave Macmillan, 2016); Richard Dunn and Rebekah Higgitt, *Finding Longitude* (Glasgow: HarperCollins, 2014); Jim Bennett, 'The Travels and Trials of Mr Harrison's Timekeeper', in Marie-Noëlle Bourguet, Christian Licoppe and H. Otto Sibum (eds), *Instruments, Travel and Science: Itineraries of Precision from the Seventeenth to the Twentieth Century* (London and New York: Routledge, 2002), 75–95.

14 J. C. Beaglehole, *The Journals of Captain James Cook on His Voyages of Discovery: The Voyage of the* Endeavour, *1768–1771* (Cambridge: Cambridge University Press, 1968), clxviii–ix.

15 Harley, 'Deconstructing the Map', 241.

16 Michael T. Bravo, 'Precision and Curiosity in Scientific Travel: James Rennell and the Orientalist Geography of the New Imperial Age (1760–1830)', in Jaś Elsner and Joan-Pau Rubiés (eds), *Voyages and Visions: Towards a Cultural History of Travel* (London: Reaktion Books, 1999), 162–83; Marie-Noëlle Bourguet, 'Landscape with Numbers: Natural History, Travel and Instruments in the Late Eighteenth and Early Nineteenth Centuries', in Bourguet et al. (eds), *Instruments, Travel and Science*, 96–125; Denis Cosgrove, 'Introduction: Mapping Meaning', in Cosgrove (ed.), *Mappings*, 1–23, at 4, 18–19. On notions of 'epistemological legitimacy' in Enlightenment mapping and travel accounts see also: Matthew H. Edney, 'Reconsidering Enlightenment Geography and Map Making: Reconnaissance, Mapping, Archive', in David N. Livingstone and Charles W. J. Withers (eds), *Geography and Enlightenment* (Chicago IL and

London: University of Chicago Press, 1999), 165–98; Innes M. Keighren, Charles W. J. Withers and Bill Bell, *Travels into Print: Exploration, Writing, and Publishing with John Murray, 1773–1859* (Chicago IL: University of Chicago Press, 2015); Dorinda Outram, 'On Being Perseus: New Knowledge, Dislocation, and Enlightenment Exploration', in Livingstone and Withers (eds), *Geography and Enlightenment*, 281–94.

17 Philosopher and anthropologist Bruno Latour talks of 'transubstantiation' from 'things' to 'signs': Bruno Latour, *Pandora's Hope: Essays on the Reality of Science Studies* (Cambridge MA and London: Harvard University Press, 1999), 64, 74.

18 Latour, 'Drawing Things'.

19 Sorrenson, 'Ship', 230–33.

20 This method is described well in contemporary treatises. See e.g. Murdoch Mackenzie, *A Treatise on Marine Surveying*, new edn by James Horsburgh (London, 1819 [1774]), 105–11, and Plate V; Thomas Charles Robson, *A Treatise on Marine Surveying* (London: Longman, Rees, & Co., 1834), 164–5; John Frederick William Herschel, *A Manual of Scientific Enquiry: Prepared for the Use of Her Majesty's Navy and Adapted for Travellers in General* (Cambridge: Cambridge University Press, 2011 [1849]), 87–90. For some scholarship on maritime surveying see: G. S. Ritchie, 'Captain Cook's Influence on Hydrographic Surveying', *Pacific Studies* 1:2 (1978), 78–95; Andrew David, 'Vancouver's Survey Methods and Surveys', in Robin Fisher and Hugh Johnston (eds), *From Maps to Metaphors: The Pacific World of George Vancouver* (Vancouver: University of British Columbia Press, 1993), 51–69, esp. at 58–64 on running surveys; M. K. Barritt, 'Matthew Flinders's Survey Practices and Records', *The Journal of the Hakluyt Society* (March 2014), 1–15 https://www.hakluyt.com/downloadable_files/Journal/Barritt_Flinders.pdf; Sorrenson, 'Ship', 229–32.

21 C. F. Beautemps-Beaupré, *An Introduction to the Practice of Nautical Surveying, and the Construction of Sea-Charts: Illustrated by Thirty-Four Plates*, trans. Richard Copeland (London: R. H. Laurie, 1823), 41–4.

22 Basil Hall, *On the Proper Method of Laying Down a Ship's Track on Sea Charts, with Some Remarks on the Importance of Time Keepers in Navigation* (1820), 1–3 (essay also published in *The Edinburgh Philosophical Journal* 2 (1820), 277–82). On Hall see James McCarthy, *That Curious Fellow: Captain Basil Hall, R.N.* (Dunbeath: Whittles, 2011). The fullest edition of his naval memoirs is Basil Hall, *Fragments of Voyages and Travels: Chiefly for the Use of Young Persons*, 2nd edn (Edinburgh and London: R. Cadell and Whittaker & Co., 1832). On his involvement with the publication of a cookbook see National Library of Scotland, Edinburgh, GB233/MS.21007, Cadell Papers: Correspondence, Letters of Captain Basil Hall, various but esp. Basil Hall to Robert Cadell, 25, 30 and 31 August 1828, ff. 10–11, 14–17.

23 Sorrenson, 'Ship', 233–4.

24 Stallard, *Antipodes*, Ch. 9; Zuber, 'Armchair Discovery'. Antarctica obviously *was* there, but much further south, and much smaller, than the mythical continent of the *philosophes*.

25 Parker, 'Pepys Island'. The term 'stepping stones' is also Parker's.

26 Louis-Antoine de Bougainville, *Voyage autour du Monde, par la Frégate du roi La Boudeuse, et la Flûte L'Étoile; en 1766, 1767, 1768 & 1769* (Paris: Saillant & Nyon, 1771), Plate 8, between 184 and 185.

27 Jean-François de Galaup, Comte de Lapérouse, letter from Macao, 3 January 1787, in *Voyage de Lapérouse autour du Monde*, 4 vols (Paris: Plassan, 1798), IV, 191 (my translation).

28 Matthew Flinders, *A Voyage to Terra Australis*, 2 vols and Atlas (London: G. and W. Nicol, 1814), I, 52–3; [George Vancouver], *A Voyage of Discovery to the North Pacific Ocean, and round the World*, 3 vols (London: G. G. and J. Robinson and J. Edwards, 1798), I, 32.

29 Edney, 'Reconsidering Enlightenment Geography', esp. 186–90; Mary Sponberg Pedley, *The Commerce of Cartography: Making and Marketing Maps in Eighteenth-Century France and England* (Chicago IL and London: University of Chicago Press, 2005), 166–74. On the role of personal travel as a source of credibility in maps see also Charles W. J. Withers, 'Mapping the Niger, 1798–1832: Trust, Testimony and "Ocular Demonstration" in the Late Enlightenment', *Imago Mundi* 56:2 (2004), 170–93.

30 [Vancouver], *Voyage*, I, 27, 73–4; III, 84, and see also 104.

31 I borrow the term 'virtual reality' from Carroll, *Empire of Air and Water*, 77.

32 Ibid., esp. 76–8.

33 '... *dans le plus vaste des déserts, entre le ciel et les flots, souvent ennemis ...*'; '... *il n'en restera pas plus de traces que son vaisseau n'en laisse sur cette onde qu'il a sillonnée*'. Cited in Ann Savours, '"A Very Interesting Point in Geography": The 1773 Phipps Expedition towards the North Pole', *Arctic* 37:4 (1984), 402–28, at 403 (my translation).

34 William Bligh, *A Voyage to the South Sea, Undertaken by Command of His Majesty, for the Purpose of Conveying the Bread-Fruit Tree to the West Indies, in His Majesty's Ship the Bounty, Commanded by Lieutenant William Bligh* (Dublin: P. Wogan et al., 1792), 81.

35 Ibid., 86, 212.

36 Adriana Craciun, 'What Is an Explorer?', *Eighteenth-Century Studies* 45:1 (2011), 29–51, quote at 31. On the Romantic construction of the 'discoverer' see, similarly, Edney, 'Creating "Discovery"'. See Chapter 4 for further discussion.

37 Schaffer, 'Scientific Discoveries'; Kuhn, 'Historical Structure'.

38 Dániel Margócsy, *Commercial Visions: Science, Trade, and Visual Culture in the Dutch Golden Age* (Chicago IL and London: University of Chicago Press, 2014).

39 Mario Biagioli, 'Patent Republic: Representing Inventions, Constructing Rights and Authors', *Social Research* 73:4 (2006), 1129–72; Oren Bracha, *Owning Ideas: The Intellectual Origins of American Intellectual Property, 1790–1909* (New York: Cambridge University Press, 2016). On the workings of the patent system in this period see also Christine MacLeod, *Inventing the Industrial Revolution: The English Patent System, 1660–1800* (Cambridge: Cambridge University Press, 1988).

40 On how in the Enlightenment the heroism of travel came to focus on the 'new' see Outram, 'On Being Perseus', 289–90.

41 Lapérouse, letter from d'Avatscha, 21 September 1787, in *Voyage de Lapérouse*, IV, 220.

42 William Robert Broughton, *A Voyage of Discovery to the North Pacific Ocean* (London: T. Cadell and W. Davies, 1804), v–vi. On Broughton see: J. K. Laughton and Roger Morriss, 'Broughton, William (1762–1821)', *Oxford Dictionary of National Biography* (2004) https://doi.org/10.1093/ref:odnb/3593; Barry Gough's Introduction in Andrew Davis (ed.), *William Robert Broughton's Voyage of Discovery to the North Pacific 1795–1798* (Abingdon and New York NY: Routledge for the Hakluyt Society, 2016).

43 Davis, *William Robert Broughton*, liv.

44 *Google NGrams* https://books.google.com/ngrams/graph?content=%22virgin+territory%22%2C%22virgin+land%22&year_start=1700&year_end=2019&corpus=29&smoothing=3; *Online Etymology Dictionary* https://www.etymonline.com/word/virgin; '"virgin" (noun & adjective)', II.7.a–b, *Oxford English Dictionary* (revised 2023) https://www.oed.com/dictionary/virgin_n?tab=meaning_and_use#15637333. A word search for 'virgin land' in the Gale Primary Sources database *Eighteenth-Century Collections Online* (14 November 2022) shows several examples from the 1770s, mainly relating to agriculture, but at times referring to countries, too. See, e.g., Abbé Raynal, *A Philosophical and Political History of the Settlements and Trade of the Europeans in the East and West Indies*, trans. J. Justamond, 5 vols, 2nd edn (London: T. Cadell, 1776), IV, 65 ('a tract of unappropriated and unbroken virgin land, which it is at his own option to clear'); *Encyclopædia Britannica*, 10 vols (Edinburgh: J. Balfour and Co. et al., 1778), III, 2055, entry for 'Coffea' or 'Coffee'; François Le Vaillant, *Travels from the Cape of Good-Hope, into the Interior Parts of Africa, Including Many Interesting Anecdotes*, 2 vols (London: William Lane, 1790), I, xxiii ('The interior parts of Africa appeared, for that purpose, a Peru. – It was a virgin land'). 'Uncharted lands' had been imagined as 'female' for centuries: Ramachandran, *Worldmakers*, 32.

45 Kathleen Wilson, *The Sense of the People: Politics, Culture and Imperialism in England, 1715–1785* (Cambridge: Cambridge University Press, 1998), 185–205; Kathleen Wilson, *The Island Race: Englishness, Empire and Gender in the Eighteenth Century* (London and New York: Routledge, 2003).

46 On place-naming in the Pacific see e.g. Jan Tent and Helen Slatyer, 'Naming Places on the "Southland": European Place-Naming Practices from 1606 to 1803', *Australian Historical Studies* 40 (2009), 5–31; Dany Bréelle, 'Matthew Flinders's Australian Toponymy and Its British Connections', *The Journal of the Hakluyt Society* (November 2013), 1–41 https://www.hakluyt.com/downloadable_files/Journal/Flinders_Toponymy.pdf; Bronwen Douglas, 'Naming "Polynesia": Cartography, Geography, and Toponymy of the "Fifth Part of the World"', *The Journal of Pacific History* 56:4 (2021), 375–414. For a literary analysis see Michel de Certeau, 'Writing the Sea: Jules Verne', in Michel de Certeau, *Heterologies: Discourse on the Other*, trans. Brian Massumi (Minneapolis MN and London: University of Minnesota Press, 1986), 137–49, at 142–5. On how indigenous voices are still visible even through this naming see Douglas, 'Naming Places'.

47 Glyndwr Williams, 'The Pacific: Exploration and Exploitation', in P. J. Marshall and Alaine Low (eds), *The Oxford History of the British Empire – Volume II: The Eighteenth Century* (Oxford: Oxford University Press, 1998), 552–75, at 559. On the double-edged quality of 'encounter' see Zoltán Biedermann, '(Dis) connected History and the Multiple Narratives of Global Early Modernity', *Modern Philology* 119:1 (2021), 13–32.

48 Epeli Hau'ofa, 'Pasts to Remember', in Epeli Hau'ofa, *We Are the Ocean: Selected Works* (Honolulu HI: University of Hawai'i Press, 2008), 60–79.

49 Nicholas Thomas, *Entangled Objects: Exchange, Material Culture, and Colonialism in the Pacific* (Cambridge MA and London: Harvard University Press, 1991), esp. Ch. 3; John Patrick Greene, 'French Encounters with Material Culture of the South Pacific', *Eighteenth-Century Life* 26:3 (2002), 225–45. On resistance to empire see also Sivasundaram, *Waves*, here esp. Ch. 2.

50 Anne Salmond, *The Trial of the Cannibal Dog: Captain Cook in the South Seas* (London: Penguin Books, 2004); Vanessa Smith, *Intimate Strangers: Friendship, Exchange and Pacific Encounters* (Cambridge: Cambridge University Press, 2010); Greg Dening, *Mr Bligh's Bad Language: Passion, Power and Theatre on the Bounty* (Cambridge: Canto, 1994), 57–8; Bernard Smith, *Imagining the Pacific in the Wake of the Cook Voyages* (Carlton, Vic.: Melbourne University Press at the Miegunyah Press, 1992); Scobie, '"Bunny!"'; Bronwen Douglas, 'Voyages, Encounters, and Agency in Oceania: Captain Cook and Indigenous People', *History Compass* 6:3 (2008), 712–37.

51 For a nuanced discussion of how 'agency' is not incompatible with victimhood see David A. Chappell, 'Active Agents versus Passive Victims: Decolonized Historiography or Problematic Paradigm?', *The Contemporary Pacific* 7:2 (1995), 303–26.

52 John Hawkesworth, *An Account of the Voyages Undertaken by the Order of His Present Majesty for Making Discoveries in the Southern Hemisphere …*, 3 vols (London: W. Strahan and T. Cadell, 1773), I, 489–90.

53 For a summary of the scholarship on this, and on potential demographic effects, see Vicki Luker, 'Disease in Pacific History: "The Fatal Impact"?', in Anne Perez Hattori and Jane Samson (eds), *The Cambridge History of the Pacific Ocean – Volume II: The Pacific Ocean since 1800* (Cambridge: Cambridge University Press, 2023), 335–48.

54 Marshall Sahlins, 'Cosmologies of Capitalism: The Trans-Pacific Sector of "the World System"', *Proceedings of the British Academy* 74 (1988), 1–51, at 30.

55 Élisabeth Rossel (ed.), *Voyage de Dentrecasteaux, Envoyé à la Recherche de Lapérouse*, 2 vols (Paris: Imprimerie Impériale, 1808), I, 347, 353–5.

56 Thomas, *Entangled Objects*, 98–103 (Marquesas), 110–18 (Fiji).

57 Bathsheba Demuth, *Floating Coast: An Environmental History of the Bering Strait* (New York: W. W. Norton & Company, 2019).

58 K. S. Inglis, 'Australia Day', *Australian Historical Studies* 13:49 (1967), 20–41, at 24–5; '"Change the Date": Vandals Attack Statues in Australia Day Protest', *SBS Korean* (28 August 2017) https://www.sbs.com.au/language/english/change-the-date-vandals-attack-statues-in-australia-day-protest; Bain Attwood, '"Change the Date": Historical Commemoration and Denial in Australia',

History Workshop (21 November 2017) https://www.historyworkshop.org.uk/
change-the-date-historical-commemoration-and-denial-in-australia; Mark
Chou and Rachel Busbridge, 'Culture Wars, Local Government, and the
Australia Day Controversy: Insights from Urban Politics Research', *Urban Policy
and Research* 37:3 (2019), 367–77; Sam Wainwright, 'Australia Day: Change the
Date', *Green Left* (16 January 2017) https://www.greenleft.org.au/content/
australia-day-change-date.

59 D. Graham Burnett, 'Hydrographic Discipline among the Navigators: Charting
an "Empire of Commerce and Science" in the Nineteenth-Century Pacific', in
James R. Akerman (ed.), *The Imperial Map: Cartography and the Mastery of
Empire* (Chicago IL: University of Chicago Press, 2009), 185–259.

60 Anne Salmond, *Aphrodite's Island: The European Discovery of Tahiti* (Berkeley
CA: University of California Press, 2009), 38–56, 134, 141; Randolph Cock,
'Precursors of Cook: The Voyages of the *Dolphin*, 1764–8', *The Mariner's Mirror*
85:1 (1999), 30–52, at 44–5; Hawkesworth, *Account*, I, 444–5.

61 See e.g. Bougainville in Tahiti: Greene, 'French Encounters', 236. On this type of
inscription see also Adriana Craciun, *Writing Arctic Disaster: Authorship and
Exploration* (Cambridge: Cambridge University Press, 2016), esp. Ch. 4.

62 Rossel, *Voyage de Dentrecasteaux*, I, 263. See also Sivasundaram, *Waves*, 50–52.

63 Broughton, *Voyage*, 124–5.

64 Anon., *A Voyage round the World, in His Majesty's Ship the Dolphin,
Commanded by the Honourable Commodore Byron* (London: J. Newbery and
F. Newbery, 1767), 38.

65 The association between imperialism and environmental impact wasn't always as
straightforward as it might appear, and it has been the subject of a vast literature.
See e.g.: Tom Griffiths and Libby Robin (eds), *Ecology and Empire:
Environmental History of Settler Societies* (Edinburgh: Keele University Press,
1997); Richard H. Grove, *Green Imperialism: Colonial Expansion, Tropical
Island Edens and the Origins of Environmentalism, 1600–1860* (Cambridge:
Cambridge University Press, 1995).

66 'Journal, In His Majesties [*sic*] Ship the Speedwell, Captain John Wood
Commander, Bound for the Discovery of a Passage to the East-Indies, by the
North-East', in *An Account of Several Late Voyages and Discoveries to the South
and North* (London: S. Smith and B. Walford, 1694), 155–70, at 162.

67 On La Pérouse see the extensive Introduction to John Dunmore (ed.), *Journal of
Jean-François de Galaup de la Pérouse, 1785–1788*, 2 vols (Farnham and
Burlington VT: Ashgate, 1994).

68 Lapérouse, letter from Macao, 3 January 1787, in *Voyage de Lapérouse*, IV,
190–91.

69 Quoted in Glyn Williams, 'Scurvy on the Pacific Voyages in the Age of Cook',
Journal for Maritime Research 15:1 (2013), 37–45, at 41; 'Jean-François de Galaup,
Comte de Lapérouse 1785–1788', *Journeys of Enlightenment: French Explorations
of Terres Australes* http://museum.wa.gov.au/exhibitions/journeys/The_
Explorers/de_Laperouse.html.

70 Rossel, *Voyage de Dentrecasteaux*, I, 445–6.

71 Myra Stanbury and Jeremy Green (eds), *Lapérouse and the Loss of the* Astrolabe

and the Boussole *(1788): Reports of the 1986 and 1990 Investigations of the Shipwrecks at Vanikoro, Solomon Islands* (Fremantle: Australian National Centre of Excellence for Maritime Archaeology and the Australasian Institute for Maritime Archaeology, 2004), 12–15, 20, 33–4.

72 Stanbury and Green (eds), *Lapérouse.*

73 Garrick Hitchcock, 'Manuscript XXXII: The Final Fate of the La Pérouse Expedition? The 1818 Account of Shaik Jumaul, A Lascar Castaway in Torres Strait', *The Journal of Pacific History* 52:2 (2017), 217–35.

74 Jacques Liozu, *Carte du voyage de Lapérouse* (1941), Musée Lapérouse https://www.laperouse-france.fr/a-la-d%C3%A9couverte-de-lap%C3%A9rouse/voyage-dans-le-pacifique.

75 Ritchie, 'Captain Cook's Influence', 90.

76 *Regulations and Instructions Relating to His Majesty's Service at Sea*, 13th edn (London, 1790), 200.

77 *The Flinders Papers*, National Maritime Museum, Greenwich, FLI25, Letter from Matthew Flinders to Ann Flinders (18 of 41), 26 August 1804, 3 https://flinders.rmg.co.uk/DisplayDocumentc409.html?ID=110&CurrentPage=1&CurrentXMLPage=3&browseBy=Date.

78 Flinders, *Voyages*, I, 19, 21; II, 135–43, 247–8, 274–5.

79 Royal Greenwich Observatory Archives, RGO 14/64, [Matthew Flinders], Log book, observations and memoir of HMS Investigator, 1795–1805, ff. 217v–218r, available at https://cudl.lib.cam.ac.uk/view/MS-RGO-00014-00064/458. This was a system suggested in contemporary manuals. See e.g. Mackenzie, *Treatise on Marine Surveying*, 182.

80 Sara Caputo, 'Exploration and Mortification: Fragile Infrastructures, Imperial Narratives, and the Self-Sufficiency of British Naval "Discovery" Vessels, 1760–1815', *History of Science* 61:1 (2023), 40–59.

81 Flinders, *Voyage*, I, 190–93; Louis Freycinet, *Voyage de Découvertes aux Terres Australes – Partie Navigation et Géographie: Atlas* (Paris: Imprimerie Royale, 1812), Plate 10.

82 On Flinders's biography, besides his *Voyages*, see: J. K. Laughton and Andrew C. F. David, 'Flinders, Matthew (1774–1814)', in *Oxford Dictionary of National Biography* (2011) http://www.oxforddnb.com/view/article/9750; Ernest Scott, *The Life of Captain Matthew Flinders, R.N.* (Cambridge: Cambridge University Press, 2011 [1914]); Kenneth Morgan, *Matthew Flinders, Maritime Explorer of Australia* (London: Bloomsbury Academic, 2016); Eóin Phillips, 'Remembering Matthew Flinders', *Journal for Maritime Research* 14:2 (2012), 111–19.

83 Savours, '"Very Interesting Point"', 427.

84 Peter Goodwin, *Nelson's Arctic Voyage: The Royal Navy's First Polar Expedition 1773* (London: Adlard Coles, 2019).

85 Constantine John Phipps, *A Voyage towards the North Pole: Undertaken by His Majesty's Command 1773* (Cambridge: Cambridge University Press, 2014 [1774]), 13–14, 24–5. On the experimental spirit of the Phipps expedition see also: Peter Fjågesund, 'When Science Came to the Arctic: Constantine Phipps's expedition to Spitsbergen in 1773', *Journal of Northern Studies* 2 (2008), 77–91; Savours, '"Very Interesting Point"', esp. 408–11, 423–4. On the commitment to

making multiple observations and instruments visible see Charles W. J. Withers, 'Geography and "Thing Knowledge": Instrument Epistemology, Failure, and Narratives of 19th-Century Exploration', *Transactions of the Institute of British Geographers* 44:4 (2019), 676–91.

86   See e.g.: Broughton, *Voyage*, 382–9; Flinders, *Voyage*, I, 255–69.

87   Flinders, *Voyage*, I, 260.

88   For a table of how this plays out see Herschel, *Manual of Scientific Enquiry*, 100.

89   On the principle of 'reasonable agreement' in experiments, which is historically constructed, see e.g. H. Otto Sibum, 'When Is Enough Enough? Accurate Measurement and the Integrity of Scientific Research', *History of Science* 58:4 (2020), 437–57.

90   Tracey P. Lauriault and Jeremy Wood, 'GPS Tracings – Personal Cartographies', *The Cartographic Journal* 46:4 (2009), 360–65, at 362–3; Jeremy Wood, 'Data Cloud: GPS Sculpture, Beatrixpark, Amsterdam', *GPS Drawing* http://www.gpsdrawing.com/projects/datacloud.html.

91   Bender, 'Enlightenment Fiction'.

Chapter 4: Storytelling

1   'Mails *via* Sydney', *South Australian Register* (Adelaide, SA) XVII:2177 (Wednesday 7 September 1853), 3, *National Library of Australia – Trove* http://nla.gov.au/nla.news-article48549639.

2   Herman Melville, *Moby Dick or The White Whale* (Boston: The St. Botolph Society, 1892), 188.

3   See, e.g., 'Speech of Hon. Rufus Choate at Salem, September 28th, 1848', *Vermont Watchman & State Journal* (Montpelier) XLII:48 (2191) (Thursday 12 October 1848), 1.

4   Edward P. Smith, *Incidents among Shot and Shell* ([Philadelphia PA?]: Edgewood Publishing Company, 1868), 379; *Court of Appeals of the State of New York – Edward M. White against Spencer H. Smith and Others* (New York: William J. Read, 1871), 15; *The Record of Crimes in the United States ...* (Buffalo: H. Faxon & Co., 1834), 255; [Fanny Fern], *Beauties of Fanny Fern* (London: Knight and Son, [1855]), 10. These instances are the result of a search across Google Books.

5   Edgar Allan Poe Society of Baltimore, Works, Letters, LTR186/RCL505, Edgar Allan Poe to Charles Anthon, about 31 October 1844 https://www.eapoe.org/works/letters/p4410000.htm.

6   Helen M. Rozwadowski, *Fathoming the Ocean: The Discovery and Exploration of the Deep Sea* (Cambridge MA and London: The Belknap Press of Harvard University Press, 2005), esp. Ch. 1; Cohen, *Novel and the Sea*, Ch. 4.

7   Paul A. Gilje, *To Swear like a Sailor: Maritime Culture in America, 1750–1850* (Cambridge: Cambridge University Press, 2016), 36–43, 63–4.

8   Delano-Smith, 'Milieus of Mobility'. On the mixed fortunes of itinerary cartography (maps supplying set routes) in the following centuries see Quentin Morcrette, 'Traverser la surface', *Terra Brasilis* 6 (2015) http://journals.openedition.org/terrabrasilis/1676.

9   Akerman, 'Finding Our Way', 23–6.

10   Woodward, 'Cartography and the Renaissance', 10.

11   Dym, *Mapping Travel*, 37–40; Catherine Delano Smith, 'Maps as Art and Science: Maps in Sixteenth Century Bibles', *Imago Mundi* 42 (1990), 65–83, images at 70.

12   See e.g. the maps collected in Pepys Library, Magdalene College, Cambridge, PL 2636, Joseph Moxon, 'Sacred Geographie. Or Scriptural Mapps' (London: at the sign of the Atlas, [1671]), nn. 2–5 ('Paradise or the garden of Eden with the countries circumjacent inhabited by the patriarchs.', 'Israels Peregrination. or the Forty Years Travels of the Children of Israel out of Egypt, through the Red Sea, and the Wildernesse, into Canaan or The Land of Promise. Newly Corrected by J. Moxon', 'Canaan or the Land of Promise. Possessed by the Children of Israel: and Travelled through by our Saviour Jesus Christ; and His Apostles' and 'The travels of St Paul and other the Apostles [*sic*] Or, a Geographical Description of those Lands and Countries, where in the Gospel of Christ was first propagated. Being a great help in the reading of the New Testament. Newly Corrected by Joseph Moxon').

13   PL 2636, Moxon, 'Sacred Geographie'.

14   Delano Smith, 'Maps as Art and Science'.

15   Dillon, 'Consuming Maps', 316.

16   1588/1590 printed map by Augustinus Ryther, reproduced in facsimile in Royal Geographical Society, London, 1.B.196. Reported in Tebel, *Schiff*, 142–3.

17   See e.g. Caird Library of the National Maritime Museum, Greenwich (henceforth NMM), PAF4697, Cooper Willyams and J. White, 'General Chart of the Mediteranean, [*sic*] with the tracks of the British Fleet Commanded by Rear Admiral S.r Horatio Nelson, K. B. and of the French Fleet, Commanded by Admiral Bruyes: Till they met in the Bay of Aboukir, off the Nile, On the First of August, 1798' (1802) https://collections.rmg.co.uk/collections/objects/128832.html.

18   Veronica Della Dora, 'Lifting the Veil of Time: Maps, Metaphor, and Antiquarianism in the Seventeenth and Eighteenth Centuries', in Wigen and Winterer (eds), *Time in Maps*, 103–25, at 114; Elizabeth Franklin Lewis, 'Mapping Don Quixote's Route: Spanish Cartography, English Travelers and National Pride', *Studies in Eighteenth-Century Culture* 46 (2017), 35–48.

19   For other surviving instances or copies see: NMM, MEC0005, Michael Mercator, 'Medal Commemorating Drake's Voyage, 1577–80', *c.*1589 https://www.rmg.co.uk/collections/objects/rmgc-object-37445; American Numismatic Society, 1907.478.1, 'White metal Medal of Michael Mercator, London (England)', 1580 http://numismatics.org/collection/1907.478.1. For more on the medal see Evans, 'Silver Medal'; Wallis, 'Cartography of Drake's Voyage', 149–51. The words '*Draci Exitus*' ('Drake's departure') follow the dotted track around its first bend out of Plymouth, in 1577.

20   Dekker, 'Globes in Renaissance Europe', esp. 148–58, quote at 153.

21   Helen M. Wallis, 'The First English Globe: A Recent Discovery', *The Geographical Journal* 117:3 (1951), 275–90, at 281, 283. For more on the 'Molyneux globes' (they were a pair, terrestrial and celestial, and more than one copy exists), and particularly their transnational propagandistic functions, see

Anna Maria Crinò and Helen Wallis, 'New Researches on the Molyneux Globes / Neue Forschungsarbeiten über die Molyneux-Globen', *Der Globusfreund* 35/37 (1987), 11–20.

22 Emma Perkins, 'The Seventeenth-Century Terrestrial Globe by Morden, Berry and Lea', *Imago Mundi* 71:1 (2019), 51–64, at 58–60.

23 Wallis, 'Cartography of Drake's Voyage', 151–5.

24 Katherine Parker, 'Pocketing the World: Globes as Commodities in the Eighteenth Century', *IMCOS Journal* 141 (2015), 47–53, at 50–51.

25 For another English example see Cambridge University Library, Royal Commonwealth Society, ORCS.1.01, 'A correct globe with the new discoveries; A correct globe with ye new constelations of Dr Halley &c', *c.*1775 https://cudl. lib.cam.ac.uk/view/MS-ORCS-00001-00001/1. This globe contains a gross mistake: its track is labelled 'Cook's Track 1760', while his first voyage took place in 1768–71. On the German globes see Rudolf Schmidt and Donna Schiller, 'Franz Ludwig Güssefeld – Wolf Paulus Jenig und das Industrie-Comtpoir [*sic*] Weimar / Franz Ludwig Güssefeld – Wolf Paulus Jenig and the Industrie-Comptoir Weimar', *Der Globusfreund* 47/48 (1999), 277–91. For an example see 'Neuester Erd-Globus [cartographic document]: zu Gaspari geographischen Lehrbüchern gehörig / entworfen von F.L. Güssefeld; gestochen von J. C. Müller' (Weimar: im Verlage des Industrie Comptoirs, [1798?]), model by Ing. Řezníček, Ing. Bílá and Prof. Pavelka. *GLÓBY Mapové sbírky Univerzity Karlovy* (2023) http://www.mapovasbirka.cz/globy/english/gallery/3d/cesty/cesty.html (general project website: http://www.mapovasbirka.cz/globy/english/index_ eng.html). Various others exist in museums and archives in Germany, Austria and New York.

26 Diane Dillon, 'Consuming Maps', in Akerman and Karrow (eds), *Maps*, 289–343, at 341–2. For some examples see e.g. the Royal Mail stamps released in August 1968, on the bicentenary of Cook's departure on his first voyage: https://www.collectgbstamps.co.uk/explore/issues/?issue=22788.

27 Judith A. Tyner, *Stitching the World: Embroidered Maps and Women's Geographical Education* (Abingdon and New York: Routledge, 2016), Ch. 1 (screen 26), Ch. 3 (screen 90), Ch. 4 (screen 112), Plate 11 ('Mary Ann Reynolds's world map, 1789'), quotes at Ch. 1 (screen 38), and see Plate 16 for another example of explorers' routes. I could only read this book in an electronic copyright deposit version, so I lack printed page numbers to cite.

28 NMM, GLB0238, George Pocock, 'Terrestrial Inflatable Globe', 1843 https:// www.rmg.co.uk/collections/objects/rmgc-object-19924; GLB0203, Philipp Cella, 'Pneumatisch Portativer Erd-Globus nach der Erfindung von Pocock', 1831 https://www.rmg.co.uk/collections/objects/rmgc-object-19890; NMM, GLB0230, George Pocock, 'Terrestrial Inflatable Globe', 1830 https://www.rmg. co.uk/collections/objects/rmgc-object-19916. The idea of silk inflatable globes was already being floated in the 1790s: *Stitching the World*, Ch. 1 (screen 36).

29 Glenn M. Stein, 'Badges for Imperial Russian & Soviet Polar Exploration and Research', *International Polar Year 2007–2008* (2006) and *academia.edu* (2016) https://www.academia.edu/22637527/ Badges_for_Imperial_Russian_and_Soviet_Polar_Exploration_and_Research.

30 'Captain James Cook Memorial', *VisitCanberra* https://visitcanberra.com.au/attractions/56b23b71d5f1565045d8031b/captain-james-cook-memorial.

31 Jeffrey R. Wigelsworth, *Selling Science in the Age of Newton: Advertising and the Commoditization of Knowledge* (Farnham and Burlington VT: Ashgate, 2010).

32 Pedley, *Commerce of Cartography*; Parker, 'Pocketing the World'; Katy Barrett, *Looking for Longitude: A Cultural History* (Liverpool: Liverpool University Press, 2022).

33 Of course, exploration voyages in new seas were a different matter: knowing longitude there really changed the game – practically and for legitimation purposes. See Sandman, 'Longitude and Latitude'.

34 Smith, *Imagining the Pacific*; Wilson, *Island Race*, 54–91; John McAleer, 'Exhibiting Exploration: Captain Cook, Voyages of Exploration and Cultures of Display', in John McAleer and John M. MacKenzie (eds), *Exhibiting the Empire: Cultures of Display and the British Empire* (Manchester: Manchester University Press, 2015), 42–63; Philippe Despoix, *Le monde mesuré: Dispositifs de l'exploration à l'âge des Lumières* (Geneva: Droz, 2005), 179–232.

35 This one is the most famous and vivid, but for earlier examples see also: National Portrait Gallery, London, NPG D12568, 'The Longitude and Latitude of Warley Camp in the Summer of 1795' (26 June 1802) https://www.npg.org.uk/collections/search/portrait/mw61973/The-longitude-and-latitude-of-Warley-Camp-in-the-summer-of-1795-James-Cecil-1st-Marquess-of-Salisbury-James-Grant; British Museum, 1859,0316.62, Isaac Cruikshank, 'Longitude & Latitude of St. Petersburgh' (1813) https://www.britishmuseum.org/collection/object/P_1859-0316-62.

36 Antoine Lilti, *The Invention of Celebrity 1750–1850*, trans. Lynn Jeffress (Cambridge and Malden MA: Polity Press, 2017).

37 See Chapter 2.

38 Perkins, 'Seventeenth-Century Terrestrial Globe', 54.

39 Raymond B. Craib, 'Beyond the Map: Landscape, History, and the Routes of Cortés', in Kathleen A. Brosnan and James R. Akerman (eds), *Mapping Nature across the Americas* (Chicago IL and London: University of Chicago Press, 2021), 180–206. Another similar example is the touristic appeal of the Lewis & Clark route across North America: James R. Akerman, 'Time, Travel, and Mapping the Landscapes of War', in Wigen and Winterer (eds), *Time in Maps*, 193–218, at 193–5.

40 Dane A. Morrison, 'Performing Cook: Early American Explorers' Appropriation of James Cook's Voyages', *Astrolabe* 49 (2020) https://crlv.org/articles/performing-cook-early-american-explorers-appropriation-of-james-cooks-voyages.

41 Simon Werrett, 'Russian Responses to the Voyages of Captain Cook', in Glyndwr Williams (ed.), *Captain Cook: Explorations and Reassessments* (Woodbridge and Rochester NY: The Boydell Press, 2004), 179–97, esp. at 188–96.

42 Simon Baker, *The Ship: Retracing Cook's* Endeavour *Voyage* (London: BBC Worldwide Ltd, 2002), quote at 6, description of navigation at 158–67. The book

includes track chart sketches of the replica's voyage, too (see 92, 132–3, 158–9, 196–7).

43 Mensun Bound, *The Ship beneath the Ice: The Discovery of Shackleton's Endurance* (London and Dublin: Macmillan, 2022).

44 Fifteenth-century Exodus maps were often identical across editions and languages: Delano-Smith, 'Maps as Art and Science', 69–73. An exception where the exact position of the track might have mattered is in maps showing the Le Maire Strait that led to Cape Horn.

45 'Carte qui indique la Route des Vaissaux de Roi le Race-horce et la Carcasse pendant l'Exepedition [*sic*] faite vers le Pole Boréal en 1773', in *Voyage au pole boréal: fait en 1773, par ordre du roi d'Angleterre, par Constantin-Jean Phipps* (Paris: Saillant & Nyon and Pissot, 1775), xiii. The map can be viewed at https:// archive.org/details/voyageaupoleboraoomulg/page/n15/mode/2up. On this edition, and a German one, see Savours, '"Very Interesting Point"', 422.

46 Helen Wallis, 'Publication of Cook's Journals: Some New Sources and Assessments', *Pacific Studies* 1:2 (1978), 163–94; W. H. Pearson, 'Hawkesworth's Alterations', *The Journal of Pacific History* 7 (1972), 45–72; Jean-Stéphane Massiani, 'What Cook Saw and What Hawkesworth Wrote: Alterations and Authorship in the Publication of Cook's Endeavour Journal', *Astrolabe* 49 (2020) https://crlv.org/articles/what-cook-saw-and-what-hawkesworth-wrote-alterations-and-authorship-in-the-publication-of; W. H. Pearson, 'Hawkesworth's Voyages', in R. F. Brissenden (ed.), *Studies in the Eighteenth Century II: Papers Presented at the Second David Nichol Smith Memorial Seminar, Canberra 1970* (Toronto: University of Toronto Press, 1973), 239–57 (239 on the Bristol library numbers).

47 J. Hawkesworth, *Relation des voyages entrepris par ordre de Sa Majesté Britannique* ..., 4 vols (Paris: Saillant et Nyon and Panckoucke, 1774); J. J. Hawkesworth, *Ausführliche und glaubwürdige Geschichte der neuesten Reisen um die Welt* ..., trans. Johann Friedrich Schiller, 4 vols (Berlin: Bey Haude und Spener, 1775); John Hawkesworth, *Reizen rondom de weereld* ... (Rotterdam: Reinier Arrenberg, 1774); Jeffrey L. Sammons, 'A New Letter of John Frederick Schiller, Friedrich Schiller's Black-Sheep Cousin', *The Yale University Library Gazette* 69:1/2 (1994), 62–7.

48 Werrett, 'Russian Responses', 188.

49 Antoine Eche, 'Jean-Nicolas Démeunier and His Translation of Cook's A Voyage to the Pacific Ocean', *Astrolabe* 49 (2020) https://crlv.org/articles/jean-nicolas-demeunier-and-his-translation-of-cooks-a-voyage-to-the-pacific-ocean.

50 Morrison, 'Performing Cook'.

51 Bruce Cumings, *Dominion from Sea to Sea: Pacific Ascendancy and American Power* (New Haven CT and London: Yale University Press, 2009), esp. Ch. 7.

52 For another example, showing the whole world and Cook's tracks, but centred on the Pacific (unlike European ones that tended to be centred on the Atlantic), see 'A Chart of the World According to Mercator's Projection. Shewing the latest Discoveries of Capt. Cook' (Philadelphia, 1814) http://purl.stanford.edu/sx256sv4177 and https://exhibits.stanford.edu/ruderman/catalog/sx256sv4177.

53 See Ezio Bassani, *Cook. Polinesia a Napoli nel Settecento. Gli oggetti dati al Museo borbonico ritrovati e illustrati* (Bologna: Calderini, 1982), 2, 7–8.

54 I found this map thanks to a mention in Papelitzky, 'Red Lines in the Ocean'. For more versions of Cook's charts in various languages see e.g. Gotha Perthes Collection, SPK-80-3 A-01, 'CARTE montrant la Route suivie Par M. COOK, en 1776, 1777, 1778, et 1779 dans son troisieme et dernier Voyage' (Benard, n.d.); 'NEUE CHARTE der in den Jahren 1777, 1778, 1779, 1780 von CAP^T. COOK und CAP.^{T} CLERKE in den Konigl. Grosbrittan. Schiffen RESOLUTION und DISCOVERY gemachten Reisen u. Entdeckungen im STILLEN WELTMEER' (1785); SPK-10.V.A C-02, F. G. Berger Senior, 'Charte von der Südlichen Halbkugel' (Berlin, after 1775); SPK-10.V.A C-03, Henri Robert, 'Carte Générale Offrant les Découvertes faites par le Capitaine Jacques Cook dans ce Voyage et dans les deux Voyages précédens' (n.d., after 1784); Heinrich Roberts and F. A. Schræmbl, 'Generalkarte sæmmtlicher Entdeckungen auf den drei grossen Weltreisen des Kapit. JAKOB COOK' (Vienna: F. A. Schræmbl, 1789). The latter two are copies of Henry Roberts, 'A General Chart Exhibiting the Discoveries made by Captn. James Cook in this and his two preceeding Voyages' (London, 1784), for a version of which see e.g. Stanford Libraries, The Barry Lawrence Ruderman Map Collection https://purl.stanford.edu/rs967qc3186.

55 Sahlins, 'Cosmologies of Capitalism', 18–19.

56 Pedley, *Commerce of Cartography*, 15, 174–89, 203.

57 See e.g. William Fitzgerald, *The Living Death of Antiquity: Neoclassical Aesthetics* (Oxford: Oxford University Press, 2022), (46–50 for a summary). It's important to note, however, that we can't speak of a single visual culture for the period: Margócsy, *Commercial Visions*; Charles Kostelnick, 'Visualizing Technology and Practical Knowledge in the *Encyclopédie*'s Plates: Rhetoric, Drawing Conventions, and Enlightenment Values', *History and Technology* 28:4 (2012), 443–54.

58 Royal Greenwich Observatory Archives, RGO 14/64, Log book, observations and memoir of HMS *Investigator*, 1795–1805, f. 217v, available at https://cudl.lib.cam.ac.uk/view/MS-RGO-00014-00064/458.

59 See various examples at https://encounter.collections.slsa.sa.gov.au.

60 For hundreds of examples of '*vues de côtes*' see e.g. the large hydrographical collections of the French Navy: Archives Nationales, Paris, MAR/5JJ/1– MAR/5JJ/437, Service hydrographique de la Marine. Voyages et missions hydrographiques (XVIIIe–XIXe siècles), 1718–1895.

61 Charles Lyell, *Travels in North America: With Geological Observations on the United States, Canada, and Nova Scotia*, 2 vols (Cambridge: Cambridge University Press, 2010 [1845]), II, 238 and frontispiece plate.

62 American Philosophical Society (Mss.B.D25.44), DCP-LETT-899: Darwin Correspondence Project, 'Letter no. 899', Charles Darwin to Charles Lyell, [30 July–2 August 1845] https://www.darwinproject.ac.uk/letter/?docId=letters/DCP-LETT-899.xml.

63 James A. Secord, *Victorian Sensation: The Extraordinary Publication, Reception, and Secret Authorship of* Vestiges of the Natural History of Creation (Chicago IL

and London: University of Chicago Press, 2000), esp. 24–76, 116–25. On how this wasn't simply a matter of technological innovation influencing culture, but rather a circular process, see also Jonathan R. Topham, 'Scientific Publishing and the Reading of Science in Nineteenth-Century Britain: A Historiographical Survey and Guide to Sources', *Stud. Hist. Phil. Sci.* 31:4 (2000), 559–612, at 575–81.

64 Lilti, *Invention of Celebrity*, Ch. 7.

65 Craciun, *Writing Arctic Disaster*, 3. On nineteenth-century notions of exploration see also Felix Driver, *Geography Militant: Cultures of Exploration and Empire* (Oxford and Malden MA: Blackwell Publishers, 2001).

66 For a good summary of the literature on this change see Wigelsworth, *Selling Science*, 9–10, 175–82. See also Aileen Fyfe and Bernard Lightman (eds), *Science in the Marketplace: Nineteenth-Century Sites and Experiences* (Chicago IL and London: University of Chicago Press, 2007). On how science was tailored for specific popular audiences (e.g. by gender, religious interest, etc.) across different periodicals see: Geoffrey Cantor and Sally Shuttleworth (eds), *Science Serialized: Representations of the Sciences in Nineteenth-Century Periodicals* (Cambridge MA and London: MIT Press, 2004); Louise Henson et al. (eds), *Culture and Science in the Nineteenth-Century Media* (Abingdon and New York: Routledge, 2016 [2004]).

67 Richard J. Cyriax, 'Sir James Clark Ross and the Franklin Expedition', *Polar Record* 3:24 (1942), 528–40, at 532–3; Russell A. Potter, *Finding Franklin: The Untold Story of a 165-Year Search* (Montreal: McGill-Queen's University Press, 2016), 8–9.

68 Among a vast literature on the search, for its general outlines see e.g. Potter, *Finding Franklin*; Janice Cavell, *Tracing the Connected Narrative: Arctic Exploration in British Print Culture, 1818–1860* (Toronto: University of Toronto Press, 2008); Cyriax, 'Sir James Clark Ross'.

69 Huw Lewis-Jones, *Imagining the Arctic: Heroism, Spectacle and Polar Exploration* (London and New York: I. B. Tauris, 2017), 200–203; Cyriax, 'Sir James Clark Ross', 588.

70 Quote from the report of Lieutenant W. H. Browne, as cited in W. Barr, 'Searching for Franklin Where He Was Ordered to Go: Captain Erasmus Ommanney's Sledging Campaign to Cape Walker and Beyond, Spring 1851', *Polar Record* 52:265 (2016), 474–98, at 478.

71 Barr, 'Searching for Franklin'.

72 On the 'inscription' of the Arctic landscape see Craciun, *Writing Arctic Disaster*, 62, 70, 73–8, 182–99.

73 On the 'Gould Map' see Potter, *Finding Franklin*, 74–9.

74 Ibid., 12–14, 225–6. On these three bodies see also Craciun, *Writing Arctic Disaster*, 59–60.

75 Cavell, *Tracing the Connected Narrative*, 204–19, 224–6; Potter, *Finding Franklin*, Ch. 6.

76 Cavell, *Tracing the Connected Narrative*, 20–26 and Ch. 9.

77 'Wrecks of HMS Erebus and HMS Terror National Historic Site', *Parks Canada* https://www.pc.gc.ca/en/lhn-nhs/nu/epaveswrecks/info/plan. For some images

and videos of the wrecks, together with a clear timeline, see 'HMS Terror and Erebus', *Royal Museums Greenwich* https://www.rmg.co.uk/stories/topics/hms-terror-erebus-history-franklin-lost-expedition.

78 Paul Watson, 'Ship Found in Arctic 168 Years after Doomed Northwest Passage Attempt', *The Guardian* (12 September 2016) https://www.theguardian.com/world/2016/sep/12/hms-terror-wreck-found-arctic-nearly-170-years-northwest-passage-attempt; Lewis-Jones, *Imagining the Arctic*, 298–302. See also Potter, *Finding Franklin*; Craciun, *Writing Arctic Disaster*, 79–81.

79 On the public debates over Franklin's fate see Cavell, *Tracing the Connected Narrative*, esp. Ch. 7.

80 *Letters on the Relief of Sir John Franklin's Expedition by an Observer* (London: Trelawney Saunders, Commenced in *The Times* newspaper; revised, 1850), quotes from 6, 16–17, 21, Letters I, IV, VI, of 1, 17, 20 January 1850. This pamphlet is available at Scott Polar Research Institute, Cambridge (henceforth SPRI), SCO: SPRI-SPC: (*41): 91(091)[1847–59 Franklin search] [Bound in: Pamphlets Franklin Search Vol. 1]. On Osborn, and for his identification as the author of these letters, see Cavell, *Tracing the Connected Narrative*, 42–9, 185–6, 188–9.

81 *Letters on the Relief of Sir John Franklin's Expedition*, 9–10, 18, Letters II and V, of 9 and 18 January 1850.

82 'The Track of Sir John Franklin', *The New Monthly Magazine and Humorist* (ed. W. Harrison Ainsworth) 90 (1850), 372–5.

83 Janice Cavell has observed how the British public followed incoming news of Arctic exploration, and of the Franklin search in particular, in the same spirit as serialised fiction by instalments: Cavell, *Tracing the Connected Narrative*, 26–38.

84 For an extended discussion of these see Craciun, *Writing Arctic Disaster*, Ch. 1.

85 *Catalogue of the Franklin Relics, in the Museum of the United Service Institution, Whitehall* (London: Kelly & Co., [1860]), in SPRI, SCO: SPRI-SPC: (*41): 91(091)[1847–59 Franklin search] [Bound in: Pamphlets Franklin Search Vol. 1].

86 James Wyld, 'Chart of the Arctic Regions From the Admiralty Surveys' (London, *c.*1855). Viewable at *Barry Lawrence Ruderman Antique Maps Inc.* https://www.raremaps.com/gallery/detail/30044/chart-of-the-arctic-regions-from-the-admiralty-surveys-pub-wyld.

87 Ralph Hyde, 'Mr. Wyld's Monster Globe', *History Today* 20:2 (1970), 118–23; Irene Javorsky, 'Pariser und Londoner Georamen des 19. Jahrhunderts', *Der Globusfreund* 38/39 (1990), 179–92, at 183–8.

88 'A Journey round the Globe', *Punch, or the London Charivari* 21 (1851), 4–5, at 5. For an introduction to scientific themes in *Punch* see Richard Noakes, '*Punch; or, The London Charivari*, 1841–1992, 1996–2002', *Science in the Nineteenth-Century Periodical* (2005–2020) https://www.sciper.org/browse/PU_desc.html. See also Richard Noakes, 'Representing "A Century of Inventions": Nineteenth-Century Technology and Victorian *Punch*', in Henson et al. (eds), *Culture and Science*, 151–63.

89 Richard Bellon, 'Science at the Crystal Focus of the World', in Fyfe and Lightman (eds), *Science in the Marketplace*, 301–35, quote at 302 (and see 316–17, briefly, on Wyld's Globe).

90 Javorsky, 'Pariser und Londoner Georamen'; Jean-Marc Besse, '"Embrasser la terre d'un seul coup d'œil": The First Parisian Georamas', Maps and Society, The Warburg Institute, London, 13 November 2003 https://shs.hal.science/halshs-00113279/document (p. 11 for the 1832 georama).

91 Bellon, 'Science at the Crystal Focus', 315–16.

92 Quote from the *Illustrated London News* 20:550 (20 March 1852), 243. Also cited in James Mangles, *Papers and Despatches Relating to the Arctic Searching Expeditions of 1850–51–52*, 2nd edn (London: Francis & John Rivington, 1852), 93.

93 [James Wyld], *Notes to Accompany Mr Wyld's Model of the Earth, Leicester Square* (London: Model of the Earth, [1851]), xiv.

94 Aileen Fyfe and Bernard Lightman, 'Science in the Marketplace: An Introduction', in Fyfe and Lightman (eds), *Science in the Marketplace*, 1–19, esp. 13–14. On the active role of 'popular' audiences see also Topham, 'Scientific Publishing'; Sally Shuttleworth and Geoffrey Cantor, 'Introduction', in Cantor and Shuttleworth (eds) *Science Serialized*, 1–15; Secord, *Victorian Sensation*.

Chapter 5: Keeping Track

1 Stephen King-Hall, *A North Sea Diary, 1914–1918* (London: Newnes, [1937?]), 156. A different version of the present chapter, written with a specifically academic audience in mind, can be found in Caputo, 'From Surveying to Surveillance'.

2 Churchill Archives Centre, Cambridge (henceforth CHU), MRDN 1/1, The Papers of Captain Charles Marsden, 'Track chart showing the positions of HMS Southampton at the Battle of Jutland, 1916-05-31'. For Marsden's record of service see The National Archives, Kew (henceforth TNA), ADM 340/94/17, Records of Service Cards – Dates of Birth before 1900, Marsden, Charles Victor Salomon Joseph, d.o.b. 3 August 1894.

3 See King-Hall, *North Sea Diary*, 134–6.

4 Ibid., 139–40.

5 Ibid., 150–53.

6 TNA, ADM 101/396, Admiralty and Predecessors: Office of the Director General of the Medical Department of the Navy and Predecessors: Medical Journals, SOUTHAMPTON, January–December 1916, n. 35.

7 TNA, ADM 53/60688, Admiralty, and Ministry of Defence, Navy Department: Ships' Logs – SOUTHAMPTON, June 1916, front page.

8 CHU, MRDN 1/3, The Papers of Captain Charles Marsden, 'Photograph album of HMS Southampton, 1916 – 1918', f. 3r.

9 CHU, MRDN 1/2, The Papers of Captain Charles Marsden, 'Notes about his career in the Royal Navy, 1970', f. 2.

10 Outram, 'On Being Perseus'; Cosgrove, *Geography and Vision*, 159–61. On surveying and embodiment see also Lachlan Fleetwood, 'Bodies in High Places: Exploration, Altitude Sickness, and the Problem of Bodily Comparison in the Himalaya, 1800–1850', *Itinerario* 43:3 (2019), 489–515. For some attempts to transcend this personal link see e.g.: Wilko Graf von Hardenberg, 'Measuring

Zero at Sea: On the Delocalization and Abstraction of the Geodetic Framework', *Journal of Historical Geography* 68 (2020), 11–20.

11 Kapil Raj, 'When Human Travellers Become Instruments: The Indo-British Exploration of Central Asia in the Nineteenth Century', in Bourguet et al. (eds), *Instruments, Travel and Science*, 156–88.

12 Steven Shapin, *A Social History of Truth: Civility and Science in Seventeenth-Century England* (Chicago IL and London: University of Chicago Press, 1994); Hellawell, '"Best and Most Practical Philosophers"'. On credibility in field science see also: Driver, *Geography Militant*, Ch. 3; Withers, 'Mapping the Niger'.

13 William Richardson, *A Mariner of England: An Account of the Career of William Richardson from Cabin Boy in the Merchant Service to Warrant Officer in the Royal Navy (1780–1819) as Told by Himself*, ed. Col. Spencer Childers (London: John Murray, 1908), 125–7. Some of the ships did make it to the Caribbean.

14 TNA, CO 318/18, Colonial Office and Predecessors: West Indies Original Correspondence – Secretary of State: Naval Despatches, 1795–1796, Admiral Hugh Christian to William Huskisson, 29 January 1796, f. 258.

15 James Davey, *Tempest: The Royal Navy and the Age of Revolutions* (New Haven CT and London: Yale University Press, 2023), 153–5.

16 The details of the whole episode as described in these three paragraphs come from TNA, CO 318/18 and from: Richardson, *A Mariner of England*, 123–32; Kenneth Breen, 'Christian, Sir Hugh Cloberry (bap. 1747, d. 1798)', *Oxford Dictionary of National Biography* (2008) https://doi.org/10.1093/ref:odnb/5357; Michael Duffy, *Soldiers, Sugar, and Seapower: The British Expeditions to the West Indies and the War against Revolutionary France* (Oxford: Clarendon Press, 1987), 199–216.

17 C. I. Hamilton, *The Making of the Modern Admiralty: British Naval Policy-Making, 1805–1927* (Cambridge: Cambridge University Press, 2011), 105. On the British Admiralty's 'paper forms of control', in particular, see Thomas Malcomson, *Order and Disorder in the British Navy, 1793–1815: Control, Resistance, Flogging and Hanging* (Woodbridge: The Boydell Press, 2016), Ch. 1.

18 Evan Wilson, AnnaSara Hammar and Jacob Seerup (eds), *Eighteenth-Century Naval Officers: A Transnational Perspective* (Cham: Palgrave Macmillan, 2019); Evan Wilson, *A Social History of British Naval Officers, 1775–1815* (Woodbridge: The Boydell Press, 2017); S. A. Cavell, *Midshipmen and Quarterdeck Boys in the British Navy, 1771–1831* (Woodbridge: The Boydell Press, 2012); Marta García Garralón, 'Ciencia e illustración en la Armada Española del siglo XVIII. La educación de la oficialidad', in Juan Marchena Fernández and Justo Cuño Bonito (eds), *Vientos de guerra: apogeo y crisis de la Real Armada, 1750–1823*, 3 vols (Aranjuez (Madrid): Ediciones Doce Calles, [2018]), III, 121–327.

19 Mark Knights, *Trust and Distrust: Corruption in Office in Britain and Its Empire, 1600–1850* (Oxford: Oxford University Press, 2021); N. A. M. Rodger, 'Honour and Duty at Sea, 1660–1815', *Historical Research* 75:190 (2002), 425–47. On the growth of 'individual accountability' see also James Poskett, 'Sounding in Silence: Men, Machines and the Changing Environment of Naval

Discipline, 1796–1815', *The British Journal for the History of Science* 48:2 (177) (2015), 213–32.

20 Cavell, *Midshipmen*, 20–24; Wilson, *Social History of British Naval Officers*, 20–32; Schotte, *Sailing School*, 96–9.

21 On the historical evolution of logbooks, inside and outside navies, see Margaret Schotte, 'Expert Records: Nautical Logbooks from Columbus to Cook', *Information & Culture* 48:3 (2013), 281–322; Gilje, *To Swear like a Sailor*, Ch. 3; W. E. May, 'The Log-books Used by Ships of the East India Company', *Journal of Navigation* 27:1 (1974), 116–18.

22 On panopticism in the dockyards see William J. Ashworth, '"System of Terror": Samuel Bentham, Accountability and Dockyard Reform during the Napoleonic Wars', *Social History* 23:1 (1998), 63–79. On the concept of Panopticon in Foucault see e.g.: David Murakami Wood, 'Beyond the Panopticon? Foucault and Surveillance Studies', in Jeremy W. Crampton and Stuart Elden (eds), *Space, Knowledge and Power: Foucault and Geography* (Aldershot and Burlington VT: Ashgate, 2007), 245–63; Jerome E. Dobson and Peter F. Fisher, 'The Panopticon's Changing Geography', *Geographical Review* 97:3 (2007), 307–23. On Jervis see also: P. K. Crimmin, 'Jervis, John, Earl of St Vincent (1735–1823)', *Oxford Dictionary of National Biography* (2006) https://doi.org/10.1093/ref:odnb/14794; N. A. M. Rodger, *The Command of the Ocean: A Naval History of Britain, 1649–1815* (London: Allen Lane, 2004), 464–5, 525–6.

23 Schotte, 'Expert Records'.

24 See e.g. John C. Rule and Ben S. Trotter, *A World of Paper: Louis XIV, Colbert de Torcy, and the Rise of the Information State* (Montreal: McGill-Queen's University Press, 2014). For a longer-term view see Edward Higgs, *The Information State in England: The Central Collection of Information on Citizens since 1500* (Basingstoke: Palgrave Macmillan, 2003). The perception of 'information overload', almost regardless of the real situation, seems to crop up across the centuries: Daniel Rosenberg, 'Early Modern Information Overload', *Journal of the History of Ideas* 64:1 (2003), 1–9.

25 *The Queen's Regulations and the Admiralty Instructions for the Government of Her Majesty's Naval Service* (London: Her Majesty's Stationery Office, 1862), 175–6 (xx.7–8, 11), 309 (xli.i.24).

26 *Queen's Regulations* (1862), 160–61 (xix.3–4).

27 TNA, ADM 1/6003, Admiralty In-Letters and Papers, From Admirals: N Mediterranean, 1867, C. Paget [Admiral Lord Clarence Edward Paget], Letter n. 338, 9 October 1867; Commander Morgan Singer, 'Reporting Proceedings', 9 October 1867 (enclosure n. 1 to letter n. 363, 5 November 1867).

28 TNA, ADM 1/6003, W. Kellett, R. Cook, G. L. Norcock, 'Report of Enquiry, "in re" Cruizer', 24 October 1867 (enclosure n. 3 to letter n. 363, 5 November 1867).

29 TNA, ADM 1/6003, 'Report of Enquiry', [ff. 4–5].

30 Joe Akintola, 'GIS Data and the Coastline Paradox', *GIS Lounge* (30 October 2014) https://www.gislounge.com/gis-data-coastline-paradox/. On the fictional quality of mapped lines see also Paul Carter, 'Dark with Excess of Bright:

Mapping the Coastlines of Knowledge', in Cosgrove (ed.), *Mappings*, 125–47, at 125–32.

31 Kevin D. Haggerty and Richard V. Ericson, 'The Surveillant Assemblage', *British Journal of Sociology* 51:4 (2000), 605–22, quote at 606. This notion owes a great deal to Gilles Deleuze's concept of 'dividual', for a particularly clear explanation of which see Olivier Aïm, *Les théories de la surveillance: Du panoptique aux Surveillance Studies* (Malakoff: Armand Colin, 2020), 77–9.

32 C. F. Noble, *The French, and English, Marine Regulations Compared* (London, 1793), as cited in Andrew S. Cook, 'Establishing the Sea Routes to India and China: Stages in the Development of Hydrographical Knowledge', in H. V. Bowen, Margarette Lincoln and Nigel Rigby (eds), *The Worlds of the East India Company* (Woodbridge and Rochester NY: The Boydell Press, 2002), 119–36, at 123.

33 Cook, 'Establishing the Sea Routes', 128–9.

34 Parker, 'Ship', 5.

35 Olivier Chapuis, Gilles Bessero and Patrick Souquière, *300 ans de cartes marines autour du monde* ([Paris]: Éditions Gallimard Loisirs and [Brest]: Shom, 2021), 46–9; Ministerio de Defensa, *Dueños del mar señores del mundo: Historia de la cartografía náutica española* ([Madrid]: Ministerio de Defensa, 2015), 120; Andrew S. Cook, 'Surveying the Seas: Establishing the Sea Routes to the East Indies', in Akerman (ed.), *Cartographies of Travel*, 69–96. On questions of reliability and copyright in the eighteenth-century mapmaking trade see also Isabella Alexander, 'Copyright and the Circulation of Geographical Knowledge in Eighteenth-Century Britain', in Louisiane Ferlier and Bénédicte Miyamoto (eds), *Forms, Formats and the Circulation of Knowledge: British Printscape's Innovations, 1688–1832* (Leiden and Boston MA: Brill, 2020), 87–111.

36 Parker, 'Ship'.

37 *The Queen's Regulations for the Government of Her Majesty's Naval Service* ([London]: [H. M. Stationery Office], [1844]), 174 (v.ix.2), 216 (vii.21).

38 *Queen's Regulations* (1862), 256 (xxxv.14), 267 (xxxv.28), 361 (xlvi.19).

39 Luciana Martins and Felix Driver, 'John Septimus Roe and the Art of Navigation, c.1815–30', in Timothy Barringer, Geoff Quilley and Douglas Fordham (eds), *Art and the British Empire* (Manchester: Manchester University Press, 2007), 53–66.

40 *Queen's Regulations* (1862), 62 (viii.ii.10).

41 NMM, MLN/140/5, Milne Family Papers, Mediterranean Station: Regulations for Track Chart Competition, 15 February 1870.

42 Archivio di Stato di Alessandria, Carbonazzi IV, 3, 2 – Carte geografiche e marittime, Faldone 25, fascicolo 5, 'Carta del viaggio nel Mediterraneo compiuto dalla R. Fregata V. Emanuele nella campagna d'istruzione della R. Marina dell'anno 1874'.

43 *Calendario generale del Regno d'Italia pel 1900 compilato a cura del Ministero dell'Interno* (Rome: L. Cecchini editrice, 1900), 186.

44 Torin Monahan, 'Surveillance as Cultural Practice', *The Sociological Quarterly* 52:4 (2011), 495–508, at 497.

45 On the Bishop of Columbia see Jean Friesen, 'Hills, George', in *Dictionary of*

Canadian Biography Vol. 12 (University of Toronto/Université Laval, 1990) http://www.biographi.ca/en/bio/hills_george_12E.html.

46 'Porcher, Edwin A., 1824–1878, Edwin Augustus Porcher Collection, 1849–1861', *Yale Center for British Art* https://collections.britishart.yale.edu/catalog/orbis:11146005. For some examples see 'Cdr Edwin A Porcher', *The British Museum* https://www.britishmuseum.org/collection/term/BIOG60142.

47 TNA, ADM 1/5969, Admiralty In-Letters and Papers, From Admirals: Y Pacific, Z Australia, 1866, Letter from Joseph Denman, 25 June 1866, and enclosures: n. 3, E. Porcher to Jos. Denman, 12 June 1866; n. 4, 'Minutes of a Court of Enquiry held on board the "Sparrowhawk" relative to the Ships getting on shore …', 12 June 1866; George Henry Richards, 'Grounding of Sparrowhawk', 13 August [1866].

48 TNA, ADM 1/5969, Joseph Denman to the Admiralty, 26 August 1866.

49 TNA, ADM 1/5969, 'Scout – Grounding 12 Aug.t 1866', and enclosures (esp. George Henry Richards, 'Grounding of the Scout', 30 October 1866).

50 The account in the following paragraphs is based on various minutes and dispatches in TNA, ADM 137/3661, Discrepancies in Track Chart of HMS CHAMPION, 7 April–4 May 1917; ADM 137/3655, Discrepancies in Track Chart in HMS CHAMPION, 8–15 April 1917.

51 'Rear-Admiral Sir Cecil Foley Lambert K.C.B.', *Royal Navy Flag Officers 1904–1945* https://web.archive.org/web/20100621053011/http://www.admirals. org.uk/admirals/individual.php?RecNo=457.

52 TNA, ADM 196/144/92, Sub Lieutenants and Lieutenants Seniority Dates Promoted from Cadets and Midshipmen – Summaries of Confidential Reports: Vol. E, 'Brownlow, Malby Donald' (d.o.b 18 April 1887, date of appointment 15 September 1903).

53 On the development of modern oceanography see: Rozwadowski, *Fathoming the Ocean*; Helen M. Rozwadowski and David K. van Keuren (eds), *The Machine in Neptune's Garden: Historical Perspectives on Technology and the Marine Environment* (Sagamore Beach MA: Science History Publications/USA, 2004); von Hardenberg, 'Measuring Zero at Sea'; Lynn K. Nyhart, 'Voyaging and the Scientific Expedition Report, 1800–1940', in Rima D. Apple, Gregory J. Downey and Stephen L. Vaughn (eds), *Science in Print: Essays on the History of Science and the Culture of Print* (Madison WI and London: The University of Wisconsin Press, 2012), 65–86; Jason W. Smith, *To Master the Boundless Sea: The U.S. Navy, the Marine Environment, and the Cartography of Empire* (Chapel Hill NC: University of North Carolina Press, [2018]).

54 TNA, ADM 199/618/20, 'Report of Proceedings by Commanding Officer, HMS Exe for the period 20 September to 4 October 1942 whilst searching for survivors of HMS Veteran', 4 October 1942, ff. 120–30.

55 Gilles Deleuze, 'Postscript on the Societies of Control', *October* 59 (1992), 3–7.

56 On the origins of RDF see Nigel West, *GCHQ: The Secret Wireless War, 1900–1986* (Barnsley: Frontline Books, 2019), 26–9, 39–44, 79, 200. On its use at sea in the Second World War, in conjunction with signal decryption and other intelligence, see David Syrett (ed.), *The Battle of the Atlantic and Signals*

Intelligence: U-Boat Tracking Papers, 1941–1947 (Aldershot: Ashgate for the Navy Records Society, 2002).

57   Priya Satia, 'The Pain of Love: The Invention of Aerial Surveillance in British Iraq', in Peter Adey, Mark Whitehead and Alison Williams (eds), *From Above: War, Violence, and Verticality* (Oxford: Oxford University Press, 2014), 223–46; Priya Satia, 'The Defense of Inhumanity: Air Control and the British Idea of Arabia', *The American Historical Review* 111:1 (2006), 16–51.

58   Beryl Markham, *West with the Night* (London: Penguin Books, 1988), 256.

59   David A. H. Wilson, 'Sea Lions, Greasepaint and the U-boat Threat: Admiralty Scientists Turn to the Music Hall', *Notes Rec. R. Soc. Lond.* 55:3 (2001), 425–55 (medium story at 433).

60   W. D. Hackmann, 'Underwater Acoustics and the Royal Navy, 1893–1930', *Annals of Science* 36:3 (1979), 255–27 (Paget's story is at 268). On Paget see also Harry Lowery and John Bosnell, 'Paget, Sir Richard Arthur Surtees, Second Baronet (1869–1955)', *Oxford Dictionary of National Biography* (2008) https://doi.org/10.1093/ref:odnb/35358.

61   TNA, ADM 199/2061, Admiralty: War History Cases and Papers, Second World War – Monthly Anti-Submarine Reports Vol. 5, 1944, *Monthly Anti-Submarine Report – March 1944* (Anti-U-Boat Division of the Naval Staff, 15 April 1944), f. 71v.

62   Edwin Hutchins, *Cognition in the Wild* (Cambridge MA and London: MIT Press, 1995).

63   Steven Morris, 'Commander of Submarine in Crash Misread Chart, Court Martial Told', *The Guardian* (15 March 2010) https://www.theguardian.com/uk/2010/mar/15/submarine-crash-navy-court-martial.

64   Natasha Dow Schüll, 'Self-Tracking', in Nanna Bonde Thylstrup et al. (eds), *Uncertain Archives: Critical Keywords for Big Data* (Cambridge MA and London: MIT Press, 2021), 457–68; Laurie Frick, 'Self-Surveillance: Should You Worry or Simply Embrace Your Personal Data?', *EMBO Reports* 15:3 (2014), 218–22.

65   Shoshana Zuboff, *The Age of Surveillance Capitalism: The Fight for a Human Future at the New Frontier of Power* (London: Profile Books, 2019), 11.

Chapter 6: A Common Highway?

1   NMM, JOD/258, 'Documents of Gilbert William Smith, steward onboard RMS vessel AVON renamed HMS AVOCA requisitioned during First World War', 1916–19. From the journal we learn that he turned 25 on 17 July 1918. On how naval requisitions affected the Royal Mail Steam Packet Company see Robert E. Forrester, *British Mail Steamers to South America, 1851–1965: A History of the Royal Mail Steam Packet Company and Royal Mail Lines* (Farnham and Burlington VT: Ashgate, 2014), Ch. 8.

2   NMM, JOD/258/1, 'Documents of Gilbert William Smith', 'Fine copy of a diary', 1916–19, 25 May 1917.

3   NMM, JOD/258/3, 'Documents of Gilbert William Smith', 'Rough copy of a diary', 1918.

4   NMM, JOD/258/4, 'Documents of Gilbert William Smith', 'A track chart of voyages', 1916–19.

5   Cunard's logbooks contained a schematic, pre-drawn 'track chart', as well as a few blank pages bearing the heading 'PASSENGER'S LOG BOOK.' (these went down from 8 in 1893 to 4 in 1895, to only 2 in 1898, as the booklets lost some pages and ads encroached): *Cunard's Passenger Log Book: A Short History of the Cunard Steamship Company and a Description of the Royal Mail Steamers Campania and Lucania* (Glasgow: David Bryce and Son, 1893, 1895 and [1898?]): Cambridge University Library, Rare Books, 1893.6.595, 1895.6.519 and 1898.6.86.

6   See, e.g., 'The Orient Line of Steamships – Passengers' Track Chart', showing, in pencil, the forty-three-day journey of SS *John Elder* from Plymouth to Melbourne: NMM, OSN/20/13, 'Passengers' Track Chart – JOHN ELDER', 1882.

7   See, e.g., 'Peninsular & Oriental Steam Navigation Company Track Chart, 1890', showing, marked in pen, travel legs of various journeys from Britain to the Indian Ocean, Australia and Japan: NMM, P&O/94/2, 'Track Chart 1890, marked with shipping routes and distances', 1890.

8   British Library, London, Cartographic Items Maps C.44.d.58, 'Wyld's outline chart from England to Australia & China for the purpose of pricking off a ships track', [*c.*1880].

9   David Jünger, 'Karte von Fritz Freudenheim', *Bundeszentrale für politische Bildung* (20 October 2021) https://www.bpb.de/themen/zeit-kulturgeschichte/geteilte-geschichte/342332/karte-von-fritz-freudenheim; '12-year-old Fritz Freudenheim's Map of his Flight from Nazi Germany' (1938), *Shared History Project: 1700 Years of Jewish Life in German Speaking Lands*, object 43 https://sharedhistoryproject.org/object/12-year-old-fritz-freudenheims-map-of-his-flight-from-nazi-germany.

10   See, e.g.: Huntington Library, San Marino, CA, ephJHK 00812, John Haskell Kemble Collection, Matson Navigation Company [JHKC-MNC], 'S. S. Monterey & S. S. Mariposa: Room Plan' (1937), 3 https://hdl.huntington.org/digital/collection/p9539coll1/id/19202/rec/4; ephJHK 00824, JHKC-MNC, 'Photograph Holder' (c.1966), back cover https://hdl.huntington.org/digital/collection/p9539coll1/id/18822/rec/8; ephJHK 00969, JHKC-MNC, 'Malolo (Flying Fish)' (1928), 35 https://hdl.huntington.org/digital/collection/p9539coll1/id/18437/rec/5; priJHK 00078, JHKC, Edward Camy, 'A Good-Natured Map of Alaska Showing the Services Offered by "The Alaska Line" and Suggesting Some of the Most Interesting Features of the Territory' (1940) https://hdl.huntington.org/digital/collection/p9539coll1/id/12340/rec/79.

11   Huntington Library, San Marino, CA, ephJHK 00511, JHKC-MNC, 'Again! Matson Lines Cruises to the South Pacific' (1956), 2 https://hdl.huntington.org/digital/collection/p9539coll1/id/15678/rec/141.

12   James R. Akerman, 'Private Journeys on Public Maps: A Look at Inscribed Road Maps', *Cartographic Perspectives* 35 (2000), 27–47; James R. Akerman, 'Twentieth-Century American Road Maps and the Making of a National Motorized Space', in Akerman (ed.), *Cartographies*, 151–206. As he puts it,

'American road maps' shared two 'tendencies': 'to release motoring tourists freely on the landscape, and to control their movement across it' ('Twentieth-Century American Road Maps', 206). This freedom applied to women, too: Christina E. Dando, *Women and Cartography in the Progressive Era* (Abingdon and New York: Routledge, 2018), Ch. 2.

13 See Chapter 2.

14 Biblioteca Nacional de España, Madrid, RES/237, 'Recueil et pourtraict d'aulcunes villes maritimes et plus memorables ports et leurs advenues et marcques servantes a la navigation en la mer oceane [Manuscrito]', 1586, ff. 34, 61, available at Biblioteca Digital Hispánica http://bdh.bne.es/bnesearch/detalle/bdh0000135241. See also f. 70 for a very schematic representation of navigation along the straight coastline of northern France and present-day Belgium. Other charts in the volume show what seem to be mainly lines of bearing rather than tracks (although a handful are slightly ambiguous). See e.g. ff. 44, 58, 67, 73, 89, 92, 95. On these charts see also Günter Schilder, 'A Dutch Manuscript Rutter: An Unique Portrait of the European Coasts in the Late Sixteenth Century', *Imago Mundi* 43 (1991), 59–71, esp. 66–9.

15 For another example, see Les Archives départementales de la Vendée, 24 Fi 103, M. de La Voye and Charles Pène, '8ème carte particulière des costes [*sic*] de Bretagne qui comprend l'entrée de la Loire et l'isle [*sic*] de Noirmoutier comme elles paroiss[en]t [*sic*] à basse mer dans les grandes marées', from the *Neptune françois* (Paris, [1753]) https://etatcivil-archives.vendee.fr/ark:/22574/s005e1362 d7e4cb9/5e1362d7e9f0f.

16 On reconnaissance see Edney, 'Reconsidering Enlightenment Geography', 175–85.

17 On Maury's career and charts, and the links with Melville, see: D. Graham Burnett, 'Matthew Fontaine Maury's "Sea of Fire": Hydrography, Biogeography, and Providence in the Tropics', in Felix Driver and Luciana Martins (eds), *Tropical Visions in an Age of Empire* (Chicago IL and London: University of Chicago Press, 2005), 113–34; Smith, *To Master the Boundless Sea*, Ch. 3.

18 Quoted in Smith, *To Master the Boundless Sea*, 88 (and see 105–6 on the notion of 'a common highway').

19 Burnett, 'Matthew Fontaine Maury', 127–30; Smith, *To Master the Boundless Sea*, 97–9.

20 *Google Books Ngram Viewer* https://books.google.com/ngrams/graph?content=trackless%2C+pathless&year_start=1500&year_end=2019&corpus=en-2019&smoothing=3; '"pathless" (adjective)', *Oxford English Dictionary* (revised 2005) https://www.oed.com/dictionary/pathless_adj?tab=meaning_and_use#31760938 (1596); '"trackless" (adjective)', a., *Oxford English Dictionary* https://www.oed.com/dictionary/trackless_adj?tab=meaning_and_use#17855400 (1656).

21 National Library of Scotland, Edinburgh, MS.9232, 'Robert Ritchie: Journal of Voyages', 1811–12, f. 1.

22 NMM, JOD/119/3, 'Book of poems kept by Richard Cotten in HMS COMUS', 1883, visible at https://www.rmg.co.uk/collections/archive/rmgc-object-550925.

23 Mystic Seaport Museum, Mystic, CT, Log of the *Halcyon*, kept by William
    George Bailey, 1843–48, Log 988, as cited in Gilje, *To Swear like a Sailor*, 92–3.

24 William Cronon, 'The Trouble with Wilderness: Or, Getting Back to the
    Wrong Nature', *Environmental History* 1:1 (1996), 7–28; Corey Ross, 'Tropical
    Nature as *Global Patrimoine*: Imperialism and International Nature Protection
    in the Early Twentieth Century', *Past & Present* 226 (Supplement 10) (2015),
    214–39; Ramachandra Guha, 'The Paradox of Global Environmentalism',
    Current History 99 (2000), 367–70. For some of the debates raised by this
    scholarly attempt to de-essentialise 'wilderness' see: Samuel P. Hays, 'Comment:
    The Trouble with Bill Cronon's Wilderness', *Environmental History* 1:1 (1996),
    29–32; William Cronon, 'The Trouble with Wilderness: A Response',
    Environmental History 1:1 (1996), 47–55.

25 Rozwadowski, *Fathoming the Ocean*, 180–82; Steinberg, *Social Construction of
    the Ocean*, Ch. 4. For a potted history of the birth of cultural associations
    between the sea and the 'empty' and 'wild' sublime see Cohen, *Novel and the
    Sea*, 106–31.

26 P. A. Nettlefold and E. Stratford, 'The Production of Climbing Landscapes-as-
    Texts', *Australian Geographical Studies* 37:2 (1999), 130–41; Peter H. Hansen,
    'Albert Smith, the Alpine Club, and the Invention of Mountaineering in
    Mid-Victorian Britain', *Journal of British Studies* 34:3 (1995), 300–324. The cult
    of untrodden wilderness and first ascents later reached skiing as well: Zac
    Robinson, 'Off the Beaten Path? Ski Mountaineering and the Weight of
    Tradition in the Canadian Rockies, 1909–1940', *The International Journal of the
    History of Sport* 24:10 (2007), 1320–43.

27 On the development of lines as conventional representational devices in rock
    climbing, in imitation of mountaineering, see J. Taylor, 'Mapping Adventure: A
    Historical Geography of Yosemite Valley Climbing Landscapes', *Journal of
    Historical Geography* 32 (2006), 190–219, at 194–9. On route-naming see Kate
    Lawrence, 'Naming (and Claiming) Vertical Territories', *Performance Research*
    24:2 (2019), 49–56.

28 Leo Tolstoy, *War and Peace*, trans. Louise and Aylmer Maude (Chicago IL:
    Encyclopædia Britannica, Inc., 1952), 575 (Book XIII, Ch. 10).

29 See Introduction.

30 Joseph Conrad, *The Mirror of the Sea* (New York and London: Harper &
    Brothers Publishers, 1906), 107.

31 'Toulon Naval Port', *VisitVar* https://www.visitvar.fr/en/explore/through-time/
    toulon-navy-port.

32 Jean-Pierre Dubreuil, 'Toulon 1830–1860: l'introduction de la vapeur dans la
    marine de guerre', *Cahiers de la Méditerranée* 5 (1972), 68–75, at 70–71.

33 D'Urville invented the term 'Melanesia' in 1832. This derives from the Greek
    '*mélas*', meaning 'black', or 'swarthy'. See: Serge Tcherkézoff (trans. Isabel
    Ollivier), 'A Long and Unfortunate Voyage towards the "Invention" of the
    Melanesia/Polynesia Distinction 1595–1832', *The Journal of Pacific History* 38:2
    (2003), 175–96.

34 For a nuanced discussion of steam as 'spectacle' in the Victorian period see

Douglas R. Burgess Jr., *Engines of Empire: Steamships and the Victorian Imagination* (Stanford CA: Stanford University Press, 2016), Part I.

35 Apostolos Delis, 'Navigating in the Age of Transition: A Voyage Analysis of Greek Sailing Ships and Steamers 1860s–1920s', in Apostolos Delis et al. (eds), *Mediterranean Seafarers in Transition: Maritime Labour, Communities, Shipping and the Challenge of Industrialization 1850–1920s* (Leiden and Boston MA: Brill, 2023), 362–411, esp. at 379–80 (on speed of travel from the Black Sea to Provence), 390–91 (on the Strait of Messina seasonal route), 400–401 (on Atlantic steamer routes – map at 401). Sailing and low-powered steamships still made tracks that were somewhat curved, even in schematic representations: NMM, G201:1/62, 'Chart of the World Showing Tracks Followed by Sailing and Low Powered Steam Vessels' (1888) https://collections.rmg.co.uk/collections/objects/544040.html. For a full-powered steam map see: 'La Salle Extension University Map of Steamship Routes of the World' (1914) https://commons.princeton.edu/mg/map-of-steamship-routes-of-the-world-1914.

36 On the slow move from paddle to screw see Basil Greenhill and Ann Giffard, *Steam, Politics and Patronage: The Transformation of the Royal Navy 1815–54* (London: Conway Maritime Press, 1994), esp. 28 (on the first steam crossing of the Channel), 108–9 (on the Suez Packet Service), 26, 41, 53–4 (on the *Great Western*). On the transatlantic race between the *Great Western* and the *Sirius* see Burgess, *Engines of Empire*, 34–40.

37 Letter from Commander Crispin to Sidney Herbert, 29 January 1845, reproduced in Greenhill and Giffard, *Steam*, 157–9. On the history of the *Great Britain* see Burgess, *Engines of Empire*, 45–53.

38 *The Times*, 8 August 1853, as cited in Peter Duckers, *The Crimean War at Sea: Naval Campaigns against Russia, 1854–6* (Barnsley: Pen & Sword Maritime, 2011), 6–7.

39 Martin J. Daunton, *Royal Mail: The Post Office Since 1840* (London and New York: Bloomsbury Academic, 2015 [1985]), 166–8, 177–8, 188–9; Francis E. Hyde, *Cunard and the North Atlantic 1840–1973: A History of Shipping and Financial Management* (London and Basingstoke: The Macmillan Press Ltd, 1975), 28–9; Torsten Feys, *The Battle for the Migrants: Introduction of Steamshipping on the North Atlantic and Its Impact on the European Exodus* (St John's, Newfoundland: International Maritime Economic History Association, 2013).

40 Freda Harcourt, *Flagships of Imperialism: The P&O Company and the Politics of Empire from Its Origins to 1867* (Manchester: Manchester University Press, 2006); Forrester, *British Mail Steamers*; Marie-Françoise Berneron-Couvenhes, *Les Messageries Maritimes: L'essor d'une grande compagnie de navigation française, 1851–1894* (Paris: Presses de l'Université Paris-Sorbonne, 2007); Hyde, *Cunard*.

41 The use of the term to mean 'a regular succession of public conveyances plying between certain places' is first attested in American English in 1786, but initially it often referred to coach lines, next to sailing packets: '"line" (noun)', III.22, *Oxford English Dictionary* https://www.oed.com/dictionary/line_n2?tab=meaning_and_use#39217041. The term 'liner' was first applied to mean

a vessel in 1838: '"liner" (noun)', II.8.a, *Oxford English Dictionary* https://www.
oed.com/dictionary/liner_n2?tab=meaning_and_use.

42   'Steam Communication with Australia', Hansard House of Commons Debate 25
July 1850 Vol. 113 cc230–53, quotes from cc240, 246 and 249, interventions by
Sir J. W. Hogg and Mr Scott https://api.parliament.uk/historic-hansard/
commons/1850/jul/25/steam-communication-with-australia#.

43   The range of potential examples is immense. For some interesting ones see e.g.
Gotha Perthes Collection, SPK-80-3 A-01, A. Petermann, 'Karte von Polynesien
und dem Litoral des Grossen Oceans, zur Übersicht der politischen Verhältnisse
im Jahre 1859' (Gotha: Justus Perthes, 1859) (for an image see https://dhb.thulb.
uni-jena.de/receive/ufb_cbu_00012625); SPK-10-V.A B-02, Ricart Giralt,
'Servicios Marìtimos de la Compañia Trasatlàntica' (Barcelona, 1884). See also
Plate 20 below.

44   Tardy de Montravel, *Instructions nautiques pour naviguer sur les côtes des Guyanes*
(Paris: Paul Dupont, 1851), 23, available at Bibliothèque numérique Manioc /
SCD Université Antilles https://issuu.com/scduag/docs/instructiot/33.

45   'The Fate of Sir John Franklin – Are There to Be More Arctic Expeditions?', *New
York Times* (17 September 1869), 4.

46   In the version I consulted, the title of this piece is bizarre (among other things,
Barrow was a strong promoter of the searches for the Passage, and dead by 1850),
leading me to suspect an imprint error: John Barrow, 'Life of Sir Francis Drake',
The British Quarterly Review 11:21 (1 February 1850), 101–11 (viewable at https://
archive.org/details/sim_british-quarterly-review_1850-02-01_11_21/page/100/
mode/2up?view=theater). The article is also cited in Cavell, *Tracing the
Connected Narrative*, 187, as 'Sir J. Franklin – The North-West Passage', *British
Quarterly Review* 9 (February 1850), 109, 102, 104.

47   Bella S. Galil, 'The Marine Caravan – The Suez Canal and the Erythrean
Invasion', in Stephan Gollasch, Bella S. Galil and Andrew N. Cohen, *Bridging
Divides: Maritime Canals as Invasion Corridors* (Dordrecht: Springer, 2006),
207–300, at 207–13.

48   John Perry, 'A Shared Sea: The Axes of French and British Imperialism in the
Mediterranean, 1798–1914', in James R. Fichter (ed.), *British and French
Colonialism in Africa, Asia and the Middle East: Connected Empires across the
Eighteenth to the Twentieth Centuries* (Cham: Palgrave Macmillan, 2019),
113–30.

49   'Suez Canal, Egypt', *Earth Watching, European Space Agency* https://earth.esa.
int/web/earth-watching/image-of-the-week/content/-/article/
suez-canal-egypt.

50   Barthélemy-Prosper Enfantin, 1833, quoted in Valeska Huber, *Channelling
Mobilities: Migration and Globalisation in the Suez Canal Region and Beyond,
1869–1914* (Cambridge: Cambridge University Press, 2013), 26.

51   On the construction of the canal see Huber, *Channelling Mobilities*, 24–30. For
general overviews of its consequences for Egypt and the sale of shares in 1875
see: Afaf Lutfi Al-Sayyid – Marsot, 'The British Occupation of Egypt from 1882',
in Andrew Porter and Wm Roger Louis (eds), *The Oxford History of the British
Empire – Volume III: The Nineteenth Century* (Oxford: Oxford University Press,

1999), 651–64; Robert L. Tignor, *Egypt: A Short History* (Princeton NJ and Oxford: Princeton University Press, 2010), 219–20. According to some scholars, protecting the canal wasn't a key motive for British occupation in 1882: A. G. Hopkins, 'The Victorians and Africa: A Reconsideration of the Occupation of Egypt, 1882', *The Journal of African History* 27:2 (1986), 363–91, at 373–4; Dan Halvorson, 'Prestige, Prudence and Public Opinion in the 1882 British Occupation of Egypt', *Australian Journal of Politics and History* 56:3 (2010), 423–40. However, the canal certainly was a factor in weakening Egypt beforehand.

52 Charles Bright, *Submarine Telegraphs: Their History, Construction, and Working* (London: Crosby Lockwood and Son, 1898), 10–13.

53 Bruce J. Hunt, 'Doing Science in a Global Empire: Cable Telegraphy and Electrical Physics in Victorian Britain', in Bernard Lightman (ed.), *Victorian Science in Context* (Chicago IL and London: University of Chicago Press, 1997), 312–33. On the scientific context of submarine telegraphy see Bruce J. Hunt, 'Electrical Theory and Practice in the Nineteenth Century', in Mary Jo Nye (ed.), *The Cambridge History of Science – Volume 5: The Modern Physical and Mathematical Sciences* (Cambridge: Cambridge University Press, 2002), 311–28.

54 Bright, *Submarine Telegraphs*, 73–7.

55 Ibid., 91–8. The 1866 Atlantic cable was 2,131 miles long (1,852 nautical miles) and sat, on average, 1.6 miles deep (1,400 fathoms) (p. 98).

56 John Tully, 'A Victorian Ecological Disaster: Imperialism, the Telegraph, and Gutta-Percha', *Journal of World History* 20:4 (2009), 559–79, figure at 575–6.

57 Hunt, 'Doing Science', 319–22. On British predominance, and for a potted history of submarine cables, see Stewart Ash, 'The Development of Submarine Cables', in Douglas R. Burnett, Robert C. Beckman and Tara M. Davenport (eds), *Submarine Cables: The Handbook of Law and Policy* (Leiden and Boston MA: Martinus Nijhoff Publishers, 2014), 9–39, esp. 19–28. For more early-twentieth-century maps representing cables see e.g. Gotha Perthes Collection, SPK-10-IV.D C-05, Bureau international de l'Union télégraphique, 'Carte officielle des stations radiotélégraphiques', 2nd edn (Berne, 1925); 'Cables sous-marins et stations télégraphiques côtières' (n.d.). Representations of cables were often coupled up with those of routes, making for very entangled maps. See e.g.: Gotha Perthes Collection, SPK-10-IV.D C-06, Hermann Leiter, 'Karte der Eisenbahnen, der transozeanischen Kabel, der Seglerwege und des Schiffsverkehrs in den bedeutenderen Häfen' (1918?); 'Johnston's Commercial and Library Chart of the World on Mercators Projection. Showing the Position of Every Place of Commercial Importance, and the Chief Railways, Steamship Routes & Telegraphs' (Edinburgh: W. & A. K. Johnston, Ltd., c.1920?). For an earlier version of the latter see also University of Wisconsin-Milwaukee Libraries, American Geographical Society Library Digital Map Collection, agsmap028988 (s1-s2) https://collections.lib.uwm.edu/digital/collection/agdm/id/31536. Older versions still, in the nineteenth century, showed oceanic currents and shipping routes only: National Library of Australia, Rex Nan Kivell Collection, MAP NK 9720, 'Johnston's Commercial Chart of the World on Mercators Projection' (Edinburgh: W. & A. K. Johnston; Glasgow: James

Lumsden and Son; London: E. Stanford, 1857) https://catalogue.nla.gov.au/Record/2702510.

58 For some weight estimates see Tully, 'Victorian Ecological Disaster', 575.

59 On cable retrieval policy and practice see Douglas Burnett, 'Out-of-Service Submarine Cables', in Burnett, Beckman and Davenport (eds), *Submarine Cables*, 213–22. On the difficulties of recovering Atlantic cables in the nineteenth century see Bright, *Submarine Telegraphs*, 90.

60 Frank Norris, *The Octopus* (London: Grant Richards, 1901), 42, as cited in Anthony Giddens, *The Nation-State and Violence: Volume Two of A Contemporary Critique of Historical Materialism* (Cambridge: Polity, 1985), 175.

61 Asif Siddiqi, 'Pan American's Flying Boats', *U.S. Centennial of Flight Commission* https://www.centennialofflight.net/essay/Commercial_Aviation/china_clipper/Tran5.htm. For many other examples see Mark Ovenden and Maxwell Roberts, *Airline Maps: A Century of Art and Design* (London: Particular Books, 2019). For an example of non-advertising chart see e.g. Boston Public Library Norman B. Leventhal Map Center, G3201.P62 1919 .B75, William A. Briesemeister, 'Airways of the world on Mercator's projection' (1919) https://collections.leventhalmap.org/search/commonwealth:7h149w30k.

62 Armand Mattelart, 'Mapping Modernity: Utopia and Communications Networks', in Cosgrove (ed.) *Mappings*, 169–92. On time, space and networks see also, e.g., Vanessa Ogle, *The Global Transformation of Time: 1870–1950* (Cambridge MA: Harvard University Press, 2015). Importantly, this modern 'mobility' explicitly excluded and 'stigmatised' 'wandering': Huber, *Channelling Mobilities*. Also, as recently demonstrated by Alexis Litvine, it *didn't* signal an 'annihilation of space' or 'shrinking' of the world, which is a philosophical commonplace not grounded in sound historical evidence: Alexis D. Litvine, 'The Annihilation of Space: A Bad (Historical) Concept', *The Historical Journal* 65 (2022), 871–900.

63 Cusack, 'Looking over the Ship Railings', 95–7.

64 Frances Steel, 'Re-Routing Empire? Steam-Age Circulations and the Making of an Anglo Pacific, c.1850–90', *Australian Historical Studies* 46:3 (2015), 356–73. I am very grateful to Professor Sujit Sivasundaram for suggesting this article to me.

65 Edmund Russell et al., 'The Nature of Power: Synthesizing the History of Technology and Environmental History', *Technology and Culture* 52:2 (2011), 246–59.

66 Peregrine Horden and Nicholas Purcell, 'Mediterranean Connectivity: A Comparative Approach', in Horden and Purcell, *Boundless Sea*, 206–18.

67 On the tensions between the construct of the Mediterranean and that of 'modernity' see: Naor Ben-Yehoyada, 'Mediterranean Modernity?', in Peregrine Horden and Sharon Kinoshita (eds), *A Companion to Mediterranean History* (Chichester: John Wiley & Sons, Ltd, 2014), 107–21; Matthew D'Auria and Fernanda Gallo, 'Introduction: Ideas of Europe and the (Modern) Mediterranean', in Matthew D'Auria and Fernanda Gallo (eds), *Mediterranean Europe(s): Rethinking Europe from Its Southern Shores* (London and New York: Routledge, 2023), 1–19.

68 Sujit Sivasundaram, 'Towards a Critical History of Connection: The Port of Colombo, the Geographical "Circuit", and the Visual Politics of New Imperialism, ca. 1880–1914', *Comparative Studies in Society and History* 59:2 (2017), 346–84; David Armitage, Alison Bashford and Sujit Sivasundaram, 'Introduction', in David Armitage, Alison Bashford and Sujit Sivasundaram (eds), *Oceanic Histories* (Cambridge: Cambridge University Press, 2017), 1–28, at 19. On the inequalities of access to 'modern' networks in the nineteenth century see also Jean-Michel Johnston, 'The Telegraphic Revolution: Speed, Space and Time in the Nineteenth Century', *German History* 38:1 (2020), 47–76.

69 I borrow the term 'fountainhead' from J. M. Blaut, *The Colonizer's Model of the World: Geographical Diffusionism and Eurocentric History* (New York: The Guilford Press, 1993), 7.

70 *Indicateur de la navigation* (26 February 1859), 4. Available at Bibliothèque nationale de France, Département Littérature et art, V-3675 https://gallica.bnf.fr/ark:/12148/bpt6k5539294k/f4.item.zoom.

71 *State of New York Department of Labor Bulletin 1904 – Volume VI (Nos. 20–23)* (Albany NY: Brandow Printing Company, 1905), 328–9 https://babel. hathitrust.org/cgi/pt?id=umn.31951d001386676&view=1up&seq=341. I found this link thanks to the extremely useful directory of sources on 'Prices and Wages by Decade: 1850–1859', *University of Missouri Libraries* (2018) https:// libraryguides.missouri.edu/pricesandwages/1850-1859.

72 In 1855, the wages for Tunis 'Arab' 'field hands' were reported as between 1.87 and 2.50 US dollars a month, after conversion: Edmund Flagg (ed.), *Report on the Commercial Relations of the United States with All Foreign Nations – Volume III* (Washington: A. O. P. Nicholson, 1857), 363 https://babel.hathitrust.org/ cgi/pt?id=miun.ahl1805.0003.001&view=1up&seq=381. The source cited in endnote 71 above sets 1.99 francs as equivalent to 0.40 USD in 1853. So, in nominal wages, a French mason made 4.8 times more than the best-paid Tunisian agricultural labourer.

73 Feys, *Battle for the Migrants*, figure at 1, quote at 67.

74 Sivasundaram, 'Towards a Critical History of Connection', 379–80; Alida Clemente, *Il mestiere dell'incertezza. La pesca nel Golfo di Napoli tra XVIII e XX secolo* (Napoli: Alfredo Guida, 2005).

75 Katerina Galani, 'From Traditional Maritime Communities to Maritime Centres. Urbanization, Social Hierarchies and the Labour Market in the Age of Steam: The Case Study of Galaxidi, 1850s–1910s', in Delis (ed.), *Mediterranean Seafarers*, 264–92; Leonardo Scavino, 'Camogli as a Maritime Community in the Age of Transition (1850s–1914)', in Delis (ed.), *Mediterranean Seafarers*, 230–63.

76 Tully, 'Victorian Ecological Disaster', 570–71. I found the Persian Gulf image originally through a reproduction in Hunt, 'Doing Science', 319.

77 Steven Gray, *Steam Power and Sea Power: Coal, the Royal Navy, and the British Empire, c.1870–1914* (London: Palgrave Macmillan, 2018), Ch. 6.

78 Memoirs of Dada Amir Haider Khan, as cited in G. Balachandran, *Globalizing Labour? Indian Seafarers and World Shipping, c.1870–1945* (Delhi: Oxford

University Press, 2012), 109. See also Berneron-Couvenhes, *Messageries Maritimes*, 477–8; Tony Lane, 'The Political Imperatives of Bureaucracy and Empire: The Case of the Coloured Alien Seamen Order, 1925', in Diane Frost (ed.), *Ethnic Labour and British Imperial Trade: A History of Ethnic Seafarers in the UK* (London: Frank Cass, 1995), 104–29, at 109–10. On the racialised division of shipboard labour and conditions see, more generally: Balachandran, *Globalizing Labour?*, 100–135; Laura Tabili, '"A Maritime Race": Masculinity and the Racial Division of Labour in British Merchant Ships, 1900–1939', in Margaret S. Creighton and Lisa Norling (eds), *Iron Men, Wooden Women: Gender and Seafaring in the Atlantic World, 1700–1920* (Baltimore MD and London: Johns Hopkins University Press, 1996), 169–88.

79 Andrew N. Cohen, 'Cutting a Canal through Central America', in Gollasch et al. (eds), *Bridging Divides*, 91–112, at 105–7. According to a contemporary medical report, during the French period one in four workers died each year: Joan Flores-Villalobos, *The Silver Women: How Black Women's Labor Made the Panama Canal* (Philadelphia PA: University of Pennsylvania Press, 2023), 10.

80 Gerald S. Graham, 'The Ascendancy of the Sailing Ship 1850–85', *The Economic History Review*, New Series, 9:1 (1956), 74–88. See also Greenhill and Giffard, *Steam*, 145.

81 For Anson's track see 'A Chart of the Southern Part of South America', in Richard Walter, *A Voyage Round the World ...*, 1st edn (London: J. and P. Knapton, 1748). An image of this is available at *Barry Lawrence Ruderman Conference on Cartography – Stanford Libraries* https://exhibits.stanford.edu/blrcc/catalog/jr204km6450 or Bibliothèque nationale de France, Médiathèque du musée du quai Branly – Jacques Chirac, Gallica https://gallica.bnf.fr/ark:/12148/btv1b23004533/f13.item.

82 NMM, MAU/8 and MSS/73/018, Arthur Goodall Maundrell, 'Track charts showing voyages of the BLACKBRAES and ELWY', 'Britsh [*sic*] Ship "Blackbraes" off Cape Horn. 1899–1900'. More details are written up on the back of the chart. For a photograph of the *Blackbraes*, see State Library of South Australia, Adelaide, PRG 1373/5/82, A. D. Edwardes Collection, 'The "Blackbraes" at Anchor', *c*.1900 https://collections.slsa.sa.gov.au/resource/PRG+1373/5/82.

83 Cited in M. S. Partridge, 'The Russell Cabinet and National Defence, 1846–1852', *History* 72:235 (1987), 231–50, at 232.

84 R. Taylor, 'Manning the Royal Navy: The Reform of the Recruiting System, 1852–1862 – First Part', *The Mariner's Mirror* 44:4 (1958), 302–13, at 305.

85 Delis, 'Navigating', 402–4.

86 Interview with Captain Paul Brick, Dartmouth, Nova Scotia, carried out by Eric W. Sager. Cited in Eric W. Sager, *Ships and Memories: Merchant Seafarers in Canada's Age of Steam* (Vancouver: UBC Press, 1993), 118–19.

87 TNA, ADM 1/6003, Commander Morgan Singer, 'Reporting proceedings', 9 October 1867 (Enclosure n. 1 to Letter n. 363 of 5 November 1861), ff. 2, 4. See Chapter 5.

88 Conrad, *Mirror of the Sea*, 105.

89 Ibid., 107–8.

90 Geo. Henry Richards and And. Clarke, 'Report on the Suez Canal', *Proceedings of the Royal Geographical Society of London* 14:3 (1869–1870), 259–73.

91 'Suez Canal: How Big are the Mega-Ships Passing along It?', *BBC Newsround* (25 March 2021) https://www.bbc.co.uk/newsround/56511717. For some data on recent accidents (from an insurer's perspective) see 'The Suez Canal Blockage – Lessons to Be Learned', *Allianz Global Corporate & Specialty* (31 March 2021) https://www.agcs.allianz.com/news-and-insights/expert-risk-articles/suez-canal-lessons-learned.html.

92 Matt Leonard, 'Suez Effects to Stretch into June, Container Shortage to Worsen', *Supply Chain Dive* (26 April 2021) https://www.supplychaindive.com/news/suez-blank-sailings-port-antwerp-sea-intelligence/599011; 'Suez: Europe Ripples Gone 1st Week of June', *Sea-Intelligence* (20 April 2021) https://www.sea-intelligence.com/press-room/62-suez-europe-ripples-gone-1st-week-of-june; Jonathan Saul and Timothy Aeppel, 'Suez Canal Blockage Continues to Disrupt Global Trade, Hitting Supply Chains', *Insurance Journal* (9 April 2021) https://www.insurancejournal.com/news/international/2021/04/09/609169.htm; Pippa Stevens, 'The Ship that Blocked the Suez Canal May Be Free, but Experts Warn the Supply Chain Impact Could Last Months', *CNBC* (29 March 2021) https://www.cnbc.com/2021/03/29/suez-canal-is-moving-but-the-supply-chain-impact-could-last-months.html.

93 Kimberly G. Ramos et al., 'Suez Canal Blockage and Its Global Impact on Healthcare amidst the COVID-19 Pandemic', *International Maritime Health* 72:2 (2021), 145–6.

94 Mary-Ann Russon, 'The Cost of the Suez Canal Blockage', *BBC News* (29 March 2021) https://www.bbc.com/news/business-56559073. See also video at https://twitter.com/MarineTraffic/status/1376447939992817664.

95 On why causal models of global science and empire are problematic see Sujit Sivasundaram, 'Sciences and the Global: On Methods, Questions, and Theory', *Isis* 101 (2010), 146–58, esp. 155.

96 Peter Jacques, *Globalization and the World Ocean* (Lanham MD: AltaMira Press, 2006), 1.

97 Steinberg, *Social Construction of the Ocean*, 13.

98 Pere Puig et al., 'Ploughing the Deep Sea Floor', *Nature* 489:7415 (2012), 286–9.

99 For a strongly positive assessment see Lionel Carter, Douglas Burnett and Tara Davenport, 'The Relationship between Submarine Cables and the Marine Environment', in Burnett et al. (eds), *Submarine Cables*, 179–212. See also, more cautious: Bastien Taormina et al., 'A Review of Potential Impacts of Submarine Power Cables on the Marine Environment: Knowledge Gaps, Recommendations and Future Directions', *Renewable and Sustainable Energy Reviews* 96 (2018), 380–91. On entanglements see Matthew Peter Wood and Lionel Carter, 'Whale Entanglements with Submarine Telecommunication Cables', *IEEE Journal of Oceanic Engineering* 33:4 (2008), 445–50.

100 Toby Tyrrell, 'Anthropogenic Modification of the Oceans', *Philosophical Transactions: Mathematical, Physical and Engineering Sciences* 369:1938 (2011), 887–908.

101 Andrés Cózar et al., 'Plastic Debris in the Open Ocean', *Proceedings of the National Academy of Sciences* 111:28 (2014), 10239–44.

102 Steinberg, *Social Construction of the Ocean*, 1; Tracey Williams, *Adrift: The Curious Tale of the Lego Lost at Sea* (London: Unicorn Publishing Group, 2022); 'Garfield Phones Beach Mystery Finally Solved after 35 Years', *BBC News* (28 March 2019) https://www.bbc.com/news/world-europe-47732553.

103 Gollasch et al. (eds), *Bridging Divides*, esp. Andrew N. Cohen, 'Species Introductions and the Panama Canal', 127–206, at 142–8.

104 See Introduction.

Chapter 7: Countertracks

1   Dane Kennedy, 'Introduction: Reinterpreting Exploration', in Dane Kennedy (ed.), *Reinterpreting Exploration: The West in the World* (Oxford: Oxford University Press, 2014), 1–18.

2   Craciun, 'What Is an Explorer?'; Edney, 'Creating "Discovery"', esp. 200 on maleness.

3   G. W. Blunt White Library, Mystic Seaport Museum, Inc., Mystic, CT, Manuscripts Collection (henceforth MSM), Coll. 89, Hotchkiss-Gray Collection, Box 2, Journal kept by Emma Hotchkiss on board the Ship Harvard of Boston, Mass, on an Oriental to European trading voyage, February–December 1856, entry for Saturday, 29 March 1856; see also 25 March for her father's condition and 28 March for the other quote. The journal is fully digitised at *Life at Sea: Seafaring in the Anglo-American Maritime World, 1600–1900* (Adam Matthew, 2022) https://lifeatsea.quartexcollections.com/Documents/Detail/journal-kept-by-emma-hotchkiss.-emma-the-daughter-of-captain-levi-j.-hotchkiss-sailed-on-board-the-ship-harvard-of-boston-mass-on-an-oriental-to-european-trading-voyage/22104181?item=22124523.

4   Ibid., 27 March 1856. I am very grateful to Pat Schaefer, of the Mystic Seaport Museum, for her help in my attempt to establish the nature of Charley's relationship to the Hotchkiss family. So far, I haven't succeeded.

5   MSM, Coll. 89, Hotchkiss-Gray Collection, Box 2, Diary kept by Emma P. (Hotchkiss) Gray on board the steamer FIREQUEEN, January–December 1868, available digitally at https://lifeatsea.quartexcollections.com/Documents/Detail/diary-kept-by-emma-p.-hotchkiss-gray-on-board-the-steamer-firequeen.-her-husband-horatio-nelson-gray-commanded-the-freight-and-passenger-service-steamer-on-the-yangtze-river-china-1-jan-31-dec-1868/22104185?item=22123819. On Emma (*c.*1841–99), her father and her husband, see the biographical notes at 'Hotchkiss-Gray Collection', *Mystic Seaport Museum* https://research.mysticseaport.org/coll/coll089.

6   James M. Dabbs, Jr., E-Lee Chang, Rebecca A. Strong and Rhonda Milun, 'Spatial Ability, Navigation Strategy, and Geographic Knowledge among Men and Women', *Evolution and Human Behavior* 19:2 (1998), 89–98; Carl W. S. Pintzka, Hallvard R. Evensmoen, Hanne Lehn and Asta K. Håberg, 'Changes in Spatial Cognition and Brain Activity after a Single Dose of Testosterone in Healthy Women', *Behavioural Brain Research* 298 (2016), 78–90.

7   Alina Nazareth, Xing Huang, Daniel Voyer and Nora Newcombe, 'A Meta-Analysis of Sex Differences in Human Navigation Skills', *Psychonomic Bulletin & Review* 26 (2019), 1503–28. This study also finds little evidence in terms of the navigating by 'survey' or by 'route' patterns: the only significant effect concerned studies in which men did better than women in egocentric, 'route'-based navigation (p. 1513)!

8   Pintzka et al., 'Changes in Spatial Cognition'.

9   Gina Rippon, *The Gendered Brain: The New Neuroscience That Shatters the Myth of the Female Brain* (London: Vintage Digital, 2019), 121–4.

10   Ascher K. Munion et al., 'Gender Differences in Spatial Navigation: Characterizing Wayfinding Behaviors', *Psychonomic Bulletin & Review* 26 (2019), 1933–40.

11   Carol A. Lawton and Janos Kallai, 'Gender Differences in Wayfinding Strategies and Anxiety about Wayfinding: A Cross-Cultural Comparison', *Sex Roles* 47:9/10 (2002), 389–401.

12   Oreskes, 'Objectivity or Heroism'.

13   Sherrill Grace, 'Inventing Mina Benson Hubbard: From Her 1905 Expedition across Labrador to Her 2005 Centennial (and Beyond)', *The Scholar and Feminist Online* 7:1 (2008) https://sfonline.barnard.edu/ice/grace_01.htm. On women's mapmaking in this period see also Dando, *Women and Cartography*.

14   Jesse Blackadder, 'Illuminations: Casting Light upon the Earliest Female Travellers to Antarctica – A Novel and Exegesis', 2 vols (unpublished PhD thesis, University of Western Sydney, 2013) https://researchdirect.westernsydney.edu.au/islandora/object/uws:22583, quote at 10 (see 9 for the 1835 spotting, 37 and 43–7 on the refusal of female applications).

15   Pamela Young (1971), quoted in Blackadder, 'Illuminations', 35.

16   For a summary of the literature on geography and masculinist constructs see e.g.: Marianna Pavlovskaya and Kevin St. Martin, 'Feminism and Geographic Information Systems: From a Missing Object to a Mapping Subject', *Geography Compass* 1:3 (2007), 583–606, esp. 587–91. Modern framings of femininity came to tar cross-dressing female sailors, specifically, as aberrations: Dianne Dugaw, 'Female Sailors Bold: Transvestite Heroines and the Markers of Gender and Class', in Creighton and Norling (eds), *Iron Men, Wooden Women*, 34–54.

17   For a few examples of wives so engaged aboard their husbands' ships see Haskell Springer, 'The Captain's Wife at Sea', in Creighton and Norling (eds), *Iron Men, Wooden Women*, 92–117, esp. 93–5, 101–2, 110–11.

18   Margarette Lincoln, *Naval Wives & Mistresses* (London: National Maritime Museum, 2007); Suzanne J. Stark, *Female Tars: Women aboard Ship in the Age of Sail*, 2nd edn (London: Pimlico, 1998); Creighton and Norling (eds), *Iron Men, Wooden Women*; Margarette Lincoln, *Trading in War: London's Maritime World in the Age of Cook and Nelson* (New Haven CT and London: Yale University Press, 2018), Ch. 5.

19   Londa Schiebinger, 'Women of Natural Knowledge', in Katharine Park and Lorraine Daston (eds), *The Cambridge History of Science – Volume 3: Early Modern Science* (New York: Cambridge University Press, 2006), 192–205, at 200.

20 David Alan Grier, *When Computers Were Human* (Princeton NJ and Oxford: Princeton University Press, 2005); Margaret W. Rossiter, '"Women's Work" in Science, 1880–1910', *Isis* 71:3 (1980), 381–98, at 383–7 (and see the whole piece for the origins of the segregation of women within specific categories of scientific work).

21 Mary Croarken, 'Mary Edwards: Computing for a Living in 18th-Century England', *IEEE Annals of the History of Computing* 25:4 (2003), 9–15.

22 Gabriella Bernardi, 'Domestic Astronomy in the Seventeenth and Eighteenth Centuries', in Claire G. Jones, Alison E. Martin and Alexis Wolf (eds), *The Palgrave Handbook of Women and Science since 1660* (Cham: Palgrave Macmillan, 2022), 269–87, at 278–9.

23 Susanna Fisher, 'Taylor [*née* Ionn], Janet (1804–1870)', *Oxford Dictionary of National Biography* (2004) https://doi.org/10.1093/ref:odnb/49543; John S. Croucher, 'Janet Taylor (1804–1870): Mathematical Instrument Maker and Teacher of Navigation', in Jones et al. (eds), *Palgrave Handbook of Women and Science*, 85–100.

24 Gray, *Steam Power*, 74–7.

25 Villalobos, *Silver Women*.

26 On 'discovery' see Ch. 3 above. For a key feminist study of women's sidelining see Margaret W. Rossiter, 'The ~~Matthew~~ Matilda Effect in Science', *Social Studies of Science* 23:2 (1993), 325–41. For a poignant twentieth-century case study see Oreskes, 'Objectivity or Heroism', 90–102.

27 Rodger, 'Anson'; Fernández-Armesto, *Straits*.

28 Dening, *Mr Bligh's Bad Language*, 62–3.

29 Lars Eckstein and Anja Schwarz, 'The Making of Tupaia's Map: A Story of the Extent and Mastery of Polynesian Navigation, Competing Systems of Wayfinding on James Cook's *Endeavour*, and the Invention of an Ingenious Cartographic System', *The Journal of Pacific History* 54:1 (2019), 1–95; Bronwen Douglas et al., 'Review Forum', *The Journal of Pacific History* 54:4 (2019), 529–61; Slappnig, 'Indigenous Map', 42–5.

30 On the intersection of gender, race and class as tools of oppression and segregation in the nineteenth-century maritime world see Tabili, '"Maritime Race"'.

31 Balachandran, *Globalizing Labour?*, 10–14.

32 *Saturday Pennsylvania Gazette* 1:48 (23 August 1828), 8. Taken 'from the *Boston Statesman*'. For later republishings, heavily rewritten and abridged, see e.g.: *The New-York Mirror: A Weekly Journal, Devoted to Literature and the Fine Arts* 9:23 (10 December 1831), 179; *American Railroad Journal, and Advocate of Internal Improvements* 4:1 (New York: D. K. Minor, January–July 1835), 333; *Atkinson's Casket: Or Gems of Literature, Wit and Sentiment* 9 (Philadelphia, September 1835), 531; *The New York Journal* 1:1 (August 1853), 38.

33 Jane Samson, 'Exploring the Pacific World', in Kennedy (ed.), *Reinterpreting Exploration*, 154–71.

34 Epeli Hau'ofa, 'Our Sea of Islands', in Hau'ofa, *We Are the Ocean*, 27–40.

35 Ben Finney, 'Rediscovering Polynesian Navigation through Experimental Voyaging', *Journal of Navigation* 46:3 (1993), 383–94; David Lewis, *We, the*

Navigators: The Ancient Art of Landfinding in the Pacific (Honolulu HI: University of Hawai'i Press, 1972); Lewis, 'Ara Moana'; Samson, 'Exploring the Pacific World'. For an accessible recent history of Polynesian sea travel in particular, see Christina Thompson, *Sea People: The Puzzle of Polynesia* (New York: HarperCollins, 2019).

36 Lewis, 'Ara Moana', 285.

37 Hau'ofa, 'Pasts to Remember', 73; Eckstein and Schwarz, 'Making of Tupaia's Map', 20–21, 31.

38 Ben Finney, 'Nautical Cartography and Traditional Navigation in Oceania', in David Woodward and G. Malcolm Lewis (eds), *The History of Cartography – Volume 2.3: Cartography in the Traditional African, American, Arctic, Australian, and Pacific Societies* (Chicago IL and London: University of Chicago Press, 1998), 443–92, at 458–9, 461–7; Lewis, *We, the Navigators*, 45–82.

39 Michael Halpern, 'Sidereal Compasses: A Case for Carolinian-Arab Links', *The Journal of the Polynesian Society* 95:4 (1986), 441–59; Finney, 'Nautical Cartography', 488–9.

40 Finney, 'Nautical Cartography', 469–75; Lewis, *We, the Navigators*, 127–50; Hutchins, *Cognition in the Wild*, Ch. 2.

41 Eckstein and Schwarz, 'Making of Tupaia's Map', 36–7.

42 Finney, 'Nautical Cartography', 475–85; Marcia Ascher, 'Models and Maps from the Marshall Islands: A Case in Ethnomathematics', *Historia Mathematica* 22 (1995), 347–70; William Davenport, 'Marshall Islands Navigational Charts', *Imago Mundi* 15:1 (1960), 19–26; Lewis, *We, the Navigators*, 181–208 (and see 84–93 on navigational uses of swells more generally). For a critical analysis of the context of these artefacts' reception in Europe see Slappnig, 'Indigenous Map', 17–54.

43 Arun Agrawal, 'Dismantling the Divide between Indigenous and Scientific Knowledge', *Development and Change* 26:3 (1995), 413–39; Lesley J. F. Green, '"Indigenous Knowledge" and "Science": Reframing the Debate on Knowledge Diversity', *Archaeologies* 4:1 (2008), 144–63. See also, on a different level, David Ludwig and Luana Poliseli, 'Relating Traditional and Academic Ecological Knowledge: Mechanistic and Holistic Epistemologies across Cultures', *Biology & Philosophy* 33 (2018), 43.

44 Ascher, 'Models and Maps'; Satia, *Spies in Arabia*, 5–6.

45 One of the most vivid expressions of this sense of specificity and obligation in scholarly practice is Max Liboiron, *Pollution Is Colonialism* (Durham NC: Duke University Press, 2021) (for definitions see esp. 7, 22–4). See also: Fikret Berkes, *Sacred Ecology: Traditional Ecological Knowledge and Resource Management* (Philadelphia PA and London: Taylor & Francis, 1999), esp. 176–83; George Nicholas, 'It's Taken Thousands of Years, but Western Science Is Finally Catching Up to Traditional Knowledge', *The Conversation* (15 February 2018) https://theconversation.com/its-taken-thousands-of-years-but-western-science-is-finally-catching-up-to-traditional-knowledge-90291; Arun Agrawal, 'Indigenous Knowledge and the Politics of Classification', *International Social Science Journal* 54:173 (2002), 287–97. On indigenous Pacific conceptions of

technology, embedded in the local context, see Hau'ofa, 'Pasts to Remember', 68–71.

46   Pearce, 'Framing the Days', 25.

47   As Denis Wood says of maps more generally, 'the relationship between signified and signifier is ever precarious, and what meant one thing in the beginning can mean its opposite today, or nothing, or everything. People are at play in the field of map signs, and the latent power of the map is waiting to be unleashed.': Wood, *Rethinking the Power of Maps*, 38.

48   Scott, *Seeing Like a State*.

49   James Cheshire and Alexander J. Kent, 'Getting to the Point? Rethinking Arrows on Maps', *The Cartographic Journal* (2023).

50   Kwan, 'Affecting Geospatial Technologies'.

51   Simon Sadler, *The Situationist City* (Cambridge MA: MIT Press, 1998), 76–103.

52   De Certeau, *Practice*, 97–9, 118–22, quotes at 97. On 'relics' at sea (or, more precisely, narratives 'which cover the space of the seas with relics and transform unknown regions into languages spelled out by the missing') see also de Certeau, 'Writing the Sea' (quote at 142).

53   Rankin, *After the Map*, 297. For a sceptical and cautious perspective see Wood, *Rethinking the Power of Maps*, Ch. 6.

54   See Chapter 6, endnote 9.

55   Chris Perkins, 'Mapping, Performative', in Audrey Kobayashi (ed.), *International Encyclopedia of Human Geography*, 2nd edn (Amsterdam: Elsevier, 2020), 291–6.

56   Wood, *Rethinking the Power of Maps*, 118–19. For the map itself, see https://static.flickr.com/45/111234775_4370a5999a_0.jpg.

57   'On Kawara: I Went, 1968–79', *Guggenheim* (3 February 2015) https://www.guggenheim.org/audio/track/on-kawara-i-went-1968-79; Wood, *Rethinking the Power of Maps*, 204.

58   Lauriault and Wood, 'GPS Tracings', 361–2.

59   Ibid.

60   As she puts it, 'Trajective maps or personal plots may take a variety of different forms that reveal not only where one moves but also who one is and/or what one does': Parks, 'Plotting the Personal', quotes at 216, 218. See also Kwan, 'Affecting Geospatial Technologies', 25. On other forms of feminist GIS see Pavlovskaya and St. Martin, 'Feminism and Geographic Information Systems'.

61   See Chapter 6.

62   Sigrid Merx, 'Mapping Invisibility: Surveillance Art and the Potential of Performative Cartography', in Martina Leeker, Imanuel Schipper and Timon Beyes (eds), *Performing the Digital: Performativity and Performance Studies in Digital Cultures* (Bielefeld: transcript Verlag, 2017), 157–67, quote at 162; Naomi Bueno de Mesquita and David Hamers, 'Mapping Invisibility', in *Proceedings of the 3rd Biennial Research Through Design Conference, 22–24 March 2017, Edinburgh, UK*, Article 27 (2017), 423–37 https://figshare.com/articles/journal_contribution/Mapping_Invisibility/4747015. I am very grateful to Dr Annja Neumann for suggesting the Merx article.

63   'Press Room & Outreach Tools' – 'Voyage and Tracking Maps', *Polynesian*

Voyaging Society – Hōkūleʻa https://worldwidevoyage.hokulea.com/press-room/; 'The Mālama Honua Worldwide Voyage', *Polynesian Voyaging Society – Hōkūleʻa* https://worldwidevoyage.hokulea.com/worldwide-voyage.

64 'The Story of Hōkūleʻa', *Polynesian Voyaging Society – Hōkūleʻa* https://worldwidevoyage.hokulea.com/voyages/our-story/. On the origins of *Hōkūleʻa* and the Polynesian Voyaging Society see: Ben R. Finney, Bernard J. Kilonsky, Stephen Somsen and Edward D. Stroup, 'Re-learning a Vanishing Art', *The Journal of the Polynesian Society* 95:1 (1986), 41–90; Finney, 'Rediscovering Polynesian Navigation'. All this is discussed in one of the most fantastic talks you could ever watch: 'Nainoa Thompson: Polynesian Voyaging Society', *Barry Lawrence Ruderman Conference on Cartography: Indigenous Mapping* (18 November 2021), available at *David Rumsey Map Center* https://www.youtube.com/watch?v=GvO_HkdkmSs.

65 These limitations are discussed in depth in Wood, *Rethinking the Power of Maps*, 129–42, 156–66.

66 David Turnbull, 'Maps Narratives and Trails: Performativity, Hodology and Distributed Knowledges in Complex Adaptive Systems – an Approach to Emergent Mapping', *Geographical Research* 45:2 (2007), 140–49. I am unsure as to whether he would subscribe to the 'however communicated' part.

67 Timothy Doyle and Sanjay Chaturvedi, 'Climate Territories: A Global Soul for the Global South?', *Geopolitics* 15:3 (2010), 516–35.

68 'Oil Tanker Spill Statistics 2022', *ITOPF* https://www.itopf.org/knowledge-resources/data-statistics/statistics.

69 Islam Abou El-Magd, Mohamed Zakzouk, Abdulaziz M. Abdulaziz and Elham M. Ali, 'The Potentiality of Operational Mapping of Oil Pollution in the Mediterranean Sea near the Entrance of the Suez Canal Using Sentinel-1 SAR Data', *Remote Sensing* 12:8 (2020), 1352, at 1.

70 S. Chesworth and P. Engel, 'Space-Based Surveillance and the Role of SAR for Operational Oil Slick Detection and Monitoring', in C. A. Brebbia (ed.), *Oil and Hydrocarbon Spills III: Modelling, Analysis and Control* (Southampton: WIT Press, 2002), 415–25; El-Magd et al., 'Potentiality of Operational Mapping'; F. Nirchio et al., 'A Method to Detect Oil Spill Based on SAR Images', in Brebbia (ed.), *Oil and Hydrocarbon Spills III*, 395–403.

71 *International Convention for the Prevention of Pollution from Ships*, London, 2 November 1973, Reg. 9, no. 3 and Reg. 10, no. 6 (available at *Center for International Earth Science Information Network (CIESIN) – Environmental Treaties and Resource Indicators (ENTRI)* https://sedac.ciesin.columbia.edu/entri/texts/pollution.from.ships.1973.html). This legislation is better known as 'MARPOL 73/78'. For an overview of the legislation and the permitted spillage limits see also: Guido Ferraro and Marko Pavliha, 'The European and International Legal Framework on Monitoring and Response to Oil Pollution from Ships', *Journal of Environmental Monitoring* 12:3 (2010), 574–80; Muslim Bin Aqeel, 'Maritime Environment and Oil Spillage: Legality and Regimes', *Maritime Study Forum* (9 November 2020) https://www.maritimestudyforum.org/maritime-environment-and-oil-spillage-legality-and-regimes.

72 A. B. Hansen, J. Avnskjold and C. Aa. Rasmussen, 'Application of PAH and

Biomarker Diagnostic Ratios in Forensic Oil Spill Identification by the Revised Nordtest Methodology', in Brebbia (ed.), *Oil and Hydrocarbon Spills III*, 59–66; P. S. Daling, L.-G. Faksness, A. B. Hansen and S. A. Stout, 'Improved and Standardized Methodology for Oil Spill Fingerprinting', in Brebbia (ed.), *Oil and Hydrocarbon Spills III*, 77–103; R. P. Philp, J. Allen and T. Kuder, 'The Use of the Isotopic Composition of Individual Compounds for Correlating Hydrocarbon Products in the Environment with Their Suspected Sources', in Brebbia (ed.), *Oil and Hydrocarbon Spills III*, 67–76.

73 Björn Hassler, 'Accidental Versus Operational Oil Spills from Shipping in the Baltic Sea: Risk Governance and Management Strategies', *Ambio* 40:2 (2011), 170–78; Magda Wilewska-Bien and Stefan Anderberg, 'Reception of Sewage in the Baltic Sea – The Port's Role in the Sustainable Management of Ship Wastes', *Marine Policy* 93 (2018), 207–13.

74 Dana D. Miller, Kathryn Tooley and U. Rashid Sumaila, 'Large-Scale Oil Spills and Flag-Use within the Global Tanker Fleet', *Environmental Conservation* 42:2 (2015), 119–26; Dana D. Miller, Ngaio Hotte and U. Rashid Sumaila, 'Mandating Responsible Flagging Practices as a Strategy for Reducing the Risk of Coastal Oil Spills', *Marine Pollution Bulletin* 81 (2014), 24–6; Weipan Zhang et al., 'Governance of Global Vessel-Source Marine Oil Spills: Characteristics and Refreshed Strategies', *Ocean and Coastal Management* 213 (2021), 105874, at 8. On flags of convenience see e.g.: Anthony van Fossen, 'Flags of Convenience and Global Capitalism', *International Critical Thought* 6:3 (2016), 359–77; Tony Alderton and Nik Winchester, 'Globalisation and De-regulation in the Maritime Industry', *Marine Policy* 26 (2002), 35–43.

75 Ian Urbina, *The Outlaw Ocean: Crime & Survival in the Last Untamed Frontier* (London: Vintage, 2019), 270–74, 286–91.

76 Urbina, *Outlaw Ocean*, 286–8.

77 An example from 2017, since taken down, is viewable at https://web.archive.org/web/20210112182526/https://www.cleanupcarnival.com/map-launch.

78 'Plastic Tracker', *The Ocean Cleanup* https://theoceancleanup.com/plastic-tracker.

Coda

1 Grotius, *Free Sea*, 28.

2 Liboiron, *Pollution Is Colonialism*.

3 I borrow the 'world as property versus world as lasting home' dichotomy, as always a brilliant way to put things, from Hau'ofa, 'Pasts to Remember', 74–5.

4 Melville, *Moby Dick*, 39.

5 J. F. Cooper, *The Pilot* (London: Henry Colburn and Richard Bentley, 1831), 410. And see, again, Cohen, *Novel and the Sea*.

6 T. E. Lawrence, *Seven Pillars of Wisdom* (Ware: Wordsworth Editions Limited, 1997). On Lawrence and the imperial imagination see e.g. Norman Etherington, *Imperium of the Soul: The Political and Aesthetic Imagination of Edwardian Imperialists* (Manchester: Manchester University Press, 2017), Ch. 7; Satia, *Spies in Arabia*, esp. Ch. 2.

7   *The Odyssey of Homer*, trans. Philip Stanhope Worsley, 2 vols (William Blackwood and Sons, 1868), II, 248 (x.53).

8   Verse x.464 in the Greek text. See e.g. the Murray edition in *Explore Homer* https://explorehomer.scaife-viewer.org/reader/urn:cts:greekLit:tlg0012.tlg002. perseus-grc2:10.464. Most other translators stick more faithfully to the text. See e.g.: *The Odyssey of Homer*, trans. William Cowper, , 2 vols, 2nd edn (London: J. Johnson, 1802), I, 285 ('all your pains and toils'); *The Odyssey of Homer*, trans. Rev. Dr Giles, 4 vols (London: James Cornish & Sons, 1872), II, 151 ('severe wandering'); *The Odyssey of Homer, with the Hymns, Epigrams, and Battle of the Frogs and Mice*, trans. Theodore Alois Buckley (London: George Bell & Sons, 1902), 143 ('severe wanderings'); *Odyssey of Homer*, [trans. Lawrence], 148 ('the evil of your wanderings').

9   John Finley, 'Introduction', [1], in *Odyssey of Homer*, trans. Lawrence (1934 impression).

10   Etherington, *Imperium*, 231.

INDEX

Page references in *italics* indicate images.